INTRUSION DETECTION SYSTEMS

Edited by **Pawel Skrobanek**

Intrusion Detection Systems
Edited by Pawel Skrobanek

Published by InTech
Janeza Trdine 9, 51000 Rijeka, Croatia

Publishing Process Manager Ana Nikolic

Technical Editor Teodora Smiljanic

Cover Designer InTech Design Team

Additional hard copies can be obtained from orders@intechopen.com

Intrusion Detection Systems, Edited by Pawel Skrobanek
p. cm.
ISBN 978-953-307-167-1

For EU product safety concerns:
IN TECH d.o.o., Prolaz Marije Krucifikse Kozulić 3, 51000 Rijeka, Croatia,
info@intechopen.com or visit our website at intechopen.com.

Meet the editor

Pawel Skrobanek was born in 1972 in Bardo, Poland. He received MSc degree in Computer Engineering at Wroclaw University of Technology in 1997. He received PhD degree in 2005. Since 2005 he has worked at Institute of Computer Engineering, Control and Robotics, Technical University of Wroclaw. His scientific interests concern: time Petri Nets, formal methods in software engineering, safety and security analysis, data warehouse, safety-critical systems.

Contents

Preface

In contrast to the typical books, this publication was created as a collection of papers of various authors from many centers around the world. The idea to show the latest achievements this way allowed for an interesting and comprehensive presentation of the area of intrusion detection systems. There is no need for convincing how important such systems are. Lately we have all witnessed exciting events related to the publication of information by WikiLeaks that resulted in increasing of various types of activities, both supporters and opponents of the portal.

Typically, the structure of a publication is planned at the beginning of a creation process, but in this situation, it reached its final shape with the completion of the content. This solution, however interesting, causes difficulties in categorization of papers. The current structure of the chapters reflects the key aspects discussed in the papers but the papers themselves contain more additional interesting information: examples of a practical application and results obtained for existing networks as well as results of experiments confirming efficacy of a synergistic analysis of anomaly detection and signature detection, and application of interesting solutions, such as an analysis of the anomalies of user behaviors and many others.

I hope that all this will make this book interesting and useful.

2011

Pawel Skrobanek
Institute of Computer Science,
Automatic Control, and Robotics
Wroclaw University of Technology,
Wroclaw,
Poland

Part 1

The Role of IDS for Global Network - An Overview of Methods, Cyber Security, Trends

1

Internet Epidemics: Attacks, Detection and Defenses, and Trends

Zesheng Chen and Chao Chen
Department of Engineering, Indiana University - Purdue University Fort Wayne
Fort Wayne, IN 46805
USA

1. Introduction

Internet epidemics are malicious software that can self-propagate across the Internet, *i.e.*, compromise vulnerable hosts and use them to attack other victims. Since the early stage of the Internet, epidemics have caused enormous damages and been a significant security threat. For example, the Morris worm infected 10% of all hosts in the Internet in 1988; the Code Red worm compromised at least 359,000 hosts in one day in 2001; and the Storm botnet affected tens of millions of hosts in 2007. Therefore, it is imperative to understand and characterize the problem of Internet epidemics including the methods of attacks, the ways of detection and defenses, and the trends of future evolution.

Internet epidemics include viruses, worms, and bots. The past more than twenty years have witnessed the evolution of Internet epidemics. Viruses infect machines through exchanged emails or disks, and dominated 1980s and 1990s. Internet active worms compromise vulnerable hosts by automatically propagating through the Internet and have caused much attention since Code Red and Nimda worms in 2001. Botnets are zombie networks controlled by attackers through Internet relay chat (IRC) systems (*e.g.*, GTBot) or peer-to-peer (P2P) systems (*e.g.*, Storm) to execute coordinated attacks, and have become the number one threat to the Internet in recent years. Since Internet epidemics have evolved to become more and more virulent and stealthy, they have been identified as one of top four security problems and targeted to be eliminated before 2014 (52).

The task of protecting the Internet from epidemic attacks has many significant challenges:

- The original Internet architecture was designed without taking into consideration inherent security mechanisms, and current security approaches are based on a collection of "add-on" capabilities.
- New network applications and technologies become increasingly complex and expand constantly, suggesting that there will exist new vulnerabilities, such as zero-day exploits, in the foreseeable future.
- As shown by the evolution of Internet epidemics, attackers and the attacking code are becoming more and more sophisticated. On the other hand, the ordinary users cannot keep up with good security practices.

In this chapter, we survey and classify Internet epidemic attacks, detection and defenses, and trends, with an emphasis on Internet epidemic attacks. The remainder of this chapter is structured as follows. Section 2 proposes a taxonomy of Internet epidemic attacks. Section 3 discusses detection and defense systems against Internet epidemics. Section 4 predicts the trends of epidemic attacks. Finally, Section 5 concludes the paper.

2. Internet epidemic attacks

In this chapter, we focus on the self-propagation characteristic of epidemics, and use the terms "Internet epidemics" and "worms" interchangeably. A machine that can be compromised by the intrusion of a worm is called a *vulnerable host*, whereas a host that has been compromised by the attack of a worm is called an *infected host* or a *compromised host* or a *bot*. The way that a worm uses to find a target is called the *scanning method* or the *target discovery strategy*. *Worm propagation* is a procedure whereby a worm infects many hosts through Internet connections. In this section, we first identify three parameters that attackers can control to change the behavior of epidemic propagation. Next, we list the scanning methods that worms have used or will potentially exploit to recruit new bots and spread the epidemics. We also explain how these worm-scanning methods adjust the three parameters. Finally, we discuss the metrics that can be applied to evaluate worm propagation performance. The left of Figure 1 summarizes our taxonomy of Internet epidemic attacks.

2.1 Parameters controlled by worms

Three parameters that worms control to design the desired epidemic behaviors include

- *Scanning space:* the IP address space among which a worm searches for vulnerable hosts. A worm can scan an entire IPv4 address space, a routable address space, or only a subnetwork address space. Different bots may scan different address spaces at the same time.
- *Scanning rate:* the rate at which a worm sends out scans in the scanning space. A worm may dispatch as many scans as possible to recruit a certain number of bots in a short time or deliver scans slowly to behave stealthy and avoid detection.
- *Scanning probability:* the probability that a worm scans a specific address in the scanning space. A worm may use a uniform scanning method that hits each address in the scanning space equally likely or use a biased strategy that prefers scanning a certain range of IP addresses. Moreover, if the scanning probability is fixed at all time, the scanning strategy is called *static*; otherwise, the scanning probability varies with time, and the strategy is called *dynamic*.

All worm-scanning strategies have to consider these three parameters, adjusting them for different purposes (4). Although the parameters are local decisions that individual infected hosts make, they may lead to global effects on the Internet, such as the worm propagation speed, total malicious traffic, and difficulties in worm detection. In the following section, we demonstrate how different worm-scanning methods exploit these parameters.

2.2 Worm-scanning methods

Many worm-scanning methods have been used in reality or developed in the research community to spread epidemics. The methods include the following twelve representative strategies.

(1) *Random Scanning (RS)*

RS selects target IPv4 addresses uniformly (35; 6). Such a strategy is the simplest method and has been widely used by Internet worms such as Code Red (26), Slammer (25), and Witty (32). Specifically, RS probes the entire (*i.e.,* 2^{32}) IPv4 address space, uses a constant scanning rate,

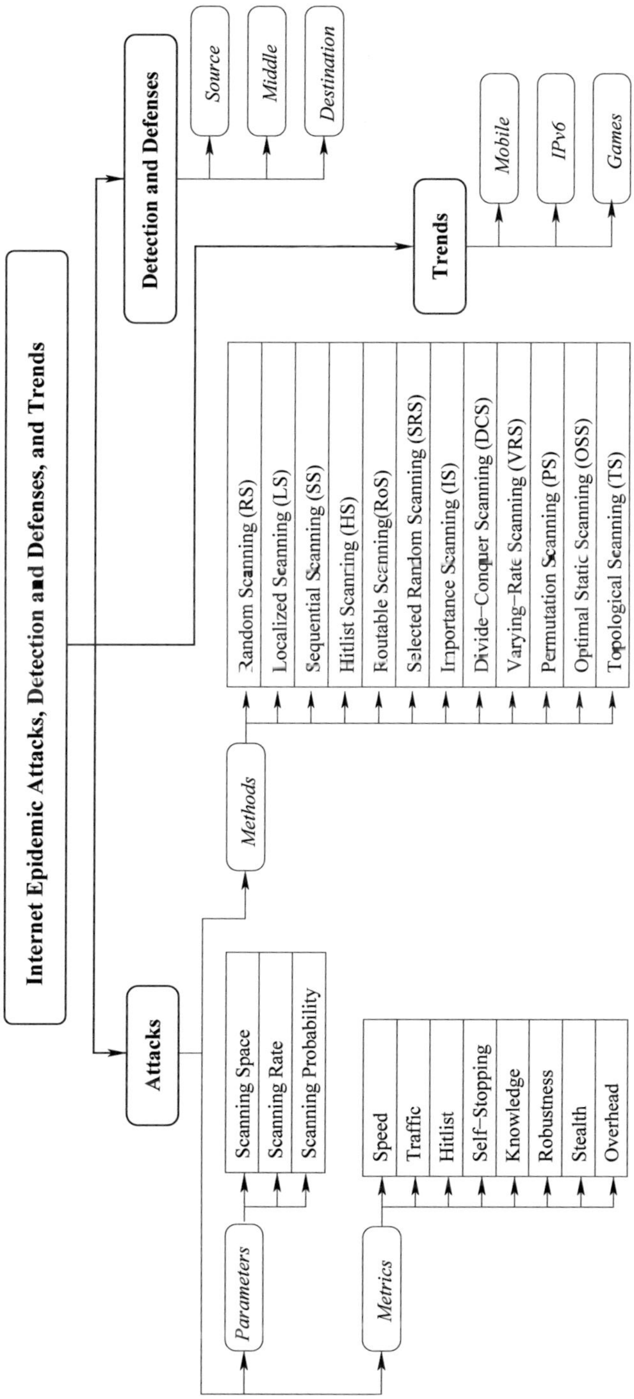

Fig. 1. A Taxonomy of Internet Epidemic Attacks, Detection and Defenses, and Trends.

and scans each address in the scanning space equally likely (*i.e.*, with the probability $1/2^{32}$).
(2) *Localized Scanning (LS)*
LS preferentially searches for targets in the "local" address space by designing the *scanning probability* parameter and has been used by such famous worms as Code Red II and Nimda (29; 5). For example, the Code Red II worm chooses a target IP address with the same first byte as the attacking machine with probability 0.5, chooses a target address with the same first two bytes with probability 0.375, and chooses a random address with probability 0.125. Similar to RS, LS probes the entire IPv4 address space and applies a constant scanning rate.
(3) *Sequential Scanning (SS)*
SS scans IP addresses sequentially from a randomly chosen starting IP address and has been exploited by the Blaster worm (49; 16; 10). Specifically, if SS is scanning address A now, it will continue to sequentially scan IP addresses $A+1$, $A+2$, $\cdots$ (or $A-1$, $A-2$, $\cdots$). Similar to RS, SS scans the entire IPv4 address space and uses a constant scanning rate. Although SS attempts to avoid re-scanning the IP addresses that have been probed, the scanning probability for SS can still be regarded as uniform. As a result, SS has a similar propagation speed as RS (49).
(4) *Hitlist Scanning (HS)*
HS collects a list of vulnerable hosts before a worm is released and attacks the hosts on the list first after the worm is set off (35; 40). Once the hosts on the list are compromised, the worm switches from HS to RS to infect the remaining vulnerable hosts. If the IP addresses of all vulnerable hosts are known to a worm in advance, HS leads to the fastest worm called the *flash worm* (34). Different from RS, HS only scans the hosts on the list before the list is exhausted. Moreover, HS is difficult to detect since each worm scan hits an existing host or service, which is indistinguishable from normal connections. But similar to RS, HS usually uses a constant scanning rate and selects targets on the list uniformly.
(5) *Routable Scanning (RoS)*
RoS scans only a routable address space (42; 50). According to the information provided by BGP routing tables, only about 28.6% of the entire IPv4 addresses are routable and can thus be used for real machines. Hence, RoS reduces the *scanning space* and spreads an epidemic much faster than RS. But similar to RS, RoS uses a constant scanning rate and selects targets in the routable address space uniformly.
(6) *Selected Random Scanning (SRS)*
Similar to RoS, SRS scans a partial IPv4 address space instead of the entire IPv4 address space (49; 31). For example, an attacker samples the Internet to detect an active IP address space before releasing a worm, and directs the worm to avoid scanning inactive addresses so that the worm can be stealthy for *network telescope* detection. Network telescopes use routable but unused IP addresses to detect worms and will be discussed in details in Section 3. Similarly, SRS applies a constant scanning rate and chooses targets in the scanning space uniformly.
(7) *Importance Scanning (IS)*
IS exploits the *scanning probability* parameter and probes different IP addresses with different probabilities (9; 8). Specifically, IS samples targets according to an underlying group distribution of vulnerable hosts. A key observation for IS is that vulnerable hosts distribute highly non-uniform in the Internet and form clusters (25; 26; 32; 29; 1; 10; 11; 38). Hence, IS concentrates on scanning groups that contain many vulnerable hosts to speed up the propagation. If a worm probes an IP address with probability 0, the worm would never scan this IP address. Therefore, RoS and SRS can be regarded as special cases of IS. Similarly, IS uses a constant scanning rate.

(8) *Divide-Conquer Scanning (DCS)*
DCS exploits the *scanning space* parameter, and different worm instances may probe different scanning spaces (42; 49; 4). Specifically, after an attacking host A infects a target B, A divides its scanning space into halves so that A would scan one half and B would scan the other half. As a result, the address space initially scanned by a worm will be partitioned into pieces that are probed by different infected hosts. Similar to RS, a worm instant uses a constant scanning rate and scans targets in its scanning space uniformly. In Section 2.3, however, it is demonstrated that DCS can spread an epidemic much faster than RS based on the realistic distribution of vulnerable hosts.
(9) *Varying-Rate Scanning (VRS)*
VRS varies the *scanning rate* over time to avoid detection (46; 47). Many worm detection methods have been developed based on change-point detection on the traffic going through routers or the unwanted traffic towards network telescopes. VRS, however, can potentially adjust its scanning rate dynamically so that it can smooth the malicious traffic. Similar to RS, VRS probes the IPv4 address space and scans targets in the scanning space uniformly.
(10) *Permutation Scanning (PS)*
PS allows all worm instances to share a common pseudo random permutation of the IP address space and to coordinate to provide comprehensive scanning (35). That is, the IPv4 address space is mapped into the permutation space, and an infected host uses SS in the permutation space. Moreover, if an infected host A hits another infected host B, A realizes that the scanning sequence starting from B in the permutation space has been probed and would switch to another scanning sequence to avoid duplicate scanning. In this way, compared with RS, PS can improve worm propagation performance (*i.e.*, the speed and the traffic) at the late stage. But at the early stage, PS behaves similar to RS in terms of the scanning space, the scanning rate, and the scanning probability.
(11) *Optimal Static Scanning (OSS)*
OSS minimizes the number of worm scans required to reach a predetermined fraction of vulnerable hosts by designing the proper *scanning probability* parameter (38). OSS is similar to IS since both methods exploit the scanning probability parameter. However, while IS emphasizes the speed of worm propagation, OSS focuses on the number of worm scans. In Section 2.3, we will further illustrate this point.
(12) *Topological Scanning (TS)*
TS exploits the information contained in the victim machines to locate new targets and has been used by Email viruses and Morris/SSH worms (40; 7). Hence, TS is a *topology-based* method, whereas the above eleven scanning strategies are *scan-based* methods. TS scans only neighbors on the topology, uses a constant scanning rate, and probes targets among neighbors uniformly.

2.3 Worm propagation performance metrics

How can we evaluate the performance of a worm-scanning method? In this section, we study several widely used performance metrics, focusing on scan-based epidemics.
(1) *Propagation Speed*
The epidemic propagation speed is the most used metric and defines how fast a worm can infect vulnerable hosts (35; 6; 49; 37; 36). Specifically, assume that two scanning methods A and B have the same initial conditions (*e.g.*, the number of vulnerable hosts and the scanning rate). If the numbers of infected hosts at time t for these two methods, $I_A(t)$ and $I_B(t)$, have the following relationship: $I_A(t) \geq I_B(t)$ for $\forall t \geq 0$, then method A has a higher propagation

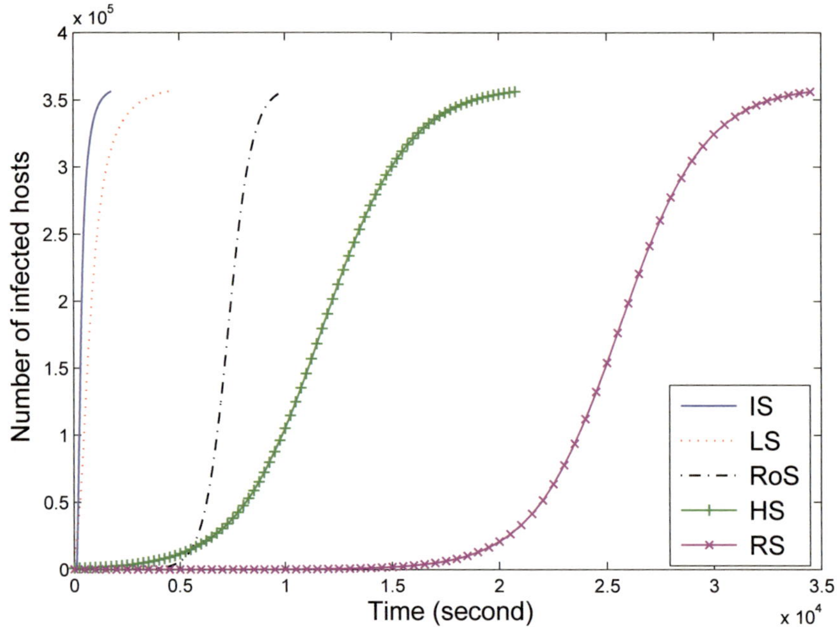

Fig. 2. Epidemic propagation speeds of different scanning methods (the vulnerable-host population is 360,000, the scanning rate is 358 per minute, the vulnerable-host distribution is from the DShield data with port 80, HS has a hitlist of 1,000, and other scanning methods start from an initially infected host).

speed than method *B*.

In Figure 2, we simulate a Code Red v2 worm using different scanning methods. Code Red v2 has a vulnerable-host population of 360,000 and a scanning rate of 358 per minute. To characterize scanning methods, we employ the analytical active worm propagation (AAWP) model and its extensions (6). The AAWP model applies a discrete-time mathematical difference equation to describe the spread of RS and has been extended to model the propagation of other advanced scanning methods. In Figure 2, we compare IS, LS, RoS, and HS with RS. We assume that except HS, a worm begins spreading from an initially infected host. HS has a hitlist size of 1,000. Since the Code Red v2 worm attacks Web servers, we use the DShield data (54) with port 80 as the distribution of vulnerable hosts. DShield collects intrusion detection system and firewall logs from the global Internet (54; 1; 11). We also assume that once a vulnerable host is infected, it will stay infected. From the figure, it is seen that IS, LS, RoS, and HS can spread an epidemic much faster than RS. Specifically, it takes RS 10 hours to infect 99% of vulnerable hosts, whereas HS uses only about 6 hours. RoS and LS can further reduce the time to 3 hours and 1 hour. IS spreads fastest and takes only 0.5 hour.

The design of most advanced scanning methods (*e.g.,* IS, LS, RoS, and OSS) roots on the fact that vulnerable hosts are not uniform distributed, but highly clustered (9; 29; 49; 38). Specifically, the Internet is partitioned into sub-networks or groups according to such standards as the first byte of IP addresses (/8 subnets), the IP prefix, autonomous systems, or DNS top-level domains. Since the distribution of vulnerable hosts over groups is highly uneven, a worm would avoid scanning groups that contain no or few vulnerable hosts and concentrate on scanning groups that have many vulnerable hosts to increase the propagation

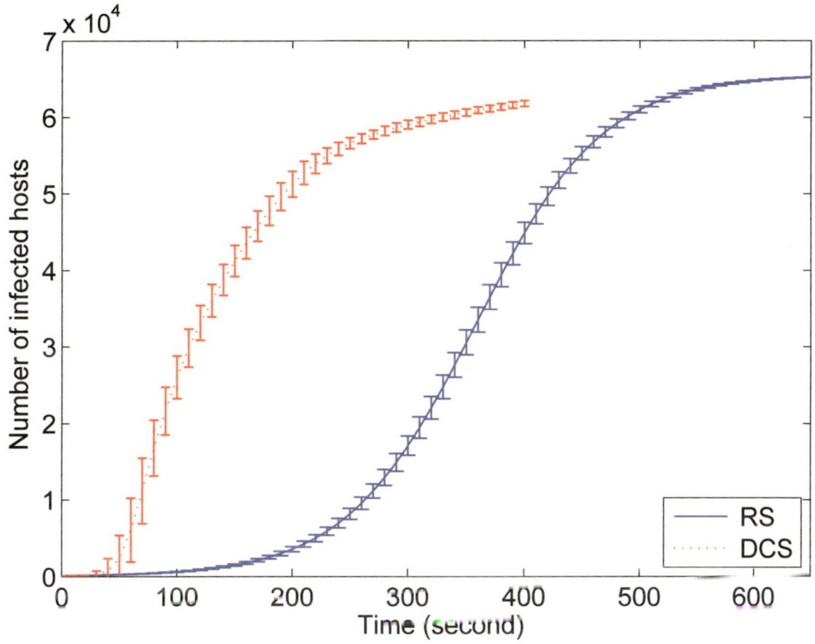

Fig. 3. Comparison of DCS and RS (the vulnerable-host population is 65,536, the scanning rate is 1,200 per minute, the vulnerable-host distribution follows that of Witty-worm victims, and a hitlist size is 100).

speed. Moreover, once a vulnerable host in a sub-network with many vulnerable hosts is infected, a LS worm can rapidly compromise all the other local vulnerable hosts (29; 5).

DCS is another scanning method that exploits the highly uneven distribution of vulnerable hosts, but has been studied little (4). Imagine a toy example where vulnerable hosts only distribute among the first half of the IPv4 address space and no vulnerable hosts exist in the second half of the space. A DCS worm starts from an initially infected host, which behaves like RS until hitting a target. After that, the initially infected host scans the first half of the space, whereas the new bot probes the other half. While the new bot cannot recruit any target, the initially infected host would find the vulnerable hosts faster with the reduced scanning space. This fast recruitment in the first half of the space would in return accelerate the infection process since the newly infected hosts in the area only scan the first half of the space. In some sense, DCS could lead an epidemic to spread towards an area with many vulnerable hosts.

Figure 3 compares DCS with RS, using a discrete event simulator. The simulator implements each worm scan through a random number generator and simulates each scenario with 100 runs using different seeds. The curves represent the mean of 100 runs, whereas the error bars show the variation over 100 runs. The worm has a vulnerable population of 65,536, a scanning rate of 1,200 per second, and a hitlist size of 100. The distribution of vulnerable hosts follows that of Witty-worm victims provided by CAIDA (56). Figure 3 demonstrates that DCS spreads an epidemic much faster than RS. Specifically, RS takes 479 seconds to infect 90% of vulnerable hosts, whereas DCS takes only 300 seconds.

(2) *Worm Traffic*

Worm traffic is defined as the total number of worm scans (38). Specifically, assuming that a worm uses a constant scanning rate s and infects $I(t)$ machines at time t, we can approximate

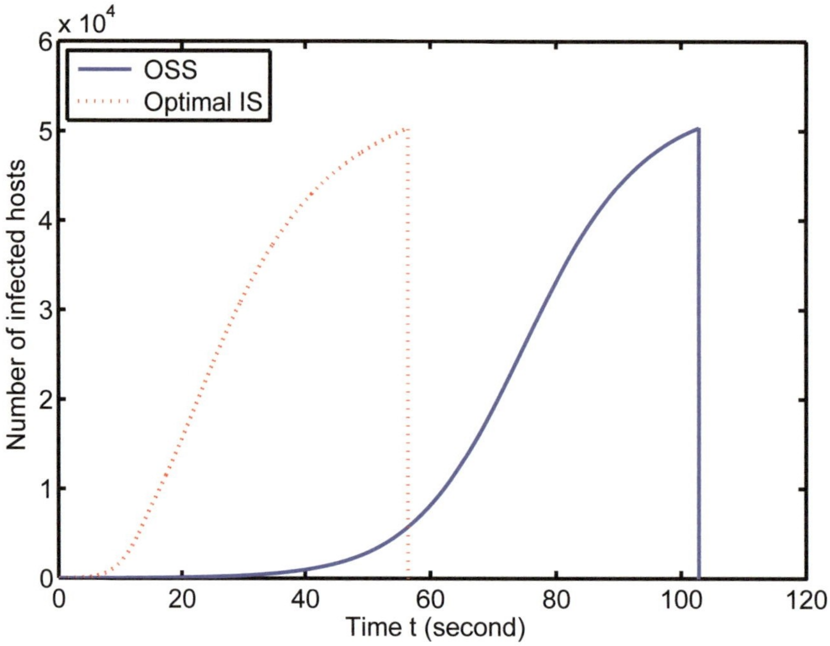

Fig. 4. Comparison of OSS and optimal IS (the vulnerable-host population is 55,909, the scanning rate is 1,200 per minute, the vulnerable-host distribution follows that of Witty-worm victims, and a hitlist size is 10).

worm traffic by time t as $s \cdot \int_0^t I(x)dx$. An epidemic may intend to reduce the worm traffic to elude detection or avoid too much scanning traffic that would slow down worm propagation in return. OSS is designed to minimize the traffic required to reach a predetermined fraction of vulnerable hosts (38).

The two metrics, the propagation speed and the worm traffic, reflect different aspects of epidemics and may not correlate. For example, two scanning methods can use the same number of worm scans to infect the same number of vulnerable hosts, but differ significantly on the propagation speed. Specifically, we apply the extensions of the AAWP model to characterize the spread of OSS and optimal IS, as shown in Figure 4. Here, we simulate the propagation of the Witty worm, where the vulnerable-host population is 55,909, the scanning rate is 1,200 per minute, the vulnerable-host distribution follows that of Witty-worm victims, and a hitlist size is 10. Both scanning methods use 1.76×10^9 worm scans to infect 90% of vulnerable hosts (*i.e.,* the scanning rate multiples the area under the curve). However, OSS uses 102 seconds to infect 90% vulnerable hosts, whereas optimal IS takes only 56 seconds.

(3) *Initially Infected Hosts (Hitlist)*

A hitlist defines the hosts that are infected at the beginning of worm propagation and reflects the attacks' ability in preparing the worm attacks (35). The curves of HS and RS in Figure 2 show that a worm can spread much faster with a larger hitlist. Hence, an attacker may use a botnet (*i.e.,* a network of bots) as a hitlist to send out worm infection (14). Moreover, the locations of the hitlist affect LS. For example, if the hitlist resides in sub-networks with few vulnerable hosts, the worm cannot spread fast at the early stage.

(4) *Self-Stopping*

If a worm can self-stop after it infects all or most vulnerable hosts, it can reduce the chance to be detected and organize the network of bots in a more stealthy way (23). One way for a bot to know the saturation of infected hosts is that it has hit other bots for several times. Another way is that a worm estimates the number of vulnerable hosts and the scanning rate, and thus predicts the time to compromise most vulnerable hosts.

(5) *Knowledge*

The use of knowledge by an attacker can help a worm speed up the propagation or reduce the traffic (8; 38). For example, IS exploits the knowledge of the vulnerable-host distribution, assuming that this distribution is either obtainable or available. Based on the knowledge, worm-scanning methods can be classified into three categories:

- *Blind:* A worm has no knowledge about vulnerable hosts and has to use oblivious scanning methods such as RS, LS, SS, and DCS.
- *Partial:* A scanning strategy exploits partial knowledge about vulnerable hosts, such as RoS, SRS, IS, and OSS.
- *Complete:* A worm has the complete knowledge about vulnerable hosts, such as a flash worm (34).

A future intelligent worm can potentially learn certain knowledge about vulnerable hosts while propagating. Specifically, a blind worm uses RS to spread and collect the information on vulnerable hosts at the very early stage, and then switches to other advanced scanning methods (*e.g.*, SRS, IS, or OSS) after estimating the underlying distribution of vulnerable hosts accurately. We call such worms *self-learning worms* (8).

(6) *Robustness*

Robustness defines a worm's ability against bot failures. For example, DCS is not robust since the failure of a bot at the early stage may lead to the consequence that a worm misses a certain range of IP addresses (4). Therefore, redundancy in probing the same scanning space may be necessary to increase the robustness of DCS. Comparatively, RS, SS, RoS, IS, PS, and OSS are robust since except extreme cases (*e.g.*, all initially infected hosts fail before recruiting a new bot), a small portion of bot failures do not affect worm infection significantly.

(7) *Stealth*

Stealth defines a worm's ability in avoiding detection. For example, many worm detection methods root on change-point detection on the unwanted traffic towards network telescopes or the traffic going through routers (51; 48; 2). These methods, however, may fail to detect VRS that adjusts the worm traffic to spread an epidemic under the radar (46; 47). Another stealthy scanning method is HS that makes worm infection undistinguishable from normal connections (35).

(8) *Overhead*

Overhead defines the size of additional packet contents required for a worm to design a scanning method. For example, the flash worm may require a very large storage to contain the IP addresses of all vulnerable hosts (34). Specifically, if there are 100,000 vulnerable hosts, the flash worm demands 400,000 bytes to store the IP addresses without compression. Such large overhead slows down the worm propagation speed and introduces extra worm traffic.

3. Internet epidemic detection and defenses

To counteract notorious epidemics, many detection and defense methods have been studied in recent years. Based on the location of detectors, we classify these methods into the following three categories. The top-right of Figure 1 summarizes our taxonomy of Internet epidemic detection and defenses.

3.1 Source detection and defenses

Source detection and defenses are deployed at the local networks, protecting local hosts and locating local infected hosts (17; 18; 41; 36; 19). For example, a defense system applies the latest patches to end systems so that these systems can be immunized to epidemic attacks that exploit known vulnerabilities. To detect infected hosts, researchers have characterized epidemic host behaviors to distinguish them from the normal host behaviors. For example, an infected host attempts to spread an epidemic as quickly as possible and sends out many scans to different destinations at the same time. Comparatively, a normal host usually does not connect to many hosts simultaneously. Hence, a detection and defense system can explore this difference and build up a connection queue with a small length (*e.g.*, 5) for an end host. Once the queue is filled up, the further connection request would be rejected. In this way, the spread of an epidemic is slowed down, while the normal hosts are affected little. Moreover, monitoring the queue length can reveal the potential appearance of a worm. Such a method is called *virus throttling* (36). Another detection method targets the inherent feature of scan-based epidemics. Specifically, since a bot does not know the (exact) locations of vulnerable hosts, it guesses the IP addresses of targets, which leads to the likely failures of connections and differs from normal connections. A *sequential hypothesis testing* method has been proposed to exploit such a difference and shown to identify an RS bot quickly (17; 18; 41).

3.2 Middle detection and defenses

Middle detection and defenses are deployed at the routers, analyzing the on-going traffic and filtering out the malicious traffic (27; 43; 33; 21). *Content filtering* and *address blacklisting* are two commonly used techniques (27). Content filtering uses the known signatures to detect and remove the attacking traffic, whereas address blacklisting filters out the traffic from known bots. Similar to source detection and defenses, middle detection and defenses can also explore the inherent behaviors of epidemics and differ the malicious traffic from the normal traffic. For example, several sampling methods have been proposed to detect the super spreader – a host sends traffic to many hosts, and thus identify potential bots (43). Another method is based on the distributions of source IP addresses, destination IP addresses, source port numbers, and destination port numbers, which would change after a worm is released (33; 21).

3.3 Destination detection and defenses

Destination detection and defenses are deployed at the *Darknet* or *network telescopes*, a globally routable address space where no active servers or services reside (51; 53; 55). Hence, most traffic arriving at Darknet is malicious or unwanted. CAIDA has used a /8 sub-network as network telescopes and observed several large-scale Internet epidemic attacks such as Code Red (26), Slammer (25), and Witty (32) worms.

We coin the term *Internet worm tomography* as inferring the characteristics of Internet epidemics from the Darknet observations (39), as illustrated in Figure 5. Since most worms use scan-based methods and have to guess target IP addresses, Darknet can observe partial scans from bots. Hence, we can combine Darknet observations with the worm propagation model and the statistical model to detect the worm appearance (42; 2) and infer the worm characteristics (*e.g.*, the number of infected hosts (6), the propagation speed (48), and the worm infection sequence (30; 39)). Internet worm tomography is named after *network tomography*, where end system observations are used to infer the characteristics of the internal network (*e.g.*, the link delay, the link loss rate, and the topology) (3; 12). The common approach to network tomography is to formulate the problem as a linear inverse problem. Internet

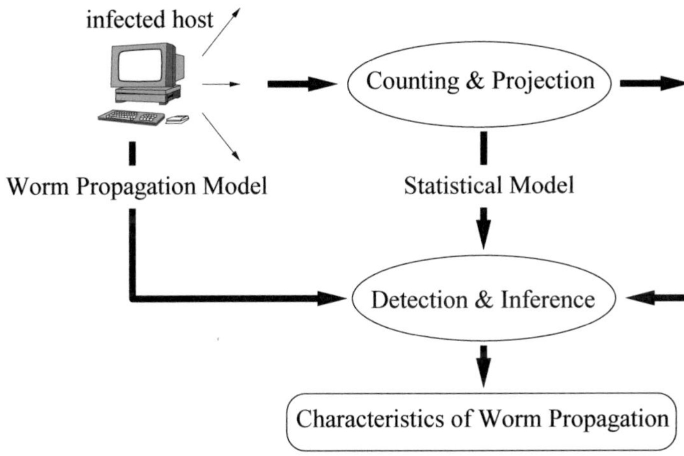

Fig. 5. Internet Worm Tomography (39).

worm tomography, however, cannot be translated into the linear inverse problem due to the complexity of epidemic spreading, and therefore presents new challenges. Several statistical detection and estimation techniques have been applied to Internet worm tomography, such as maximum likelihood estimation (39), Kalman filter estimation (48), and change-point detection (2).

Figure 6 further illustrates an example of Internet worm tomography on estimating when a host gets infected, *i.e.*, the host infection time, from our previous work (39). Specifically, a host is infected at time instant t_0. The Darknet monitors a portion of the IPv4 address space and can receive some scans from the host. The time instants when scans hit the Darknet are t_1, t_2, $\cdots$, t_n, where n is the number of scans received by the Darknet. Given Darknet observations $t_1, t_2, \cdots, t_n$, we then attempt to infer t_0 by applying advanced estimation techniques such as maximum likelihood estimation.

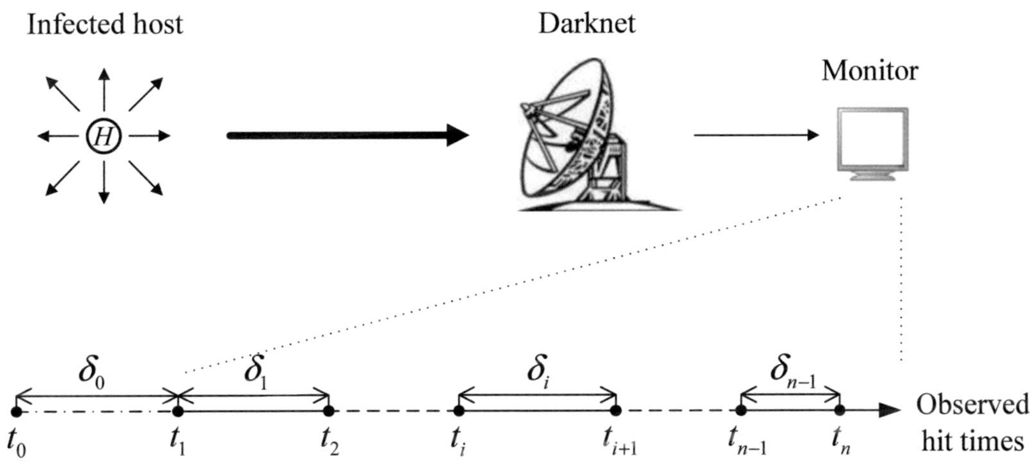

Fig. 6. An illustration of Darknet observations (39).

4. Internet epidemic trends

Internet epidemics have evolved in the past more than twenty years and will continue developing in the future. In this section, we discuss three prominent trends of epidemic attacks. The bottom-right of Figure 1 summarizes our taxonomy of Internet epidemic trends.

4.1 Mobile epidemics

Over the past few years, a new type of worms has emerged that specifically targets portable devices such as cell phones, PDAs, and laptops. These mobile worms can use Internet connectivity for their propagation. But more importantly, they can apply TS and spread directly from device to device, using a short-range wireless communication technology such as WiFi or Bluetooth (20; 44). The first mobile epidemic, Cabir, appeared in 2004 and used Bluetooth channels on cell phones running the Symbian operation system to spread onto other phones. As WiFi/Bluetooth devices become increasing popular and wireless networks become an important integrated part of the Internet, it is predicted that epidemic attacks will soon become pervasive among mobile devices, which strongly connect to our everyday lives.

4.2 IPv6 worms

IPv6 is the future of the Internet. IPv6 can increase the scanning space significantly, and therefore, it is very difficult for an RS worm to find a target among the 2^{128} IP address space (50). The future epidemics, however, can still spread relatively fast in the IPv6 Internet. For example, we find that if vulnerable hosts are still clustered in IPv6, an IS worm can be a zero-day worm (10). Moreover, a TS epidemic can spread by exploiting the topological information, similar to Morris and SSH worms. Another example of advanced worms would propagate by guessing DNS names in IPv6, instead of IP addresses (15).

4.3 Propagation games

To react to worm attacks, a promising method generates self-certifying alerts (SCAs) or patches from detected bots or known vulnerabilities and uses an overlay network for broadcasting SCAs or patches (13; 37). A key factor for this method to be effective is indeed that SCAs or patches can be disseminated much faster than worm propagation. This introduces propagation games between attackers and defenders, since both sides apply epidemic spreading techniques. Such a weapon race would continue in the foreseeable future.

5. Conclusions

In this chapter, we have surveyed a variety of techniques that Internet epidemics have used or will potentially exploit to locate targets in the Internet. We have examined and classified existing mechanisms against epidemic attacks. We have also predicted the coming threats of future epidemics.

In addition to survey, we have compared different worm scanning methods based on the three important worm-propagation parameters and different performance metrics. Specifically, we have demonstrated that many advanced scanning methods can spread a worm much faster than random scanning. Moreover, the worm propagation speed and the worm traffic reflect different aspects of Internet epidemics and may not correlate. We have also emphasized Internet worm tomography as a framework to infer the characteristics of Internet epidemics from Darknet observations. Finally, we have contemplated that epidemics can spread among mobile devices and in IPv6, and have a far-reaching effect to our everyday lives.

6. References

[1] P. Barford, R. Nowak, R. Willett, and V. Yegneswaran, "Toward a model for sources of Internet background radiation," in *Proc. of the Passive and Active Measurement Conference (PAM'06)*, Mar. 2006.

[2] T. Bu, A. Chen, S. V. Wiel, and T. Woo, "Design and evaluation of a fast and robust worm detection algorithm," in *Proc. of INFOCOM'06*, Barcelona, Spain, April 2006.

[3] R. Caceres, N.G. Duffield, J. Horowitz, and D. Towsley, "Multicast-based inference of network-internal loss characteristics," *IEEE Transactions on Information Theory*, vol. 45, no. 7, Nov. 1999, pp. 2462-2480.

[4] C. Chen, Z. Chen, and Y. Li, "Characterizing and defending against divide-conquer-scanning worms," *Computer Networks*, vol. 54, no. 18, Dec. 2010, pp. 3210-3222.

[5] Z. Chen, C. Chen, and C. Ji, "Understanding localized-scanning worms," in *Proc. of 26th IEEE International Performance Computing and Communications Conference (IPCCC'07)*, New Orleans, LA, Apr. 2007, pp. 186-193.

[6] Z. Chen, L. Gao, and K. Kwiat, "Modeling the spread of active worms," in *Proc. of INFOCOM'03*, vol. 3, San Francisco, CA, Apr. 2003, pp. 1890-1900.

[7] Z. Chen and C. Ji, "Spatial-temporal modeling of malware propagation in networks," *IEEE Transactions on Neural Networks: Special Issue on Adaptive Learning Systems in Communication Networks*, vol. 16, no. 5, Sept. 2005, pp. 1291-1303.

[8] Z. Chen and C. Ji, "A self-learning worm using importance scanning," in *Proc. ACM/CCS Workshop on Rapid Malcode (WORM'05)*, Fairfax, VA, Nov. 2005, pp. 22-29.

[9] Z. Chen and C. Ji, "Optimal worm-scanning method using vulnerable-host distributions," *International Journal of Security and Networks: Special Issue on Computer and Network Security*, vol. 2, no. 1/2, 2007.

[10] Z. Chen and C. Ji, "An information-theoretic view of network-aware malware attacks," *IEEE Transactions on Information Forensics and Security*, vol. 4, no. 3, Sept. 2009, pp. 530-541.

[11] Z. Chen, C. Ji, and P. Barford, "Spatial-temporal characteristics of Internet malicious sources," in *Proc. of INFOCOM'08 Mini-Conference*, Phoenix, AZ, Apr. 2008.

[12] M. Coates, A. Hero, R. Nowak, and B. Yu, "Internet Tomography," *IEEE Signal Processing Magazine*, May 2002, pp. 47-65.

[13] M. Costa, J. Crowcroft, M. Castro, A. Rowstron, L. Zhou, L. Zhang, and P. Barham, "Vigilante: End-to-end containment of Internet worms,", in Proc. of SOSP'05, Brighton, UK, Oct. 2005.

[14] D. Dagon, C. C. Zou, and W. Lee, "Modeling botnet propagation using time zones," in *Proc. 13th Annual Network and Distributed System Security Symposium (NDSS'06)*, San Diego, CA, Feb. 2006.

[15] H. Feng, A. Kamra, V. Misra, and A. D. Keromytis, "The effect of DNS delays on worm propagation in an IPv6 Internet," in *Proc. of INFOCOM'05*, vol. 4, Miami, FL, Mar. 2005, pp. 2405-2414.

[16] G. Gu, M. Sharif, X. Qin, D. Dagon, W. Lee, and G. Riley, "Worm detection, early warning and response based on local victim information," in *Proc. 20th Ann. Computer Security Applications Conf. (ACSAC'04)*, Tucson, AZ, Dec. 2004.

[17] J. Jung, V. Paxson, A. Berger, and H. Balakrishnan, "Fast portscan detection using sequential hypothesis testing," in *Proc. of IEEE Symposium on Security and Privacy*, Oakland, CA, May 2004.

[18] J. Jung, S. Schechter, and A. Berger, "Fast detection of scanning worm infections," in *7th International Symposium on Recent Advances in Intrusion Detection (RAID'04)*, Sophia Antipolis, French Riviera, France, Sept. 2004
[19] S. A. Khayam, H. Radha, and D. Loguinov, "Worm detection at network endpoints using information-theoretic traffic perturbations," in *Proc. of IEEE International Conference on Communications (ICC'08)*, Beijing, China, May 2008.
[20] J. Kleinberg, "The wireless epidemic," *Nature (News and Views)*, vol. 449, Sept. 2007, pp. 287-288.
[21] A. Lakhina, M. Crovella, and C. Diot, "Mining anomalies using traffic feature distributions," in *Proc. of ACM SIGCOMM'05*, Philadelphia, PA, Aug. 2005.
[22] M. Lelarge and J. Bolot, "Network externalities and the deployment of security features and protocols in the Internet," in *Proc. of the 2008 ACM SIGMETRICS*, June 2008, pp. 37-48.
[23] J. Ma, G. M. Voelker, and S. Savage, "Self-stopping worms," in *Proc. ACM/CCS Workshop on Rapid Malcode (WORM'05)*, Fairfax, VA, Nov. 2005, pp. 12-21.
[24] J. Mirkovic and P. Reiher, "A taxonomy of DDoS attacks and defense mechanisms," *ACM SIGCOMM Computer Communications Review*, vol. 34, no. 2, April 2004, pp. 39-54.
[25] D. Moore, V. Paxson, S. Savage, C. Shannon, S. Staniford, and N. Weaver, "Inside the Slammer worm," *IEEE Security and Privacy*, vol. 1, no. 4, July 2003, pp. 33-39.
[26] D. Moore, C. Shannon, and J. Brown, "Code-Red: a case study on the spread and victims of an Internet worm," in *ACM SIGCOMM/USENIX Internet Measurement Workshop*, Marseille, France, Nov. 2002.
[27] D. Moore, C. Shannon, G. Voelker, and S. Savage, "Internet quarantine: Requirements for containing self-propagating code," in *Proc. of INFOCOM'03*, vol. 3, San Francisco, CA, Apr., 2003, pp. 1901-1910.
[28] J. Nazario, *Defense and Detection Strategies Against Internet Worms*. Artech House, Inc., Norwood, MA, 2003.
[29] M. A. Rajab, F. Monrose, and A. Terzis, "On the effectiveness of distributed worm monitoring," in *Proc. of the 14th USENIX Security Symposium (Security'05)*, Baltimore, MD, Aug. 2005, pp. 225-237.
[30] M. A. Rajab, F. Monrose, and A. Terzis, "Worm evolution tracking via timing analysis," in *Proc. ACM/CCS Workshop on Rapid Malcode (WORM'05)*, Fairfax, VA, Nov. 2005, pp. 52-59.
[31] M. A. Rajab, F. Monrose, and A. Terzis, "Fast and evasive attacks: highlighting the challenges ahead," in *Proc. of the 9th International Symposium on Recent Advances in Intrusion Detection (RAID'06)*, Hamburg, Germany, Sept. 2006.
[32] C. Shannon and D. Moore, "The spread of the Witty worm," *IEEE Security and Privacy*, vol. 2, no 4, Jul-Aug 2004, pp. 46-50.
[33] S. Singh, C. Estan, G. Varghese, and S. Savage, "Automated worm fingerprinting," in *Proc. of the 6th ACM/USENIX Symposium on Operating System Design and Implementation (OSDI'04)*, San Francisco, CA, Dec. 2004, pp. 45-60.
[34] S. Staniford, D. Moore, V. Paxson, and N. Weaver, "The top speed of flash worms," in *Proc. ACM/CCS Workshop on Rapid Malcode (WORM'04)*, Washington DC, Oct. 2004, pp. 33-42.
[35] S. Staniford, V. Paxson, and N. Weaver, "How to 0wn the Internet in your spare time," in *Proc. of the 11th USENIX Security Symposium (Security'02)*, San Francisco, CA, Aug. 2002, pp. 149-167.

[36] J. Twycross and M. M. Williamson, "Implementing and testing a virus throttle," in *Proc. of the 12th USENIX Security Symposium (Security'03)*, Washington, DC, Aug. 2003, pp. 285-294.
[37] M. Vojnovic and A. J. Ganesh, "On the race of worms, alerts and patches," *IEEE/ACM Transactions on Networking*, vol. 16 , no. 5, Oct. 2008, pp. 1066-1079.
[38] M. Vojnovic, V. Gupta, T. Karagiannis, and C. Gkantsidis, "Sampling strategies for epidemic-style information dissemination," in *Proc. of INFOCOM'08*, Phoenix, AZ, April 2008, pp. 1678-1686.
[39] Q. Wang, Z. Chen, K. Makki, N. Pissinou, and C. Chen, "Inferring Internet worm temporal characteristics," in *Proc. IEEE GLOBECOM'08*, New Orleans, LA, Dec. 2008.
[40] N. Weaver, V. Paxson, S. Staniford, and R. Cunningham, "A taxonomy of computer worms," in *Proc. of ACM CCS Workshop on Rapid Malcode*, Oct. 2003, pp. 11-18.
[41] N. Weaver, S. Staniford, and V. Paxson, "Very fast containment of scanning worms," in *Proc. of 13th Usenix Security Conference (Security'04)*, San Diego, CA, Aug. 2004.
[42] J. Xia, S. Vangala, J. Wu, L. Gao, and K. Kwiat, "Effective worm detection for various scan techniques," *Journal of Computer Security*, vol. 14, no. 4, 2006, pp. 359-387.
[43] Y. Xie, V. Sekar, D. A. Maltz, M. K. Reiter, and H. Zhang, "Worm origin identification using random moonwalks," in *Proc. of the IEEE Symposium on Security and Privacy (Oakland'05)*,Oakland, CA, May 2005.
[44] G. Yan and S. Eidenbenz, "Modeling propagation dynamics of bluetooth worms (extended version)," *IEEE Transactions on Mobile Computing*, vol. 8, no. 3, March 2009, pp. 353-368.
[45] V. Yegneswaran, P. Barford, and D. Plonka, "On the design and utility of internet sinks for network abuse monitoring," in *Symposium on Recent Advances in Intrusion Detection (RAID'04)*, Sept. 2004.
[46] W. Yu, X. Wang, D. Xuan, and D. Lee, "Effective detection of active smart worms with varying scan rate," in *Proc. of IEEE Communications Society/CreateNet International Conference on Security and Privacy in Communication Networks (SecureComm'06)*, Aug. 2006.
[47] W. Yu, X. Wang, D. Xuan, and W. Zhao, "On detecting camouflaging worm," in *Proc. of Annual Computer Security Applications Conference (ACSAC'06)*, Dec. 2006.
[48] C. C. Zou, W. Gong, D. Towsley, and L. Gao, "The monitoring and early detection of Internet worms," *IEEE/ACM Transactions on Networking*, vol. 13, no. 5, Oct. 2005, pp. 961-974.
[49] C. C. Zou, D. Towsley, and W. Gong, "On the performance of Internet worm scanning strategies," *Elsevier Journal of Performance Evaluation*, vol. 63. no. 7, July 2006, pp. 700-723.
[50] C. C. Zou, D. Towsley, W. Gong, and S. Cai, "Advanced routing worm and its security challenges," *Simulation: Transactions of the Society for Modeling and Simulation International*, vol. 82, no. 1, 2006, pp.75-85.
[51] CAIDA, "Network telescope," [Online]. Available: http://www.caida.org/research/security/telescope/ (Aug./2010 accessed).
[52] Computing Research Association, "Grand research challenges in information security & assurance," [Online]. Available: http://archive.cra.org /Activities /grand.challenges /security /home.html (Aug./2010 accessed).
[53] Darknet. [Online]. Available: http://www.cymru.com/Darknet/. (Oct./2010 accessed).
[54] Distributed Intrusion Detection System (DShield), http://www.dshield.org/.

(Oct./2010 accessed).
[55] Honeypots: Tracking Hackers. [Online]. Available: http : // www. tracking - hackers. com/ . (Oct./2010 accessed).
[56] The CAIDA Dataset on the Witty Worm - March 19-24, 2004, Colleen Shannon and David Moore, http://www.caida.org/data/passive/witty_worm_dataset.xml. Support for the Witty Worm Dataset and the UCSD Network Telescope are provided by Cisco Systems, Limelight Networks, the US Department of Homeland Security, the National Science Foundation, DARPA, Digital Envoy, and CAIDA Members.

2

Anomaly Based Intrusion Detection and Artificial Intelligence

Benoît Morel
Carnegie Mellon University
United States

1. Introduction

"The internet can be regarded as the most complex machine mankind ever built. We barely understand how it works, let alone how to secure it" [Schneier 2008]. The introduction of new technologies like the proliferation of new web applications or the increasing use of wireless, have exacerbated this fact. Cybersecurity, a spin-off of the phenomenal growth of the internet, has probably become the most complex threat to modern societies. The development of cybersecurity has been reactive and driven by the ingeniosity and imagination of cyberattackers. In the words of Carl Landwehr in IEEE security and Privacy (Landwehr 2008), "defense has consisted in "fixing the plumbing". What we need is to put more Artificial Intelligence (AI) in cybersecurity". This is the theme of this chapter.

Cyberspace is a rather brittle infrastructure, not designed to support what it does today, and on which more and more functionality is build. The fact that the internet is used for all sorts of critical activities at the level of individuals, firms, organizations and even at the level of nations has attracted all sorts of malicious activities. Cyber-attacks can take all sorts of forms. Some attacks like Denial of Service are easy to detect. The problem is what to do against them. For many other forms of attack, detection is a problem and sometimes the main problem.

The art of cyber-attack never stops improving. The Conficker worm or malware (which was unleashed in Fall 2008 and is still infecting millions of computers worldwide two years later) ushered us in an era of higher sophistication. As far as detection goes, Conficker in a sense was not difficult to detect as it spreads generously and infected many honeypots. But as is the case for any other new malware, there are no existing tool which would automatically detect it and protect users. In the case of Conficker, the situation is worse in the sense that being a dll malware, direct detection and removal of the malware in compromise computers is problematic. One additional problem with Conficker is the sophistication of the code (which has been studied and reverse engineered ad nauseam) and of the malware itself (it had many functionality, was using encryption techniques to communicate (MD6) which had never been used before). It spreads generously worldwide using a variety of vectors, within networks, into a variety of military organizations, hospitals etc…). In fact the challenge became such that the security industry made the unprecedented move of joining forces in a group called the Conficker working group. The only indication that this approach met with some success is that even if the botnet that Conficker build involves millions of infected computers, that botnet does not seem to have been used into any attack, at least not yet....

Conficker is only but one evidence that cyber-attackers have reached a level of sophistication and expertise such that they can routinely build malware specifically for some targeted attacks (against private networks for example), i.e. malware that are not mere variations of a previous one. Existing tools do not provide any protection against that kind of threat and do not have the potential to do so. What is needed are tools which detect autonomously new attacks against specific targets, networks or even individual computers. I.e. what is needed are intelligent tools. Defense based on reactively protecting against the possibility of a re-use of a malware or repeat of a type of attack (which is what we are doing today) is simply inadequate.

With the advent of the web, the "threat spectrum" has broadened considerably. A lot of critical activity takes place through web application. HTML, HTTP, JavaScript among others offer many points of entry for malicious activity through many forms of code injections. Trusted sessions between a user and a bank for example can be compromised or hijacked in a variety of ways.

The security response against those new threats is tentative and suboptimal. It is tentative in the sense that new attacks are discovered regularly and we are far from having a clear picture of threat spectrum on web application. It is suboptimal in the sense that the "response" typically consists in limiting functionality (through measure such as "same origin policy", for example), or complicating and making more cumbersome the protocol of trusted session in different ways. The beauty and attraction of the web stem from those functionalities. This approach to security potentially stifles the drive for innovations, which underlie the progress of the internet.

Cybersecurity is a challenge, which calls for a more sophisticated answer than is the case today. In this chapter, we focus on intrusion detection. But there is a role for Artificial Intelligence practically everywhere in cybersecurity,

The aspect of the problem that Intrusion Detection addresses is to alert users or networks that they are under attack or as is the case with web application may not even involve any malware but is based on abusing a protocol. What kind of attributes should an Intrusion Detection System (IDS) have to provide that kind of protection? It should be intelligent, hence the interest in AI.

The idea of using AI in intrusion detection is not new. In fact it is, now decades old, i.e. almost as old as the field of intrusion detection. Still today AI is not used intensely in intrusion detection. That AI could potentially improve radically the performance of IDS is obvious, but what is less obvious is how to operationalize this idea. There are several reasons for that. The most important one is that AI is a difficult subject, far from mature and only security people seem to be interested in using AI in intrusion detection. People involved in AI seem much more interested in other applications, although in many ways cybersecurity should be a natural domain of application for AI. The problem may lie more with cybersecurity than the AI community. Cybersecurity projects the impression of a chaotic world devoid of coherence and lacking codification.

As a result of that situation, most of the attempts to introduce AI in intrusion detection consisted in trying to apply existing tools developed or used in AI to cybersecurity. But in AI tools tend to be developed around applications and optimized for them. There are no AI tools optimized for cybersecurity. AI is a vast field which goes from the rather "primitive" to the very sophisticated. Many AI related attempts to use AI in cybersecurity, were in fact using the more basic tools. More recently there has been interest in the more sophisticated approaches like knowledge base approach to AI.

In the spirit of the Turing test (Turing 1950), it is tempting to define what an AI based intrusion detector should accomplish, is to replicate as well as possible what a human expert would do. Said otherwise, if a human expert with the same information as an IDS is able to detect that something anomalous/ malicious is taking place, there is hope that an AI based system could do the job. Since cyber attacks necessarily differ somehow from legitimate activities, this suggest that an AI based detector should be also an anomaly-based detector, whatever one means by "anomaly" (we elaborate on that later in this chapter). A closer look at the comparison between human beings and machine suggests that there are irreducible differences between the two which translate in differences in the limit of their performance. Human beings learn faster and "reason" better. But those differences do not go only in favor of the human: machines compute faster and better...

Today's AI based IDS's are very far from the kind of level of performance that makes such comparisons relevant. To provide adequate protection to the increasing level of functionality and complexity that is happening in the internet, the AI systems involved in cybersecurity of the future would have to be hugely more sophisticated than anything we can imagine today, to the point of raising the issue of what size they would have and the amount of CPU they would need. Is it possible to conceive a future cyberworld where so much artificial intelligence could coexist with so much functionality without suffocating it? The answer has to be yes. The alternative would be tantamount to assume before trying that AI will be at best a small part of cybersecurity. Where would the rest, the bulk of cybersecurity come from?

In fact there is a precedent: the immune system. The immune system co-evolved with the rest of biological evolution to become a dual use (huge) organ in our body. There are as many immune cells in our body as nervous cells ($\sim 10^{12}$). The human body is constantly "visited" by thousands of "antigens" (the biological equivalent of malware) and the immune system is able to discriminate between what is dangerous or not with a high degree of accuracy. In the same way one could envision in the long run computers being provided with a "cyber-immune system" which would autonomously acquire a sense of situational awareness from which it could protect the users. This is at best a vision for the long run. In the short run, more modest steps have to be made.

The first detection of any attack is anomaly-based. Today most if not all of the time the anomaly-based detector is a human being. The interest in anomaly-based detection by machines has an history which overlaps the history of attempts of introducing AI in cybersecurity. In fact most of the attempts to introduce AI in intrusion detection was in the context of anomaly-based detection.

Basically all new attacks are detected through anomalies, and in most cases they are detected by human beings. Considering the variety of forms that attacks can take, it is rather obvious that anomalies can take all sorts of forms. Anomaly based Intrusion Detection has been a subject of research for decades.. If it has failed to deliver a widely used product, this is not for lack of imagination of where to look to find anomalies. One of the most promising attempts, which had an inspirational effect on the research in that field, was to use system calls.

The nemesis of anomaly-based detection has been the false positive. A detection system cannot be perfect (even if it uses a human expert). It produces false positive (it thinks it has detected a malicious event, which in fact is legitimate) and has false negative (it fails to detect actual malicious events). Often there is a trade-off between the two: when one puts the threshold very low to avoid false negative, one often ends up with a higher rate of false positive. If a detector has a false positive probability of 1%, this does not imply that if it raises a flag it will be a false alert only 1% of the time (and 99% probability that it detected an actual malicious event). It means that when it analyzes random legitimate events 1% of the time it will raise a flag. If the detector analysis 10,000 events, it will flag 100 legitimate events. If out of the 10,000 events one was malicious, it will raise an additional flag, making its total 101.Out of the 101 events detected, 1 was malicious and 100 were legitimate. In other words, out of the 101 alerts only one is real and 100 out of 101, i.e. more than 99% of the time the alert was a false positive.

Those numbers were illustrative but taken totally by chance. 1% is a typical performance for "good" anomaly based detection systems thus far proposed. The actual frequency of malicious activity in the traffic (if one neglects spam) is not precisely known, but malicious events are relatively rare. I.e. they represent between 0 and maybe 10^{-4} of the traffic. Before anomaly-based detection can be considered operational, one has to find ways to reduce the probability of false positive by orders of magnitude. It is fair to say that we are at a stage where a new idea in anomaly-based intrusion detection, inspired by AI or anything else, lives or dies on its potential to put the false positive under control. In this chapter, two algorithms or mechanisms are offered which can reduce the probability of false positives to that extent: one uses Bayesian updating, the other generalizing an old idea of von Neumann (von Neumann 1956) to the analysis of events by many detectors.

Those two algorithms represent the "original" or technical contributions of this chapter, but this chapter is also concerned more generally by the interface between AI and cybersecurity and discusses ways in which this interface could be made more active.

2. Framing the problem

a. The new Threat environment

The "threat environment" has evolved as has the art of cyber-attack. Buffer overflow vulnerabilities have been known for a long time - the Morris worm of 1988, that for many was the real beginning of cybersecurity, exploited a buffer overflow vulnerabilities. They became a real preoccupation a few years later and progressively people realize that most software written in C have exploitable buffer overflow vulnerabilities.

Buffer overflows are still around today. Although they have not been "solved" they now represent only one class in what has become a zoology of exploitable vulnerabilities. In most cases after those vulnerabilities are discovered, the vendor produces a patch, which is reverse engineered by hackers and an exploit is produced within hours of the release of the patch... Many well-known malware (Conficker is an example) exploit vulnerabilities for which there is a patch. They use the fact that for a variety of reasons, the patch is not deployed in vulnerable - of such attacks, where the attacker discovers the vulnerability before the vendor and susceptible computers are helpless. The attack in the fall 2009 against Google and a few more companies originating in China, called Aurora, was an example of an exploitable dangling pointers vulnerability in a Microsoft browser, that had not been discovered yet.

A good defense strategy should rely on the ability of anticipating attacks and produce patches in time. A really good defense system should be able to protect computers from the exploitation of yet undiscovered exploitable vulnerability.

With advent of the web new classes of vulnerabilities emerge. Some websites are not immune against code injection, which can have all sorts of implications. Some website are vulnerable to Java-script instructions. This can be used for a variety of purpose, one being to compromise the website and makes its access dangerous to users. Protecting websites against all forms of code injection is easy in the case where it does not involve a lot of functionality. But interactive websites providing a lot of functionality are far more difficult to protect against every possible scenario of attack.

In the case of web application security, the Browser plays a central role. The interaction between users and severs go through the Browser, which in principle sees everything. In practice browsers have some security embedded in them, but not of the kind that could alert the user that he is victim of a cross site request forgery (CSRF) attack, for example. A really good defense system would be able to achieve a degree of situational awareness of what is taking place within the browser to detect that kind of attack and other forms of attack.

b. What are anomalies

The concept of anomalies is problematic, as is their relation with malicious activities (Tan and Maxion, 2005). By definition an anomaly is a "rare event", in other words, the concept of anomaly is statistical in nature. A noteworthy attempt to define anomaly was the idea of S. Forrest et al to make statistics of system calls (Hofmeyr et al. 1998). The idea was inspired by the concept of self and non-self ion immunology. The building blocks of proteins and antigens are amino acids. There are about 20 of them, some more essential than others. This means that there is an enormous variety of sequence of amino acids. Antigens are recognized by the immune systems as "non-self", i.e. having sequences that are not represented in the body. In principle the immune system attacks only the tissues which are non-self (This is what happens in the rejection of transplants). Auto-immune diseases would represent the "false positive" and they are relatively very rare. What is remarkable is that the distinction self non-self in immunology is based on short sequences (typically 9) of amino acids, called peptides.

The idea is that users can be recognized by the statistics of system calls, and that the equivalent of peptides would be short set of successive system calls. The number six (Tan and Maxion 2002) turned out to be "optimum". In that approach one can choose to define what is "anomalous", through its frequency of occurrence: 1%, 0.1%, .. The connection between abnormality and maliciousness is based on assumptions.

One advantage of this approach is that every user is supposed to be different. That puts potential attackers in situation of added complexity as it is difficult for them to fool many users with the same attack at the same time.

Among the other obstacles in using this approach is the fact that users change habits, the concept of what is normal is not constant. and that can potentially be exploited through so-called "mimicry attacks", i.e. manipulation of the concept of normality by a shrewd attacker. The fact that in modern computers there is a lot of activity taking place in the background, out of the control of the user introduces an additional noise. Furthermore that kind of approach has limited use for web security. In the context of web applications, the information to analyze statistically is buried in the set of HTTP requests that reach and are conveyed by the browser.

3. Review of previous relevant work

One can find many papers dealing with intrusion detection and using the word "AI" in their title. By AI, often is meant data mining, neural network, fuzzy logic (Idris et al 2005),

Hidden Markov Model (Choy and Cho, 2001), self-organizing maps and the like. Considering that all these papers deal with anomaly-based intrusion detection, the key figure of merit to gauge their contribution is whether their approach has the potential to tame the false positives. Those papers are remotely related to this chapter, as the problem of false positives is not as central and unlike this chapter, in those papers the machine learning and Knowledge base aspects of AI are not as prominent as in the discussion of this chapter.

A lot but not all of the AI "machinery" is statistical (Mitchell 1997) in nature (and therefore is threatened by the curse of the false positives... There is branch of AI concerned by "reasoning" (Brachman et al. 2004, Bacchus et al 1999, Baral et al. 2000), making context dependent decision and the like. Among the papers dealing with AI in the context of intrusion detection, the paper of Gagnon and Esfandiari 2007 is probably the closest to this chapter. Its discussion is in fact less general than this chapter and is organized around a very specific use of a Knowledge based approach to AI. The discussion illustrates the challenges in trying to use sophisticated AI techniques in cybersecurity.

4. Reducing the false positives using Bayesian updating

As stated in the introduction the nemesis of anomaly based IDS systems is the probability of false positive. When the probability that an event is malicious does not exceed 10^{-4}, the probability of false positive should be less than that.

Little or no thought has been put in exploiting the fact that a cyber-attack is in general a protracted affair. In the same way that a human expert monitoring an suspicious events would see whether the evidence that what he is witnessing is indeed an attack or not, an IDS system could make a more protracted analysis of suspicion before raising a flag, thereby reducing the probability of false positive.

We sketch here how the math of such an iterated procedure would work, starting by spending some time defining what false positive means. It can mean more than one thing...

Let the Boolean variable ζ refer to whether one deals with a malicious event or not. By definition: $\zeta = 1$ means that the event is malicious. Otherwise $\zeta = 0$. The variable of interest is: $P(\zeta = 1)$, the probability that it was a malicious event. All the paraphernalia of data, measurements and detection, can be represented by another Boolean variable X. By definition $X = 1$ means that there is evidence for something malicious, i.e. something abnormal.

The famous Bayes theorem states that:

$$P(X=1,\zeta=0) = P(X=1|\zeta=0)P(\zeta=0) = P(\zeta=0|X=1)P(X=1) \quad (1)$$

In EQ1 there are three probabilities, which can be referred to as "false positive", but should be distinguished:

$P(X=1,\zeta=0)$ is the probability that, an attack is being detected while in fact no attack took place.

$P(X=1|\zeta=0)$ is the conditional probability that even if there is no attack, the system of detection will detect one.

$P(\zeta = 0 \mid X = 1)$ is the conditional probability that when there is evidence of an attack, in fact this is a false alert.
From EQ 1, it is clear that they are three different numbers.
The conditional probabilities $P(X = 1 \mid \zeta = 0)$ and $P(X = 0 \mid \zeta = 1)$ are figures of merit of the detection system. They determined whether or not the information generated by the detection system should be used or not. The number of interest is: that an attack is taking place.
What is referred to as "false positive" in this chapter is $P(X = 1 \mid \zeta = 0)$, i.e. it is an attribute of the detection system. In the same way $P(X = 0 \mid \zeta = 1)$ represents the false negative, also an attribute of the detection system
One can then use the fundamental assumption underlying the so-called "Bayesian updating": if at a given time the probability that there is a malicious event is $P(\zeta = 1)$, then after a new measurement where X is either 1 or 0, the new value of $P(\zeta = 1)$ is:

$$\tilde{p}(\zeta = 1) = \{X p(\zeta = 1 | X = 1) + (1 - X) p(\zeta = 1 | X = 0)\} \tag{2}$$

In order to have this expression in terms of "false positive" and false negative" , we rewrite EQ. 2, using EQ.1, as:

$$\widetilde{P}(\zeta = 1) = \left\{ \frac{(1 - X) P(X = 0 \mid \zeta = 1)}{P(X = 0)} + \frac{X P(X = 1 \mid \zeta = 1)}{P(X = 1)} \right\} P(\zeta = 1) \tag{3}$$

$\vartheta = P(\zeta = 1)$ is a dynamical variable. Each time a measurement is made, the value of $\vartheta = P(\zeta = 1)$ is updated into $\tilde{\vartheta}$:

$$\begin{aligned} \frac{\tilde{\vartheta}}{\vartheta} = & \frac{(1 - X) P(X = 0 \mid \zeta = 1)}{\vartheta P(X = 0 \mid \zeta = 1) + (1 - \vartheta) P(X = 0 \mid \zeta = 0)} + \\ & + \frac{X P(X = 1 \mid \zeta = 1)}{\vartheta P(X = 1 \mid \zeta = 1) + (1 - \vartheta) P(X = 1 \mid \zeta = 0)} \end{aligned} \tag{4}$$

To show the potential power of using Bayesian updating, let assume that as a prior we take $\vartheta = P(\zeta = 1) \approx 10^{-4}$. We also assume that the detection system has 1% false positive ($P(X = 1 | \zeta = 0) = 0.01$), we also assume that $P(X = 1 | \zeta = 1) = 0.99$, and consistently in EQ.4 each measurement is suspicious, i.e: $X = 1$. The evolution of the value of $\vartheta = P(\zeta = 1)$ is shown in Figure 1. It takes 4 successive evidences of suspicion to put the probability that there is a malicious activity close to 1. The probability that the detector will make 4 mistakes in a row (if there is no correlation) is $(10^{-2})^4 = 10^{-8}$.
The possibility of using Bayesian updating in the context of anomaly-based detection has not yet been seriously contemplated. This is only one avenue toward making an AI based systems much less prone to false positives. Another is using several computers networked together.

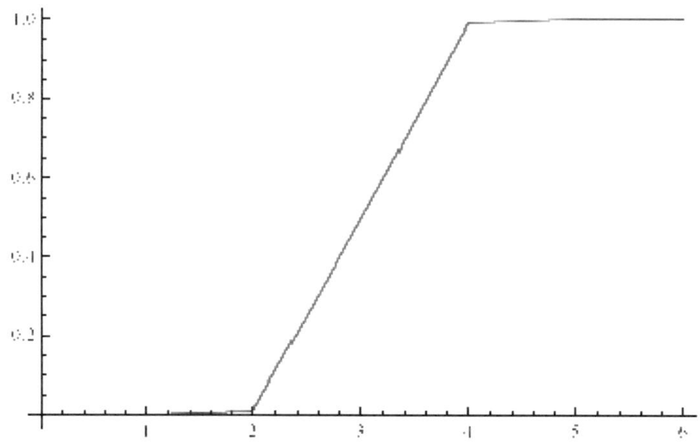

Fig. 1. Evolution of $P(\zeta = 1)$ through Bayesian updating, using EQ.4 starting at $P(\zeta = 1) = 10^{-4}$, assuming $P(X = 1|\zeta = 0) = 0.01$ and $P(X = 1|\zeta = 1) = 0.99$ and assuming that at each measurement $X = 1$.

5. Reducing the false positives using networked computers

Another avenue, which offers a lot of promises too, is using the observation that what one computer may have difficulty to do, several computers networked intelligently could.
John von Neumann (von Neumann 1956) wrote a paper entitled "Probabilistic logics and the synthesis of reliable organisms from unreliable components", which supports this notion. The paper, which culminated several years of study was not about anomaly-based intrusion detection, but understanding how the brain works. The goal was to sow how a logical system can perform better than its component and thereby establish some foundations for AI.
A way to interpret some of the results of von Neumann is that it is possible if one has a system involving a large number of components, to combine the components in such a way that they build a kind of information processor such that the resulting uncertainty on the outcome can in principle be made arbitrarily small if the number of components can be large enough.
Ostensibly the paper of John von Neumann (von Neumann 1956), addresses the question of how to reduce the error due to unreliable components to an arbitrary small level using multiplexing and large numbers. In practice, the ideas developed in that paper have the potential to be applied to a large variety of problems involving unreliable components and we think among others the problem of early detection of new malware. Here we described succinctly some relevant observations of von Neumann.

a. Logical 3- gates

A majority rule 3-gate receives information from three sources. The probability that the gate yields a false information is the probability that at least two of the three sources were providing a false information. If χ_i is the probability that line "i" gives a false positive, the probability that at least two of the three incoming lines give a wrong information and that the gate is sending a false positive signal is:

$$\pi_g = \chi_1\chi_2(1-\chi_3)+\chi_1\chi_3(1-\chi_2)+\chi_2\chi_3(1-\chi_1)+\chi_1\chi_2\chi_3 \quad (1)$$

Or equivalently:

$$\pi_g = \chi_1\chi_2+\chi_1\chi_3+\chi_2\chi_3-2\chi_1\chi_2\chi_3 \quad (2)$$

If one assumes that $\chi_i \approx 10\%$, then the probability of false positive of the system made of three detectors, feeding on a majority 3-gate will be $\pi_g \approx 3\%$ (Cf Figure 2).

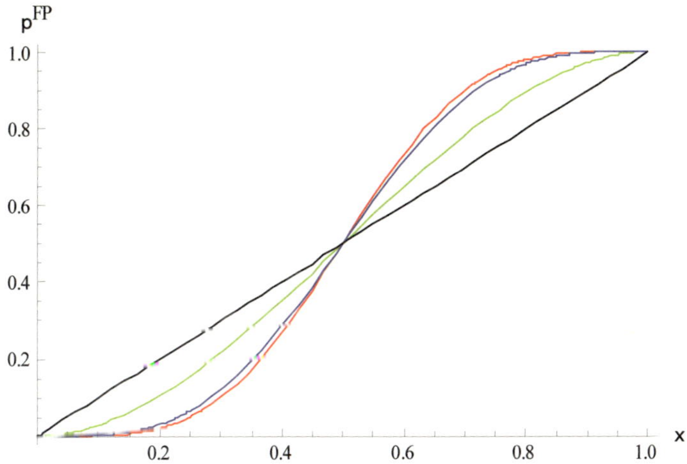

Fig. 2. Output of majority rule gates: The green curve is for the case with three detectors assuming that: $\chi_1=\chi_2=\chi_3=\xi$, i.e. that: $\pi_g = 3\xi^2-2\xi^3$. In that case: $\pi_{FP}^3 = 3\xi^2-2\xi^3$. The two other curves are for the case where there are nine detectors. The red curve corresponds to the simple majority rule π_{MR}^9, the other one (blue) corresponds to the case where the nine detectors are distributed in three majority 3 rules feeding a majority 3 rule. I.e. it corresponds to: π_{FP}^9.

b. With 3 N computers Logical 3-gates

Grouping the signal emanating from detectors in three and make them feed a majority rule gate would produce an aggregate with a somewhat improved probability of false positive (and this can be used for the false negative too).

For illustration let us assume that the number of detectors is nine, In the first scenario (construct of majority 3-gates), the probability π_{FP}^9 of false positive that nine computers (each with the same probability of false positive ξ) feeding three majority rule gates (each gate has a false positive probability $\pi_{FP}^3 = 3\xi^2-2\xi^3$), is therefore:

$$\pi_{FP}^9 = 3\left(\pi_{FP}^3\right)^2-2\left(\pi_{FP}^3\right)^3 = \left(3\xi^2-2\xi^3\right)^2\left\{3-2\left(3\xi^2-2\xi^3\right)\right\} \quad (3)$$

The generalization of this formula to the case of 3N detectors is:

$$\pi_{FP}^{3N} = 3\left(\pi_{FP}^{3(N-1)}\right)^2-2\left(\pi_{FP}^{3(N-1)}\right)^3 \quad (4)$$

The speed at which the false positive rate decreases when N grows is shown in Table 1, where the individual probability of false positive is assumed to be 10% ($\xi = 0.1$). What in table 1 is referred to as N=27 in EQ. 4 would correspond to 3N=27, i.e. N=9.Table 1 compares the situation of computers distributed into networked 3 gates, with the scenario where they build one logical N gates.

c. Logical N-gates

In this scenario (one majority rule gate), the probability of false positive π_{MR}^{N} has the general form:

$$\pi_{MR}^{N} = \sum_{i>\frac{N}{2}}^{N} \binom{N}{i} \xi^{i} (1-\xi)^{N-i} \tag{4}$$

In that scenario the overall probability of false positive decreases with N even faster than in the scenario of the networked 3-gates, as illustrated in Table 1.
When the number of computers increases, the improvement increases as well and it increases fast, in particular in the majority rule case. For example for $\xi = 0.1$:

	$\pi_{MR}^{N} = \sum_{i=\frac{N}{2}+1}^{N} \binom{N}{i} \xi^{i} (1-\xi)^{N-i}$	$\pi_{FP}^{N} = 3\left(\pi_{FP}^{\frac{N}{3}}\right)^{2} - 2\left(\pi_{FP}^{\frac{N}{3}}\right)^{3}$
N=3	0.028	0.028
N=9	0.00089	0.0023
N=27	5.6 x 10^{-8}	0.0000159
N=81	3.5 x 10^{--20}	7.6 x 10^{-10}
Set-up	Majority rule	3-gates

Those results assume that the probabilities of false positive of the different detectors are independent. This is clearly not always the case. This idea inspired from von Neumann could benefit significantly anomaly-based network intrusion detection.

d. Operationalizing such ideas and the need for more AI

If one could exploit the full implications of Bayesian updating and/or when possible use logical N-Gates, the fact that anomaly-based detection generate intrinsically too many false positive, would not constitute an insuperable obstacle to build a full anomaly-based system.

Logical N-gates and network security:

The multi computer approach inspired from von Neumann would be appropriate for network intrusion detection. If several computers detect anomalies simultaneously and they are appropriately connected, this could lead to a powerful system of detection with few false positives and few false negatives at the same time.
Ghostnet (and its follow up "Shadows in the Cloud") refers to a Trojans which penetrated several networks associated with government agencies, most notoriously the network of the Dalai Lama in 2008 and of Indian agencies involved in national Security in 2009/2010. In both cases it was traced back to China. Ghostnet was eventually discovered when the Dalai

Lama began to suspect that his network must have been penetrated by the Chinese and asked infowar in the university of Toronto to investigate. Using honeypot they uncovered the presence of a Trojan, which was spying on the e-mails and reporting to servers scattered in the world. The investigation established that the compound of the Dalai Lama was only one of several networks that had been penetrated. A close monitoring of the traffic coming in and out of the network, by the computers of the networks, could have detected some suspicious queries. But the probability that those suspicious queries were false positive would have been large. If the evidence of those suspicions had been sent to a centralized server, by an algorithm similar to the logic N-gates scenario, it may have been able to establish the suspicion with far more certainty, much earlier.
The same kind of argument can be made about malware like Agent.btz which "traumatized" the US military and malware like Silent Banker that roam in the networks of Banks. In each case an individual computer would not be able to do a very good job at detecting a malicious activity with high level of certainty. But those malware do not infect only one computer. They need to infect quite a few, which therefore could cooperate to establish the presence of the malware.

Operationalizing Bayesian updating:

Bayesian updating is somewhat reminiscent of the implications of the observation that if one uses more than one measurement, the two best measurements may not be the best two (Cover 1970). A way to operationalize the Bayesian updating technique would be for example through a tool making periodic assessments of whether a sequence of events involves an increasing number of evidences that it is suspicious or not. For example, the tool could be embedded in the Browser of a client monitoring all the HTTP requests. If the tool detects suspicious activity it would trigger this updating procedure by analyzing subsequent events and see whether the suspicion tends to increase or not.
Ideally the tool would be designed in such a way that it would be able to "reason" about those events and analyze them. The important part here is that the tool would use a protracted analysis of the event to reach a decision about the event. Its reasoning would be probabilistic, but not necessarily statistically based.

6. Web applications

Although the web is only one aspect of the internet, web applications are becoming a dominant feature of the internet and this trend is growing. From the perspective of cybersecurity, the world of web applications is very complicated and seems to offer an infinite numbers of opportunities for abuse. Some exploitable vulnerabilities are difficult to understand or anticipate as they result from technical details of protocols, implementation of application or are consequences of abusing functionalities which otherwise are very useful or valuable (vanKesteren et al. 2008). Each time a new vulnerability is discovered, suggestions are made on how to avoid them (Barth et al. 2008b, Zeller and Felten 2008). Those suggestions are often not very attractive because they are based on reducing some functionality or they include adding complications in the implementation of applications. To the credit of system administrators, many of them spontaneously find ways to avoid potentially exploitable vulnerabilities. This is one reason why it is not so easy to find popular websites with obvious cross-site scripting (XSS) or cross site forgery request (CSRF) vulnerabilities (Zeller and Felten 2008). On the other hand, new forms of attacks appear regularly (for example "ClickJacking"

(Grossman 2008), login CSRF (Barth et al. 2008) and more will appear. Still in the same way that the semantic web is based on the culture of AI, the new level of complexity of cybersecurity accompanying this development, would benefit from relying more on AI.

a. The example of Cross Site Request Forgery (CSRF)

In a CSRF attack, the attacker manages to pose as the legitimate user to a trusted website (Zeller and Felten 2008). CSRF is in fact not a new form of attack. In 1988 it was known as "confused deputy". For a long time it was a "sleeping giant" (Grossman 2006), which came to prominence only recently.

CSRF can take many forms, some of them not so easy to understand. But a simple instantiation of CSRF would run the following way. A user has a trusted session (trust being guaranteed by cookies) with his bank website. If without having logged out from the session, the user goes to a malicious website and is induced to click on a link, a CSRF could occur. If HTTP request the user makes an HTTP Get request to the bank website, the browser of the user will make the query to the bank website. Since the cookies of the session are still active, the website will not be able to realize that the query technically originates from the malicious site and will execute it and it could be a instruction to transfer money from the account of the user. This is one (there are others) of the possible abuses of HTTP requests. This is an unfortunate consequence of what otherwise makes HTTP such a powerful protocol allowing a lot of functionalities in web applications.

In order for the attack to be successful, not only should the user omit to log off from the trusted session with the bank, but the attacker should know all the coordinates of the bank and user. There are several ways to do that. One, which is simple to understand is if the website of the bank has been compromised in the first place by another form of popular web attack: Cross Site Scripting (XSS) (Foggie et al. 2007). Then the user can find himself been send to a spurious website and induce into But there are many other ways to lure a hapless user into going a malicious website or let an attacker hijack a trusted session.

A few suggestions have been made for defense against CSRF, either on the server side (Zeller and Felten 2008) or on the user side (for example RequestRodeo (Johns and Winter 2006)). But "to be useful in practice, a mitigation technique for CSRF attacks has to satisfy two properties. First, it has to be effective in detecting and preventing CSRF attacks with a very low false negative and false positive rate. Second, it should be generic and spare web site administrators and programmers from application-specific modifications. Basically all the existing approaches fail in at least one of the two aspects" (Jovanovic et al. 2006).

Would an expert monitoring each HTTP request and everything that goes through the browser always be able to realize that a CSRF attack is unfolding? The answer is not obvious. But it is safe to say that in most cases he would. That suggests that a AI-based defense system located within the browser could in principle also detect attacks.

b. Web Application Firewalls (WAF)

Firewalls have been part of the arsenal of cyberdefense for many years. The simplest and also the most reliable ones deny access based on port number. The filtering can be more sophisticated, like being based on a deeper analysis of the incoming traffic, like deep packet inspection.

Web applications firewalls (WAF) cannot rely on port number as most web applications use the same port as the rest of the web traffic, i.e. port 80. WAFs are supposed to tell the difference between benign and malicious web applications. This has to be made through deep packet inspection.

The idea of firewalls operating at the application layer is not new. They were introduced as "third generation" firewalls in the early 1990's. They are used to protect data bases against SQL injections, for example. WAFs, are sometimes treated as a specialized form of application layer firewalls. WAFs began to enter the market at the end of the 90's and tended to find their niche around specific applications. However sophisticated as they sometimes seem or are made to seem, as of today WAFs are not the reliable and performant tools that web security requires.

WAFs are in a sense very illustrative of what this chapter is about: to become what cybersecurity requires, WAFs need more Artificial Intelligence. One reason WAFs progress so slowly is that putting AI in security tools in general and in WAFs in particular is difficult. AI tends to be developed around specific applications. Many areas of applications have inspired aggressive AI research. Cybersecurity is not one of them, at least not yet, although it seems a very natural area of application as it is about computers. Human beings are completely in control of the rules and protocol and they could be designed to facilitate the use of AI.

7. Artificial Intelligence

a. The need for a new paradigm for defense

Instead of being adaptive, defense is purely reactive. In most cases it involves or essentially consists in limiting or foregoing some functionality. When a new attack has been discovered, more often than not the "security" solution consists in reducing the functionality. One major reason to turn toward AI, is to put an end at the present situation.

The move from DNS to DNSSEC illustrates somewhat the problem with the present approach. It has improved the security of the internet. But the cost is a complicated system of keys, whose renewal opens the door for scenarios of failures, which did not exist before. With DNSSEC the internet is less vulnerable to malicious exploitations of the weaknesses of the DNS system, but the use of a cumbersome system of authentication for all the servers involved does not make it more reliable.

The world of web applications is growing fast in importance and size, but in parallel it raises increasing concerns about security, which will not be solved adequately within the present paradigm of defense.

Same Origin Policy (SOP) is another example of the "old-fashioned" approach to cybersecurity. SOP (a policy adopted by most browsers) was designed to prevent the possibility that scripts originating from other than one site can be run on a web site (admittedly this has potentially dangerous consequences). Not only attacks such CSRF show that it is possible to circumvent the same origin policy, but that policy blocks other functionalities, which could be useful. In the words of Douglas Crockford: "[The Same Origin Policy] allows dangerous things while preventing useful ones". The way out of that dilemma may lie in a much more intelligent defense.

In the case of CSRF, the proposed defenses are either in the website (alerting the system administrator that the website in its present design allows CSRF attacks) or in the client side. Typically the solutions suggested either reduce the functionality of the website, changes the protocol of trusted session by requiring more authentication, or (as is the case with request rodeo) offers a tool which limits partially the access to websites from the clients. In other

words, the solutions tend to make the protocols safer by making them more cumbersome and the protection often involves a reduction of functionality, i.e. it goes exactly against the logic, which underlies the success of the internet.
What and AI-based approach potentially offer is a way to address the multiple threats associated with cybersecurity, without having to rely on an increasing list of changing rules or security procedures for diagnostic and recovery procedures. If security tools were expert systems, which could not be abused as easily, the situation would be very different. Ideally they would understand what users are trying to do and make sure that this is what is happening. They would develop a sense of "situational awareness", from which they would be able to tell malicious activity from legitimate ones. They would be able to make context dependent determinations.

b. Prospects of AI in cybersecurity

If AI means introducing intelligence in an automated system, there is no doubt that the future of cybersecurity lies in AI. But AI is at the same time an advanced field and at a very early stage of development.
The limits of the possible with AI are not known. The limits of the capabilities of AI are a moving frontier. In a "post biological intelligence" world (P. Davies, 2010), the division between natural and artificial intelligence will be blurred.
We are still far away from that world, but it is not too early to envision it. And the question is how should AI be introduced in the world of cybersecurity with maximum effect in the short term. Should we have a vision of AI-based cybersecurity as a cyber-equivalent of what happen with the immune system during biological evolution? I.e. of the creation over time of a large and complex organ inseparable from the rest of the organism? Should the first phase attempt to build the equivalent of a rudimentary immune system, with the vision of an eventual large and sophisticated one? Or should the search be more random and based on trying to introduce more intelligence in security tool whenever possible and wherever possible? In fact the two approaches differ only on paper. The immune system must have developed out of a random search as we are told the rest of biological evolution, leading in the long run to high levels of organization.
To what extent does AI in its present state provide a framework to start building such a system? It is impossible and not useful here to try and describe a field like AI. On the one hand it is a large body of academic knowledge (Russel and Novig 2003). When it comes to its applications, it looks more like a vast and fragmented field. Through expert systems AI has found applications in numerous fields from medical diagnosis to helping manufacture to finance management to fault analysis to advanced optimization, and to a too limited extent to cybersecurity.
Of the many techniques used in AI, when it comes to anomaly-based intrusion detection the techniques, which seem the most natural are either "statistics" based (Mitchell 1997) or "knowledge-based"(Kerkar and Srinivas 2009).
The whole area of machine learning tends to make heavy use of statistics. The a priori caveat with that kind of approach in the context of intrusion detection is the possibility that the problem (or curse) with false positive re-emerges. If it is possible to set-up the system in such a way it can "reason" probabilistically (Pearl 1988) about events along the lines of the iterative Bayesian updating described previously, this problem may turn out manageable. Statistically based machine learning traditionally needs huge amount of data. This may turn problematic in many situations of interest for intrusion detection.

This points to the fact that there are fundamental cognitive differences between human beings and machines. Human beings need much less data to "learn" than machines and get a better power of discrimination. One implication of that remark is to invalidate partially the assumption that what human beings can do, machines will also be able to do.
Still an approach based on statistical learning in cybersecurity is not hopeless, quite the opposite. But this suggests that the best use of AI may not be to try to find a way to have machines replicating what human beings do.
An alternative to statistical learning is Knowledge Based systems (KBS) (kerkhar, 2009), although that approach raises also challenging issues. KBS tends also to be specialized. The system can acquire its knowledge in a variety of ways. It can be made to learn. A lot rides on the way knowledge is stored and represented. Those systems can reason and make inferences. In principle they could be used to make autonomous determination of whether a malicious attack is unfolding.
In practice in the case of web applications, for example, the information they have is what the browser sees: http requests, they can parse ad nauseam, website contents etc... One immediate challenge is to set up a knowledge base, which can make sense of such information.
Other approaches used in AI may turn out quite powerful in cybersecurity. Intrusion detection has some features in common with problem solving. Techniques using formal logic and theorem proving may turn out to be quite useful. If it were possible to reformulate the problem of intrusion detection as solving a logical problem, we would know better what the limits of the possible are.
As of now probabilistic reasoning seems to be the most natural and easiest way to introduce AI in intrusion detection, but this may not be the only one in the long run.
In the context of cybersecurity, AI applications could take several forms. But it is clear that to be useful any AI will have to be used intensively. Even if the processing power of computers is increasing impressively, one has to be concerned by the potential CPU overhead associated with any intensive AI technique. Considering that there is hardly any alternative in the long run to AI in cybersecurity, one has to be prepared to see cybersecurity to be part of the rest of cyber in the same way as the immune system is part of the animal's organisms. Instead of being a protection added at the end, it will be an integral part of the system, and as is the case with the immune system, it could be made "dual use". I.e. its function may not be limited to protection.

8. Conclusions

Cybersecurity is a real challenge and the future of the internet partially depends on how that challenge is met. For a long time it has been clear that the cybersecurity response to the fast evolving threat needs to be much smarter than has been the case. The alternative is bound to lead to the situation predicted by Jonathan Zittrain [Zittrain 2008]: "If the problems associated with the Internet [...] are not addressed, a set of blunt solutions will likely be applied to solve problems at the expense of much of what we love about today's information ecosystem".
This chapter focused on anomaly-based intrusion detection. But the role of AI in cybersecurity should not be seen as limited to that. Some cybersecurity problems needs urgent attention: for example the BGP (Border Gateway Protocol). In that case as was the case with the DNS system, the origin of the problem has to do with authentication. It seems

that there is little that a human expert can do let alone an AI system without an authentication protocol. Today that means a cumbersome system of keys, which slows down everything and introduces new failure modes. Furthermore as we saw recently with MD5, encryption protocols get eventually broken.
BGP does not have a system of authentication based on keys. It has no authentication system at all. It is vulnerable to any rogue routers. That is not sustainable. Eventually BGP may also use an authentication system based on keys, with the same negative consequences. A very nice scenario would be that AI could offer other ways toward authentication, which is one of the major basically unsolved problem in cybersecurity.
There is an imperative to put far more artificial intelligence in cybersecurity. The question is how best to do it.
Artificial intelligence is a vast and advanced field still relatively immature and definitely not optimized for cybersecurity. Specific work will be needed in artificial intelligence to facilitate its application to cybersecurity. Progress on that front will go faster if the possibility of applying AI techniques in cybersecurity inspires more interest to the AI community.
Cybersecurity could turn out a very good field of application for AI. It has the computer to computer interaction dimension and some of the problem solving culture (Newel and Simon 1972) developed in AI may find a natural area of application there.
One obstacle to the development of the interface between the two communities (security and AI) is the way security world operates. In cybersecurity, there is no real repository of knowledge. The knowledge exists, there is a lot of it, but it is scattered and not codified. Instead of looking at AI to try and find some "tools" which could be applied directly to cybersecurity, security people should have a harder look at their field, to make it more easily penetrable to outsiders, like AI people. As long as the approach to security is organized around the specific of attacks and the defense consists in looking for ways to prevent them, through some tweaking of existing protocols or functionalities, this will not happen soon. A possibility would be to be able to develop some sense of "situational awareness" which could be communicated or inoculated to the AI based tools.
AI systems and human beings differ in significant ways. The implications of those differences will be clearer when operational AI based tools become far more common in cybersecurity. Although the limit of the possible in AI is really ill-defined, it exists.

9. References

Bacchus, Fahiem, Halpern, Joseph Y., and Levesque, Hector J., 1999, “Reasoning about noisy sensors and effectors in the situation calculus”, *Artificial Intelligence,* 111(1-2): 171-208.

Baral, Chitta and Gelfond, Michael, 2000, “Reasoning agents in dynamic domains”, in *Logic-Based Artificial Intelligence,* Jack Minker, ed., Dordrecht: Kluwer Academic Publishers, 257-279.

Baral, Chitta, McIlraith, Sheila, and San, Tran Cao, 2000, “Formulating diagnostic reasoning using an action language with narratives and sensing”, in *KR2000: Principles of Knowledge Representation and Reasoning,* Anthony G. Cohn, Fausto Giunchiglia, and Bart Selman, eds., San Francisco: Morgan Kaufmann, 311-322.

A. Barth, C. Jackson, and J. C. Mitchell. Robust Defenses for Cross-Site Request Forgery. In Proceedings of 15th ACM Conference, CCS,2008

Christopher M. Bishop. Pattern recognition and machine learning. Springer Verlag, Berlin, Germany, 2006

Brachman, R. J., Levesque, H. J.: Knowledge Representation and Reasoning, Morgan Kaufmann, San Francisco, chapters 10 and 11 (2004).

Alan Belasco et al. (2004). "Representing Knowledge Gaps Effectively". In: D. Karagiannis, U. Reimer (Eds.): *Practical Aspects of Knowledge Management, Proceedings of PAKM 2004, Vienna, Austria, December 2-3, 2004.* Springer-Verlag, Berlin Heidelberg.

Jongho Choy and Sung-Bae Cho, Anomaly Detection of Computer Usage Using Artificial Intelligence Techniques_ R. Kowalczyk et al. (Eds.): PRICAI 2000 Workshop Reader, LNAI 2112, pp. 31–43, 2001. Springer-Verlag Berlin Heidelberg 2001

Roberto Cordeschi: The role of heuristics in automated theorem proving. J.A. Robinson's resolution principle, *Mathware & Soft Computing* (1996) 3: 281-293

Marco Cova, Davide Balzarotti, Viktoria Felmetsger, and Giovanni Vigna: Swaddler: An Approach for the Anomaly-Based Detection of State Violations in Web Applications, C. Kruegel, R. Lippmann, and A. Clark (Eds.): RAID 2007, LNCS 4637, pp. 63–86, 2007. Springer-Verlag Berlin Heidelberg 20

T. Cover. The Best Two Independent Measurements are Not the Two Best. *IEEE Trans. on Systems, Man and Cybernetics*, SMC-4(1):116--117, January 1974

Davies Paul: Eerie Silence, Renewing our Search for Alien Intelligence, Penguins Book 2010.

Stefan Edelkamp and Carsten Elfers and Mirko Horstmann and Marcus-Sebastian Schröder and Karsten Sohr and Thomas Wagner, Early Warning and Intrusion Detection based on Combined AI Methods, Bremen, 2009.

Scott E. Fahlman: *Marker-Passing Inference in the Scone Knowledge-Base System,* J. Lang, F. Lin, and J. Wang (Eds.): KSEM 2006, LNAI 4092, pp. 114 - 126, 2006. Springer-Verlag Berlin Heidelberg 2006

Fahlman, S. E.: *NETL: A System for Representing and Using Real-World Knowledge,* MIT Press, Cambridge MA (1979)

Feigenbaum, E.A.: Some Challenges and Grand Challenges for Computational Intelligence, Journal of the ACM, Vol. 50, No. 1, January 2003, pp. 32–40.

Fogie, S., Jeremiah Grossman, Robert Hansen, Anton Rager, and Petko D. Petkov. XSS Attacks: Cross Site Scripting Exploits and Defense. Syngress, 2007

S. Forrest, S.A. Hofmeyr and A. Somayaji, "Computer immunology," *CACM,*

vol. 40, no. 10, pp. 88–96, October 1997

Francois Gagnon and Babak Esfandiari, "Using Artificial Intelligence for Intrusion Detection", in Frontiers in Artificial Intelligence and Applications, Vol. 160, "Emerging Artificial Intelligence Applications in Computer Engineering", Edited by Ilias Maglogiannis, Kostas Karpouzis, Manolis Wallace, John Soldatos, IOS Press, ISBN 978-1-58603-780-2, 2007, pp. 295 - 306.

A.K. Ghosh, A. Schwartzbard and M. Schatz, "Learning program behavior profiles for intrusion detection," *Proc. Workshop on Intrusion Detection and Network Monitoring*, pp. 51–62, Santa Clara, USA, April 1999.

J. Grossman. CSRF, the sleeping giant. http://jeremiahgrossman.blogspot.com/2006/09/csrf-sleeping-giant.html,Sep 2006

S. A. Hofmeyr, S. Forrest, A. Somayaji, Intrusion Detection using Sequences of System Calls, Journal of Computer Security,6:151--180, 1998

Norbik Bashah Idris and Bharanidlran Shanmugam, Artificial Intelligence Techniques Applied to Intrusion Detection IEEE Indicon 2005 Conference, Chennai, India, I I - 1 3 Dec. 2005, pp52-55.

Norbik Bashah, Idris Bharanidharan Shanmugam, and Abdul Manan Ahmed, Hybrid Intelligent Intrusion Detection System, World Academy of Science, Engineering and Technology 11 2005, pp.23-26

M. Johns and J. Winter. RequestRodeo: Client Side Protection against Session Riding. In F. Piessens, editor, Proceedings of the OWASP Europe 2006 Conference, refereed papers track, Report CW448, pages 5 – 17. Departement Computerwetenschappen, Katholieke Universiteit Leuven, May 2006.

N. Jovanovic, E. Kirda, and C. Kruegel. Preventing Cross Site Request Forgery Attacks. Securecomm and Workshops, 2006, pages 1–10, Aug. 28 2006- Sept. 1 2006

Kerkar RA and Sajja Priti Srinivas: "*Knowledge-based systems*", Jones & Bartlett Publishers, Sudbury, MA, USA (2009)

Landwehr,Carl, Cybersecurity and Artificial Intelligence: From Fixing the Plumbing to Smart Water, IEEE, Security and privacy, September/October 2008, p.3

Lee, W., S. J. Stolfo, Data Mining Approaches for Intrusion Detection, Columbia University, 1996

Loveland D. (1978), *Automated theorem proving: a logical basis,* Amsterdam, North Holland.

McCarthy, John, 1959, "Programs with common sense", in *Proceedings of the Teddington Conference on the Mechanization of Thought Processes*, London: Her Majesty's Stationary Office, 75-91.

McCarthy, John, 1979, "First order theories of individual concepts and propositions", in *Machine Intelligence 9*, J.E. Hayes, D. Mitchie, and L.I. Mikulich, eds., Chichester, England: Ellis Horwood, 129-148.

Meltzer B. (1969), The use of symbolic logic in proving mathematical theorems by means of a digital computer, in Bulloff J.J., Holyoke T.C., Hahn S.W. (eds),

Foundations of mathematics, Berlin, Springer, 39-45.

Meltzer B. (1971), Prolegomena to a theory of efficiency of proof procedures, in Findler N.V., Meltzer B. (eds), *Artificial intelligence and heuristic programming*, Edinburgh, Edinburgh University Press, 15-33.

Minsky M. (1975), A framework for representing knowledge, in Winston P. (ed.), *Psychology of computer vision*, New York, McGraw-Hill, 211-280.

Tom M. Mitchell. Machine learning. McGraw-Hill, New York, NY, 1997.

Moore, Robert C., 1985, "A formal theory of knowledge and action", in *Formal Theories of the Commonsense World*, Jerry R. Hobbs and Robert C. Moore, eds., Norwood, New Jersey: Ablex Publishing Corporation, 319-358.

B. Morel, Anomaly-Based Intrusion detection using Distributed Intelligent Systems, Proceedings of the 3rd Conference on Risks and Security of the Internet and Systems, Tunis , October 28-30, 2008, Tozeur, Tunisia

J. von Neumann, "Probabilistic logics and the synthesis of reliable organisms from unreliable components", in C. E. Shannon and J. McCarthy, editors, Annals of Math Studies, numbers 34, pages 43-98. Princeton Univ. Press, 1956

Newell A., Shaw J.C., Simon H.A. (1958), Elements of a theory of human problem solving, *Psychological Review, 65,* 151-166.

Newell A., Simon H.A. (1965), Simulation of human processing of information, *American Mathematical Monthly, 72,* 111-118.

Newell A., Simon H.A. (1972), *Human problem solving,* Englewood Cliffs, Prentice-Hall.

Nilsson N.J. (1971), *Problem solving methods in Artificial Intelligence,* New York,McGraw-Hill.

Judea Pearl. Probabilistic Reasoning in Intelligent Systems: Networks of Plausible Inference. Morgan Kaufmann, San Mateo, CA, 1988.

Pearl, Judea, 2000, *Causality: Models, Reasoning, and Inference,* Cambridge, England: Cambridge University Press, ISBN 0-521-77362-8.

T. Pietraszek Using Adaptive Alert Classification to Reduce False Positives in Intrusion Detection E. Jonsson et al. (Eds.): RAID 2004, LNCS 3224, pp. 102–124, 2004. Springer-Verlag Berlin Heidelberg 2004

Mario Castro Ponce, Intrusion Detection System with Artificial Intelligence, FIST Conference - June 2004

Robinson J.A. (1965), A machine oriented logic based on the resolution principle, *Journal of the Association for Computing Machinery, 12,* 23-41.

Robinson J.A. (1967a), Heuristic and complete processes in the mechanization of theorem-proving, in Hart J.T., Takasu S. (eds.), *Systems and computer science,* Toronto, University of Toronto Press, 116-124.

Russell, Stuart and Norvig, Peter, 2003, *Artificial Intelligence: A Modern Approach,* Englewood Cliffs, New Jersey: Prentice Hall, 2 ed.

Blake Shepard et al. (2005). "A Knowledge-Based Approach to Network Security: Applying Cyc in the Domain of Network Risk Assessment". In: *Proceedings of the Seventeenth Innovative Applications of Artificial Intelligence Conference*. Pittsburgh, Pennsylvania, July 2005.

Schneier, Bruce. On Security, 2008

K. C. Tan, R. Maxion, The Effects of Algorithmic Diversity on anomaly detector performance", International Conference on Dependable Systems and networks, Yokohama Japan, 2005, p.216

K.C. Tan, R. Maxion: "Why 6? Defining the Operational Limits of stide, an Anomaly- Based Intrusion Detector", Proc. IEEE Symposium on Security and Privacy, (2002)

Turing, A. M. 1950. Computing machinery and intelligence. *Mind 59,* 433–460.

Anne van Kesteren et al. Access control for cross-site requests. http://www.w3.org/TR/access-control/. 2008

C. Warrender, S. Forrest and B. Pearlmutter, "Detecting intrusions using system calls: Alternative data models," *Proc. IEEE Symposium on Security and Privacy,* pp. 133–145, May 1999

William Zeller and Edward W. Felten; Cross-Site Request Forgeries: Exploitation and Prevention, Princeton (2008);
http://citp.princeton.edu/csrf/
Jonathan Zittrain: The Future of the Internet and how to stop it, Blog, 2008

Part 2

Solutions and New Possibilities of IDS Constructed Based on Agent Systems

3

A Sustainable Component of Intrusion Detection System using Survival Architecture on Mobile Agent

Sartid Vongpradhip, Ph.D., and Wichet Plaimart
Chulalongkorn University, Rajamangala Thanyaburi University of Technology
Thailand

1. Introduction

The rapid growth of the Internet uses all over the world, estimation from the statistics up to December, 2010 [1], found that there are 6,845 Million Internet users worldwide. However, it comes with problems about threats; especially the Distributed denial-of-service attack (DDoS) that make the victim cannot services as usual. This threat is one of the computer network security problems that attack the confidentiality, authentication, integrity, non-repudiation, access control, and availability [2]. The major objective of these types of attack is to make the victim cannot access the resource or service the user as usual [3]. Those problem not only important for the security of the organizations network, but also can cause those organizations cannot connect to the Internet connection, especially if that organization having the transactions via the Internet, this will cause the huge effect that is hard to forecast. Moreover, nowadays there is still no method that can completely prevent or avoid those attacks [4]. IDS is defined as [5] the problem of identifying individuals who are using a computer system without authorization (i.e., 'cracker') and those who have legitimate access to the system but are abusing their privileges (i.e., the 'insider threat'). For our work, we add to this definition the identification of attempts to use a computer system without authorization or to abuse existing privileges. Thus, intrusion is defined as "any set of actions that attempt to compromise the integrity, confidentiality, or availability of a resource".

IDS acts like the gate-keeper that has a duty to screen the people who come in and out the network. It will detect and block the intruder to access the network, therefore one of the objectives of IDS is to classify correctly between the real intrusion activity and the activity that similar to the intrusion but not the intrusion. Now, IDS is the software that detects, specifies, and reacts on the activities without the permission or the activities that are unusual on the target system. Various form of IDS are use as the main tool to detect and protect all of the computer system resources in the organization, may be the specific tool or the software that can install on the system that need to be protected.

Furthermore, IDS is used as the major tool in the detecting and preventing the computer network resources in the organizations. So, IDS is the first target that the intruder will be attacked. I they can make IDS not convenient; all of the computer network resources have no prevention. However, as we cannot avoid the attack, the problem is how we can survive from the attack. For that, we must design the intrusion detection system that is based on the basic of the architecture that is durable and can survive when there is an attack. So, the research about the intrusion detection system architecture design which is durable is the challenge.

The content in this paper divided into 7 sections. Firstly, the section is introduction. Secondly, the section is the related work. Thirdly, this section will explain about our architecture and model description. Fourthly, the section is architecture analysis. Fifthly, the section is analytical result. Sixthly, the section is our architecture proofing. And the last section is conclusion, recommendation and future work.

2. Related work.

The research in the field of the intrusion detection system that use the agent-based detection representative program technology can be separated to 3 levels, approach level [6], [7], [8], [9], [10], [11] implementation level [12], [13], and evaluation level [14], [15]. At present, the research about the technology of the Mobile Agent that uses the intrusion detection system is rapid growth. From our study the present IDS in the both of commercial and research, we found that most IDS use the architecture that has hierarchical structure that has both host-based and network-based sensor, which collect the data, fundamental compile and pass on the result from the server that is the central analyzer. Here is the conclusion of the intrusion detection system main problem.

Firstly, the single point of failure, the server that use for system analysis can found the single point of failure, if the intruder can make the server cause problem, slower or fail, for example, attack with DDoS. The system will have no protection.

Secondly, the scalability problem, the architecture that compile with one computer make the system cannot be larger, because the analyzer unit that use to analyze the system will be limited with the size of the network that is detected. Moreover, the process that the server must handle the communication from many other hosts, this not only causes the heavy traffic on the network, but also leads to the bottleneck too.

Thirdly, the difficulties of the adjusting of the configuration or ad the new abilities onto the components of the network, because mostly to the adjusting, correcting, and increasing the configuration, we must modify the configuration file, add or delete configuration file, or add new modules. These kinds of actions must restart the system, so the IDS can be used. Even if the third problem had been solved by implementing the mobile agent technology in the IDS architecture, however, the first two problems still not solved indeed.

In summary, the major problem of current IDS is not resistant to the attack of the IDS. This consequence from structural weaknesses of the lack of robust IDS that, lack of dynamic elements that can not escape the attack and lack of rapid backup and recovery mechanism.

3. Overview of our proposed architecture

This research goes to the effort to design the IDS architecture that is durable and survived after the attack. It is mainly use mobile agent technology to design and let IDS has more ability to the Distributed IDS.

In this research, we interest in the architecture design that still has the detecting function and response to prevent the computer system resource, but durable from the attack and survived by using mobile agent technology with the network topology design. To deals with the ability to be the Survival architecture for IDS, the design will be based on the topics as bellow.

3.1 Survival architecture.

Our conceptual framework to design for survival architecture based on highly available service of fault tolerant model which the model and description as the bellow.

A. Highly available service of fault tolerant model.

Our design concept based on highly available service of fault tolerant model. The framework for implementing highly available service by replicating data close to the points where group of clients need it. The replica manager exchange messages periodically in order to convey the update they have each received from clients. The service model provides two basic of operations: queries are read only operations and update modify but do not read the state. A key feature is that front ends send queries and updates to any replica manager they choose any that is available and can provide reasonable response time [18]. The system as shown in Fig. 1 make two guarantees, even though replica manager may be temporarily unable to communicate with one another, each client obtains a consistent service over time - or- relaxed consistency between replicas.

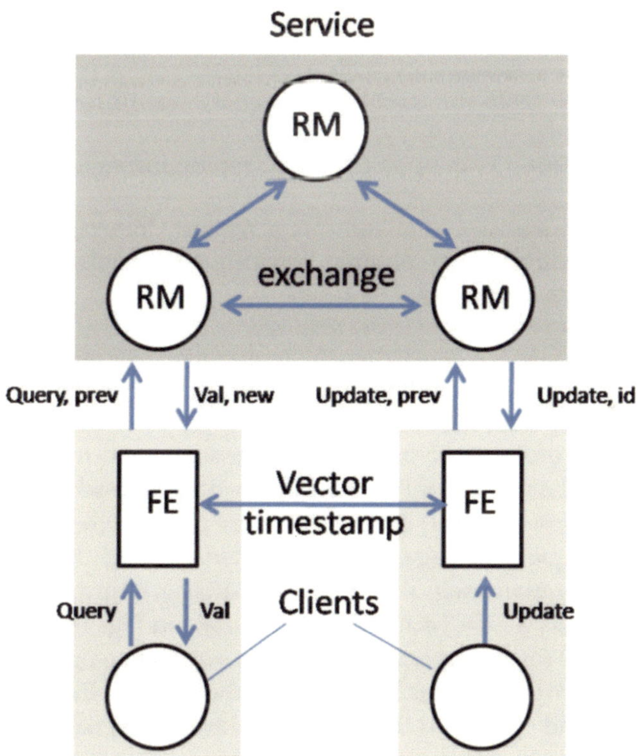

Fig. 1. Highly available service of fault tolerant model

The highly available service is a fault tolerant model that ability of the system will continue to work in conditions that damage occurred. The goal of a durable system of corruption is preventing failure of the system as possible. There have key three properties [18]; fault avoidance, fault masking and fault tolerance. Fault Avoidance is a technique to avoid damage that may occur. Avoiding damage is in the form of IDS architectural design. We use this property as a separate architectural design system divided by the critical resources of the network into three sections includes Critical asset, Proxy partition and region. The enterprise network perimeter by zoning to break the trust-host and untrust host separated to the mechanism used to secure appropriate.

Fault Masking is the process to prevent fault that occur not to affect overall system performance. Our design of system architecture and network zoning this property to hide the fault of some of the elements and use the rapid backup and recovery mechanism to work instead.

Fault Tolerance is the ability of the system will continue to work in conditions that damage occurred. The goal of a durable system of corruption is preventing failure of the system as possible. The architecture, we use several techniques designed to sustain damage, including fault detection, fault location, fault containment and fault recovery. These techniques can all work under the Mobile Agent technology.

B. The Model Description

To explain our basic replication model, how a model processes queries and update operations is as follows.

Request: The front end (FE) normally sends request to only a single replica manager (RM) at a time. A front end will communicate with a different replica manager when the one it normally uses fails or becomes unreachable. It may try one or more others if the normal manager is heavily loaded.

Update Response: If the request is an update then the replica manager replies as soon as it has received the update.

Coordination: The replica manager that receives a request does not process it until it can apply the request according to the required ordering constraints. No other coordination between replica managers is involved.

Execution: The replica manager executes the request.

Query Response: If the request is a query then the replica manager replies at this point.

Agreement: The replica managers update one another by exchanging the messages, which contain the most recent updates they have received.

In order to control the ordering of operation processing, each front end keeps a vector timestamp that reflects the version of the latest data values accessed by the front end or the client. This timestamp (prev in Fig. 1) contains an entry for every replica manager. The front end sends it in every request message to a replica manager, together with a description of the query or update operation itself. When replica manager returns a value as a result of a query operation, it applies a new vector timestamp (new in Fig. 1). Since the replicas may have been updated since the last operation. Similarly, an update operation returns a vector timestamp (update id in Fig. 1) that is unique to the update. Each return timestamp is merged with the front end's previous timestamp to record the version of the replicated data that has been observed by the client.

3.2 System architecture

Allocate all the network resources into parts as shown in Fig. 2. Each part will be composed of Critical asset, Proxy partition and region. In the Critical asset there is Critical host which include the important Application server and Critical IDS hosts. In Proxy partition, there are the proxy agents' multicast groups and the intermediate layer hosts or network elements. The communication between this internal component and the communication with the

Critical asset has to use the high-speed transmission line or the network backbone that is hard to be attacked and region means the leaf LAN in the network.

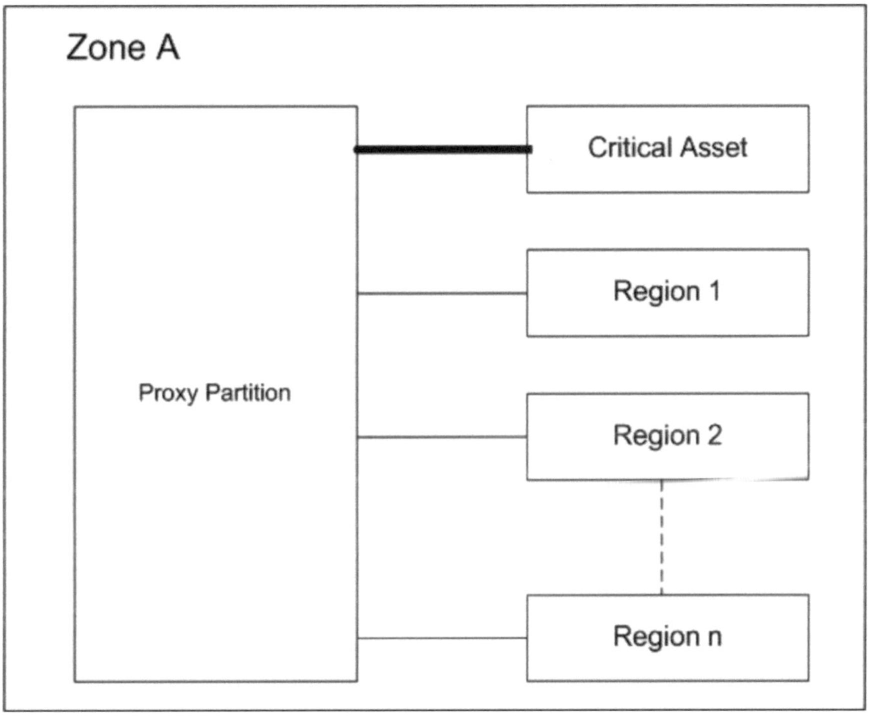

Fig. 2. System architecture

Using Proxy partition concept that has the proxy agent as the medium for the communication between the components for hiding the major resources from the approach an attack directly, having shadow agent as the redundancy mechanism and the backup and recovery mechanism design, makes the system durable for the attack and can be survived. Proxy agent in the proxy partition is the multicast group that composed of the group members; each group will have the shadow agent as the mirror group communicates with other groups. The objective of this structure is to make the shadow agent, uses for preventing the proxy agent as shown in Fig. 3.

Design the main components of the detection and response system is divided into groups, each group communicate by using the multicast group and asynchronous information transferring to reduce the amount of the information that are transferred in the network.

3.3 Enterprise network perimeter by zoning

The designs that will be divide all of organization's network resources into separate parts, according to the separate design concept as shown in Fig.4. Define the region of the network to support both trusted-hosts and untrusted-hosts. The network will be dividing to 4 zones, external network zone, internal network zone, wireless zone and DMZ (Demilitarized zone), as shown in Fig. 4 and has monitoring zone with the use of the network topology that has NAT (Network Address Translation) technique to hide the network resources from the outsider.

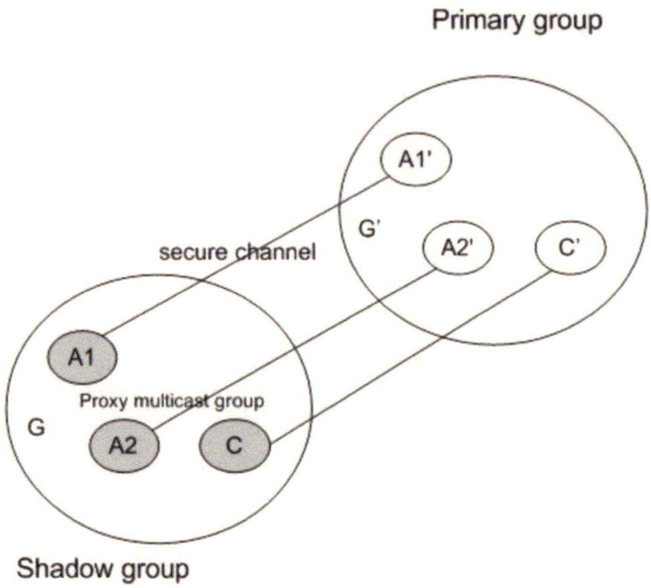

Fig. 3. Proxy agent and shadow agent

Although designed for corporate network security, this is actually not new. But today, most organization's network still does not focus much. They remain vulnerable to intruders use to attack at any time.

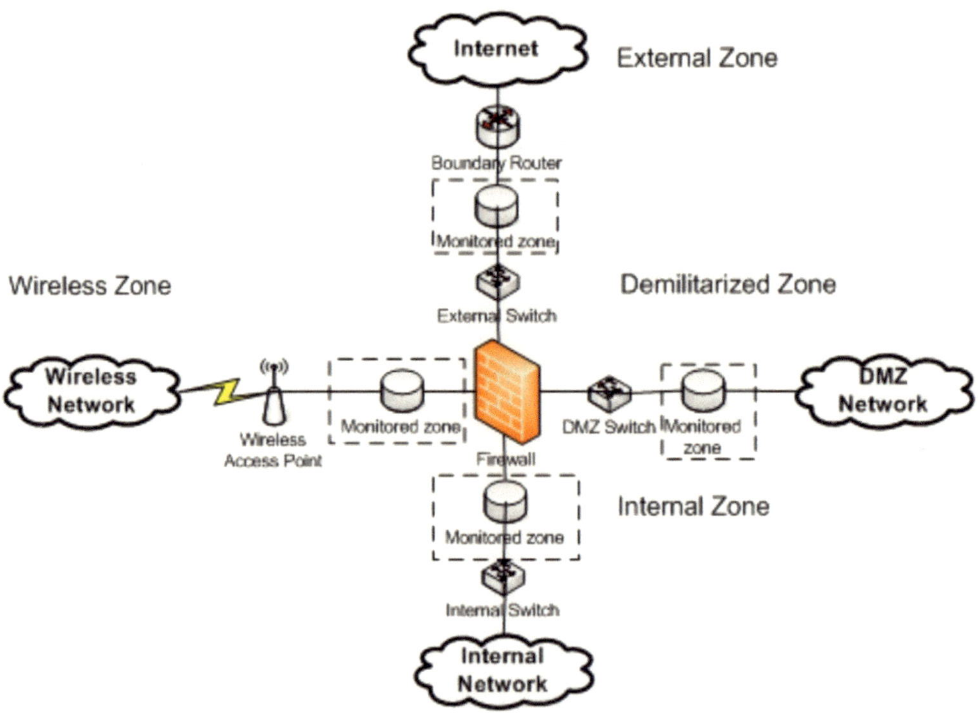

Fig. 4. Enterprise network zoning with monitored zone

This idea has the objective to not being the target that can attack easily and from the attacking. It also and limit the damage when there is an attack. Therefore, these are 5 class of the attacker, the outside attacker that intruding via the Internet (class 1), the outside attacker who intrude via wireless segment (class 2), the internal attacker who intrude via the wired LAN (class 3), and the internal attacker that intrude via the wireless segment (class 4).
This network consists of 4 monitoring zone, installing at the area that there is the inbound and outbound access of traffic, by using firewall as the tool to separate the network into 4 zones in the physical level featured with;
External network zone composed of the external firewall interface through the boundary router, and to the Internet. Internal network zone composed of the internal firewall interface, including every host that is connected until reach the internal switch.
Wireless zone composed of devices and hosts that connect to the wireless. DMZ composed of firewall DMZ interface, including every host that is connected with DMZ switch. The separation of the network into zones will support good security framework, specifying about the rule and security policy that conform with the traffic from each zone clearly and concisely. This make the system can clearly monitor and detect the intrusion.

3.4 Backup and recovery mechanism

To ensure that the survival system, in case of the agent that is one of the components of this architecture stops its process, which might because the lost while transmitting, being attacked, or fail to communicate with other agents in the proper time limit. It will suddenly resume perfectly, do not make others process in IDS being destroyed. This is because we design the rapid backup and recovery mechanism, it is the major part of this architecture because it is the protection using the agent system, and every agent will has more than 1 agent backup as shown in Fig. 5.

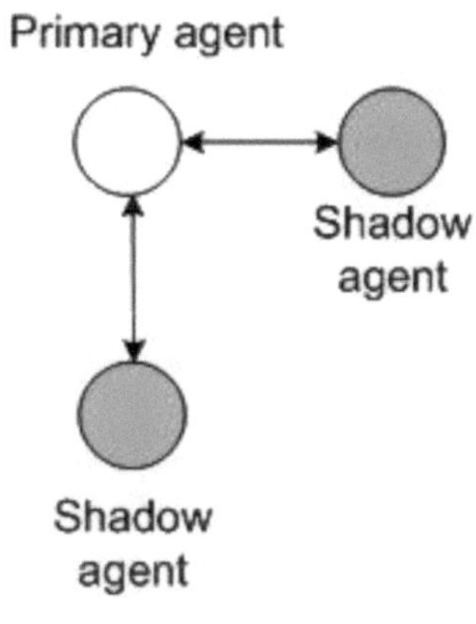

Fig. 5. Agent Backup

Backup agent will keeps all the information or some part of the agent that it is backup as shown in Fig. 6. The recovery process will (1) operational agent with 2 backup agents (2). When the original agent is corrupts. (3) Both backup agents will make a deal to choose the selected the successor. (4) When the successor is selected, it will create the new backup (5), agent that is broken discovers their ability, but the original agent will be terminated.

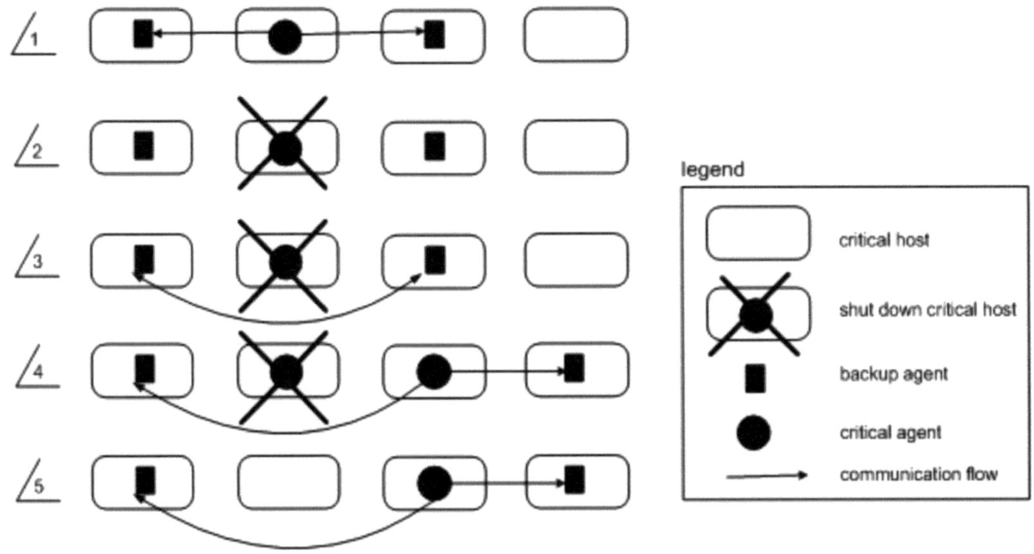

Fig. 6. Backup and recovery mechanism

3.5 Security techniques

To ensure the correctness of the message integrity, we make all of the communications in the components pass only the secured channel, by using the Public-key cryptography that is the Asymmetric scheme encryption and prevent the information by using HMAC (Hashed Message Authentication Code), which is the one component of the Digital signature. We do not need to encrypt overall document, but encrypt only with hash-value that received from the original document for the more execution speed and reduces the density of the transmission on the network.

Moreover, the communication between the groups of the major components will force to communicate via the secure transmission channel, using the VPN (Virtual private network) technique. To reduce network congress ion, we design all communication between components using asymmetric multicasting group.

4. Architecture analysis

For considering whether our designed architecture can be survived or not, we will consider.

4.1 Phase of compromise analysis

If we want to detect the intrusion, we need to understand the actions to make the victim compromised from scanning, infiltrating, until the ability to control over the victim. There are 5 phases [17] to compromise a target, including (1) reconnaissance, (2) exploitation, (3) reinforcement, (4) consolidation, and (5) pillage. Reconnaissance is the process to detect the connection and the number of hosts, the number and type of services, and examine the vulnerability of the application. Exploitation is the process that using those vulnerabilities in the wrong way, changing, or make the victim's service unusable.

Reinforcement is the step of trying to make strength of the intruder, by using the ability of it while infiltrating on the victim. Consolidation is the step that occur when the intruder communicate to the server of the victim via the Back door and use the victim as the base to intercept the traffic of the communication between the server and the other host. Pillage is the last step of the aim of the intruder; this may be stealing important data, attack the victim, or command to attack other system that is identified, using the victim as the base for attacking, terminating the process, destroying the resource, or spoil the target's whole organization reputation. After understand the procedure and the activities of the attacking, we can design the intruder detection system to handle, detect, analyze, and response to the intrusion easily.

4.2 Attack pattern analysis

From the previous section, we can conclude the attacking pattern from the attacking model into 4 patterns, that are the external attacker that intruding through the Internet (class 1), the external attacker that intruding through the wireless network (class 2), the internal attacker that intruding through the wired LAN (class 3), and the internal attacker that intruding through the wireless network (class 4). Therefore, we can divide the intruder into two groups, the first group is the external intruder that intruding through the Internet and the wireless network, the second group is the internal intruder through the organization network and the wireless network, both group have the bad objective to the organization's resources. However, with the architecture we designed in this research. Although we can see the channel (that comes from which route), the direction (of the attacking), and the intruder type (who, internal or external), but we cannot close these channels for forbid the intruder, because the usual user also use them. It is impossible that the organization do not allow their officers use the internet from the internal hosts. So, we defined the way to access the network for getting to the resources certainly and limited. We divided the network resource into 4 zones, internal network zone, external network zone, wireless zone, and DMZ. Each zone has the certainly controlled in and out path, using firewall to control the flow of the inbound and outbound traffic, defined the 4 zones as the monitored zone and install the monitored host in each zone also. With our proposed architecture, we assume that there is no attacking type, by which channel, and by who can avoid the detecting of our system. Our system can certainly see the intrusion that occurs in any time and any where. Although this assumption does not guarantee that the intrusion detection system will oppose and survive if there is an attack, but we can find the conclusion in the next topic.

4.3 Attack analysis

We defined the attacking type into 4 types, that are (1) penetrate attack, (2) passive sniffing attack, (3) active probing attack, and (4) denial-of-service attack. As considering the sequence of the intrusion in the previous topic, usually the intruder will use type (2) and type (3) for the first phase of the attack to explore the target network, and then in phases 2-5, it will use type (1) and type (2) with the target victim. By considering those 4 attacking types with our designed system architecture, we can analyze the region that the intruder can attack into 3 partitions, which are the region, the proxy partition, and the critical asset partition.

A. Region attacking

Every host in the leaf region can be penetrated. If there hosts can be breaking through, the attacker can certainly use the same pattern to break through other host, for example, the attacker can use the port of the host that is made to listen to the passing packet of the network that it goes through and enclosing the channel, so every other hosts in the network cannot be use. Moreover, it can use the active probing attack to attack the hosts in other region of the network. If there is the attacker that can break through large amount of hosts without detection, we can conclude that the intrusion detection system is unsafe. We propose the intruder detection system architecture that can continue function and the attacker cannot destroy the critical region that is the main resource of the host. Although the attacker can destroy some segment of the agent that work in this host, the attacker might correct the encoding of the agent for the bad objective. In this case, the backup mechanism for the agent that is in the leaf LAN still can recover the agent back and continue its function.

B. Proxy partition attacking

Although our proposed architecture can hide the important resources of the system invisible for the address and the real IP address by using NAT. This method can protect only Class 1 and Class 2 attacking, but the attacker can know the location of the proxy agent while connecting with the leaf via the region agent. So, the proxy partition can be the target of the attacking. In our architecture, we will change the location of the proxy agent every time after finish each duty with the region agent, but if the attacker that know the location of those agent still can break through those host as in our assumption and if s/he is fast enough, s/he can control that host before the agent get off from the location. In this case, proxy agent that is in the multicast group can be in the danger situation, because the attacker may destroy the agent or waiting in that host to sniff the traffic package of the network. With this method, the attacker will see the address of the shadowed agent; s/he may attack with the fourth method (DoS) on the multicast group until it is failed or attack with the first method to break through the shadowed agent. By the reason that the members of the multicast group are distributed all over the infrastructure of the system, the attack that make the victim failed will not have an effect to all the network and cannot make the group of the left agent stop, and for the first method attacking, the attacker must be fast enough to break through the host that the shadowed agent is exist, because these agents can move its address at any time. The agents will randomly move all over the region, hard to be the still target for probing or penetrating. Under our assumption, the attacker will be detected before it will attack other target.

For the proxy agent partition, the traffic analysis does not help the attacker to find the coordinator agent of the group, because the whole group communicates through the secured channel. So, it is not possible to sniff or analyze the traffic.

For the shadowed agent, our proposed architecture allows to use the public key cryptography for the couple of the agent and the shadowed agent to guarantee the integrity of both of them. In this case, the traffic analysis also cannot be used. In case of both agents do not use the security mechanisms because of wanting to reduce the operating cost or reduce the traffic congestion, it is the cause that the attacker can find the group coordinator and attack that coordinator, making the system failed. However, the shadowed agent of the coordinator can be recovered the process of the system without stopped, and for the segment that do not have the agent, it is not possible to analyze the traffic definitely.

C. Critical asset partition attacking

With the property of survivability of our proposed architecture, it is hard to penetrate the critical section. Because we cannot use the sniffing or probing to get the communicating data between these critical agents and these critical agent is set up not to response other information types than the agreement. The probing of the attacker is not useful, the attacker may random critical host or uses the critical host's IP address to attack the proxy agent and the shadowed agent simultaneously, after that uses the information to attack the critical host in the future. However, even if the critical agent is attacked, it can recover by using backup and recovery mechanism as presented.

Therefore, we can say that the intrusion detection system in this architecture will not be shutdown whether it is attacked by any attacking pattern. It is truth that if the intrusion detection system cans still function, there is also the ability to detect the intrusion perfectly and countered that intrusion until it can get rid of it. The intrusion detection system in this architecture can recover its process by using backup and recovery mechanism.

5. Analytical result

By analytical result as the previous section, we can found the survival properties of our architecture. The survivability is the idea for continue designing the system that has ability to progress all of the missions, even there is an attack, objection, or situation [17]. The system that has the survivability must have 3 important characteristics that are the resistance, which is the ability to avoid the attack, the recognition, which is the ability to remember the attacking pattern and limit the damage, and the recovery, which is the ability to recover the important services during the attack and recover all the services after the attack.

Using dynamic and sustainable components based on mobile agent technology and conceptual design framework based on fault tolerance model, leads to reduce the problem on single point of failure and emphasis fault tolerant properties.

5.1 Resistance

The designed Survival Architecture for Distributed Intrusion Detection using Mobile Agent has the main characteristics in the durability and avoid the attack by hiding the main components of the system by using proxy agent as the medium in the communication between components, together with using the network topology that separate network resources into zones, make the main components can move around the network by using the mobile agent and use the shadow agent reserved for every agents that have strong reserve mechanism.

5.2 Recognition

Survival Architecture can remember the attacking patterns, because it has the knowledge database that keeps the signature of the intrusion and the system that use the mobile agent can get rid of the damage when it was attacked.

5.3 Recovery

In case of some parts or every part failed, it can recover some of the processes or all of the processes by using the shadow agent together with the fast recovery.

5.4 Single point of failure (SPoF) reduction

The design that moves the Central directory server of all the components to the critical asset and do not allow the communication with other components directly via the Proxy partition will make the Central directory server hind effectively. The single point of failure problem also has been solved.

5.5 Fault avoidance
Avoiding damage is in the form of IDS architectural design. We use this property as a separate architectural design system divided by the critical resources of the network into three sections includes Critical asset, Proxy partition and region. The enterprise network perimeter by zoning to break the trust-host and untrust host separated to the mechanism used to secure appropriate.

5.6 Fault masking
Our design of system architecture and network zoning this property to hide the fault of some of the elements and use the rapid backup and recovery mechanism to work instead.

5.7 Fault tolerance
The architecture, we use several techniques designed to sustain damage, including fault detection, fault location, fault containment and fault recovery. These techniques can all work under the Mobile Agent technology.

6. Proofing

For proofing that our proposed intrusion detection system architecture can be survived.

Theorem:

The architecture of the intrusion detection system using mobile agent that is proposed can be survived.

Proof:

In case of the attacker can attack only the region, proxy partition, and the critical asset partition as in above analysis.
In bad condition, the attacking at the region might be the cause to make the agent at the leaf of the network failed, but can recover rapidly by using the agent in the proxy partition.
In worst case, the intruder may penetrate the region to the agent in the proxy partition, having the possibility to attack the agent in the proxy partition until it is failed. But these agents still can recover by using the shadowed agent.
In worst case, if the attacker can stop the operation of the proxy partition, and may be able to attack the critical agent later. Causing the malfunction in some sections of the critical agent, but those the critical agent still can be recovered by using the recovery mechanism.
In worst case, since it is so little possibility, but if there is the possibility that there is the attacks partly malfunction the intrusion detection system, but those attack cannot destroy all of the intrusion detection system architecture, because we propose the strong and fast backup and recovery mechanism for each section of the architecture.
Therefore, we have proven that the intrusion detection system architecture that is proposed can be survived even if it is attacked.

7. Conclusion, recommendation and future work

7.1 Conclusion
The current research topics about the architecture for Distributed IDS using mobile agent technology is being growth both in approach level and implementation level, but the main

problem of the design that use this concept is dIDS still has some mistakes, especially dIDS has no strength, it cannot deals with the big attack. Our research design the dIDS architecture is robust architecture improvement that is durable and can be survived by using the mobile agent technology with the network topology design, which allocate the resources into 4 separated parts, installs the monitored host onto each of network segment in order to resist the 5 class of the attacker and hides the main resource of the network behind the intrusion detection system. The design avoid the single point of failure, using shadow agent, together with proxy agent, fast backup and recovery mechanism, multicast group and the encryption of the communication between components of IDS. So, our architecture has the survivability that is resistance, recognition and recovery when there is the attacking from the intruder.

Using dynamic and sustainable components based on mobile agent technology and conceptual design framework based on fault tolerance model, leads to reduce the problem on single point of failure and emphasis fault tolerant properties.

7.2 Recommendation

However, our designed architecture, have some main issues that is the interoperability and traffic congestion. Interoperability Because our architecture is the distributed intrusion detection system (dIDS) that is able to detect the distributed intrusion detection system, one of the issue of this system is the limit of the interoperability, in case of working with other distributed intrusion detection systems, especially the real implementation, because the standard of each dIDS are not match with each other. This is the common problem of the researching and developing the distributed intruder detection system.

Traffic congestion

The concept of this designed architecture aim to the strength of the structure, able to handle any intruder, and survived from any pattern of the attack. Therefore, our architecture must be designed for having the secured communication route, using every security technique, by force every communication between components to pass only the secured channel. However, those security techniques will increase the operation cost and also can lead to the traffic congestion in the network.

From this problem, we use HMAC as the security technique for contents integrity, this technique do not need to encrypt all the contents, we will encrypt only hash value that comes from the original for the velocity in the processing and specify to have the asynchronous communication via multicast group for reducing the traffic.

However, for the cryptography that is used in every section of our architecture, we can consider to use Symmetric-key cryptography instead of the Public-key cryptography in some section to reduce the operation cost, having almost the same security standard.

7.3 Future work

We will work on implementation level using the model to evaluate the performance and proofing the model with survival analysis statistic on the next phase.

8. References

[1] [online]. Available http://www.internetworldstats.com/stats.htm

[2] William Stallings, 2002, Network and Internetwork Security 3th edition, Prentice Hall.

[3] [online]. Available http://staff.washington.edu/dittrich/misc/ddos/
[4] CERT Householder et al., October 2001, Managing the Threat of Denial-of-Service Attacks. [online]. Available http://www.cert.org/archive/pdf/Managing_DoS.pdf
[5] Mukherjee et al., Network intrusion detection, IEEE Network, 8(3):26-41, May/June 1994.
[6] Jai Sundar Balasubramaniyan, Jose Omar Garcia-Fernandez, David Isacoff, Eugene Spafford and Diego Zamboni, An Architecture for Intrusion Detection using Autonomous Agents, COAST Technical Report 98/05, Purdue University, 1998.
[7] Perter Mell, Donald Marks and Mark McLarnon, A denial-of-service resistant intrusion detection architecture, Computer Network, Special Issue on Intrusion Detection, Elsevier Science BV, 2000.
[8] Kruegel et al., Applying Mobile Agent technology to Intrusion Detection. Distributed Systems Group, Technical University of Vienna, 2002
[9] Tieyan Li, Wai-Meng Chew and Kwok-Yan Lam, Defending Against Distributed Denial of Service Attacks using Resistant Mobile Agent Architecture. In Proceedings of the International Parallel and Distributed Processing Symposium (IPDPS'02), IEEE, 2002.
[10] Chunsheng Li, Qingfeng Song and Chengqi Zhang, MA-IDS Architecture for Distributed Intrusion Detection using Mobile Agents. In Proceedings of the 2nd International Conference on Information Technology for Applications (ICITA2004), IEEE, 2004.
[11] Sartid Vongpradhip and Wichet Plaimart, Survival Architecture for Distributed Intrusion Detection System (dIDS) using Mobile Agent. In Proceedings of Sixth IEEE International Symposium on Network Computing and Applications (NCA2007), IEEE, USA, 2007.
[12] P.C.Chan and V.K.Wei, "Preemptive distributed intrusion detection using mobile agents", in Proceedings of Eleventh IEEE International Workshops on Enable Technologies: Infrastructure for Collaborative Enterprises, Jun, 2002.
[13] E. Amoroso and R. Kwapniewski, A selection criteria for intrusion detection systems, in Proceedings of 14th Annual Computer Security Applications Conference, Phoenix, USA, Dec 1998.
[14] A. Birch, Technical evaluation of rapid deployment and re-deployable intrusion detection systems, in Proceedings of IEEE, 1992, International Carnahan Conference on Security Technology, Atlanta, USA, 1992.
[15] Survivable Network, Technology Team, Technical Report, Survivable Network Systems, Software Engineering Institute, Carnegie Mellon University, CMU/SEI-97-TR-013, ESC-TR-97-013, November 1997.
[16] Richard Bejtlich, The Tao of Network Security Monitoring: Beyond Intrusion Detection, Addison-Wesley, 2005.
[17] Pankaj Jalote (1994) Fault tolerance in distributed systems. Prentice-Hall, USA.
[18] George Coulouris, Jean Dollimore And Tim Kindberg, (2001). Distributed Systems, Concept and Design, third edition, Addison-Wesley.

4

Advanced Methods for Botnet Intrusion Detection Systems

Son T. Vuong and Mohammed S. Alam
University of British Columbia
Canada

1. Introduction

Today, our dependence on the internet has grown manifold. So has the need to protect our vast personal information accessible via web interfaces such as online passwords, corporate secrets, online banking accounts, and social networking accounts like Facebook. The appearance of botnets in the internet scene over the last decade, and their ever changing behavior has caused real challenges that cannot be easily remedied.

According to literature, a *botnet* is defined to be a set of infected hosts (also called bots or zombies) that run autonomously and automatically, controlled by a botmaster (bot herder) who can co-ordinate his/her malicious intentions using the infected bots. Some of the prominent malicious tasks that can be credited to botnets include DDoS (Distributed denial-of-service), spam, phishing, ransomwares and identity theft.

In a botnet DDoS attack, the botmaster can command all its bots to attack a particular server (example: update.microsoft.com) at a particular date, time and for a duration via a malicious or anonymous proxy used as a stepping-stone to hide the actual commanding node. In a spam campaign, the nodes that form the bot network are responsible for sending spam by behaving as spam relay points, delivering spam mails to a list of intended victim email addresses selected by the botmaster. For example: a node which is part of a spam botnet could be sent a list of email addresses to spam for the day with a payload of the spam that is to be mailed. These spam messages could advertise pharmaceutical products and may also deliver further infection executables via email links or attachments to recruit more bots, as done by botnets such as *Storm* and *Waledac*. In a phishing scam, botnets are responsible for acting as web proxies or web servers to deliver hoax site content to benign users to gather their e-banking or credit card credentials. For example, the sites could host content which looks like a banking site requesting for login details credentials which when entered by the user, can be used by the botmaster to access legitimate banking sites. Eventually the funds are transferred to accounts that leave no trails (Nazario & Holz, 2008).

Botnets such as *Storm* have been known to infect over 2 million hosts while *Conficker* has infected over 9 million hosts according to some estimates. As can be seen, the far reaching effects of malicious intentions of botnets and their masters are a real threat.

This chapter will cover a concise survey of botnet detection systems as well as provide a novel mobile-agent based method that has been adapted from mobile-agent based intrusion detection systems, for handling botnets. We provide the necessary background needed to understand botnets such as the offensive techniques utilized by botnets; the defensive techniques developed by researchers; and also focus on a mobile agent based technique to detect infected hosts.

2. Botnet offense

In order to better understand the challenges that the security community faces in order to dismantle botnets, we first need to understand how botnets function, and the many tools and techniques employed by them.

2.1 Setting up a command and control server

The first step in creating a botnet is to setup the Command and Control (C&C) server. This is the location where the infected hosts report to the botmaster, letting it know that a host has been infected successfully. This is also the location where the infected hosts retrieve the full list of commands that the infected bot should run. Section 2.3 covers some of the communication features of a C&C server.

2.2 Bot lifecycle

Unlike the initial advanced botnets such as *Agobot* which carried a list of exploits to perform on a vulnerable host and its entire command set at the time of initial infection, every advanced bot today uses multiple stages in order to form a botnet (Schiller et al., 2007; Gu et al., 2007). This was mainly done first, to avoid signature detection by network intrusion detection systems such as snort (Roesch, 1999) and second, to reduce the initial infection size of the bot binary to make it less traceable while using *drive-by-download* attacks.
Stage 1 of a bot's lifecycle is the initial infection/exploit of a host. In this step the bot binary has to first infect the host by attempting to exploit one or more security vulnerabilities that might pre-exist on a system. Section 2.4 provides further details on the associated techniques that botmasters could use in this step. Once infected, *stage 2* is the process by which the bot reports back to the botmaster using the command and control (C&C) channel to inform him that the host has been successfully compromised. Information related to the host such as opened backdoors, host operation system settings and network capabilities are just some of the details that are reported back during this phase. In *stage 3* the bot downloads new executables. This process is also referred to as *egg downloading*. This could be the component that detects and disables antivirus software, or could provide potential updates to the bot malware with its full command list to make it more functional. In *stage 4* the downloaded malware is executed on the bot. The bot at this stage has become fully functional. In *stage 5*, the bot starts listening to the command-and-control channel to retrieve payload information from peers or servers and could execute the commands that are passed on using the payload. It is not necessary that the channel used in stage 3 is the same channel used in stage 5. In *stage 6*, the bot could optionally report the results of executing the commands to the server. This feature is used by many botnets to track the functionality of the bot so that the botnet could be load-balanced.

2.3 Botnet communication structure

The most important component of a botnet that decides if it can be easily dismantled is its communication structure which is used to command and control the infected hosts of a botnet. The type of communication used between a bot client and its command-and-control server or between any two bot clients can be differentiated into two types: *Push-based* commanding or *pull-based* commanding. Each method has its own advantages and disadvantages.

In a push-based communication, the bot master "pushes" the command that the bots are to run. The advantage of push-based communication lies in the fact that botmasters can instantaneously ask bots to perform a certain task. This allows for tighter control. However, the inherent disadvantage of such a method is the amount of traffic that can be observed leaving the server, or the tight timing correlation between various monitored nodes that are part of the same botnet, leading to easier detection of infected hosts. This weakness has been utilized by most botnet detection techniques such as *Botsniffer* (Gu et al., 2008). An example of push-based communication is the use of IRC servers for command-and-control.

In a pull-based communication, each bot is allowed to periodically retrieve the next command to run from a server. This helps not only to avoid flash-crowds at a command-and-control server, but the injection of random delays in command retrieval from bot to server makes it more difficult to trace a command-and-control server. This allows the server to hide behind traditional web traffic. Most existing botnets used for spamming (5 of top 9) use http protocol, a pull-based communication, to masquerade communication as legitimate users (Steward, 2009). In addition to the primary channel of communications, bots also have a secondary communication usually in the form of backdoors created by Trojans/bot software installed in each infected host. This channel is only used by the botmaster if the primary communication channel has been compromised.

We now elaborate a little on some of the more common communication structures used by botnets.

2.3.1 IRC (Internet Relay Chat)

In the beginning, most botnets used a centralized approach for managing botnets (Bacher et al., 2005). This was done using the IRC (internet relay chat) protocol or modified versions of the protocol using freely available sources such as *UnrealIRCd* (unrealircd, 2010). As per (Schiller et al., 2007), the main reasons for using IRC were its interactive nature for two way communication between server-client; readily available source code for easy modifications; ability to control multiple botnets using nicknames for bots and password protected channels; and redundancy achieved by linking several servers together.

Most IRC servers are modified from the original IRC protocol so that not all clients are visible to each channel member, or the server only listens to commands entered by the botmaster. Most bots parse the channel subject to be the command issued by the botmaster (Bacher et al., 2005). However, since these servers become the single point of failure and are easily detected, botnets have moved to other decentralized methods of control such as P2P; use of other less detectable protocols (http web servers); or use of IRC in combination to DNS fast-flux techniques, as explained in section 2.4.1. This was mainly due to the increased ability of the research community to reverse engineer the bot binary using tools such as *IDA pro* (Hex-rays, 2010) and mimic the behavior of a bot by joining and monitoring a botnet (Bacher et al., 2005; Rajab et al., 2006).

2.3.2 Web based botnet

The most prominent communication structure for botnets after IRC is the used of web servers. This is mainly done since most firewalls cannot distinguish between web-based bot traffic, and legitimate web traffic. The botmaster could be informed via an http request of the backdoor port to be used for communication along with a password to connect to the bot in case a secondary channel is required for communication.

2.3.3 P2P (peer-to-peer)

Probably the most complex botnet that had been studied to use a P2P scheme was the *Storm/Zhelatin/Pecomm/Nuwar* botnet and its variants. This botnet used a P2P approach to communicate commands between its bot members (Holz et al., 2008) based on the edonkey (*Overnet* protocol based on the Kademlia P2P algorithm) protocol followed by its custom *stormnet* (XOR encrypted communications) protocol to communicate. Using an off-the-shelf protocol that relied on unauthenticated publish-subscribe system allowed researchers to infiltrate the botnet. The number of botnets that use the P2P approach is less mainly due to the complicated nature of the C&C structure and due to the fact that once defenders have control of one infected host, it is easier for them to detect other infected peers connecting to it. *Nugache* is another P2P based botnet that uses encrypted peer communications. A noteworthy feature of *Storm* is the additional feature of automatically attacking anyone attempting to track it i.e. any storm infected node that was not behaving appropriately would be DDoSed by the system. This made it increasingly difficult for researchers to understand how the botnet functioned (Holz et al., 2008).

2.3.4 Other communication protocols and proposed botnet features

Botnets have also been detected to use one of many other uncommon protocols such as instant messaging for C&C. Using instant messaging for C&C has the drawback of being easily tracked and taken down by the instant messaging provider. ftp *dropzones* for banking Trojans have also been observed by (Holz et al., 2009). As per the authors, botnets used for stealing banking credentials submit keylogged data from phishing attacks into dropzones. The authors discovered a few authentication free *dropzones* during their investigations.
Some researchers have also proposed advanced techniques that could be used by botnets in the future. (Singh et al., 2008) discusses the use of email as C&C by using a combination of encryption and steganography in email content. The email content could be send to the user's inbox or spam folder at the direction of the botmaster by picking the right keywords. (Bambenek & Klus, 2008) proposed the possibility of using RSS feeds or XML for communication via websites maintained by botmasters, or public bulletin boards not controlled by the botmaster. (Hund et al., 2008) proposed a new bot design called *Rambot* that uses peer-to-peer technology in addition to using strong cryptography (2048 bit RSA keys) where the public key of botmaster would be hardcoded into the bot binary. Use of Diffie-Hellman symmetric key between bot-bot communications was also proposed by the authors in addition to the possibility of using a credit-point system to build trust among bots. The authors also discuss about peers only sharing partial peer lists with other bots to avoid detection of all peers in the botnet. In order to avoid allowing defenders to simulate multiple nodes on a single host, the authors also discuss about presenting a challenge(5-15 minute task) to any node before it communicates. This however has the drawback of the bot being detected by regular users. (Wang et al., 2007) proposes concepts similar to (Hund et al., 2008) in the use of asymmetric keys for bot-botmaster communication, symmetric keys for bot-bot communication and the use of peer-list exchange where only a partial list of peers are exchanged only during reinfection attempts. (Vogt et al., 2007) proposes creating

infections where thousands of smaller botnets are created with each having its own C&C server. Also all commands require a decryption key based on both the public key of the botmaster and another key that is partitioned such that each botnet has a partial key K_i. Defenders would need to infiltrate each separate botnet to gather the entire decryption key.

2.4 Infecting the user

The primary step that creates the botnet is the initial infection of the user which converts a clean host into a bot. Users can be infected in one of three ways.

Drive-by-downloads

As noted in numerous papers (Provos et al., 2007; Wang et al., 2006; Ikinci et al., 2008; Siefert et al., 2007; Provos et al., 2008) drive-by-downloads have become an emergent threat that exploit weaknesses often seen in web browsers and browser plugins.
In this process, the user is infected by a malicious link embedded in the site that based on the *user-agent* (browser) starts off a series of attacks (attack vector) to download malware into the user's machine without any acceptance by the user other than to have visited the site. This malicious site could be hosted by a malicious entity; could have 3rd party advertisement links which load malicious content; or be a legitimate site that has been infected earlier. 3rd Party advertisements could include the action of syndication (Daswani & Stoppelman, 2007) by which space on a site is sold for advertisement links to 3rd party sites that serve the ad content. Legitimate sites could be infected by a SQL injection attack which would then contain malicious iframe pointers to malicious servers. Unlike network scanning for vulnerabilities, which are blocked by firewalls and NATs, drive-by-download uses a pull-based technique that bypasses most filters. (Provos et al., 2008) notes that many of the infected hosts show connections to IRC servers or HTTP requests soon after infection confirming the fact that drive-by-downloads lead to creation of botnets. The malware or malicious iframe pointers are usually obfuscated within the html source. Instead of reinventing the exploits, these malicious links use ready-made exploit packs such as *Mpack, IcePack* or *EL Fiesta* that contain customized infection vectors. Though (Provos et al., 2008) mentions scanning well known URLs to check for maliciousness, a URL may seem benign in the beginning during initial scan, but might start behaving maliciously at a later time. The authors reported the presence of over 3 million malicious URLs detected over a 10 month period, and 1.3% of search results returning malicious URLs in Google searches.

Malicious attachments (social engineering)

A few botnets such as *Storm* & *Waledac* use social engineering as the attack vector. In this process, users are emailed a web link, hosted by a node in the bot network that a benign user would be enticed to visit. Once the URL is visited, the botmaster uses social engineering such as the need for missing flash plug-in or video codec to entice the user into downloading an executable and thus infecting the user. The use of custom packers and added encryption makes it almost impossible for antivirus software to detect maliciousness of the downloaded binary.

Vulnerable hosts

Most botnet attack vectors still target hosts that have not been fully patched. For example, some of the initial botnets such as *SDBot, Rbot, Agobot, Spybot* and *Mytob* were formed due to various windows vulnerabilities. Similarly the recent worm having a botnet commanding structure (*Downadup/Conficker/Kido*) that exploits MS08-067 spreads primarily due to inadequate patching. As pointed out by (Brumley et al., 2007; Brumley et al., 2008), attack vectors for a vulnerability can be created within hours of a patch being made available by a vendor. The difference between a patched and an unpatched version of the software allows malware authors to detect the underlying vulnerability that unpatched systems are vulnerable to.

2.5 Advanced botnet features

2.5.1 Obfuscation

The primary reason for using obfuscation is to make it difficult for botnet defenders to detect and tear down the inner functioning of a bot malware by simple signature matching. This is accomplished in many ways. For example, web-based malware (used for drive-by-downloads) uses JavaScript obfuscation to hide the attack vector. Web based malware is easier to obfuscate than memory corruption vulnerabilities and cannot be caught by state of the art polymorphic worm detectors such as Hamsa (Li et al., 2006) and Polygraph (Newsome et al., 2005). Another method includes the use of *packing* followed by *encryption* of bot binaries that causes bot binaries to go undetected by signature detectors. For example, storm is packed every minute by a custom packer built into its code whereby the size and thus MD5 hash no longer match to previous bot binary samples of the same malware.

2.5.2 Fast-flux

Most advanced botnets (*Storm, Waledac*) used primarily for phishing and spam use fast-flux techniques to hide the actual servers responsible for updated copies of the malware. In a fast-flux technique, the DNS to IP mapping of the download location of the malware constantly changes such that blocking an IP address does not really help, or correlating information about a particular infection based on just the IP is no longer useful enough. Some botnets use double fast flux using multihoming to change both the A record and NS record of DNS (Holz et al., 2009; Nazario & Holz, 2008; Siefert et al., 2007).

2.5.3 Virtual-machine detection

Quite a few malicious bot applications have inbuilt functionality to check if the host that has been infected is running in a virtual machine. Some characteristics include registry entries caused as artifacts of running various virtual machine software; list of running processes and services; or attempt remote timing attacks (Franklin et al., 2008) where the bot code runs a set of instructions in a loop leading to difference in results compared to a real system. It has also been noted by researchers in the virtual machine field that virtual machines will continue to be detected regardless of hardware support for virtualization (Garfinkel et al., 2007) mainly due to the difference in goals of the virtualization community.

2.5.4 Rootkits

Most bot code packages such as *Rustock, Storm* and *rxbot* uses rootkits to hide its presence to antivirus and malware detection tools. In these cases the bot binary package contains an executable which causes inline-function-hooking of important windows kernel dll functions such as kernel32.dll to hide the actual bot binary files from detection. An example rootkit used by hackers include *Hacker Defender*.

2.5.5 Random generation of domain names

Some newer botnets such as *Conficker* and *Kraken/Bobax* use random generation of domain names in search of the Command and Control servers. While *Kraken* walked through its generated list in serial order, *Conficker* generates a new list every day that has not been registered yet. Once the first C&C server is connected to, *Conficker* could activate its botnet structure (Pierce, 2008). This feature of trying to connect to non-existent servers could act as a give-away in detecting bot infections.

3. Botnet defense

In trying to keep pace with botnets, defenders have constantly tried to mitigate the harmful intentions of botnets by coming up with novel solutions, targeted at the core architectural footprint of botnets. Some of the solutions use static analysis techniques via reverse engineering the bot binaries using programs such as *IDA pro* or *peryleyez* (Holz et al., 2008; Grizzard et al., 2007; Chiang & Lloyd, 2007). Other approaches have used a dynamic analysis approach using tools such as *cwsandbox* (Sunbelt, 2010) or *norman* sandbox by performing windows API hooking; or performing system wide dynamic taint tracking (Tucek et al., 2007; Yin et al., 2007).

Botnet emulation approaches testbeds such as EMUlab/ DETER/ WAIL (Barford & Blodgett, 2007) have also been used to emulate an entire botnet by setting up command-and-control servers, infected clients and local DNS resolvers.

Work related to the area of drive-by-downloads has been done by (Provos et al., 2007; Provos et al., 2008) using honeynets to monitor URLs that might be malicious. These honeynets browse the URL using internet explorer via client-honeypots and track the number of new processes created, number of registries modified, and number of files creates due to visiting a site. The use of honey-clients to monitor changes while visiting URLs such as the Strider Honey monkey project (Wang et al., 2006), the Monkey spider project (Ikinci et al., 2008) or the use of behavior analysis tools such as Capture-BAT (Seifert, 2008) fall under the category of detecting drive-by-downloads. DNS monitor approaches have been used for lookup behaviors commonly used by bots using active methods such as DNS hijacking (Dagon et al., 2006) or passive methods such as DNS Black listing (Ramachandran et al, 2006). We now discuss some of the broader approaches that have been taken for botnet detection.

3.1 Botnet detection using honeypots

The main research methodology to detect and infiltrate botnets in the past few years has been via the use of honeypots. A honeypot can be loosely defined to be a machine that is closely monitored to watch for potential infiltration. The honeypot machine could be a real vulnerable machine but is usually a machine running in a virtual environment. The use of honeypots lies in the fact that any traffic that tries to penetrate or contact a honeypot can be considered as inherently malicious since by default, honeypots do not by themselves contact other hosts unless instructed to do so and hence should not exhibit any network traffic. The use of more than one honeypot in a network is called a *honeynet.* The purpose of a honeypot defines its type. Some of them include (Riden & Seifert, 2008):

Client honeypots: A Client honeypot is a machine that looks for malicious servers, behaving as a client. Some of the prominent projects in this area includes *Strider Honeymonkeys* (Wang et al., 2006), *Monkey Spider* (Ikinci et al., 2008), *Capture HPC* (Seifert, 2008), *Shelia*

(Rocaspana, 2007) and the *MITRE Honeyclient* (Mitre, 2007). Most of these projects use links (URL) gathered from spam traps as seed values, and then actively visit the sites using a virtual machine that contains different levels of patching. This allows the system to detect the vulnerability attacked, and the configuration of the vulnerable machine.
High Interaction Honeypot: 3rd generation honeywall ('Roo") (Roo, 2005) is a high interaction honeypot that allows the attacker to interact at all levels. The honeywall is placed between a honeynet and the outside world, collecting data from network. Roo uses *snort-inline* (snort-inline, 2005) to block all outgoing attack traffic from the honeynet.
Low Interaction Honeypot: A low interaction honeypot emulates vulnerabilities rather than hosting an actual vulnerable system. Thus these types of honeypots can be easily detected if an attacker interacts with this node. These are mainly useful for automated worm like bots that spread. Some known examples include:

- *Nepenthes* (Baecher, 2006): Emulates multiple windows vulnerabilities on various windows ports via stateful finite state machine. It has the ability to emulate 16,000 IP addresses on a single machine. Meant to collect self replicating malware automatically. Contains 21 different vulnerability modules. Has a module for parsing shell codes that are XOR encoded and a module for retrieving binary from remote server obtained by parsing shell code.
- *Honeyd* (Provos, 2007b): Implements a small daemon which creates virtual hosts on a network. Allows one to create a simulated network of over 60,000 hosts on a single host allowing real hosts to co-exist among virtual hosts, thus making it extremely difficult for attackers to track down the real hosts in the network. Each host feature can be configured separately. (Li et al., 2008) used one year worth of honeynet data captured using half darknet sensors and half honeyd sensors to reach the conclusion that most botnet nodes scan randomly rather than scanning just a specific local IP range in most cases.

3.2 Spamming botnet detection

Given that the primary utility of botnets is in sending spam, many researchers have looked into analyzing botnets that are used exclusively for sending spam such as the *Storm, Srizbi* and *Rustock* botnets. Though the size of spamming botnets has reduced significantly due to internet service providers blocking C&C servers as well as the domain providers for these botnets, spamming botnets remain an active threat (Steward, 2009). (Ramachandran et al., 2008) used a DNS blacklisting technique (DNSBL) where it creates a graph of nodes that are in any way linked to the known *srizbi* botnet. If a bot belonging to *srizbi* queries a large DNSBL of an internet service provider, correlation of the querying node or the one being queried with the *srizbi* list gives a list of new peers who are infected by *srizbi*. This process could be repeated multiple rounds to find out all associated bots which send spam. Spamming botnets have also been detected based on using hotmail spam mail as seed data and detecting source of the mail using domain-agnostic signature detection (Xie et al., 2008; Brodsky & Brodsky, 2007).

3.3 Network-based botnet detection

Some botnet detection systems have relied on detecting bot traffic using network level data. This is mainly done using network sniffing intrusion detection tools such as snort in addition to other network flow monitors.

Bothunter (Gu et al., 2007) uses a vertical correlation algorithm which tries to capture the different steps of a bot life-cycle. The 5 stages of a bot used in Bothunter are *Inbound scanning* where network monitoring is done to see if an internal host is scanned for from external host; *Exploit usage* where an exploit packet is sent from external to internal host; *egg downloading* where a binary of the malware is retrieved by the infected host from the outside network; Outbound *bot coordination* dialog where Command and Control traffic is observed; Outbound *attack propagation* where the internal host attempts to attack an external host. The system throws a warning if atleast 2 outbound bot attempt stages are seen or evidence of localhost infection followed by a single outward communication from infected host is seen. The authors use a combination of snort and anomaly detection tools called SCADE and SLADE for detection.

BotSniffer (Gu et al., 2008a) uses network-based anomaly detection approach to detect C&C channel for IRC in a local area network by implementing modules as snort preprocessors. Their algorithm is based on the fact that IRC has a tight spatial-temporal correlation on the size and duration of packet lengths observed during an n-gram (2-gram) analysis for homogeneity check of communication packets.

BotMiner (Gu et al., 2008b) uses a horizontal correlation algorithm to detect bot traffic which detects both centralized command-and-control structures and peer-to-peer command-and-control structures. The authors partition every network flow into an Activity-plane (A-plane) and a Communication plane (C-plane) based on the type of traffic. A-plane is monitored by snort and modules from the BotHunter program. C-plane uses binning technique to read four network quantities such as flows per hour, packets per flow, average number of bytes per packet and average number of bytes per second. Once flows that have the same C-plane state are clustered, a cross-correlation plane is calculated to figure out which nodes are part of the same botnets based on a scoring function.

(Strayer et al., 2008) uses network monitoring to try to correlate traffic in a local area network to detect bots based on the tight correlation in the timing of IRC-based bot traffic to the server. The authors used a modified version of the *Kaiten* bot to connect to their own internal IRC server (*UnrealIRCd*) to collect data via *TCPdump*.

Some IRC-based botnet detection work has also been done by (Karasaridis et al., 2007) which looks at traffic flows obtained by a Tier-1 ISP and correlates the data to locate the commanding server and hosts.

Some botnet defense techniques rely on cooperation from every Autonomous System (AS) which is currently not feasible due to privacy issues. (Liu et al., 2008) proposes the use of *Stop-It* servers that are supposed to stop internal nodes from performing denial of service attacks if reported by another autonomous system. Similarly (Simon et al., 2007) also relies on setting an evil-bit for traffic arriving from an autonomous system that cannot be trusted. Overall the system behaves similar to the system proposed by (Liu et al., 2008).

(Stinson & Mitchell, 2008) discusses the evasion techniques that can be used to defeat the various network based botnet detection approaches used. They come to the conclusion that network-based botnet detection systems that rely on packet timings and size of packets can be easily defeated by random modifications to the measured variables associated to a network packet. Similarly (Cooke et al., 2005) reports that there is no simple connection based invariant useful for network detection. Their conclusion was based on data collected from the Internet Motion Sensor project. They measured that the length of the outgoing connection from bot to botmaster varied from 9 hours to less than a second. Some botnets had traffic that was encrypted along with random noise insertions to thwart signature detection.

3.4 Behavior analysis based botnet detection

More recently, researchers have attempted to detect botnets by tracking their network and host behavior. (Bayer et al., 2009) recently proposed the correlation of behavior analysis of malware via clustering of behavior of host system calls via their ANUBIS dynamic analysis tool and the use of Locality Sensitive Hashing (LSH) clustering algorithm. Their tool works by performing an offline analysis of a malware sample similar to CWSandBox. The authors mention that capturing behavior at a system call level causes data explosion and increased false positives and negatives if an adversary has the knowledge that a system is tracked at a system call level.

(Bailey et al., 2007) uses hierarchical clustering based on measuring normalized compression distance where distances are measured by computing the zlib compressing of features, stored in random order. Each feature is represented by registry modifications made, processes created, file modifications made.

(Rieck et al., 2008) uses support vector machines to calculate which malware group a malicious executable represents, based on supervised learning using 10-fold cross validation of certain bot families. They compute feature vectors computed from CWSandbox reports.

(Lee & Mody, 2006) perform k-medoid clustering of events generated by running malicious executables. Each event is represented by file modifications or registry changes. They use edit distance of events among executables to cluster. They showed that edit distance measurements for distance do not work when the number of events goes higher than 500. Using k-medoid also has the drawback that the actual number of clusters has to be predetermined. Having a *k* which is less than the actual number of clusters cause outliers to be included, thus significantly impacting the cluster features.

(Gao et al., 2005) had proposed the use of applying DNA behavior distance of sequence of system call subsets by calculating distance between *system call phrases* of a given process and its replica. Their approach works by computing the edit distance between any two system call phrases, where a phrase is a sequence of system calls. However their work has limitations as the distance between system calls can be artificially increased by malicious adversaries by making unnecessary system calls.

4. Agent technology

Though various methodologies have existed for botnet detection, the use of agent technology has been mostly overlooked. Given the distributed nature of botnets, and their modular structure allowing for constant updates, it is more intuitive to use a similar technology that is inherently distributed and allows similar kind of code updates for defensive purposes. The need for a clear understanding of agents is necessitated due to the fact that the system that we have developed and extended, is layered on top of an agent platform, *Grasshopper* (Bäumer & Magedanz, 1999), based on the first mobile agent standard MASIF (Mobile Agent System Interoperability Facility), an interoperability standard that allows agents from different mobile agent platforms to interact with each other. Researchers could use other mobile-agent based platforms such as *Aglets* that allow for similar functionality. The term agent or software agent is usually deciphered well in the artificial intelligence community, where it stands for a program that can behave autonomously to perform a multitude of dynamic tasks based on the logistics that have been programmed into it by a user.

4.1 Agent classification

Based on the mobility of agents, they can be classified into three main types:

Static Agents: The first is the concept of static agents. Static agents are fragments of code that do not move to different locations, and stay at a constant position throughout its life cycle.

Semi-Mobile Agents: Semi-mobile agents, as the name suggests, have some mobility. They are in fact an inherent type of mobile agents, which are created at one logical or physical location, but are moved to another location for its functional life cycle.

Mobile Agents: Mobile agents are a fragment of code, which can move around, from host to host during its life cycle depending on the runtime task allocated to it. Mobile agents are based on a terminology, well known in literature as *mobile code* (Fuggetta et al., 1998). The term mobile code can be defined as the capability to change the binding between the pieces of code, and the location where they are executed.

The scope of the advantages or disadvantages of using any of the above mentioned agent types can vary based on the functionality of the agent based system that is being deployed. If latency is a big issue in the system, one should opt for static and/or semi-mobile agents. This is because the greater the mobility of an agent, the higher the latency introduced into the system caused by the time required to create it at a new location and to transfer the runtime state of the agent. If the host where the agent runs is very fragile or more prone to destruction or tampering, it would be best to use a mobile agent rather than a static agent, as it is easier for mobile agents to find a new location to run at than static agents.

4.2 Advantages and disadvantages of agents

The use of mobile agents offers wide advantages especially in distributed systems that cannot be overlooked. Some of the advantages offered by agents have been clearly listed in (Bieszczad et al., 1998). The major categories of these are summarized as follows:

Reduction in Network Traffic: In case of mobile agents, the agents themselves move to data. i.e. we move the agent code to the data rather than moving the data to the agent code. This allows for a dramatic reduction in the amount of bandwidth consumed in the log correlation process (explained in later sections) as data is almost always larger than the few kilobyte size of agents in general.

Asynchronous autonomous interaction: This is vital in a network where network connections are volatile, such as wireless networks. In such cases, the agent could migrate to a mobile device to gather data. Even if the connection breaks, the agent could continue processing data on the mobile device and report back whenever the connection is reestablished. This adds to the agent's capability to work in a fault tolerant mode.

Software Upgrades: Usually in order to update software on multiple hosts, an administrator has to first stop the server functionality, then uninstall the old version of the software, and then reinstall the new version. The entire software system has to be stopped for upgrades. The advantage of mobile agents or agents in general in this situation is that if each component of the upgraded software is managed by an agent, then it is as easy as disabling the old agent and deploying a new agent which has the required functionality. In this way one could avoid bringing down the entire system and instead stop just a single agent-based component.

Functionality in heterogeneous environments: Most agents today can work in heterogeneous environments. This is due to the fact that these agents are usually written in a language which is portable to multiple platforms, such as java or perl. Since agents sit on top of an agent framework, they can easily function regardless of if the host runs a version of Linux or Windows operating system. The significant reduction in costs of placing agent frameworks in hosts over the past few years have added to the benefits of running agents.

Just like there are advantages to using agents, there are also drawbacks to using agents. The applicability of advantages or disadvantages to using agents is based immensely on the specific user needs or goals that have been put forward. The shortcomings of using a mobile agent-based system have been clearly summarized by (Vigna, 2004).

Agent Security: The one and only reason that has hindered the wide usage of mobile agents in the real world has been its security constraints. One of the key problems associated with mobile agent security is the *malicious host* problem i.e. how much trust can be placed on a host where the agent travels to, given that the agent may have valuable data. Other security concerns that have been mentioned in literature include the concept of *malicious agents* (Vigna et al., 2002) where given the availability of an agent platform in a host, how much trust can be placed on the agent that travels to the host to gather information? This problem has been solved in the agent-security field by allowing a host to run only certain digitally signed agents. Last but not the least, agents can be *tampered* with which means, a legitimate agent could be *brainwashed* while traveling from host to host. (Vigna et al., 2002) has provided a means for auditing an agents trail to detect attacks that modify agents legitimate access permissions and authorization mechanisms for the aglets mobile agent platform.

Lack of Shared Language: Even though many tasks have been overtaken by FIPA (The Foundation for Intelligent Physical Agents) to create a standard ACL (Agent communication language), most agent platforms do not adhere to this language. Hence it is hard for agents to communicate with each other when they are based on different platforms.

Required Agent Platform: Any piece of agent code available today needs to run on an agent platform that contributes to the control and deployment of agents. For example, our system has to use the Grasshopper agent platform to execute its tasks currently. Similarly, to run java applets, the system has to have a java runtime environment available. The dependence of mobile agents on an agent platform is an extra requirement that has to be made, without which they cannot function. The problem is further compounded by the fact that not all agent platforms follow a given set of rules and procedures thus hindering interoperability issues even with the existence of standards such as MASIF.

4.3 Intrusion detection system data correlation

Most detection systems today use the process of *log correlation*, which is a process that takes the alerts generated by multiple intrusion detection systems and produce a brief report on the network being protected (Valeur et al., 2004). The advantage of this method is that if there are multiple intrusion detector sensors deployed in the network, on the occurrence of an intrusion attack, each of these sensors would generate a report on the intrusion type. Allowing log correlation of the information generated by all these sensors would provide a system administrator with a compact but detailed report on the attack allowing him or her to pinpoint the vulnerability easily.

In the conventional log correlation model, distributed sensors, after gathering the data, send all the alerts to a centralized location for correlation purposes. But the major disadvantage of this model is that if the amount of logs generated is large, it would clog the network system in a low-bandwidth network. Also a centralized approach would overload a node that receives too many correlation tasks at a given time, causing system overload and hence delay in producing the analyzed results.

4.4 Agent based security systems

The earliest relevant work in this area was started by Purdue University's CERIAS (The Center for Education and Research in Information Assurance and Security) group in 1995 when they put forward a proposal for building an autonomous agent based security model by using genetic programming (Crosbie & Spafford, 1995). This was followed up by their work in implementing the earlier proposal (Balasubramaniyan et al., 1998).This system was called AAFID (Autonomous Agents for Intrusion Detection) written earlier in Perl, Tcl/Tk and C, and later revised and written in the perl language to make it more portable. (Helmer et al., 1998) used an anomaly detection technique by using the *Ripper* algorithm on *sendmail* system calls. The architecture mimicked a portion of the Java Agents for Meta-Learning (JAM) project (Stolfo et al., 1997). A distributed hierarchical IDS was proposed by (Mell & McLarnon, 1999) that tries to randomize the location of agents and decentralizing directory services. The system also resurrects agents killed by an intruder as there always exists multiple copies that track the original agent and vice versa. The *Micael* IDS was proposed by (Queiroz et al., 1999). They proposed an additional feature of periodically checking if all agents are active in the system. Another prominent work that detects intrusions using mobile agents is the IDA system (Asaka et al., 1999). This system tries to backtrack intrusion attempts by looking into MLSI (Mark Left by Suspected Intruders) left at each host. They also emphasize tracking the steps that an attacker takes.
The *Sparta* system by (Krügel et al., 2001; Krügel & Toth, 2002) is the most extensive work done till date on using mobile agents and intrusion detection. Sparta, which stands for Security Policy Adaptation Reinforced Through Agents, is an architecture that is capable of monitoring a network to detect intrusions and security policy violations by providing a query like functionality to reconstruct patterns of events across multiple hosts. This is a network-based IDS that *correlates* data from multiple sensors located throughout the network. The authors have created an EQL (Event Query Language) with syntax similar to SQL (Sequence Query Language) used in databases.
Other mobile agent based IDS's include a P2P based IDS (Ramachandran & Hart, 2004) that works in a *neighborhood watch* manner where each agent looks after other agents in its vicinity by using a voting procedure to take action against a compromised agent; the MA-IDS system (Li et al., 2004) which uses encrypted communication between the mobile agents in the system, and use a threshold mechanism to detect the probability for each intrusion depending on the quantity of each intrusion type obtained allowing it to learn in a one dimensional method. Some other mobile agent based IDS's include a position paper (Aslam et al., 2001) that claims to work on D'Agents environment; and work by (Foukia et al., 2001; Foukia et al., 2003) which uses a social insect metaphor and immune systems to model an intrusion detection system.

5. Agent-based botnet detection

Based on our previous experience on mobile agent based intrusion detection systems (Alam et al., 2005; Alam & Vuong, 2007), and an in-depth understanding of the behavior of botnets, we believe the appropriate approach to defend against botnets is to adapt a *mobile-agent*

based paradigm in combination with current host monitoring techniques, to detect bot infected hosts based on bot *behavior analysis*.
Our proposed approach predominantly would work for a local or remote environment with a single administrative entity with access to network level data of monitored hosts and optionally, access to the host machine via mobile-agent middleware if host-based bot behavior features are need. We use network and host behavior monitoring of hosts to detect bot infections based on calculating feature vectors stored as a bot DNA.
As mentioned in previous sections, each botnet exhibits certain traits/features. For example, the *storm* botnet used technique of fast-flux; used a peer-to-peer modeling based on edonkey (kademlia) protocol; used rootkits; certain variants exhibited detection of virtual machines; and infected bots either are used to DDoS, send phishing emails, or advertisements. We believe that each of these attributes could be considered a feature of the botnet. Some of the features describe the communication methods of a botnet while others describe their activity (Gu et al., 2008). Some of these can be detected using network monitoring while others by monitoring host changes. Each variant of a bot over time modifies some of its functionality (features), but the change is subtle from variant to variant in most cases. There are certain exceptions, such as *Conficker.C* which retains only 15 percent of its code intact from *Conficker.B* (Porras et al., 2009) and extensively modifies both its network and host behavior.
With our primary goals to:

1. detect hosts that exhibit botnet traits with a certain confidence level, and
2. detect which bot an infected host behaves like,

we believe that our first goal can be captured by calculating an *infection score* based on *weighted botnet features* exhibited by a host. The weights could be calculated based on using machine learning methods such as support vector machines (SVM) on predominant bot families. Our second goal can be accomplished by first learning the behavior of botnet infected hosts by capturing host and network behavior of known bot infections. This is followed by converting the behavior to a set of features represented as a vector stored in synthetic DNA format, allowing application of clustering or hashing algorithms as discussed in section 3.4.

5.1 Mapping bot feature vector

In order to apply the botnet detection problem to DNA, we map labeled buckets representing the range of values exhibited per bot feature/attribute. The purpose of using marked bins is to emphasize the more bot-like feature a host exhibits.

	A	T	C	G
#failed connection	<5	5-10	10-15	>15
Fast-flux TTL	> 3 minutes	2-3	30 seconds-2min	<30 seconds
Exhibits fast-flux?	No	-	-	Yes

→ Increasing Bot-like Behavior

Fig. 1. Assigning labels to botnet attributes

For example, if an infected node exhibits fast-flux, we only need two possible attribute states: *yes* or *no*. But measuring features such as the rate of outgoing connection, or average packet sizes cannot be captured by a *yes/no* solution. This can be solved to an extent by using a bucket/binning technique by partitioning such numbers into multiple marked bins. Whereas there exists a small number (4) of allowed variations in DNA nucleotides, it reduces the ability to measure accuracy in case of botnet detection. An example labeling is shown in Fig. 1. One also has to assign appropriate bin ranges that distinguish benign traffic from bot-like traffic. These are some of the challenges we are trying to solve based on measuring current bot features.

5.2 Sequencing of hosts

A system administrator would keep multiple DNA sequences of each host in its network: a set of sequences representing network-based DNA and a set representing host-based DNA. We partition the space into two since there might be cases when only one set of sequences are available. For example cellular devices using local wifi access cannot contribute to a host-based sequencing due to the absence of host-monitoring applications on the device in some cases. Fig. 2 shows an example DNA of a host as maintained by the administrator.
Two hosts that exhibit similar DNA sequences behave similarly. Thus if a host shows DNA sequencing similar to a bot DNA sequence with subtle mutations, we know the type of infection and can mark the infected host. Similarly if a host exhibits DNA sequences similar to innocuous DNA, we know it is clean.

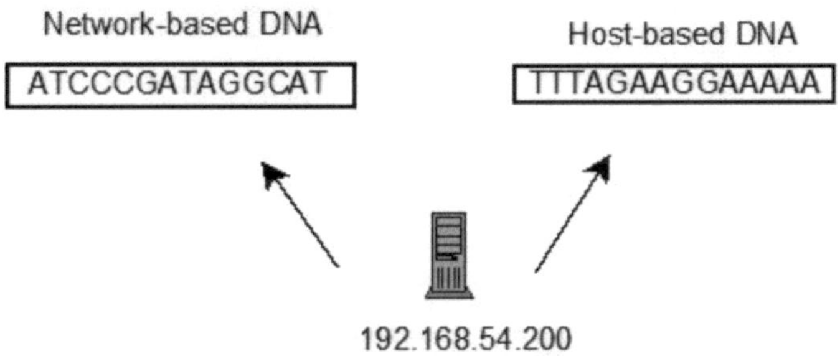

Fig. 2. An example of the DNA structure maintained per host basis

5.3 Capturing the attributes

The effectiveness of our solution is based on selecting the appropriate network or host attributes exhibited by botnets. These lists of attributes are based on the behavior depicted by various botnets over time as discussed in sections earlier. One or more of the attributes requires maintaining some sort of state information. Table 1 provides some of the higher layer network features that are currently tracked.

Fast-flux TTL, Rate of failed connections to ip, Rate of failed connection to dns, IRC, (Incoming http request, Outgoing http response, Outgoing http request, (Failed http response, Successful http response)), Incoming network scanning, (Outgoing network scanning, (Outgoing network scanning, Rate of Scanning)), (Retrieve Binary, (Binary MD5 match, Size of Binary)), (P2P traffic, Active connection rates, P2p active connections), Source IP spoofing, Outgoing SMTP traffic

Table 1. Network features tracked

5.4 Depth of attributes

As shown in Fig. 3, the depth at which a collected attribute resides, decides the length of the feature vector, and associated runtime and memory costs. The depth of the feature also decides if a bot can be appropriately distinguished or categorized under a known botnet. This is a trade-off that has to be kept into consideration. If the features vector comprises a sequence of system call API, this would cause a feature vector explosion (Bayer et al., 2009). In order to tackle this issue, some have abstracted system call objects (Bayer et al., 2009) , or created feature vector generated from system registry changes, file read/write and processes created for host-based attributes (Bailey et al., 2007; Rieck et al., 2008; Lee & Mody, 2006).

The attribute collection strategy regarding host-based behavior is based on the decisions of the researcher designing the agents. We envision having a multi-tiered strategy for host-based attributes where some attributes are collected at a higher layer than others depending on required time sensitivity.

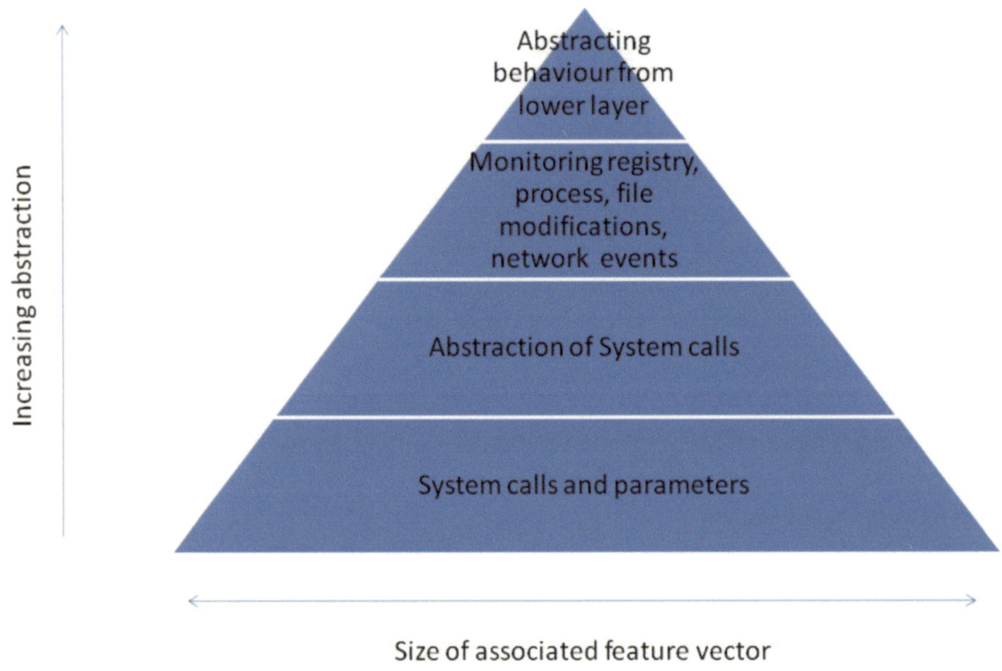

Fig. 3. Feature vector size vs. level of abstraction

5.5 Network attributes

A network-based DNA could be computed by capturing network packets by network-based packet filters such as *snort-inline* by monitoring all network connections between internal hosts and the external network. The primary advantage of *snort-inline* is that it allows active dropping of network packets if needed based on snort rules triggered.

We envision that one would need two sets of network attributes. Those that can be computed based on just packet header traces, and those that can be computed via deep packet inspection. The difficulty in capturing the later is the amount of encrypted channels used by botnets today. Due to the extensive obfuscation technology and encryption used, we have to take into account that some of the attributes that requires deep packet inspection will not be able to detect some bot traffic, and thus should be weighed differently.

5.6 Host attributes

Host-based attributes need to be captured using multiple methods. We could run host monitoring tools such as *Sebek* (Sebek, 2010) in a host that provide some of the host-based DNA, for example: list of dll and system files created, registry entries modifies, their modification dates, running processes, etc. This information and the analysis code that computes the host DNA could reside on the host. But there is an inherent problem in capturing host infections.

No data obtained using analysis tools already present on a host once it has been infected can be trusted. Moreover, the infected host could modify results sent by the infected host. For example most bots such as *storm, rxbot* and *rustock* use rootkits to modify results obtained using windows system API to hide monitoring of processes, network connections, file visibility and file sizes. Similarly *Conficker* (Porras et al., 2009) modifies in memory versions of windows system API leaving the actual dll file on disk untouched. This leads us to the case for using mobile agents.

5.7 The case for mobile agents

The main reason why using a mobile agent based approach is viable in host-based behavior detection is the fact that if our evidence gathering code is already available on an infected node, we cannot trust its result. Thus in order to analyze a host, our evidence gathering code has to travel to the host being analyzed. This could be the code which computes an MD5 hash of some important system files, or retrieve analysis data stored in a pseudo random file stored on the host in an encrypted format to hide from the infection code, or the code that detects the presence of rootkitted files similar to *Rootkit Revealer* or *Rootkit Unhooker*. Similarly, if more than one host exhibits similar malicious activities, or if multiple network sensors are deployed, mobile agents would allow processing of multiple hosts in a parallel manner, minimizing the time to detect infections. Mobile agents would allow us to replace outdated monitoring agents, with new agent code that has updated tracking abilities.

5.8 Protecting the agent and the infected host

An approach that can be taken to protect the infected host from malicious agent is the use of strong asymmetric cryptography. Some mobile agent platforms such as *Grasshopper* and *Aglets* allow only agent code signed and verified to run on a given host with access control policies. Using strong asymmetric key to sign the agent and its verification by the infected host environment would protect the host.

Similarly, once the agent performs its analysis task, the mobile agent would travel back to the analyzing host where it would be marked as tainted. The analyzing host could perform a check such as performing an MD5 hash on the agent to see that the agent code has not been modified before its results are processed.

Any agent travelling to an infected host also has to verify that the agent middleware has not been compromised in any way before starting its processing. The absence of an agent middleware that is supposed to exist could act as a sign of maliciousness. Using Aglets agent middleware has the added advantage of us being able to add functionality to the agent middleware as required since it is open-sourced.

5.9 Feature extraction (infection score)

Though we rely on measuring the various network and host-based attributes, not all attributes have equal weight in detecting botnet communication or activity. Moreover certain botnet families exhibit higher frequency of a certain attribute versus others. For example, certain attributes such as the use of fast-flux for communication or a user machine exhibiting SMTP traffic are symtoms of botnet behavior in case of botnets such as *Storm* and *Waledac*, but these features may not be utilized by IRC based bots such as *Agobot*. Thus, we see that not all attributes should be weighed equally for all botnets.
One approach would be to partition the features into multiple sets each assigned to a weight category, or each feature assigned an individual appropriate weight. This would constitute a part of feature extraction, where certain features are brought into focus while other probably noise given less emphasis. Whereas taking the first approach is easier, it is also prone to more inaccuracy. The second approach is more accurate but harder to compute.

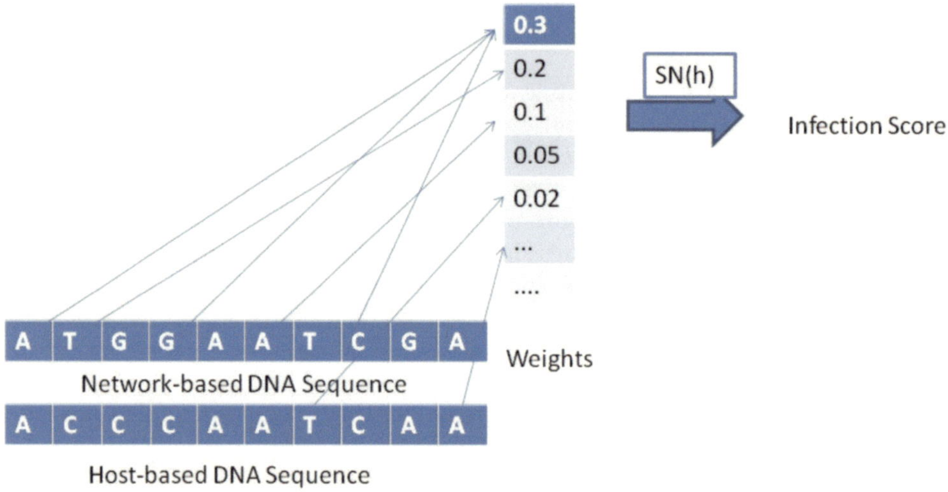

Fig. 4. Computing an infection score for a botnet infected host

The second approach could be accomplished by using Support Vector Machine (SVM), a supervised machine learning approach which is less prone to noise in the data sample. Creating an SVM for each bot family, and comparing the host DNA to each bot family SVM would allow us to measure which bot a host behaves like. The purpose of an SVM is to compute an optimal hyperplane that separates one class of n-dimensional points from another class (Rieck et al., 2008). Thus the main reason for using SVM in our case would be to compute actual weight assignments. This allows us to compute the infection score as shown in figure 4 where SN(h) is the computed infection score.

A host that exhibits a higher infection score, and if the infection score exceeds a threshold score set by an administrator, would automatically trigger a correlation requirement of host and network features exhibited and a further analysis.
Similarly, if the host or network DNA exhibits similar patterns to a known infection (based on distance measurement) after clustering bot behavior, it would also trigger a DNA-based correlation.

5.10 Scenario of use

In this section we describe the scenario of use of our approach.
A system administrator will receive continuous updating of the DNA sequencing of a given host and its probability of infection. The network-based DNA of a host will be updated based on the network traffic seen by the snort-inline processor. The host-based DNA will be reported periodically by individual hosts within the local network.
If the probability of the host being infected crosses a certain threshold based on the infection score, or a host approaches a DNA match close to a botnet, a bot correlation trigger flag will be raised.
Based on the infection model seen, a mobile agent would be created with the required host-detection functionality.
The agent would be deployed to the infected host, where it would perform analysis tasks as described in earlier sections. If the infected host denies a real agent to run, this could be a sign of maliciousness.
The agent could return with advanced-detailed results such as an encrypted list of rootkitted processes/files, or just the host-based DNA results. The agent is placed in the tainted bin, to verify the integrity of the agent, since it had travelled to a probable infected host. If the agent has retained its integrity its results are measured to be valid.
Based on both the host and network-based results, the node could block all incoming/outgoing network traffic by automatically modifying snort-inline for the given host. It could also provide details such as if the infection matches a known botnet, or is a new botnet pattern. It would also allow us to correlate hosts that have exhibited similar bot behavior pattern.

6. Conclusion

In this chapter, we have primarily focused on the various mechanisms utilized by botnet owners to maintain and protect their botnets; and the defensive mechanisms designed by researchers to study, detect and dismantle the malicious botnets. As can be understood, botnets utilize multiple advanced technologies that are constantly updated. Hence we have proposed the use of mobile agents which too can be constantly updated to defend against the ever changing behavior of bot binaries.

7. References

Alam, M.; Gupta, A.; Wires, J. & Vuong, S. (2005). APHIDS++: Evolution of a Programmable Hybrid Intrusion Detection System, *Proceedings of Mobility Aware Technologies and Applications*, pp. 22-31, Volume 3744/2005, Montreal, January, 2007, SpringerLink.

Alam, M. & Vuong, S. (2007). APHIDS++ : A Mobile Agent Based Intrusion Detection System, *Proceedings of 2nd International conference on Communication Systems Software and Middleware*, pp. 1-6, ISBN 1-4244-0613-7, Bangalore, January, 2007.

Asaka, M.; Taquchi, A. & Goto, S. (1999). The Implementation of IDA: An Intrusion Detection Agent System. *Proceedings of the 11th conference on Forum of Incident Response and Security Teams*. Brisbane Australia, July, 2007.

Aslam, J.; Cremonini, M.; Kotz, D. & Rus, D. (2001). Using Mobile Agents for Analyzing Intrusion in Computer Networks. *Proceedings of the Workshop on Mobile Object Systems at ECOOP 2001*. Budapest, Hungary, June, 2001.

Bacher, P. ; Holz, T. ; Kotter, M. & Wicherski, G. (2005). Know your Enemy : Tracking Botnets using Honeynets to learn more about bots. Honeynet Project, [online] Available at: http://www.honeynet.org/papers/bots, [Accessed 10 September 2010].

Baecher, P; Koetter, M;Dornseif, M. & Freiling, F. (2006). The nepenthes platform: An efficient approach to collect malware. *Proceedings of the 9th International Symposium on Recent Advances in Intrusion Detection*, pp. 165-184, Springer Link, Hamburg, Germany, September, 2006.

Bailey, M.; Oberheide, J.; Andersen, J.; Mao, Z. M.; Jahanian, F. & Nazario, J. (2007). Automated classification and analysis of internet malware. *Proceedings of the 10th international Conference on Recent Advances in intrusion Detection* (Gold Goast, Australia, September 05 - 07, 2007, pp 178-197 C. Kruegel, R. Lippmann, and A. Clark, Eds. Lecture Notes In Computer Science. Springer-Verlag, Berlin, Heidelberg.

Balasubramaniyan, J. S., Garcia-Fernandez, J. O., Isacoff, D., Spafford, E. & Zamboni, D. (1998). An Architecture for Intrusion Detection Using Autonomous Agents, *Proceedings of the 14th Annual Computer Security Applications Conference* (ACSAC), ISBN 8186-8789-4, IEEE Computer Society, Washington, DC, December, 1998.

Bambenek, J. & Klus, A. (2008). Botnets and proactive system defense. Botnet Detection: Countering the Largest Security Threat, edited by Wenke Lee, Cliff Wang, and David Dagon, ISBN 978-0-387-68766-7, Springer-Verlag, 2008.

Barford, P. & Blodgett, M. (2007). Toward botnet mesocosms. *Proceedings of the First Conference on First Workshop on Hot Topics in Understanding Botnets,* Cambridge, MA, April, 2007, USENIX Association, Berkeley, CA.

Bäumer, C. & Magedanz, T. (1999). The Grasshopper Mobile Agent Platform Enabling Shortterm Active Broadband Intelligent Network Implementation. *Proceedings of the First international Working Conference on Active Networks* S. Covaci, pp 109-116, Ed. Lecture Notes In Computer Science, vol. 1653. Springer-Verlag, London.

Bayer, U; Comparetti, P; Hlauschek, C; Kruegel, C & Kirda, E. (2009). Scalable Behavior-based Malware Custering. *Proceedings of the 16th Annual Network and Distributed System Security Symposium,* ISOC, SanDiego, CA, February, 2009.

Bieszczad, A; White, T & Pagurek, B. (1998). Mobile Agents for Network Management, *Proceedings of IEEE Communications Surveys*, September 1998.

Brodsky, A. & Brodsky, D. (2007). A distributed content independent method for spam detection. *Proceedings of the First Conference on First Workshop on Hot Topics in Understanding Botnets,* Cambridge, MA, April, 2007, USENIX Association, Berkeley, CA.

Brumley, D.; Caballero, J.; Liang, Z.; Newsome, J. & Song, D. (2007). Towards automatic discovery of deviations in binary implementations with applications to error detection and fingerprint generation, *Proceedings of 16th USENIX Security Symposium on USENIX Security Symposium*, pp. 1-16, Boston, MA, N. Provos, Ed. USENIX Association, Berkeley, CA.

Brumley, D.; Poosankam, P.; Song, D. & Zheng, J. (2008). Automatic Patch-Based Exploit Generation is Possible: Techniques and Implications. *Proceedings of the 2008 IEEE Symposium on Security and Privacy*, pp. 143-157, SP. IEEE Computer Society, Washington, DC, May, 2008.

Chiang, K. & Lloyd, L. (2007). A case study of the rustock rootkit and spam bot. *Proceedings of the First Conference on First Workshop on Hot Topics in Understanding Botnets*, Cambridge, MA, April, 2007, USENIX Association, Berkeley, CA

Cooke, E.; Jahanian, F., & McPherson, D. (2005). The Zombie roundup: understanding, detecting, and disrupting botnets. *Proceedings of the Steps To Reducing Unwanted Traffic on the internet on Steps To Reducing Unwanted Traffic on the internet Workshop*, Cambridge, MA, July, 2005, USENIX Association, Berkeley, CA.

Crosbie, M. & Sapfford, G. (1995). Defending a Computer System using Autonomous Agents. *Proceedings of the 8th National Information Systems Security Conference.*

Dagon, D ;Zou, C & Lee, W. (2006). Modelling Botnet Propagation using time zones. *Proceedings of The 13th Annual Network and Distributed System Security Symposium (NDSS 2006)*, San Diego, CA, February 2006, ISOC.

Daswani, N. & Stoppelman, M. (2007). The anatomy of Clickbot.A. *Proceedings of the First Conference on First Workshop on Hot Topics in Understanding Botnets*, Cambridge, MA, April 2007, USENIX Association, Berkeley, CA.

Foukia, N.; Billard, D. & Harms, J. (2001). Computer System Immunity using Mobile Agents. *Proceedings of HP Openview University Association 8th Annual Workshop*. 2001.

Foukia, N.; Hassan, S.; Fenet, S. & Albequerque, P. (2003). Combining Immune System and Social Insect Metaphors: A Paradimg for Intrusion detection and response system. *Proceedings of the 5th International Workshop for Mobile Agents for Telecommunication Applications*, Marakech, Morocco, October, 2003, Lecture Notes in Computer Science, Springer.

Franklin, J.; Luk, M.; McCune, J.M.; Seshadri, A.; Perrig, A., & van Doorn, L. (2008). Towards Sound Detection of Virtual Machines, *Botnet Detection: Countering the Largest Security Threat*, edited by by Wenke Lee, Cliff Wang, and David Dagon, ISBN 978-0-387-68766-7, Springer-Verlag, 2008.

Fuggetta, A.; Picco, G.& Vigna, G. (1998). Understanding Code Mobility, *Proceedings of IEEE Transactions on Software Engineering*, pp. 342-361, May, 1998

Gao, D.; Reiter, M. & Song, D. (2005). Behavioral Distance for Intrusion Detection. *Proceedings of the 8th International Symposium on Recent Advances in Intrusion Detection*, pp. 63-81, Seattle, Washington, September 2005, Springer.

Garfinkel, T.; Adams, K.; Warfield, A.; & Franklin, J. (2007). Compatibility is not transparency: VMM detection myths and realities. *Proceedings of the 11th USENIX Workshop on Hot Topics in Operating Systems*, pp. 1-6, San Diego, CA, May, 2007, G. Hunt, Ed. USENIX Association, Berkeley, CA.

Grizzard, J. B.; Sharma, V.; Nunnery, C.; Kang, B. B. & Dagon, D. (2007). Peer-to-peer botnets: overview and case study. *Proceedings of the First Conference on First*

Workshop on Hot Topics in Understanding Botnets, Cambridge, MA, USENIX Association, Berkeley, CA.

Gu, G.; Porras, P.; Yegneswaran, V.; Fong, M. & Lee, W. (2007). BotHunter: detecting malware infection through IDS-driven dialog correlation. *Proceedings of 16th USENIX Security Symposium on USENIX Security Symposium,* pp. 1-16, Boston, MA, August 2007, N. Provos, Ed. USENIX Association, Berkeley, CA.

Gu, G.; Zhang, J.; Lee, W. (2008). BotSniffer: Detecting Botnet Command and Control Channels in Network Traffic. *Proceedings of The 15th Annual Network and Distributed System Security Symposium (NDSS 2008),* San Diego, CA, February 2008, ISOC.

Gu, G.; Perdisci, R.; Zhang, J. & Lee, W. (2008). BotMiner: clustering analysis of network traffic for protocol- and structure-independent botnet detection. *Proceedings of the 17th Conference on Security Symposium* , pp. 139-154, San Jose, CA, July 28 - August 01, 2008, USENIX Association, Berkeley, CA.

Helmer, G.; Wong, J.S.K.; Honavar, V. & Miller, L. (1998). Intelligent agents for intrusion detection. *Proceedings of IEEE Information Technology Conference,* pp. 121-124, Syracuse, NY, USA, September 1998.

Holz, T.; Steiner, M.; Dahl, F.; Biersack, E. & Freiling, F. (2008). Measurements and mitigation of peer-to-peer-based botnets: a case study on storm worm. *Proceedings of the 1st Usenix Workshop on Large-Scale Exploits and Emergent Threats,* pp. 1-9, San Francisco, California, April 2008, F. Monrose, Ed. USENIX Association, Berkeley, CA.

Holz, T.; Engelberth, M. & Freiling, F. (2009). Learning more about the underground economy: a case-study of keyloggers and dropzones. *Proceedings of the 14th European Conference on Research in Computer Security,* pp. 1-18, Saint-Malo, France, September 21 - 23, 2009, M. Backes and P. Ning, Eds. Lecture Notes In Computer Science. Springer-Verlag, Berlin, Heidelberg.

Hund, R.; Hamann, M. & Holz, T. (2008). Towards Next-Generation Botnets. *Proceedings of the 2008 European Conference on Computer Network Defense* , pp. 33-40, Dublin, Ireland, December 11 - 12, 2008, EC2ND, IEEE Computer Society, Washington, DC.

Hex-rays. (2010). IDA Pro. [Online] Available at: http://www.hex-rays.com/idapro/

Ikinci, A.; Holz, T. & Freiling, F. (2008). Monkey-Spider: Detecting Malicious Websites with Low-Interaction Honeyclients. *Proceedings of Sicherheit, Schutz und Zuverlssigkeit,* pp. 407-421, April 2008, Germany.

Jansen, W & Karigiannis, T. (1999). Mobile Agent Security. *NIST Special Publications,* Computer Security Resource Center. [Online] Available at: http://csrc.nist.gov/publications/nistpubs/800-19/sp800-19.pdf [Accessed 12 September 2010]

Karasaridis, A.; Rexroad, B. & Hoeflin, D. (2007). Wide-scale botnet detection and characterization. *Proceedings of the First Conference on First Workshop on Hot Topics in Understanding Botnets* , Cambridge, MA, April 2007, USENIX Association, Berkeley, CA.

Lee, T. & Mody, J. (2006). Behavioral classification. *Proceedings of European Expert Group For IT-Security,* EICAR 2006, Hamburg, Germany, May 2006.

Li, Z.; Goyal, A. & Chen, Y. Honeynet-based Botnet Scan Traffic Analysis. (2008). *Botnet Detection: Countering the Largest Security Threat,* pp. 25-44, ISBN 978-0-387-68766-7, edited by Wenke Lee, Cliff Wang, and David Dagon, Springer-Verlag.

Krügel, C.; Toth, T. & Kirda, E. (2001). SPARTA, a Mobile Agent Based Instrusion Detection System. *Proceedings of the IFIP Tc11 Wg11.4 First Annual Working Conference on Network Security: Advances in Network and Distributed Systems Security*, pp. 187-200, Belgium, November 26 - 27, 2001, B. D. Decker, F. Piessens, J. Smits, and E. V. Herreweghen, Eds. IFIP Conference Proceedings, vol. 206. Kluwer B.V., Deventer, The Netherlands.

Krügel, C.& Toth, T;. (2002).Flexible, Mobile Agent based Intrusion Detection for Dynamic Network. *Proceedings of the European Wireless*. February 2002.

Li, C.; Song, Q.; Zhang, C. (2004). MA-IDS Architecture for Distributed Intrusion Detection using Mobile Agents. *Proceedings of the 2nd International Conference on Information Technology for Application (ICITA 2004).*

Li, Z.; Sanghi, M.; Chen, Y.; Kao, M. & Chavez, B. (2006). Hamsa: Fast Signature Generation for Zero-day PolymorphicWorms with Provable Attack Resilience. *Proceedings of the 2006 IEEE Symposium on Security and Privacy* , pp. 32-47, Oakland, CA, May 21 - 24, 2006. SP. IEEE Computer Society, Washington, DC.

Liu, X.; Yang, X. & Lu, Y. (2008). To filter or to authorize: network-layer DoS defense against multimillion-node botnets. *Proceedings of the ACM SIGCOMM 2008 Conference on Data Communication,* pp. 195-206, Seattle, WA, USA, August 17 - 22, 2008. SIGCOMM '08. ACM, New York, NY.

Mell, P. & McLarnon, M. (1999). Mobile Agent Attack Resistant Distributed Hierarchical Intrusion Detection Systems. *Proceedings of the Second International Workshop on Recent Advances in Intrusion Detection*. Purdue, IN, USA, September 1999, [Online] Available at: http://www.raid-symposium.org/raid99/

MITRE Honey Client Project. (2007). [Online] Available at: http://www.honeyclient.org/trac

Queiroz, J.; Carmo, L. & Pirmez, L. (1999). Micael: An autonomous mobile agent system to protect new generation networked applications. *Proceedings of the Second International Workshop on Recent Advances in Intrusion Detection.* Purdue, IN, USA, September 1999, [Online] Available at: http://www.raid-symposium.org/raid99/

Nazario, J. & Holz T. (2008). As the net churns : fast-flux Botnet Observations. *Proceedings of 3rd International Conference on Malicious and Unwanted Software*, Virginia, October 2008, IEEE.

Newsome, J.; Karp, B. & Song, D. (2005). Polygraph: automatically generating signatures for polymorphic worms, *In Proceedings of IEEE Symposium on Security and Privacy, 2005,* pp. 226- 241, Oakland, CA, 8-11 May 2005. IEEE.

Pierce, C. (2008). Owning Kraken Zombies, A detailed Dissection. [Online] Available at: http://dvlabs.tippingpoint.com/blog/2008/04/28/owning-kraken-zombies . Last accessed: 12th September, 2010.

Porras, P.; Saidi, H. & Yegneswaran, V. (2009). Conficker C Analysis. [Online] Available at: http://mtc.sri.com/Conficker/addendumC/ , Last Updated: 4 April, 2009.

Provos, N.; McNamee, D.; Mavrommatis, P.; Wang, K. & Modadugu, N. (2007). The ghost in the browser analysis of web-based malware. *Proceedings of the First Conference on First Workshop on Hot Topics in Understanding Botnets*, Cambridge, MA, April 2007, USENIX Association, Berkeley, CA.

Provos, N. (2007). HoneyD. [Online] Available at: http://www.honeyd.org. Last accessed: 7th September 2010.

Provos, N.; Mavrommatis, P., Rajab, M. A., & Monrose, F. (2008). All your iFRAMEs point to Us. *Proceedings of the 17th Conference on Security Symposium*, pp. 1-15, San Jose, CA, July 28 - August 01, 2008. USENIX Association, Berkeley, CA.

Rajab, M.; Zarfoss, J.; Monrose, F. & Terzis, A. (2006). A multifaceted approach to understanding the botnet phenomenon. *Proceedings of the 6th ACM SIGCOMM Conference on internet Measurement*, pp. 41-52, Rio de Janeriro, Brazil, October 25 - 27, 2006, ACM, New York, NY.

Ramachandran, A.; Feamster, N. & Dagon, D. (2006). Revealing botnet membership using DNSBL counter-intelligence. *Proceedings of the 2nd Conference on Steps To Reducing Unwanted Traffic on the internet - Volume 2*, pp. 49-54, San Jose, CA, July, 2006, USENIX Association, Berkeley, CA.

Ramachandran, G. & Hart, D. (2004). A P2P intrusion detection system based on mobile agents. *Proceedings of the 42nd Annual Southeast Regional Conference*, pp. 185-190, Huntsville, Alabama, April 02 - 03, 2004. ACM-SE 42. ACM, New York, NY.

Riden, J. & Seifert, C. (2008). A guide to different kinds of honeypots. [Online] Available at: http://www.symantec.com/connect/articles/guide-different-kinds-honeypots, February 2008, Symantec.

Rieck, K.; Holz, T.; Willems, C.; Düssel, P. & Laskov, P. (2008). Learning and Classification of Malware Behavior. *Proceedings of the 5th international Conference on Detection of intrusions and Malware, and Vulnerability Assessment*, pp. 108-125, Paris, France, July 10 - 11, 2008, D. Zamboni, Ed. Lecture Notes In Computer Science, vol. 5137. Springer-Verlag, Berlin, Heidelberg.

Rocaspana, J. (2007). Shelia: a client-side honeypot for attach detection. [Online] Available at: http://www.cs.vu.nl/~herbertb/misc/shelia/. Last accessed: 10 September, 2010.

Roesch, M. (1999). Snort – lightweight intrusion detection system for networks. *Proceedings of USENIX LISA'99*. Seattle, Washington, November 1999.

Roo. (2005). Honeywall. The Honeynet Project. [Online] Available at: https://projects.honeynet.org/honeywall/

Sebek. (2010). Sebek. The Honeynet Project. [Online] Available at: https://projects.honeynet.org/sebek/

Schiller, C. ; Binkley J.; Evron G. ; Willems, C ; Bradley, T. ; Harley D. ; Cross M. (2007). *Botnets : The Killer Web Application*, ISBN 1597491357, Syngress.

Siefert, C; Steenson, R.; Holz, T.; Davis, M. (2007). Know Your Enemy: Behind the scenes of Malicious WebServers. Honeynet.org. Nov 2007, [Online]: Available at: http://www.honeynet.org/papers/mws. Last Accessed: 12 September, 2010.

Siefert. C. (2008). Capture-HPC Client Honeypot. [Online] Available at: https://projects.honeynet.org/capture-hpc . Last Accessed: 12 September, 2010.

Simon, D. R.; Agarwal, S. & Maltz, D. A. (2007). AS-based accountability as a cost-effective DDoS defense. *Proceedings of the First Conference on First Workshop on Hot Topics in Understanding Botnets*, Cambridge, MA, April 2007, USENIX Association, Berkeley, CA.

Singh, K.; Srivastava, A.; Giffin, J.& Lee, W. (2008). Evaluating Email's Feasibility for Botnet Command and Control. *Proceedings of the 38th IEEE/IFIP International Conference on Dependable Systems and Networks (DSN)*, Anchorage, Alaska, USA, June, 2008, IEEE.

Snort-inline. (2005). [Online] Available at: http://snort-inline.sourceforge.net/

Steward, J. (2009). Spam Botnets to Watch 2009. [Online] Available at: http://www.secureworks.com/research/threats/botnets2009/. Secureworks, January, 2009.

Stinson, E. & Mitchell, J. C. (2008). Towards systematic evaluation of the evadability of bot/botnet detection methods. *Proceedings of the 2nd Conference on USENIX Workshop on offensive Technologies*, pp. 1-9, San Jose, CA, USENIX Association, Berkeley, CA.

Stolfo, S.; Prodromidis, A.; Tselepis, S.; Lee, W.; Fan, D. & Chan P. (1997). JAM: Java Agents for Meta-Learning over Distributed Databases. Proceedings of the third international conference on Knowledge Discovery and Data mining, pp. 74-81, Newport Beach, CA, USA, August, 1997, ISBN 1-57735-027-8, AAAI Press.

Strayer, W.; Lapsely, D; Walsh, R & Livadas, C. (2008). Botnet Detection Based on Network Behavior. *Botnet Detection: Countering the Largest Security Threat*, pp. 1-24, edited by Wenke Lee, Cliff Wang, and David Dagon, ISBN 978-0-387-68766-7, Springer-Verlag, 2008.

Sunbelt. (2010). CWSandbox. [Online] Available at: http://www.sunbeltsoftware.com/Malware-Research-Analysis-Tools/Sunbelt-CWSandbox.

Tucek, J.; Newsome, J.; Lu, S.; Huang, C.; Xanthos, S.; Brumley, D.; Zhou, Y. & Song, D. (2007). Sweeper: a lightweight end-to-end system for defending against fast worms. *Proceedings of Special Interest Group on Operating Systems Operating Systems Review*, pp. 115-128, Volume 41, No. 3, June 2007, ACM, Newyork, NY, USA.

Unrealircd. (2010). [Online] Available at: http://www.unrealircd.com/. Last accessed: 12 September, 2010.

Valeur, F.; Vigna, G.; Kruegel, C. & Kemmerer, R. A. (2004). A Comprehensive Approach to Intrusion Detection Alert Correlation. *Proceedings of IEEE Transactions on Dependable and Secure Computing*, pp. 146-169, Volume 1, No. 3, July 2004, IEEE.

Vigna, G. (2004). Mobile agents: ten reasons for failure. *Proceedings of the IEEE International Conference on Mobile Data Management (MDM '04)*, pp. 298-299, Berkeley, CA. IEEE.

Vigna, G.; Cassell, B. & Fayram, D. (2002). An Intrusion Detection System for Aglets. *Proceedings of the 6th international Conference on Mobile Agents*, pp. 64-77, Barcelona, Spain, October 22 - 25, 2002, N. Suri, Ed. Lecture Notes In Computer Science, vol. 2535, ISBN 3-540-00085-2, Springer-Verlag, London.

Vogt, R.; Aycock, J. & Jacobson Jr, M. (2007). Army of Botnets. *Proceedings of the Network and Distributed System Security Symposium, NDSS 2007*, San Diego, California, USA, 28th February - 2nd March 2007, ISOC.

Wang, P.; Sparks, S. & Zou, C. (2007). An advanced hybrid peer-to-peer botnet. *Proceedings of the First Conference on First Workshop on Hot Topics in Understanding Botnets*, Cambridge, MA, April 2007, USENIX Association, Berkeley, CA.

Wang, Y.; Beck, D; Jiang, X.; Roussev, R.; Verbowski, C.; Chen, X. & King, S. (2006). Automated Web Patrol with Strider HoneyMonkeys: Finding web sites that exploit Browser vulnerabilities. *Proceedings of the Network and Distributed System Security Symposium, NDSS 2006*, San Diego, California, USA, February 2006, ISBN 1-891562-22-3, ISOC

Xie, Y.; Yu, F.; Achan, K.; Panigrahy, R.; Hulten, G., & Osipkov, I. (2008). Spamming botnets: signatures and characteristics. *Proceedings of SIGCOMM Computer*

Communication Review, pp. 171-182, Volume 38,No. 4, October 2008, ACM, Newy York, NY, USA.

Yin, H.; Song, D.; Egele, M.; Kruegel, C. & Kirda, E. (2007). Panorama: capturing system-wide information flow for malware detection and analysis. *Proceedings of the 14th ACM Conference on Computer and Communications Security,* pp. 116-127, Alexandria, Virginia, USA, October 28 - 31, 2007, ACM, New York, NY.

5

Social Network Approach to Anomaly Detection in Network Systems

Grzegorz Kołaczek and Agnieszka Prusiewicz
Wroclaw University of Technology
Poland

1. Introduction

The problem of the network security is taken up since eighties (Denning et al., 1987) and is developed up today (Beltilch et al., 2004, Bera, 2010, Dasgupta, 1999, Basile, 2007, Wilson, 1999). A major problem of automatic intrusion detection is that, it is difficult to make a difference between normal and abnormal user behaviour. Intrusion detection system should not only recognise the previously known patterns of attacks, but also react in case of appearance of the new events that violate the network security policy. The distributed nature of the task of the network security monitoring requires applying of the distributed tools for network security maintaining. The most important postulate addressed to the intrusion detection systems is that, such systems should automatically react in case of detecting the security policy breach to prevent the attack execution or to reduce the potential loss in the network systems. Intrusion detection systems should be equipped with the components responsible for the permanent observation of the states of monitored nodes and components that integrate the results of these observations and diagnose the security level of the system (Kolaczek et al., 2005, Nguyen et al., 2006).

A comprehensive survey of anomaly detection systems is presented in (Patcha & Park, 2007) and a comparison of different approaches to intrusion detection systems is given in (Bejtlich, 2004). One of the first agent systems for network security monitoring has been proposed in works (Balasubramaniyet et al., 1998, Spafford & Zamboni, 2000). In work (Kolaczek et al., 2005) a framework of an original proposal of the intrusion detection system based on the multi-agent approach was presented. In particular, the architecture of such a system and the task of agents were specified. Proposed ideas were further developed and in work (Nguyen et al., 2006) the problem of anomalies detection on the basis of the nodes traffic analysis was discussed. The proposal of the method for Denial of Service Attack detection was given in (Prusiewicz, 2008a).

In this work we propose a novel framework of a multi-agent system for anomaly detection. The originality of our solution consists of applying the social network approach to Man in the Middle Attack (MITM) detection in a network system. Our proposal is based on the social networks discovery and their characteristics measurement to detect anomalies in network traffic. We assume that network communication between nodes constitutes social network of users and their applications, so the appropriate methods of social network formal analysis can be applied. The other important assumption is that values of these social

network parameters for a given node and their distribution for all nodes tend to be constant under normal conditions (Golbeck, 2005, Jamali, 2006, Park, 2007).
We measure the values of the parameters that describe the social network consisted of the nodes and then verify whether the communication patterns between the members of the social network have been violated. The organization of the remaining part of this chapter is as follows. In Section 2 the social networks and the properties of social network are introduced. Then in section 3 the architecture of the multi-agent monitoring system is given. In section 4 the problem of anomaly detection in a social network is taken up. In particular the general schema of anomaly detection procedure is given, the case study of man-in-the-middle attack is carried and the method for this type of attack detection is proposed.

2. Social networks

The basic idea about social networks is very simple. It could be understood as a social structure made of actors which can be represented as network nodes (which are generally individuals or organizations) that are tied by one or more specific types of interdependency, such as values, visions, idea, financial exchange, friends, kinship, dislike, conflict, trade, web links, etc. The resulting structures are often very complex (Butts, 2008, Jamali, 2006, Golbeck , 2005). Social relationships in terms of nodes and ties among them could be used in various types of analysis. A number of academic researches have shown that dependences form social fields play a critical role also in many other fields and could be used in determining the way problems could be solved.

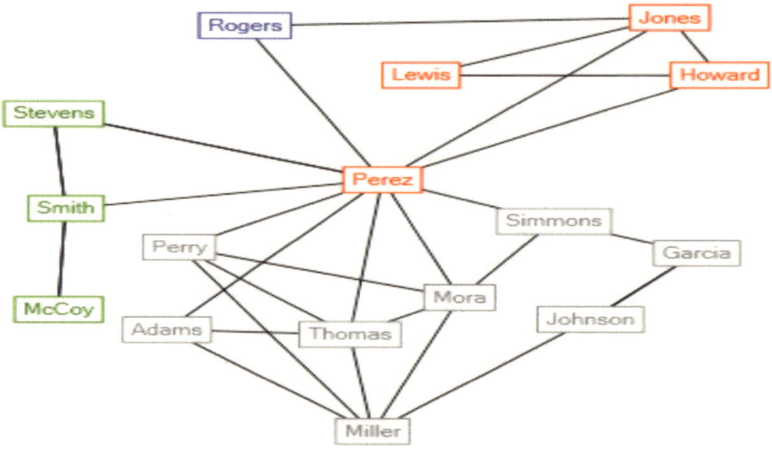

Fig. 1. The example of social network structure (Batchelor, 2010)

Better understanding of social networks requires a complete and rigorous description of a pattern of social relationships as a necessary starting point for analysis. The most convenient situation is when we have complete knowledge about all of the relationships between each pair of actors in the population. To manage all pieces of information related to social network the mathematical and graphical techniques have been used. This formal apparatus allows us to represent the description of networks compactly and systematically. In this context, social network analysts use two kinds of tools from mathematics to represent information about patterns of ties among social actors: graphs and matrices.

Network analysis uses one kind of graphic display that consists of nodes to represent community members and edges to represent ties or relations. There are two general types of situation when there are a single type of relations among the community members and more than one kind of relation. The first one can be represented by the simplex graph while in the second case we use multiplex graphs. Additionally, each social tie or relation represented by graph may be directed or undirected (tie that represents cooccurrence, co-presence, or a bonded-tie between the pair of community members). Another important feature related to the social networks and their graph representation is the strength of ties among community members. In a graph it may be one of the following types: nominal or binary (represents presence or absence of a tie); signed (represents a negative tie, a positive tie, or no tie); ordinal (represents whether the tie is the strongest, next strongest, etc.); or valued (measured on an interval or ratio level).

Other basic social network proprieties that can be formally described and so can constitute a good background for analysis of community dynamics and which can be applied to detect various types of security breaches are as follows (Scott , 2000):

- The Connections between nodes
  The number of immediate connections may be critical in explaining how community members view the world, and how the world views them, so it could be also important factor while modelling trust relations within community. The number and kinds of ties are a basis for similarity or dissimilarity to other community members the direction of connections may be helpful to describe the role of the community member in the society, it can be "a source" of ties, "a sink", or both.

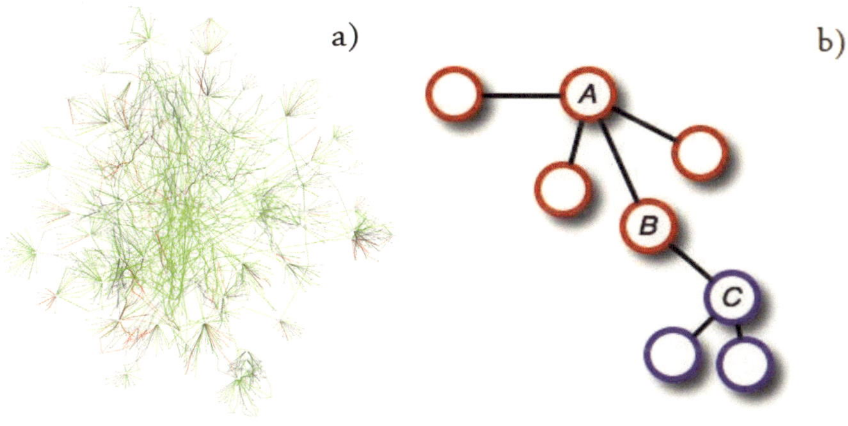

Fig. 2. A network with large number of connection between nodes (a) and small number of connections (b)

- The size of a network
  The size of a network is indexed simply by counting the number of nodes, critical element for the structure of social relations because of the limited resources and capacities that each community member has for building and maintaining ties. The size of a network also influences trust relations while in bigger group it is easier to preserve anonymity and it is more difficult to evaluate trust values.
- The density of a social network
  The density of a social network is defined as the number of existing connections divided by the number of maximum possible connections. The number of logically

possible relationships grows exponentially as the number of actors increases linearly. In communities with greater value of density parameter it should be easier to maintain relations between nodes as we get more information about the other community members.

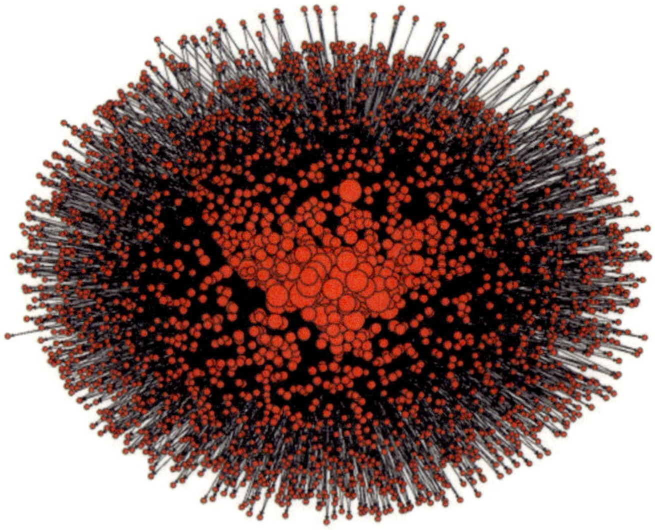

Fig. 3. High density social network (Morrison, 2008)

- The degree of a network node
  It tells us how many connections a community member has. Where out-degree is the sum of the connections from the community member to others and in-degree is the sum of the connections to the particular community member from others. Out-degree and in-degree are also referred as fan-out and fan-in parameters. This type of parameter has been proved to be invariant for a long time periods and different scales (subnet sizes) or traffic types (protocols) of data flows in communication networks (Allmanz, 2005). Experiments showed that both Fan-in and Fan-out for a given node and their distribution for all nodes tend to be constant under normal conditions. While network is affected by some type of attack the structure of communication is often heavily affected and the distribution changes. There is also a detectible dependence between type of the attack and communication pattern disturbance (Kohler, 2002). At the other hand, community members that receive information from many sources may also be more powerful community members. However, these nodes could also suffer from "information overload" or "noise and interference" due to contradictory messages from different sources. Impact for the social relations between nodes is similar to that described in a case of density, dependently from in/out-degree when an individual has more or less information about its neighbourhood.
- The reachability of community members
  A community member is "reachable" by another if there exists any set of connections by which we can find link from the source to the target entity, regardless of how many others fall between them. If some community members in a network cannot reach others, there is the potential of a division of the network. For example, disconnected community members could have more problems to evaluate trust value.

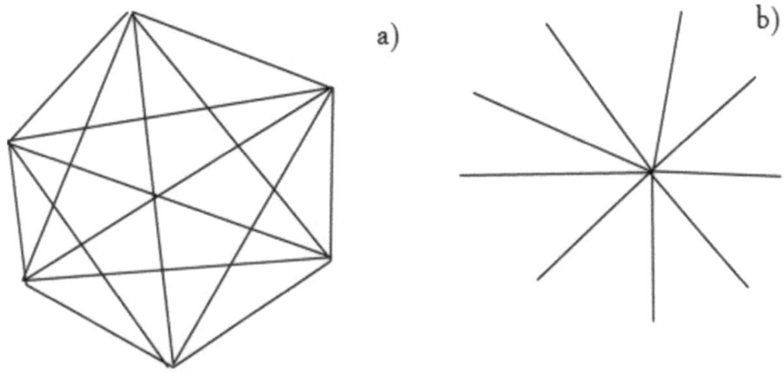

Fig. 4. The examples of networks with different node degree parameter values (a) Perfect graph of n nodes with avg. node degree n-1. (b) Star graph of n+1 nodes with avg. node degree (2n)/(n+1)

- The transivity of network nodes connections
  The transitivity principle holds that, if A is tied to B, and B is tied to C, then A should be tied to C. The triadic relationships (where there are ties among the actors) should tend toward transitivity as an equilibrium condition. One of the most important type of social relation as trust is not strictly transitive and so this propriety not necessarily influences trust evaluation process.
- The distance between the network nodes
  An aspect of how individuals are embedded in networks, two actors are adjacent when the distance between them is one. How many community members are at various distances from each other can be important for understanding the differences among community members in the constraints and opportunities they have as a result of their network location. Community members located more far apart from each other in the community have more problems with establishing new relations than the members, which are close.
- The geodesic distance between the network nodes
  The geodesic distance is defined as the number of relations in the shortest possible walk from one community member to another. Many algorithms in network analysis assume that community members will use the geodesic path when communicating with each other.
- The diameter of a network
  The diameter of a network is the largest geodesic distance in the connected network which tells us how "big" the community is, in one sense quantity in that it can be used to set an upper bound on the lengths of connections that we study.
- The cohesion of a social network
  The degree to which nodes are connected directly to each other by communication links. Count the total connections between actors more strong connection between community members should determine grater trust values.
- Centrality, Power, Betweenness
  Centrality, closeness, betweenness describe the locations of individuals in terms of how close they are to the "center" of the action in a network - though there are a few different definition of what it means to be at the canter. The more important community member is, the more important its opinions should be.

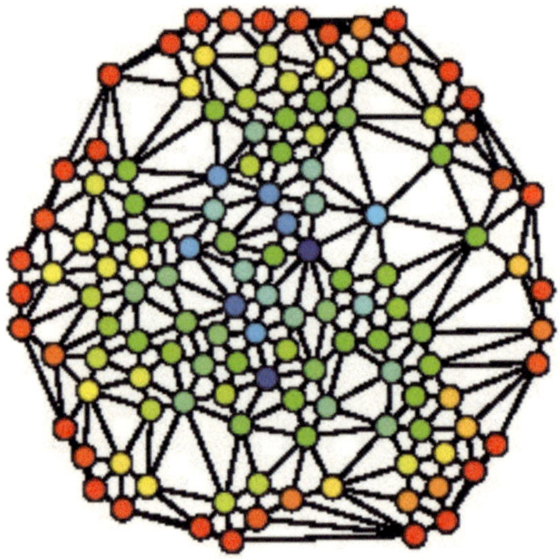

Fig. 5. Example of betweenness centrality. Red colour indicates the lowest betweenness centrality value and blue the highest (Bailin, 2009)

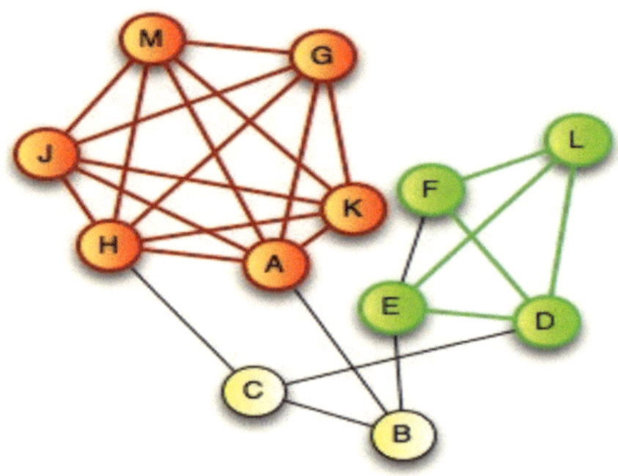

Fig. 6. Cliques example. Network with two cliques - first one is composed of nodes: A,G,H,J,K,M, the second: D,E,F,L

- The eigenvector of the geodesic distances
  An effort to find the most central community members in terms of the "global" or "overall" structure of the network, and to pay less attention to patterns that are more "local"
- The cliques in the network
  A subset of community members who are more closely tied to each other. A clique typically is a subset of community in which every node is connected to every other node of the group and which is not part of any other clique. Idea of cliques within a network is a powerful tool for understanding social structure and the embeddedness of individuals. Cliques reflect the groups of community members with strong relationship.

So, sudden change in communication pattern within such a group may be related to security breaches.

- The clustering coefficient
  The probability that two nearest neighbours of a given node are also neighbours of each other. The value of clustering coefficient provides a quantitative measure for cliques in communication graph.

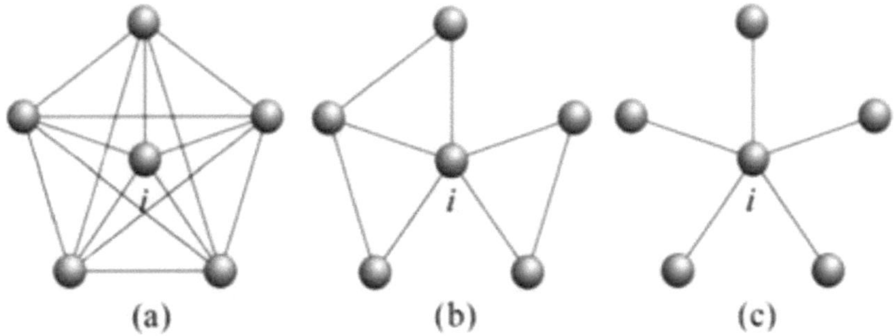

Fig. 7. Example of clustering coefficients (cc) for different networks. a) cc=1, b) cc=0.3, c) cc=0

3. The architecture of the multi-agent monitoring system

It is assumed that there are two layers in the architecture of the multi-agent monitoring system: monitoring layer and control layer (Fig. 8). Monitoring layer consists of the nodes that are monitored by the monitoring agents. While control layer consists of the security control agents that are responsible for collecting data from monitoring agents and determining general characteristics of the network traffic in the monitored region. These characteristics describe communication patterns in the monitored region. We assume that communicating nodes constitutes the social network. Each security control agent is responsible for controlling one region (social network).
The patterns of discovered social networks are temporally collated by security control agents with communication patterns stored in security control agents private databases in order to verify if any security policy breach has been occurred.

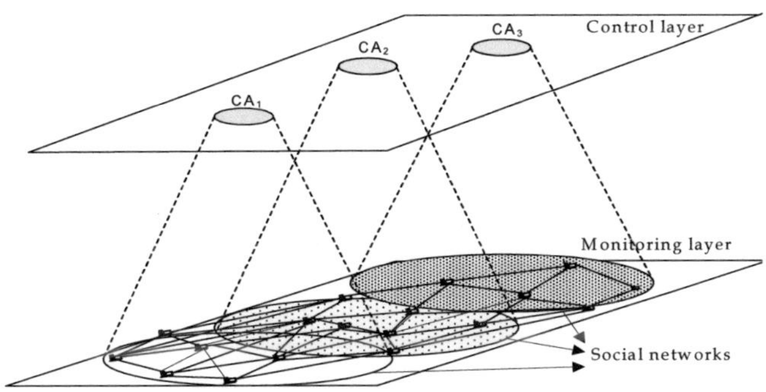

Fig. 8. Two-layers multi-agent monitoring system architecture

Before the internal organization of the monitoring and security control agents will be given, let us denote: V as the set of the nodes, $V = \{v_1, v_2, \ldots, v_k, \ldots, v_K\}$, $K \in N$, MA

($MA = \{MA^1, MA^2, ..., MA^k, ...MA^K\}$) as the set of the monitoring agents, SA ($SA = \{SA^1, SA^2, ..., SA^g, ...SA^G\}$), $G \in N$ as the set of security control agents, SN ($SN = \{SN^g : SN^g \subseteq V\}$) as the set of the social networks (monitoring regions) and $P = \{P_1, P_2, ..., P_Z\}$ as the set of the observed parameters describing the nodes from V.

3.1 Monitoring agent's internal organization

Each monitoring agent $MA^k \in MA$ observes the states of one node from V in their monitoring regions (social networks) from SN with the reference to the values of the parameters from the set P. The results of the observations are captured in their private set of observations.

Definition 1. A single observation of agent MA^k is stored as a tuple [Prusiewicz, 2008a]:

$$O^k\left(\left(P_j, x\right), t_n\right) \in DB^k \tag{1}$$

where: $P_j \in P$, $t_n \in T$ and T is the universe of the timestamps and DB^k denotes the database of the agent MA^k.

Such observation refers to the situation that at the timestamp t_n the agent MA^k has observed in the node v_k the value of the parameter P_j equals x.

3.2 Security control agents internal organization

Security control agents control the monitoring regions. The size of the monitoring regions may change by adding or removing nodes as a consequence of the social networks evolutions. Security control agent SA^g, $SA^g \in SA$ is built from three modules: Data Storage Module, Social Network Module and Security Control Module. Security control agent SA^g collects data from databases of the monitoring agents and builds communication matrix in Data Storage Module [Prusiewicz, 2008b].

Definition 2. The communication matrix CM^g is defined as:

$$CM^g = [a_{mn}]_{GxG} \tag{2}$$

where a_{mn} is the set of time stamps of communication acts between nodes v_m and v_n. The node v_m is a sender and v_n - receiver.

	v_1	v_2	v_5	v_{12}	v_{13}	v_{17}	v_{31}
v_1							
v_2					a_{213}	a_{217}	
v_5				(t_2, t_5, t_9, t_{23}, t_{28}, t_{34})			
v_{12}							
v_{13}							
v_{17}			a_{175}				
v_{31}							

Table 1. En example of communication matrix: the node v_2 communicated with the node v_{12} at the timestamps: t_2, t_5, t_9, t_{23}, t_{28}, t_{34}

On the basis of data from communication matrix CM^g the values of the parameters describing the social network SN^g, $SN^g \in SN$ are determined in Social Network Module. Additionally in Social Network Module the patterns of communication between nodes are determined that a are the basis for the social networks discovery. In Security Control Module the procedures for anomalies detections are implemented. In this case the procedure for Man-In-The Middle attack is implemented.

3.3 Determining of the social network characteristics

Social network characteristics are determined on the basis of the data from communication matrix CM^g by the Social Network Module. In this module two data structure are used in order to control the security of the monitoring region: Social Network Patterns and Temporal Communication Patterns defined as follows:

Definition 3. A Social Network Patterns is defined as:

$$SNP^g_{[t_b,t_e]} = \left\langle f^{[t_b,t_e]}_{in,v_i}, f^{[t_b,t_e]}_{out,v_i}, cl^{[t_b,t_e]}_{v_i}, c^{[t_b,t_e]}_{v_i} \right\rangle \tag{3}$$

where:

- $f^{[t_b,t_e]}_{in,v_i}$ is the number of nodes that originate data exchange with node v_i during observation period $[t_b, t_e]$
- $f^{[t_b,t_e]}_{out,v_i}$ is the number of nodes to which v_i initiates conversations during observation period $[t_b, t_e]$
- $cl^{[t_b,t_e]}_{v_i}$ is the clustering coefficient defined according to the following equation:

$$cl^{[t_b,t_e]}_{v_i} = \frac{2\left|E\left(G1\left(v_i^{[t_b,t_e]}\right)\right)\right|}{\deg\left(v_i^{[t_b,t_e]}\right)\left(\deg\left(v_i^{[t_b,t_e]}\right)-1\right)} \tag{4}$$

where:

- $f^{[t_b,t_e]}_{in,v_i}$ is the number of nodes that originate data exchange with node v_i during observation period $[t_b, t_e]$
- $\deg(v_i^{[t_b,t_e]})$ - denotes degree of node v_i during observation period $[t_b, t_e]$
- $G1(v_i^{[t_b,t_e]})$ - is the set of nodes which are connected with v_i via single link (its immediate neighbors) during observation period $[t_b, t_e]$
- $E(G1(v_i^{[t_b,t_e]}))|$ – is the number of edges among nodes in 1–neighbourhood of node v_i during observation period $[t_b, t_e]$
- $c^{[t_b,t_e]}_{v_i}$ is the centrality of the node, it describes the temporal location of the node v_i during observation period $[t_b, t_e]$ in terms of how close it is to the "canter" of the action in a network.

There are four measures of centrality that are widely used in network analysis: degree centrality, betweenness, closeness, and eigenvector centrality. The proposed method uses Eigenvector centrality measure which assigns relative scores to all nodes in the network based on the principle that connections to high-scoring nodes contribute more to the score of the node in question than equal connections to low-scoring nodes. For examle Google's PageRank is a variant of the Eigenvector centrality measure (Page, 1998). For the node v_i the centrality score is proportional to the sum of the scores of all nodes which are connected to it within observation period $[t_b, t_e]$:

$$c_{v_i}^{[t_b,t_e]} = \frac{1}{\lambda}\sum_{j\in M^{[t_b,t_e]}(i)} v_j^{[t_b,t_e]} = \frac{1}{\lambda}\sum_{j=1}^{N} A_{i,j}^{[t_b,t_e]} v_j^{[t_b,t_e]} \tag{5}$$

where:

- $M^{[t_b,t_e]}(i)$ is the set of nodes that are connected to the node v_i during observation period $[t_b, t_e]$,
- N is the total number of nodes,
- $A_{i,j}^{[t_b,t_e]}$ is the adjacency matrix of the network during observation period $[t_b, t_e]$,
- λ is a constant.

Definition 4. A Temporal Communication Patterns is the set of social network characteristics that has been determined at the time intervals, defined as:

$$TCP^g = \left\langle TCP^g_{[t_b^{'},t_e^{'}]} \middle| TCP^g_{[t_b^{'},t_e^{'}]} = \left\langle f_{in,v_i}^{[t_b^{'},t_e^{'}]}, f_{out,v_i}^{[t_b^{'},t_e^{'}]}, cl_{v_i}^{[t_b^{'},t_e^{'}]}, c_{v_i}^{[t_b^{'},t_e^{'}]} \right\rangle \right\rangle \tag{6}$$

where each element of the set TCP^g has the same structure as Social Network Patterns. The difference is that the values of $SNP^g_{[t_b,t_e]}$ are the patterns that describe the monitored social network SN^g ($SN^g \subseteq V$). They are discovered on the basis of the historical network traffic data analysis. Social Network Patterns are used to discover any security policy breaches in a network system. While the values from Temporal Communication Patterns describe the current communication characteristics of monitored region. The last element of the TCP^g is a current characteristics of communication patterns of a social network SN^g.

Having the values of the parameters from Social Network Patterns and current social network characteristics the procedure for anomaly detection might be applied.

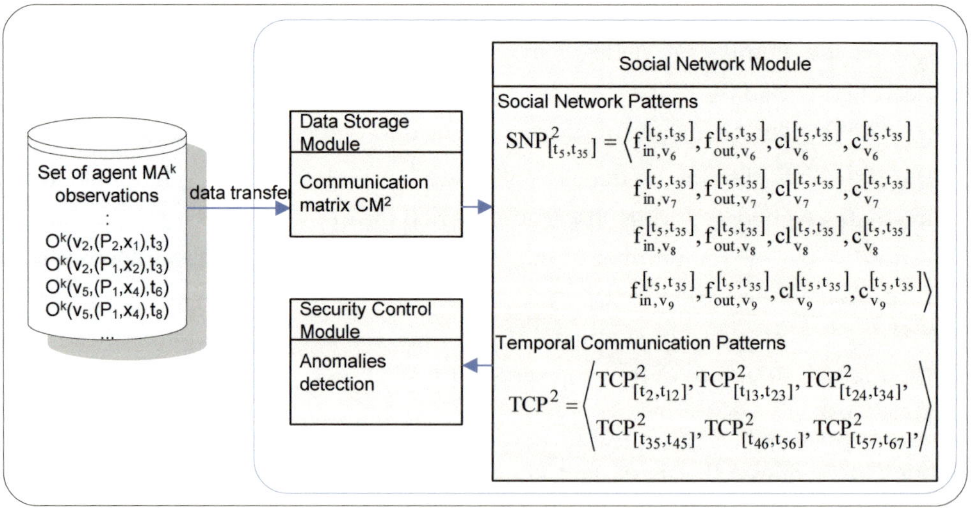

Fig. 9. The process of determining of the social network characteristics and anomaly detection

On the fig. 9 the process of anomaly detection carried out by the security control agent is illustrated. First the observations from the monitoring agents embodied in the nodes v_6, v_7, v_8, v_9 are captured by the Data Storage Module and used to determine communication matrix CM^2. Data from CM^2 are sent to Social Network Module, responsible for determining the patterns of communications in an observed network. The social network patterns $SNP^2_{[t_5,t_{35}]}$ have been determined for the nodes: v_6, v_7, v_8, v_9 and the time interval $[t_5,t_{35}]$ to control the security. The current communication patterns TCP^2 are compared with $SNP^2_{[t_5,t_{35}]}$ to control the security of SN^2.

4. Man-in-the-middle attack detection

The man-in-the-middle attack (often abbreviated MITM) is a form of active eavesdropping in which the attacker makes independent connections with the victims and relays messages between them, making them believe that they are talking directly to each other over a private connection when in fact the entire conversation is controlled by the attacker. To perform the effective attack, the attacker must be able to intercept all messages going between the two victims and inject new ones, which is straightforward in many circumstances (Fields, 1995).

This type of attack can be as analyzed as a general problem resulting from the presence of intermediate parties acting as proxy for clients on either side (Asokan, 2002, Shim, 2003, Welch, 2003). The problems related to the MITM attacks are also related to trust relation among geographically distributed subjects. If communicating with each other subjects are trustworthy and competent the risk of the MITM attack is low. If communicating parts do not know each other or has no trust relation, the risk of the attack increases. By acting as proxy and appearing as the trusted client to each side, the intermediate attacker can carry out much mischief, including various attacks against the confidentiality or integrity of the data passing through it. So, one of the most urgent question is how one can detect MITM attacks.

It is important to notice, that MITM attack is a general security problem not only related to cryptographic applications. An example of such non-cryptographic man-in-the-middle attack was caused by one version of a Belkin wireless network router in 2003 (Leyden, 2003). This router periodically would take over an HTTP connection being routed through it: it would fail to pass the traffic on to destination, but instead itself respond as the intended server. The reply it sent, in place of the requested web page, was an advertisement for another Belkin product. This 'feature' was removed from later versions of the router's firmware (Scott, 2000).

Another example of such type of man-in-the-middle attack could be the "Turing porn farm". This schema of the attack potentially could be used by spammers to defeat CAPTCHAs (Petmail). The general idea is that the spammer sets up a pornographic web site where access requires that the user solves the CAPTCHAs in question. However, this attack is merely theoretical because there is no evidence of building Turing porn farm by the time being (Atwood, 2006). There are available several ready to use tools which implement the MITM idea and which can be used for communication interception in various environments, e.g. dsniff - a tool for SSH and SSL MITM attacks, Ettercap - a tool for LAN based MITM attacks, AirJack - a tool that demonstrates 802.11 based MITM attacks, and many others.

4.1 Evaluation of MITM event probability value

We assume tracking four communication patterns: Fan-in (from here on denoted as $f_{in,v_i}^{\Delta t}$ for node v_i during the observation period Δt), Fan-out ($f_{out,v_i}^{\Delta t}$), clustering coefficient ($cl_{v_i}^{\Delta t}$) and centrality ($c_{v_i}^{\Delta t}$).

According to the assumption presented by (Allmanz, 2005) that these types of parameter has been proved to be invariant for a long time periods and different subnet sizes or traffic types of data flows, the risk of the MITM incident will be estimated as the abnormal change of the characteristic parameters values for a given social network member.

Let us assume that the collected history record consists of a number of observations of Fan-in values from some starting point up to current time t. So we have $f_{in,v_i}^{\Delta t_1}, f_{in,v_i}^{\Delta t_2}, f_{in,v_i}^{\Delta t_3}, \ldots, f_{in,v_i}^{\Delta t_k}$. Now, consider the Fan-in as a random variable F_{in,v_i}. Thus, ($f_{in,v_i}^{\Delta t_1}, f_{in,v_i}^{\Delta t_2}, f_{in,v_i}^{\Delta t_3}, \ldots, f_{in,v_i}^{\Delta t_k}$) is a sample of size k of F_{in,v_i}. We also assume all of the $f_{in,v_i}^{\Delta t}$ to be independent. It is commonly known that the mean value and the variance of F_{in,v_i} can be estimated by using the following formulae:

$$\overline{F}_{in,v_i} = \frac{1}{m}\sum_{j=1}^{k} f_{in,v_i}^{\Delta t_j} \tag{7}$$

$$S_{in,v_i} = \frac{1}{k-1}\sum_{j=1}^{k} (f_{in,v_i}^{\Delta t_j} - \overline{F}_{in,v_i})^2 \tag{8}$$

$\overline{F}_{in,v_i}$ and S_{in,v_i} are thus the estimations (based on the data being at our disposal) of mean value and the variance of F_{in,v_i}. Obviously the bigger our sample is, the better they approximate E(F_{in,v_i}) (expected value of random variable) F_{in,v_i} and Var(F_{in,v_i}) (variance of random variable F_{in,v_i}) respectively. From this point we assume that the observations 'number is big enough to state that E(F_{in,v_i}) and Var(F_{in,v_i}) are known.

Let also E(F_{out,v_i}) and Var(F_{out,v_i}) for the Fan-out, as well as E($cl_{v_i}^{\Delta t}$) and Var($cl_{v_i}^{\Delta t}$) for clustering coefficient and centrality E($c_{v_i}^{\Delta t}$), Var($c_{v_i}^{\Delta t}$) be defined in the same way.

In our approach, we will detect the possible MITM events by evaluation of some weighted value related to mean value and variance of fan-in, fan-out, clustering coefficient and centrality. At this stage of research we assume that we will analyze all four parameters independently. This means that it is enough to assume MITM incident if only one of the parameters exceeds threshold value.

From the Chebyshev's inequality we can estimate the upper bound of the probability that $|\overline{F} - x|$ is greater than kS. Where $\overline{F}$ and S are mean value and the variance of X, while X denotes the random variable related to x (in this case one of the following: $f_{in,v_i}^{\Delta t}, f_{out,v_i}^{\Delta t}, c_{v_i}^{\Delta t}, cl_{v_i}^{\Delta t}$).

According to this estimation the probability expectation E (ϖ_{v_i}) value of the MITM event for a given parameter will be evaluated using the following formula:

$$E(\omega_{v_i}) = 1 - \frac{1}{\alpha k^2} \tag{9}$$

Where α is a coefficient, which value should be set during a process of tuning-up the detection system to the real network conditions. Parameter k is defined as follows:

$$k = \begin{cases} 1 & \text{if} \left\lfloor \frac{\bar{F} - x}{\sqrt{S}} \right\rfloor < 1 \\ \left\lfloor \frac{\bar{F} - x}{\sqrt{S}} \right\rfloor & \text{if} \left\lfloor \frac{\bar{F} - x}{\sqrt{S}} \right\rfloor \geq 1 \end{cases} \tag{10}$$

4.2 The procedure of the Man-in-the-middle attack detection

Our approach of MITM attack detection has been dedicated especially to effectively detect automated attacks of this type. For example this method should be convenient for detection HoneyBot-based attacks as it has been described in their work by researchers from Institut EURECOM in France (Lauinger, 2010), who are working on automation of social engineering attacks on social networks.

French researchers have developed an automated social engineering tool that uses a man-in-the middle attack and strikes up online conversations with potential victims. In the work (Lauinger, 2010) the proof-of-concept HoneyBot has been presented that poses convincingly as a real human in Internet Relay Chats (IRC) and instant messaging sessions. It lets an attacker collect personal and other valuable information from victims via these chats, or tempt them into clicking on malicious links. The researchers had proved the feasibility and effectiveness of their MITM attack variant. During the tests they were able to get users to click onto malicious links sent via their chat messages 76 percent of the time.

We propose the following idea of algorithm for MITM detection using social network patterns.

Input: D - set of data that can be used to derive and observe patterns of the social network (e.g. e-mail logs, chat rooms records, network traffic, etc.)

Output: $R \in \{Y,N\}$ - information about the social network state according to risk of MITM incidents

BEGIN

1. Take the data set D and derive the social network structure (e.g. using one of the approach presented in section 3.1)
2. For each node find the current value of the monitored social network patterns (fan-in, fan-out, centrality, clustering)
3. Analyze the history of network patterns changes. As we treat the network patterns values as the realization of the random variable, mean value and variance will be calculated for each pattern.
4. For each node compare the latest change of the patterns values to the assumed threshold value.
5. If the result of the step 4 is that the observed parameter value exceeded the threshold, the value of the result variable is set to Y - the high risk of the MITM incident, otherwise it is set to N - small risk of MITM incident.
6. Return to step 2.

END

Remarks:

- due to the social network dynamics, we may consider some periodic more thorough updates of the network structure; it could be represented in the above algorithm by adding a time related condition in step 6 and then by return to step 1 instead of returning to step 2

- it is possible to consider situation when we are interested only in monitoring for one particular or some specific subset of all nodes (bank client, chat room participant, etc.), then we may investigate some additional information about its activity and use some data fusion methods to improve the accurateness of the final decision (e.g. we may concurrently track the node's activity within several different social network and so build more comprehensive profile of the network identity).
- we should consider if some "suspicious" behaviour in the context of the only one observed parameter is enough to assume MITM incident or we would prefer to wait for more premises or else we will combine the values of all parameters and only after using data fusion methods set up the final decision.

The algorithm for MITM attack detection

Input: Social Network Patterns $SNP^{g}_{[t_b, t_e]}$

Temporal Network Patterns $TNP^{g}_{[t_{b'}, t_{e'}]}$

Threshold values: F_{in,v_i-max}, F_{out,v_i-max}, C_{v_i-max}, Cl_{v_i-max}.

Output: The risk of the MITM incidents in the nodes of SN^g

BEGIN

1. For each node $v_i \in SN^g$ determine the probability expectation values: $E(\omega_{F_{in,v_i}})$, $E(\omega_{F_{out,v_i}})$, $E(\omega_{Cl_{v_i}})$, $E(\omega_{C_{v_i}})$ according to the formula 9.
2. If $E(\omega_{F_{in,v_i}}) > F_{in,v_i\text{-}max}$ or $E(\omega_{F_{out,v_i}}) > F_{out,v_i\text{-}max}$ or $E(\omega_{Cl_{v_i}}) > Cl_{v_i\text{-}max}$ or $E(\omega_{C_{v_i}}) > c_{v_i\text{-}max}$

   then the risk of MITM incident in the node V_i: $R_{v_i} := \{Y\}$ else $R_{v_i} := \{N\}$

END

5. Conclusion

Generally the aim of the network security systems is to protect computational and communication resources from any security policy breaches. Such systems should be equipped with the meachnisms for permanent monitoring the values of the parameters describing their states in order to diangose and protect of their resources. The most important postulate addressed to the intrusion detection systems is that, such systems should automatically react in case of detecting the security policy breaches to prevent the attack executions or to reduce the potential loss in the network systems. Although the problem of the network security has been studied for decades and several methods and approaches have been proposed there is still open problem how to differentiate normal and abnormal states of the network system. In this work we proposed the social network approach to evaluate the security state of the network. The values of the chosen coefficients that characterise the users behaviour are used to discover security breaches occurrence. The idea of our proposal is as follows. First the user behaviours are monitored and the social networks are discovered. Then having the pattern values of social networks characteristics we are able to compare them with the current observations and detect any aberrances.

We proposed two-layers multi-agent system for security monitoring and the algorithm for MITM attack detection.

6. Acknowledgements

The research presented in this work has been partially supported by the European Union within the European Regional Development Fund program no. POIG.01.03.01-00-008/08

7. References

Allmanz M. et.al. (2005). A First Look at Modern Enterprise Traffic, In *Proc. Internet Measurement Conference*, pp. 217-231.

Asokan N, Niemi V, Nyberg K (2002) Man-in-the-middle in tunnelled authentication protocols, *Technical Report 2002*/163, IACR ePrint archive

Atwood J., (2006). CAPTCHA Effectiveness, http://www.codinghorror.com/, last access 01 September 2010

Bailin A., (2009). Measuring digital engagement, http://coi.gov.uk/blogs/digigov/, last access 01 September 2010

Balasubramaniyan, J.S., Garcia-Fernandez, J.O., Isacoff, D., Spafford, E., Zamboni, D. (1998) An Architecture for Intrusion Detection Using Autonomous Agents, Proceedings of the 14th Annual Computer Security Applications Conference

Basile C., Lioy A., Prez G. M., Clemente F. J. G., and Skarmeta A. F. G. (2007). POSITIF: a policy-based security management system, In 8th *IEEE International Workshop on Policies for Distributed Systems and Networks* (POLICY07), pp.280-280

Batchelor J., (2010). What the naked eye cannot see, http://thesocionomicaffect.wordpress.com/, last access 01 September 2010

Bejtlich, R. (2004). Tao of Network Security Monitoring, The: Beyond Intrusion Detection, Addison-Wesley.

Bera P., Ghosh SK., Dasgupta P. (2010) A Spatio-Temporal Role-Based Access Control Model for Wireless LAN Security Policy Management, *4th International Conference on Information Systems,Technology and Management* (ICISTM 2010), LNCS Springer Berlin, vol.54, pp.76-88

Biermann, E., Cloete, E., Venter, L.M., (2001). A comparison of Intrusion Detection systems, *Computers and Security*, vol. 20 Issue: 8, pp. 676-683

Butts J. and Carter T. (2008). Social network analysis: A methodological introduction. Asian *Journal of Social Psychology* 11 (1), 13-41.

Dasgupta, D. (1999). Immunity-Based Intrusion Detection. System: A General Framework. *Proceedings of the 22nd National Information Systems Security Conference*, USA

Denning, D.E, Edwards, D.L, Jagannathan, R., Lunt, T.F., Neumann, P.G. (1987). A prototype IDES: A real-time intrusiondetection expert system. Technical report, Computer Science Laboratory, SRI International, Menlo Park.

Fields A., Ringel M. (1995). Who do you trust? Trust Hierarchies Over Insecure Communications Channels

Golbeck J. and Hendler J. (2005) Inferring trust relationships in web-based social networks, *ACM Transactions on Internet Technology*, pp. 145-165

Jamali M., Abolhassani H. (2006). Different Aspects of Social Network Analysis, 2006. [Online]. Available: http://dx.doi.org/10.1109/WI.2006.61

Kohler E., Liy J., Paxson V., Shenker S. (2002). Observed Structure of Addresses in IP Traffic, In *Proc. SIGCOMM Internet Measurement Workshop*, pp. 253 - 266.

Kołaczek, G., Prusiewicz, A., Juszczyszyn, K., Grzech, A., Katarzyniak, R., Nguyen, N.T. (2005). A mobile agent approach to intrusion detection in network systems, Lecture Notes in Computer Science, *Lecture Notes in Artificial Intelligence*. vol. 3682, pp. 514-519

Lauinger T., Pankakoski F., Balzarotti D., Kirda E. (2010). Honeybot: Your Man in the Middle for Automated Social Engineering, *3rd USENIX Workshop on Large-Scale Exploits and Emergent Threats* (LEET), San Jose

Leyden J. (2003). Help! my Belkin router is spamming me, http://www.theregister.co.uk, last access 01 September 2010

Morrison M.(2008). Map of top 50 UK PR twitter people and their followers http://blog.magicbeanlab.com/, last access 01 September 2010

Nguyen, N.T., Juszczyszyn, K., Kołaczek, G., Grzech, A., Prusiewicz, A., Katarzyniak, R. (2006). Agent-based approach for distributed intrusion detection system design, *Lecture Notes in Computer Science*, vol. 3993, pp. 224-231

Onnela J.P., Saramaki, J., Szabo, G., Lazer, D., Kaski, K., Kertesz, J., Barabasi, Hyvönen, A.L. (2007). Structure and tie strengths in mobile communication networks, *Proceedings of the National Academy of Sciences* 18, 7332-7336, 2007.

Page L., Brin S., Motwani R., Winograd T. (1998). The PageRank Citation Ranking: Bringing order to the Web. Technical Report, Computer Science Department, Stanford University (1998).

Park J. and A. L. Barabási (2007). Distribution of node characteristics in complex networks. *Proceedings of the National Academy of Sciences of the United States of America* 104 (46), 17916-17920.

Patcha, A., Park, J.-M. (2007). An overview of anomaly detection techniques: Existing solutions and latest technological trends, *Computer Networks*, vol. 51, Issue: 12, pp. 3448-3470

Petmail Documentation: Steal People's Time To Solve CAPTCHA Challenges, http://petmail.lothar.com/, last access 01 September 2010

Prusiewicz, A. (2008a). On some method for intrusion detection used by the multi-agent monitoring system, *Lecture Notes in Computer Science*, vol. 5103, pp. 614-623, Kraków, Poland

Prusiewicz, A. (2008b). A multi-agent system for computer network security monitoring. *Lecture Notes in Artificial Intelligence*. 2008, vol. 4953, s. 842-849.

Scott J. (2000). Social Network Analysis: A Handbook. 2nd Ed. Sage, London

Shim K, (2003) A man-in-the-middle attack on Nalla-Reddy's ID-based tripartite authenticated key agreement protocol, http://eprint.iacr.org/2003/115.pdf, last access 01 September 2010

Spafford, E., Zamboni, D. (2000). Intrusion detection using autonomous agents, Computer Networks. *The International Journal of Computer and Telecommunications Networking*, vol.34 , Issue 4, pp. 547-570

Welch, D., Lathrop, S. (2003). Wireless security threat taxonomy, Information Assurance Workshop, *IEEE Systems, Man and Cybernetics Society* , vol., no., pp. 76- 83

Wilson, E. (1999). Network Monitoring and Analysis: A Protocol Approach to Troubleshooting, Prentice Hall.

6

An Agent Based Intrusion Detection System with Internal Security

Rafael Páez
Pontificia Universidad Javeriana, Bogotá
Colombia

1. Introduction

Intrusion Detection Systems (IDS) are software or hardware products that automate the analysis process of traffic on a network or a host. and they are a complementary security tool in computer networks; it can be deployed at different points depending on the application, host or network segment to be monitored. Accordingly to its location, the IDS must be parameterized in a different way, for example, an IDS located in a Demilitarized Zone (DMZ) must be more flexible than an IDS located inside the internal network to reduce false alarms or to avoid system overload, allowing intrusions without generating an alarm. Likewise the IDS can receive different kinds of attacks if it is located in a DMZ or in the intranet zone.

Due to the increasing rate of attacks, Intrusion Detection Systems has become a complementary and mandatory security tool to any organization, and in addition it is useful to perform forensic analysis procedures in order to complement the IDS use. An IDS performs passive monitoring and captures information to be analyzed subsequently, it can launch an alarm to a server or send an email warning about possible intrusions but it cannot modify its environment, otherwise it is named Intrusion Prevention System (IPS). An IPS responds in real time if an intrusion is detected, the IPS takes an action modifying its environment; it could modify the firewall by closing a suspicious connection, or reconfigure the router, etc.

In the last two decades many research studies about technologies, architectures, methodologies and technologies have been proposed in order to increase the IDS effectiveness. One of them is the agent technology. Agents offer many advantages to IDS like scalability, independence, solution to complex tasks, reduction of network traffic, etc. For these reasons, agents are appropriate but they have inherent security drawbacks and they must be tackled. There are four risk scenarios: agent against agent, agent against platform, others against agent and platform against agent. The most difficult problem to face is the last one because the platform can be accessed by the agent code and it could eventually modify it. The internal security of a system is treated in few research works and it is a critical situation because it is a barrier for attackers, and one of their first challenges is to cheat or attack defence systems.

In previous studies (Páez et al., 2005), many IDS architectures based on agents were analyzed, and it was possible to conclude that it was necessary to propose techniques to protect internally an agent based IDS, by securing its different entities. The new IDS's architecture proposed is named Laocoonte and it is a work on progress, using an open framework developed in the Pontificia Universidad Javeriana named BESA (*Behaviour-oriented, Event-driven and Social-based agent framework*) (González et al., 2003).

BESA is a platform developed in Java in order to take advantage of its portability. BESA allows the deployment of a Multi agent Systems (MAS), its environment is object oriented and offers multithreading and transparency in communications among entities. The abstract model of BESA is based on three fundamentals concepts: Behaviour-Oriented, Event-Driven and Social-Based. Moreover BESA uses a set of containers located in each host on the system, and each container contains several agents performing specific functions. Likewise, each agent has a set of guards; each guard has two associated procedures. The first one is executed automatically by the firing mechanism to verify a boolean condition. The second is executed by behaviour when the guard has fired. The code implementing behaviour is generic and can be written independently of the agent specificity. Behaviour receives an event, and depending on its type executes a program. In this way, the internal structure of each agent can be constructed.

2. Important

An IDS is a software or hardware tool which allows to detect and warn about an attack or intrusion from authorized or non authorized users to the system which is being protected. The intrusion can be from inside or outside the protected system and it can be intentional or accidental. An intrusion is an unauthorized or non wanted activity that puts in risk any security service like confidentiality, integrity and/or availability of the information or computer resource.

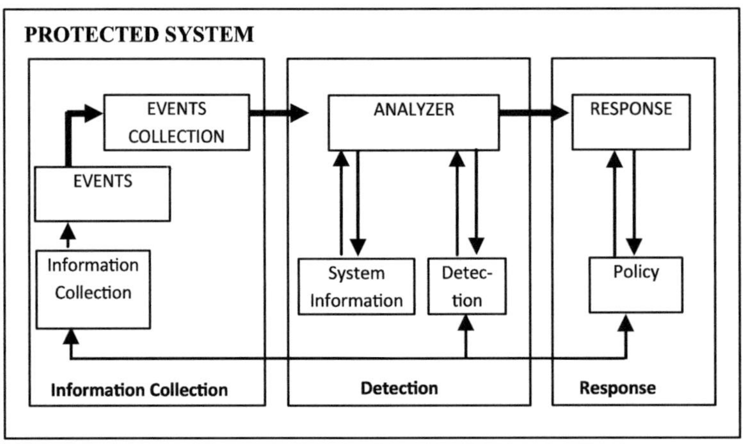

Fig. 1. Basic IDS architecture

The basic architecture of an IDS consists of three main modules: The information collection module, detection module and Response module (Páez et al., 2006). The information collection module contains: an event generator, an event collection sub-module and a reference to detect an intrusion (Database of attacks, behaviour profile, etc.). Fig. 1 illustrates the basic architecture of an IDS.

The event generator sub module can be the operating system, the network or an application. The events generator sub module sends the information to the event collection sub module, and then it sends the traffic to the detection module.

The detection module has an analyzer or sensor which decides if actually there is an intrusion. Finally, the detection module sends the suspicious traffic to the response module which acts accordingly, based on a policy database.
There are many ways to classify an IDS [Debar et al., 1999]. Debar et al classify IDS´s accordingly to the detection method, the behaviour on detection, the audit source location and usage frequency.
The main concern of researchers in Intrusion Detection Systems is to avoid false negative and positive events because they are common drawbacks to IDS's, a false positive occurs when the IDS detects an intrusion and reacts accordingly to its configuration but actually is not malicious traffic, and a false positive occurs when the IDS does not alert about a real intrusion. Both factors affect negatively the IDS but maybe the second one is the most dangerous because it would allow an attack, but the first one would reduce the IDS' reliability and distracts network administrators from real issues. Thus, an IDS must to minimize false negative and positive events and keep updated the system. Moreover, a well configured IDS is also another resource to perform forensic analysis through its log files, and depending on its location it can offer many information about inside or outside attacks. An IDS is a complementary security tool; in neither case, it would replace other security tools like firewalls, antivirus, etc.
Moreover false positive and negatives events, there are many other problems regarding IDS's such as evasion, in this case an intruder may try to avoid detection by fragmenting communication packets, in this way, the signature database would not match what the IDS expects to see. Fragmented packets are put back together into its original form and the attack is performed without being detected by the IDS. Another problem to solve is related to cryptographic techniques; because a network based IDS cannot access raw data and it could not detect a possible attack or intrusion. Finally, depending on the used technology other problems could arise inside the IDS.
We have focused our work in an IDS based on autonomous and mobile agents. Agents have many characteristics appropriates to IDS (Balasubramaniyan et al., 1998) because they can perform simple tasks individually without supervision (i.e. traffic monitoring; event correlation of results), they can solve complex tasks such as detect an intrusion or attack. Agents can be classified according to their mobility, they can be static or mobile; according to their behaviour, they can be deliberative or reactive and according to their attributes, they can be autonomous, cooperative or intelligent. By combining these properties, they can be classified as: collaborative agents, interface agents, information or internet agents, hybrids or heterogeneous agents.
On the other hand, mobile agents have inherent security drawbacks due to their nature, because of this its use has not been widely spread in industrial environments. These security problems can be summarized in the following four scenarios (Fig. 2): agent against agent, agent against platform, others against platform and platform against agent (Jansen, 2000). These scenarios have common attacks and they are: masquerade, denial of service and unauthorized access; A masquerade attack occurs when an entity (platform, agent, etc.) claims the identity of another entity in order to impersonate it and obtain access to services and resources; A denial of service attack occurs when an entity consumes an excessive amount of computing resources; this attack can be launched intentionally or unintentionally. The denial of service can occur on a resource (i.e. printer) or on information; An unauthorized access attack occurs when an entity access resources' information to which it has not granted permission. Additionally, attacks from agent to agent scenario can suffer repudiation attacks, this occurs when an entity which have participated in a transaction or communication, later it

denies its participation. In the case of attacks from others entities to agent, exists the copy and replay attack, it means that a malicious entity intercepts an agent or agent's message and then tries to copy the agent or message in order to clone or retransmit it. Finally, in the platform to agent scenario, the eavesdropping attack is a passive attack and occurs when an entity, in this case the platform, intercepts and monitors secret communications.

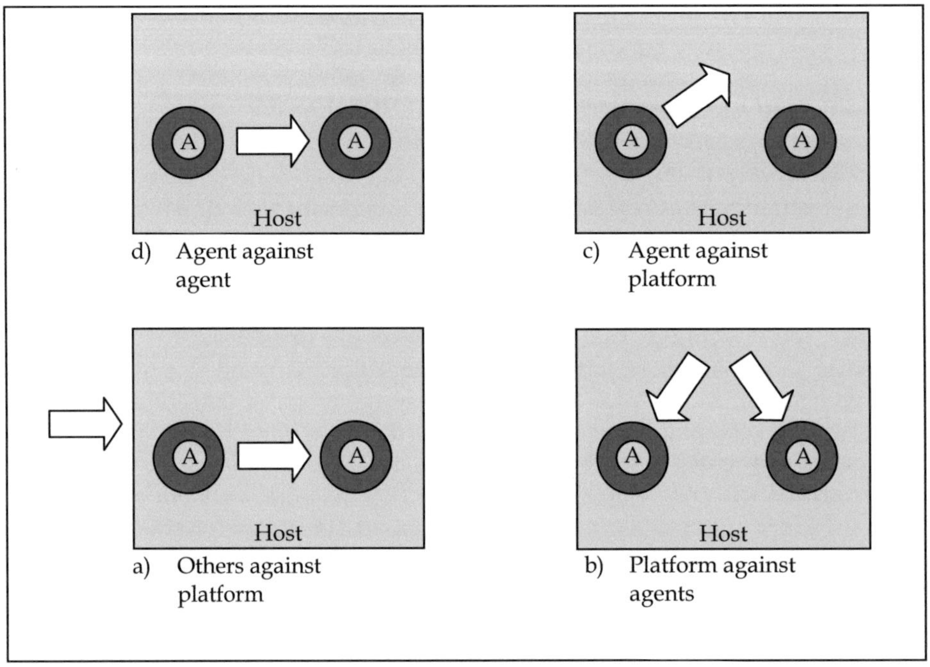

Fig. 2. Different attacks in an agent environment

There are some proposals to protect both agents and platform (Jansen, 2000) (Collberg, 2002) (Knoll et al., 2001), but many of them have general purpose to any agent based systems. Some of these proposals are not viable to all systems, because they add overload to the system or use cryptographic techniques which have significant drawbacks in response time. The most difficult problem to solve is the attack from a platform against agents. This is because the platform has access to the data, code and results of the agents located on it. In this way, if a host is malicious, it can perform an active or passive attack. In the case of a passive attack, the host obtains secret information as electronic money, private keys, certificates or secrets that the agent uses for its own security requests. On the other hand, to perform an active attack, the host would be able to corrupt or to modify the code or the state of the agents. A malicious host can also carry out a combination of passive and active attacks, for example, by analyzing the operation of the agent and applying reverse engineering to introduce subtle changes, so the agent shows malicious behaviour and reports false results. Some authors consider two phases in a Mobile Agents System (MAS), transferring phase and running phase (Xiaobin, 2004). Thus, an agent could be attacked either when it is moving or when it is located in a malicious host performing its job. In an IDS based on mobile agents the threats are transferred, but they must be treated in a particular way. It is important to provide internal security in order to avoid or detect an attack but without adding overload to the system and using simple techniques which do not consume excessive response time.

We have centred our research in the worst scenario: attacks from platform against agent. Several IDS based on agent architectures have been analyzed in order to investigate about its protection mechanisms, in order to provide internal security, because all of them must face the same issues. Among them are: IDA [Asaka et al., 1999], MA-IDS [Shao-Chun et al., 2003], JAM [Salvatore et al., 1997] and Sparta system [Kruegel et al., 2001] and others systems based on agents.

2.1 IDA´s architecture

The IDA´s (Intrusion Detection Agent system) architecture (Fig. 3) uses a sensor agent that resides at a node in search of an MLSI (Marks Left by Suspected Intruder) from the system's log; and upon discovery, notifies the Manager who dispatches a tracing agent to the host where the MLSI was detected. This agent activates an information-gathering agent. The information-gathering agent collects, in a independent way, information related to the MLSI on the target system. The information-gathering agent returns to the Manager with its results and logs them on a bulletin board. The tracing agent moves to the next targeted system and activates a new information gathering agent. Meanwhile, the bulletin board integrates information collected about the intrusion, using the gathered information from several involved agents. So, bulletin board and message board are a common use area and can be accessed by tracing agents and information-gathering agents. The manager accumulates, analyzes and weighs the information entered on the bulletin board by the mobile agents and, if the weights exceed a threshold, it concludes that an intrusion has occurred and issues an alarm.

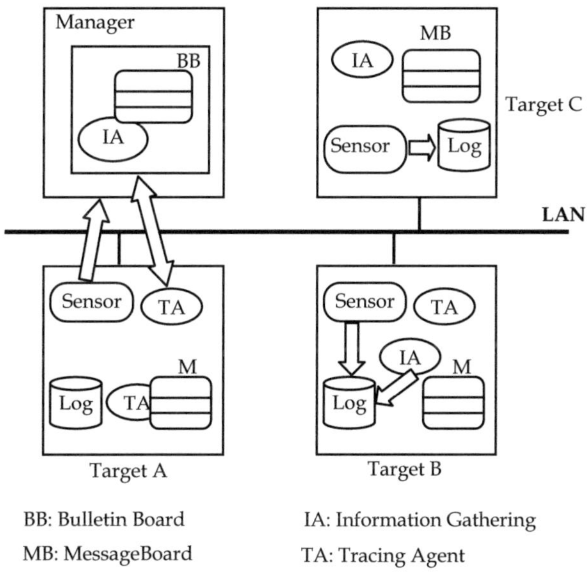

Fig. 3. The IDA´s architecture

2.2 MAID's architecture

The MAID's (Mobile Agents Intrusion Detection System) architecture is a distributed IDS which includes a Manager, Assistant Monitor Agent, Response Monitor Agent and a Host Monitoring Agent. There is a Monitor Agent (MA) in each host. If an agent detects an intrusion, it reports it directly to the Manager. The host Monitor Agent can request aid to the manager. If a Manager receives an Assistant's request, it will send an Assistant MA to patrol the network in order to gather information, and thus to determine if some suspicious activities in different hosts can be combined to carry out a distributed intrusion. Finally, the manager analyzes the gathered information and if it detects a plausible distribution intrusion it will dispatch a Response MA. The manager is a central point of correlation and therefore, if it is located by any attacker, the system would be in a dangerous situation. The mobile agents (Assistant MA and the Response MA) are encrypted using a symmetric key algorithm with a one-time session key. Then, this session key is encrypted using a public key algorithm, this turns the MAIDS's runtime environment slow. The MAID's architecture is shown in the Fig. 4.

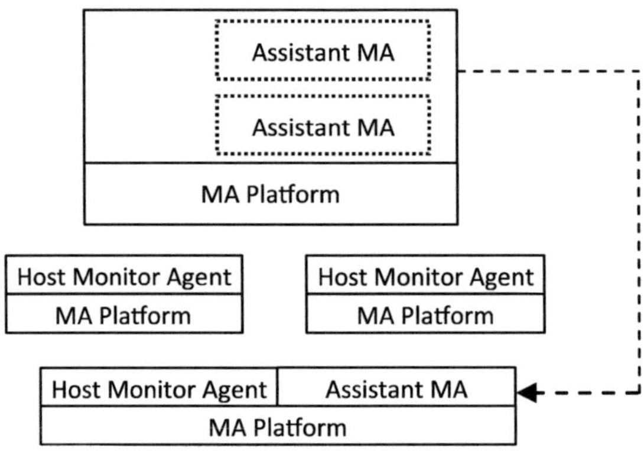

Fig. 4. MAID's architecture

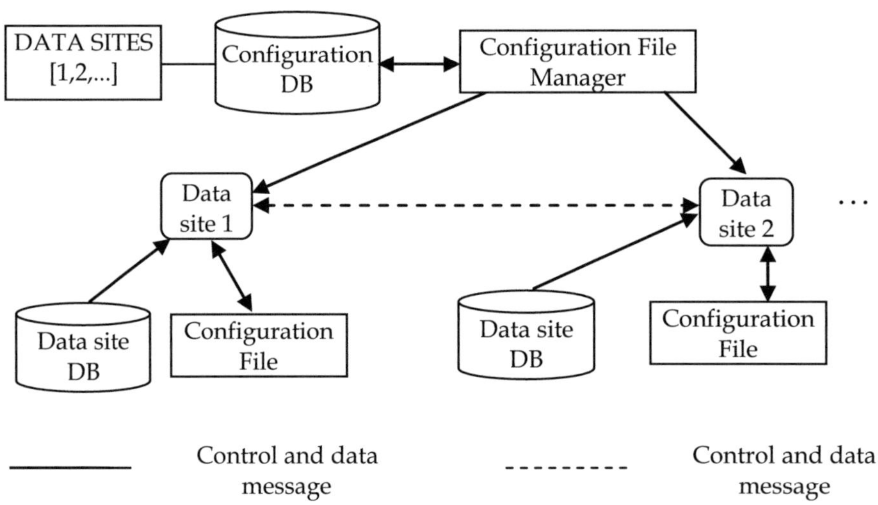

Fig. 5. JAM's architecture

2.3 JAM's architecture

The JAM's (Java Agents for Meta-learning) architecture (Fig. 5) applies learning and meta-learning agents to distributed database sites and the system's configuration is maintained by a Configuration File Manager (CFM), which is a server that provides information about the participating data sites and log events, and the CFM is in charge of keeping the state of the system up-to-date.

2.4 Sparta's architecture

The Sparta (Security Policy Adaptation Reinforced Through Agents) system uses correlation mechanisms among agents in order to identify and relate suspect events in a distributed manner. Three different types of users can be recognized by a host in this system: Administrators, regular users and owners of agents. Moreover, each node belonging to the system, has a Loacal even generator (sensor), event storage component, mobile agent platform and agent launch and query unit (optional). Sparta can detect network intrusion in a dynamic environment using a pattern language (Event Definition Language-EDL) to express intrusions in a declarative way. Each host has at least a sensor (local event generator), a storage component and the mobile agent platform installed (Fig. 6). Sensors monitor interesting occurrences on the network or at the host itself and this information is stored in a local database for later retrieval by agents; the mobile agent subsystem provides an execution environment, communication layer, clock synchronization and a directory service.

The Sparta's architecture provides mechanisms to protect agents and platforms implementing a Public Key Infrastructure (PKI). Agents are encrypted and signed during its transportation and authenticated on arrival.

The use of a public key introduces delay on the system, which is not a desirable attribute on an IDS.

We have analyzed others proposals [Yonggang Chu et al., 2005], [Zaman & Carray, 2009] but none provide internal security or there is no information is available. So, we propose complementary techniques in order to avoid and/or prevent an intrusion or attack providing internal security to an agent based IDS. Few authors treat the internal security of an IDS and it is in our opinion an important factor because it is one of the first barriers that an intruder would find when trying to access a network. So, the IDS become a susceptible objective to be attacked.

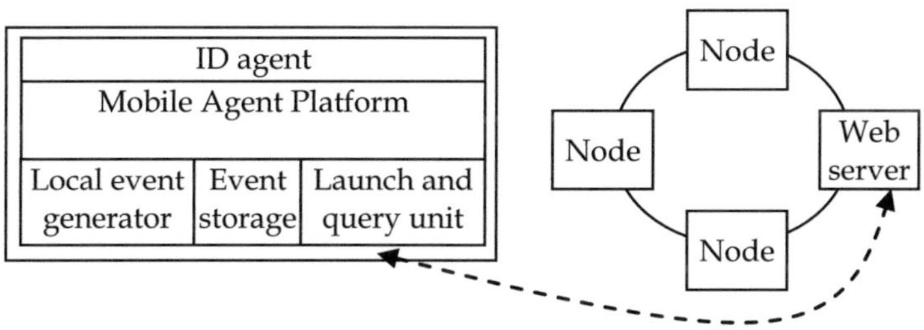

Fig. 6. SPARTA's architecture

Our proposed system is named Laocoonte. Laocoonte is a distributed and hierarchic IDS based on AAFID project [Balasubramaniyan et al., 1998] but we have made modifications to the architecture in order to increase the internal security level. We have added Cooperative Itinerant Agents (CIA) as an intermediary agent to request for a particular mark, all entities are mobile inside a network segment. Moreover we use different techniques to prove the integrity on central point of failure, such as transceivers or monitors. Laocoonte uses autonomous and mobile agents but its main characteristic is its internal security.

3. Laocoonte's architecture

Laocoonte is a hierarchical IDS with three main levels. Each level has different entities performing a particular job in a cooperative manner, but the entities which belong to the same level cannot communicate directly among them. Each entity is an agent but with different characteristics and duties. Fig. 7 depicts Laocoonte's architecture. In the lower lever are located collector agents, in the middle level are located the transceivers and in the higher level are located the monitors. Finally, there is an interface which is not considered as component of the architecture but it is necessary for the system administrator in order to set different parameters on each entity to configure the system.
On each host, there are one or more collector agents, monitoring the information which travels on the network or host. Each collector agent is specialized on a particular kind of traffic (TCP, UDP, ICMP). Collector agents determine if a determined traffic is malicious based on a database of attacks. When it occurs, the collector agent sends this information to the transceiver. So the only two functions performed by a collector agent are: monitoring and report its findings.

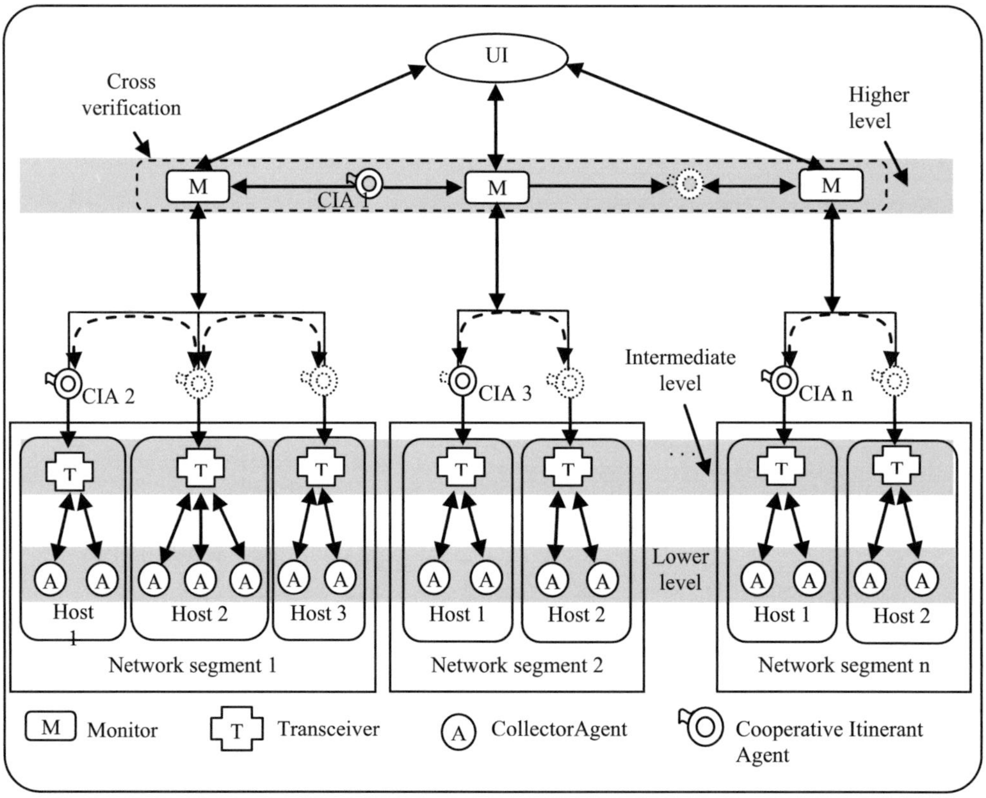

Fig. 7. Laocoonte's architecture

Transceivers are agents located in the intermediate level, and they must take the findings of the collector agents and perform correlation of events in order to identify a possible attack or intrusion in the host on which it is located. There is only a transceiver for each host and it can detect an intrusion or attack in a local way. Moreover, a transceiver can perform control

functions on collector agents (create, stop... etc.). If the transceiver identifies an attack, it reports this information to the corresponding monitor.
Monitors are agents located in the upper level of the infrastructure, and they are in charge of controlling the transceivers. When a Monitor creates a transceiver, sends it to a host and waits for results. The Monitor collects the information from its transceivers and performs high correlation functions, in this way it can detect a distributed attack because the information comes from different network segments. A Monitor could depend of another Monitor; it is because in large distributed systems a monitor could receive large amounts of information. Thus, to avoid any overload it is necessary to create another level.
Cooperative Itinerant Agents (CIA) are mobile entities and they are created by a Monitor. CIA agents are part of the internal security scheme. It must ask for a particular mark to a transceiver located in each host and sends the response to the monitor, and then it continues its itinerary inside a network segment. There is an exception in the upper level because monitors do not have another superior entity performing control activities. In this case, the CIA agent must travel among different network segments to ask for the mark to each monitor.
We have discussed the general IDS architecture. Next we will present and explain the internal security scheme.

4. Laocoonte's security scheme

The objective of this proposal is to ensure the integrity of a mobile agent which could be attacked by an untrusted platform. The proposed technique, consist on the inclusion of a marks matrix inside the code of the entities which are going to be verified (transceivers and monitors), and also store a copy of the verifying entities. The matrix is composed by a set number of cells which can be determined by the protected hosts' processing capabilities. In each cell of the matrix there is a prime number (sub-mark). The Monitor which will behave as a verifier, informs the cooperative agent which are the coordinates that are to be verified from the matrix; in this way what is really requested is not a mark itself, but the result of an operation between primer numbers (the sub-marks) which are located in the given coordinates. The sub-marks involved in the operation are different every time a request is generated, and every time a set of coordinates is used, the position in the matrix gets blocked from being used again in the subsequent processes. The result is then masked though a module function and a randomly generated coefficient value generated by the verified entity. when the cooperative agent warns the Monitor about its transfer to a host, the Monitor sends the coordinates which will be used in the operations, the CIA agent serves as an intermediary and sends the petition to the entity that is going to be verified (transceiver or monitor), then the entity returns the product of the requested sub-marks.
The reason to use module functions is to mask the result of the operation performed on the given sub-marks. Also the prime number product increments security by means that if the result is captured by an attacker, it would not be trivial to find the values, and then protecting the information that is going to be received by the verifying entity, in this case the Monitor which controls the verified entity. The Monitor knows the module that has been applied to the verified entity, and then it would only have to repeat the product of the two sub-marks and then apply the correspondent module, and finally compare the results.
The Monitor's request is also performed using randomly generated prime numbers as coefficients from a previously established module. The result of the product of such given

prime numbers and the random variable are in fact the coordinates of the sub-masks in the matrix. In this way if the result is intercepted, the attacker would not be able to identify the requested coordinates.

The procedure since the creation of the entity (monitor or transceiver), through the verification of it is as follows:

1. The Monitor generates the transceiver.
2. The Monitor assigns the prime number matrix; it inserts it as a mark to the transceiver and keeps a copy of the matrix and its contents.
3. The Monitor generates a prime number x, which will be used as module for the function (1). The transceiver also stores this value.
4. The Monitor sends the transceiver to the correspondent host.
5. When the CIA agent announces the host's change, the Monitor generates the random numbers and solves function (1). In this way it sends the masked coordinates of the sub-marks matrix.
6. The CIA agent requests the result of function (2) to the verified entity (the transceiver), giving it the masked coordinates generated by the Monitor.
7. The transceiver gets the module x of the given coordinates. With this information it can obtain the values of the sub-marks in those coordinates.
8. The transceiver generates t as a multiplicative factor and solves function (2) with the given sub-marks. then it send the results to the CIA agent
9. The CIA agent resends the results to the Monitor.
10. The Monitor receives the result from the CIA agent and applies the module y having S1. Then solves the product of the sub-marks and having then S2.
11. The Monitor then compares S1 and S2. If the values match, then there is a high probability that the transceiver has not been compromised.

And now we proceed to present the mathematical definition of the variables used in Laocoonte's proposal.

Being M a matrix of dimensions fxc, where f means rows and c columns, and the set represented by (f_i, c_j) indicates a cell in the matrix where $(i,j)=(0..f,0..c)$. In each cell a randomly generated prime number is stored by the corresponding Monitor. Each prime number is a sub-mark of the main mark (the matrix). The verifying entity (the monitor which controls the CIA Agent and the transceiver) will request a set of sub-marks in order to test the integrity of the agent (transceiver or monitor). The requested sub-marks will be different each time the request is generated (because of the actual blocking of previously used coordinates). when the CIA agent arrives to a host, the Monitor sends the coordinates of the sub-marks that wants to verify. The CIA agent issues a request to the transceiver, and when it gets an answer it resends it to the Monitor. The Monitor uses the information on the request in function (1):

$$f_1(x)=\{(x*p_1+f_1),(x*p_2+c_1),(x*p_3+f_2),(x*p_4+c_2),\ldots,(x*p_k+f_n),(x*p_n+c_n)\} \quad (1)$$

Where x is an integer greater or equal to zero. The value of x corresponds to a fixated value, randomly generated by the Monitor and known by the transceiver. This value represents the module used by the Monitor to mask the values. The values p_1, p_2, p_3, p_k, p_n are integer random variables generated by the monitor, and the variables $f_1, c_1, f_2, c_2,$ correspond to the two sets of coordinates of the sub-marks in the matrix generated randomly by the Monitor every time the cooperative agent issues a request of marks to the transceiver. In some cases the set of requested sub-marks can be more than two. This coordinates are given to the transceiver and it calculates the correspondent module to get the sub-marks from the matrix. Knowing the coordinates the sub-marks values w_1, w_2 are multiplied in function (2):

$$f_2(y) = \{(y * t) + (w_1 * w_2)\} \quad (2)$$

Where y corresponds to a fixed number which represents the previously assigned module. This model is known by the Monitor and it is used to mask the sub-marks; in this way there will not be inferred information about the given values of the sub-marks. Parameter t is a randomly generated integer by the transceiver every time it uses function (2). The agent receives this parameter and sends it back to the Monitor. The Monitor then applies the

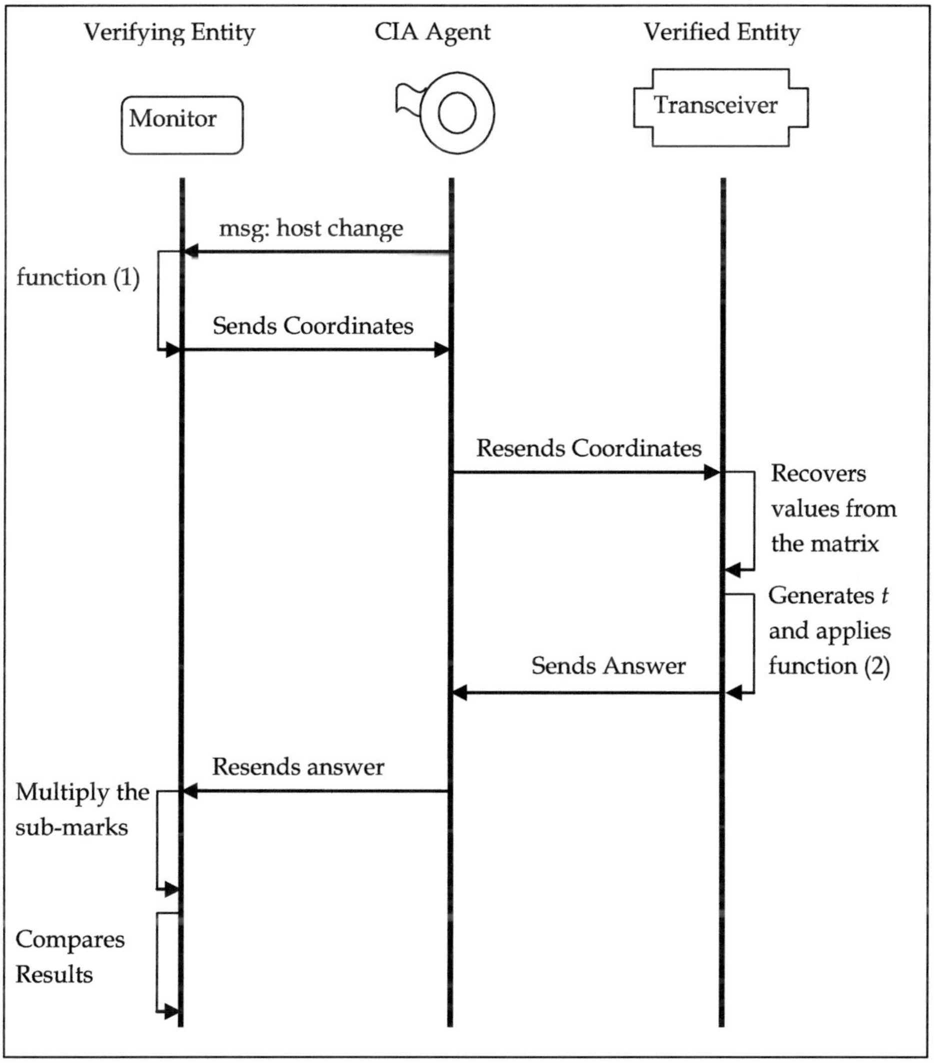

Fig. 8. Sequences diagram among entities for marks' verification

accorded module function and compares it to the given value obtained of applying the same module to the product of the requested values. If the result of the module function does not match, it means that the transceiver has been compromised and it must be considered as malicious. Otherwise, there is a high probability that the integrity of the agent has not been compromised.

Fig. 8 presents a sequence diagram which depicts the processes performed by each entity. The proposed integrity verification process of a transceiver or a monitor can be considered as a Zero-Knowledge Proof or ZKP. The concept was introduced in 1985 for systems verification identity [U. Fiege et al., 1985], but it can be applied to cryptographic applications. A ZKP is an interactive protocol between two parts, which gives a test, a tester (verified entity, in our case, a transceiver or a monitor) and the verifier of the test (the monitor). The Verified entity must convince the verifier that it knows the answer to a given theorem without revealing any kind of additional information [Yang & Liu, 2005]. This means, an entity probes its identity by showing it knows a secret, without giving the secret away, this is particularly useful in the case the messages are being intercepted, since the attacker will not receive any information related to the secret. Another important characteristic is that the messages are always different and randomly generated in order that the attacker could not memorize a concrete sequence.

4.1 Generating the matrix

In the following section we will describe the process used by the Monitor to generate the sub-mark matrix and the actual verification of the sub-marks. After generation the transceiver, the Monitor creates a matrix of size f by c which will be used as a mark. this matrix must be stored in the Monitor and in the transceiver and it must be unique for each transceiver. For the example we are going to present, the matrix will be of size 4 by 4 (16 sub-marks) and two sub-marks will be requested. It also will be generated a module (x) which will remain constant during the process to be used on function (1). Several additional random values will be generated to multiply the module and to pick the two sets of coordinates from the matrix.

For simplicity, small values have been chosen for the given example. It is also possible for a CIA agent to request more than two sets of coordinates (sub-marks) to verify. In this case the Monitor must provide the different sets of coordinates; also the transceiver must get such values in order to replace them in function (2).

The set of modules and the values of the sub-marks in the matrix are:

1. Sub-marks Matrix:

0	68813	79687	36599	98663
1	59879	16993	98689	36997
2	79657	11383	35729	21991
3	78643	41299	86323	59693
	0	1	2	3

Table 1. Transceiver Sub-marks

The Monitor generates the transceiver, the sub-marks matrix, the prime numbers in the matrix (Table 1), module x and y. After this the Monitor sends the transceiver to the corresponding host. These given values remain constant and will be used later in the verification process.

2. The values given to the modules in this example are (Table 2):

Variable	Value	Description
x	17	Module of function (1)
y	53	Module of function (2)

Table 2. Fixed Values

3. The Monitor's randomly generated values, used to issue a sub-mark request to the transceiver (for this example) are (Table 3):

Variable	Value	Description
P_1	37	Random values that multiplies the module of function (1).
P_2	13	
p_3	7	
p_4	23	
t	53	Random value, generated by the transceiver which multiplies the module in function (2).
f_1	0	Raw coordinate of the first sub-mark (w1) to be verified. f1 < m (m is the number of rows in the matrix)
c_1	2	Column coordinate of the first sub-mark (w1) to be verified. c1 < n (n is the number of columns in the matrix)
f_2	2	Raw coordinate of the first sub-mark (w2) to be verified. f2 < m (m is the number of rows in the matrix)
c_2	3	Column coordinate of the first sub-mark (w2) to be verified. c2 < n (n is the number of columns in the matrix)

Table 3. Randomly Generated Values

The sub-marks in the coordinates $f_1, c_1 = (0,2)$ y $f_2, c_2 = (2,3)$; correspond to the values 36599 and 21991 in the sub-marks matrix.
The Monitor generates the random values $(p_1, p_2, p_3, p_4, f_1, c_1, c_2)$ and applies function (1):

$$f_1(x) = \{(x * p_1 + f_1), (x * p_2 + c_1), (x * p_3 + f_2), (x * p_4 + c_2)\}$$

$$f_1(x) = \{(17 * 37 + 0), (17 * 13 + 2), (17 * 7 + 2), (17 * 23 + 3)\}$$

$$f_1(x) = \{629, 223, 121, 394\}$$

The Monitor gives the result to the CIA agent, and the CIA agent resends it to the transceiver. The transceiver uses those values and applies the corresponding module in order to obtain the coordinates of the requested sub-marks:

$$C = \{(629) mod_x, (223) mod_x, (121) mod_x, (394) mod_x\}$$

$$C = \{(629)mod_{17}, (223)mod_{17}, (121)mod_{17}, (394)mod_{17}\}$$

$$C = \{0,2,2,3\}$$

The values of the sub-marks in the given coordinates (w_1, w_2) are respectively (36599 y 21991). The transceiver uses function (2). For this example the values will be y = 53 y t = 3571, y is generated by the Monitor and t is generated by the transceiver.

$$f_2(y) = \{(y * t) + (w_1 * w_2))\}$$

$$f_2(y) = \{(53 * 3571) + (36599 * 21991))\}$$

$$f_2(y) = \{805037872\}$$

The CIA agent receives the answer from the transceiver and resends it to the Monitor. The Monitor uses the value of y and obtains the module of the given value:

$$S_1 = \{f(2)mod_y\}$$

$$S_1 = \{(805037872)mod_{53}\}$$

$$S_1 = \{43\}$$

Then it gets the module of the product of the two requested sub-marks:

$$S_2 = \{(36599 * 21991)mod_y\}$$

$$S_2 = \{(804848609)mod_{53}\}$$

$$S_2 = \{43\}$$

After getting S_2, it verifies if the result is equal to the module of the product of the two sub-marks (36599, 21991), this is if $S_1 = S_2$ then it means that there is a high probability that the transceiver has not been compromised.

For the example we have used a four rows by four columns matrix, in this case the number of possible combinations of a couple of marks which can be obtained is given by (3):

$$\frac{n!}{w!(n-w)!} = \frac{16!}{2!(16-2)!} = 120 \quad (3)$$

Each time a CIA agent issues a reuest for sub-marks, the monitor randomly picks the cells coordinates. With a 16 cell matrix there are 120 possibilities of obtaining the same pair of sub-marks, thus the probability that a set of sub-marks are repeated on a request is 1/120. If the number of requested marks is greater than two, the probability that an attacker could guess the sub-marks is smaller. If the matrix grows (more rows and columns), the probability gets closer to 0. Table 4 presents the different sets of combinations that can be achieved for matrixes size 16, 32, 64 y 128, by choosing 2, 3 or 4 sub-marks.

Cells	2 *sub-marks*	3 *sub-marks*	4 *sub-marks*
16	120	560	1.820
32	496	4.960	35.960
64	2.016	41.664	635.376
128	8.128	341.376	10.668.000

Table 4. Possible Combinations by Number of cells in the matrix and sub-marks to be verified

Table 4 shows that the probability to find a set of 4 sub-marks from a 128 cells matrix is minimal (1/10'668.000). Accordingly to the amount of requested sub-marks and the length of the prime numbers (the actual sub-marks) special care must be taken because the returned value of function (2) may be too large and generate a stack overflow. The next graphic is the representation of previous values on the table, presenting a logarithmic projection.

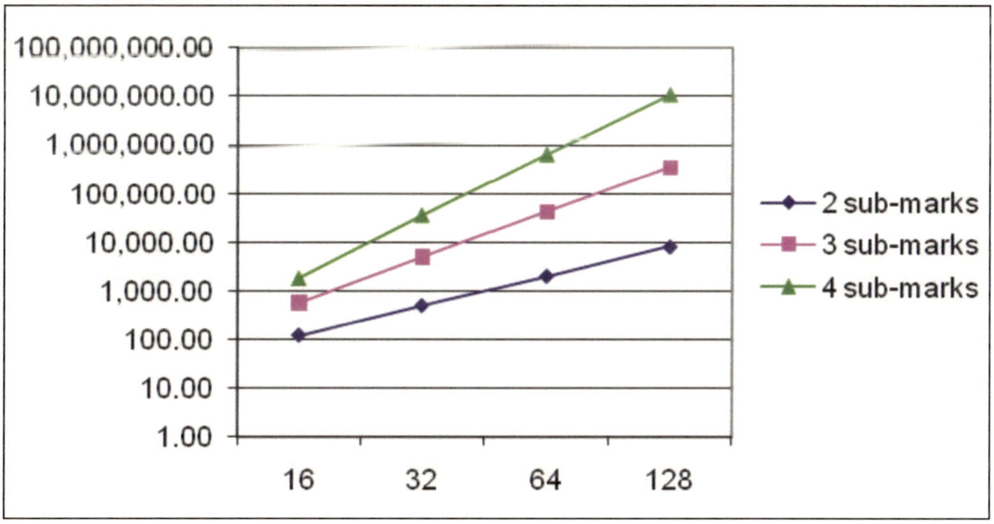

Graphic 1. Number of cells and sub-marks to be proved

5. The BESA framework

BESA (Behavior-oriented, Event-driven, and Social-based agent framework) is a Multi-Agent Development Framework, which allows multithreading, and is FIPA (Foundation for Intelligent Physical Agents) compliant; this allows interoperability with other platforms. BESA is based on three main concepts: Behavior-oriented, Event-driven, and Social-based, behavior allows and agent to encapsulate the needed characteristics that will guarantee the fulfillment of a well defined purpose, by forming cooperative societies and giving as a result agents composed by a set of concurrent behaviors; Event-driven means that the agent must react accordingly to its knowledge to a change in the environment. Finally the social-based concept, allows that different entities interact forming microsocieties. The way in which internal cooperation is achieved is by the implementation of a social mediator agent which also works as an external representative. BESA is structured in three different levels: the agent level, the social level and the system level.

Agent level: at this level the behavior of the agents is specified as well as the events of the environment. An agent is composed by a channel, a set of behaviors and a state. Each agent uses mutual exclusion synchronization, in this way it avoids concurrency issues.

Social level: At this level the mediator agent is incorporated in order to form the actual abstraction of the intermediate levels. The mediator agent is a facilitator of the cooperative work between agents and acts as a receiver o thrower of events.

System level: At this level the life cycle of the agents is specified and managed.

6. Laocoonte's implementation on BESA

An agent based system implemented in BESA is a distributed system composed by one or many containers which are instantiated on a physical or virtual machine. Each container is processing space in itself, with a local administrator which supports the communication among agents and provides yellow and white pages services. The white pages service is used by the administrator to register the instantiation of an agent in the container. The yellow pages service is used by the contained agents to publish its own services. When there is a change in the agent's life cycle, the white and yellow pages services are updated and a copy mechanism is triggered in order to maintain the consistency among local administrators. The system includes a single FIPA compatible communication port, which communicates and receives queries from other systems using FIPA ACL (Agent Communication Language).

BESA is formed by container instances, each one belongs to the same group and they share the same IP address and a multicast port. Each event can reach any agent located on any container of the group, and notify the group members if some change has happened in the life cycle of the container or the agent. In this way, in order to implement a Laocoonte's collector agent, it must be located inside a container. The collector agent can monitor any kind of traffic (TCP. UDP, ICMP), but the agent must be specialized in only one kind. The collector agent filters and identifies suspicious events, then sending this information to its correspondent transceiver. Theses collector agents are located in the bottom of the architecture, one or several of them can be located on a container verifying the same o different kinds of traffic.

Transceivers are located in the middle layer of the architecture and they must be located inside a container. It can only exist one in each container. The transceiver has the local view of what is happening in the system, meaning that the transceiver is capable of identifying an intrusion in the host in which it is located. The transceiver must execute information correlation functions, based on the information gathered from the collector agents which in turn are managed by the collector agent (create, activate, sleep or delete).

The Monitor is an agent located on the highest level of the architecture; it is also located in a container. There is only one Monitor for each network segment and it controls all the transceivers in the network segment. The Monitor also executes correlation functions, but to a higher level than the transceivers, by filtering the information the Monitor gathers from the transceiver in its network segment. A Monitor can detect if an distributed attack or intrusion are being performed on the system. Eventually some Monitors could depend on other monitors in order to give some scalability to the system. At the root level (the highest level of the architecture), there must be at least two Monitors, in order that they could verify each other.

The CIA agents are generated by a Monitor and they have the mission of requesting the marks to each transceiver. The CIA agent is a mobile agent which is moving through network segments. When a CIA agent reaches a container, it must verify its identity requesting a hash function. This hash function corresponds to the sub-marks matrix of the transceiver; in this the container ensures that the CIA agent is not a malicious agent.

At the highest level of the architecture every Monitor must generate a CIA agent in order to verify other monitors at its same level, executing a cross verification.

7. Conclusions

Agents are appropriate entities to define an IDS, but they have inherent security risk due to its nature. These risks must be controlled in an efficient way in order to avoid interferences with the proper function of the system.

An IDS is a security tool which is one of the first barriers reached by an intruder, thus becoming a potential target of attack, it must also be configured in such a way that avoids the production of false positive and false negative alerts, it also must incorporate security techniques in order to avoid malfunctioning of the internal entities of the system.

With the proposed mark verification technique, using module arithmetic, the use of public key cryptography is avoided, reducing the integrity verification of the agents to simple mathematical operations. It also avoids overloading of the system and obtains acceptable response times for the IDS.

Accordingly to the proposed technique, if the sub-marks matrix grows, and the number of requested sub-marks also grows, the probability of being attacked is close to zero, making the deduction of requested or answered information by an attacker almost impossible.

8. References

Asaka, M., Okazawa, S., Taguchi, A., Goto, S. A Method of Tracing Intruders by Use of Mobile Agents. *INET99*, June 1999.

Balasubramaniyan, J.O. Garcia-Fernandez, D. Isaco, E. Spafford, D. Zamboni. An Architecture for Intrusion Detection using Autonomous Agents, *14th IEEE Computer Security Applications Conference ACSAC '98*. 1998.

C. Kruegel, C., Toth, T. Sparta - A mobile agent based intrusion detection system; In *Proceedings of the IFIP Conference on Network Security* (I-NetSec). (2001)

Collberg Christian S., Watermarking,Tamper-Proffing and Obfuscation-Tools for Software Protection, *IEEE Transactions on Software Engineering*. Vol 28,No,8,August 2002.

González E.; Avila J.A. y Bustacara C.J., 2003. BESA: Behavior-oriented, Event-Driven and Social-based Agent Framework. En: *PDPTA'03*, Las Vegas-USA, CSREA Press, vol. 3.

Hervé Debar, Marc Dacier, and Andreas Wespi. Towards a taxonomy of intrusion-detection systems. Computer Networks: *The International Journal of Computer and Telecommunications Networking*, ISSN:1389-1286, Vol. 31, Pag. 805–822, April 1999.

J.S Balasubramaniyan, J.O. Garcia-Fernandez, D. Isacoff, E. Spafford, D. Zamboni, An Architecture for Intrusion Detection using Autonomous Agents, *Proceedings., 14th Annual Computer Security Applications Conference*, 1998, 13 - 24

Jansen W.A., Countermeasures for Mobile Agent Security, National Institute of Standards and Technology. *Computer Communications*, 23(17), 1667-1676, 2000

Knoll G. Suri and J.M. Bradshaw, Path-Based Security for Mobile Agents. *Proceedings 1st International Workshop Security of Mobile Multiagent Systems and 5th International Conf. Autonomous Agents*. ACM Press, New York, 2001, pp. 54-60.

Páez, R., Satizábal, C., Forné, J., Analysis of Intrusion Detection Systems Based on Autonomous Agents and their Security In: IPSI 2005 France, 2005, Carcassonne. *IPSI-2005 FRANCE International Conference on Advances in the Internet, Processing, System and Interdisciplinary Research*. 2005.

Páez, R. Satizábal C., Forné J. Cooperative Itinerant Agents (CIA): Security Scheme for Intrusion Detection Systems, *Proceedings of the International Conference on Internet Surveillance and Protection* (ICISP). ISBN:0-7695-2649-7. Pag. 26-32. 2006

Shao-Chun Zhong; Qing-Feng Song; Xiao-Chun Cheng; Yan Zhang. A safe mobile agent system for distributed intrusion detection. *Machine Learning and Cybernetics, 2003 International Conference on* , Volume: 4 , 2-5 Nov. 2003 Pages:2009 - 2014 Vol.4

Salvatore Stolfo, Andreas L. Prodromidis, Shelley Tselepis, Wenke Lee, and Dave W. Fan, JAM: Java Agents for Meta-Learning over Distributed Databases, The Third *International Conference on Knowledge Discovery & Data Mining* (David Heckerman, Heikki Mannila, Daryl Pregibon, and Ramasamy Uthurusamy, eds.), AAAI Press, August 1997.

U. Fiege, A. Fiat, A. Shamir, Annual ACM Symposium on Theory of Computing archive *Proceedings of the nineteenth annual ACM symposium on Theory of computing*. ISBN:0-89791-221-7 New York, United States. Pages: 210 – 217, 1987.

Xiaobin Li, Aijuan Zhang, Jinfei Sun and Zhaolin Yin. (2004). The Research of Mobile Agent Security. In: *Grid and Cooperative Computing*. Springer Berlin / Heidelberg. Springer. Pag. 187-190. ISBN: 978-3-540-21993-4.

Yang, Z. and Liu, M., ZKp based identification protocol on conic curve in distributed environment, *The Fifth International Conference on Computer and Information Technology*, IEEE, pp. 690-694, 2005.

Yonggang Chu, Jun Li, Yixian Yang, The Architecture of the Large-scale Distributed Intrusion Detection System, *Parallel and Distributed Computing Applications and Technologies*, International Conference on, pp. 130-133, Sixth International Conference on Parallel and Distributed Computing Applications and Technologies (PDCAT'05), 2005.

Zaman, S.; Karray, F.; Collaborative architecture for distributed intrusion detection system. *IEEE Symposium on Computational Intelligence for Security and Defense Applications* (CISDA), 2009. ISBN: 978-1-4244-3763-4 Ottawa, Canada

Part 3

Data Processing Techniques and Other Algorithms using Intrusion Detection Systems – Simultaneously Analysis Different Detection Approach

7

Intrusion Detection System and Artificial Intelligent

Khattab M. Alheeti
Alanbar University
Iraq

1. Introduction

In this chapter we will look to the essential demonstrates the basic concepts of Intrusion Detection System and explain the role of artificial intelligence in the promotion and development of Intrusion Detection System using artificial intelligence. We will then explain the model the new intelligent, who has much on the distinction between regular normal connection and unusual or abnormal connection, Use of neural networks with data normal with out Fuzzification to build a new predicative model, and we have another predicative model but the data that is entered into by the Fuzzification data. And what follows mention of the topics that will take them in our chapter.

On completing this chapter, you will be able to:

- Explain the major categorized and classification of the IDSs.
- Describe network-based IDSs.
- Describe host-based IDSs.
- Explain how IDS management communication works.
- Explain the principles of artificial intelligence.
- Describe the type of the neural network.
- Explain Crisp set and Fuzzy set.
- Describe the predicative model with normal data
- Describe the predicative model with Fuzzification data.
- Conclusion.
- Future works.
- References.

2. Overview of intrusion detection system

An intrusion can be defined as "an act of a person of proxy attempting to break into or misuse a system in violation of an established policy" [Malik 2002]. So to protect systems from intruders, intrusion detection system is needed. IDS is software and/or hardware system for monitoring and detecting data traffic or user behavior to identify attempts of illegitimate accessing system manipulation through a network by malware and/or intruders (crackers, or disgruntled employees). ID has been used to protect information systems along with prevention-based mechanisms such as authentication and access control. An ID cannot directly detect attacks within properly encrypted traffic.

Intrusion detection systems can be classified as *network-based* and *host-based* according to the information source of the detection. Network-based IDS monitors the network traffic and looks for network-based attacks, while host-based IDS is installed on host and monitors the host audit trail. Intrusion detection systems can be roughly classified as *anomaly detection* and *misuse detection*. Anomaly detection is based on the normal behavior of a subject (e.g., a user or a system). Any action that significantly deviates from the normal behavior is considered intrusive. Misuse detection is based on the characteristics of known attacks or system vulnerabilities, which are also called *signatures*. Any action that matches the signature is considered intrusive. Both anomaly detection and misuse detection have their limitations.

Misuse-base detection detects attacks based on signatures (known attacks signatures), at which the traffic pattern compared with these signatures, if a match is found, then it is reported as an attack, otherwise it is not. So misuse detection cannot detect novel attacks. On the other hand, anomaly-based detection depends on monitoring system activity and classifying it as either normal or anomalous. The classification is based on heuristics or rules, rather than patterns or signatures, and will detect any type of misuse that falls out of normal system behavior.

The strength of the anomaly detection approach is that prior knowledge of the security flaws of the target systems is not required. Thus, it is able to detect not only known intrusion but also unknown intrusion. In addition, this approach can detect the intrusion that is achieved by the abuse of legitimate users or masqueraders without breaking security policy [Denning 1987, Porras 1992]. However, it has several limitations, such as high false positive detection error, the difficulty of handling gradual misbehavior and expensive computation [Mykerjee and et al 1994]. In contrast, the misuse detection approach detects only previously known intrusion signatures. The advantage of this approach is that it rarely fails to detect previously notified intrusions [Denning 1987]. However, this approach cannot detect new intrusions that have never previously been monitored. Furthermore, this approach is known to have other drawbacks such as the inflexibility of misuse signature rules and the difficulty of creating and updating intrusion signature rules [Porras 1992, Kumar 1995]. These strengths and limitations of the two approaches imply that effective IDS should employ an anomaly detector and a misuse detector in parallel [Mykerjee and et al 1994]. However, most available commercial IDS's use only misuse detection because most developed anomaly detector still cannot overcome the limitations described above. This trend motivates many research efforts to build anomaly detectors for the purpose of ID [Kim 2002]. However, the nature of current and future threats in conjunction with ever larger Information Technologies (IT) system systems urgently requires the development of automated and adaptive defensive tools.

2.1 Intrusion Detection System (IDS)

To understand what is ID, the meaning of intrusion should be declared. An intrusion can be defined as [Kumar 1995, Bace & Peter 2001]: "Any set of actions that attempt to compromise the integrity, confidentiality, or availability of a resource". Intrusion detection becomes essential security mechanism to protect systems and networks. It attempts to detect improper or inconsistent activity in a computer network, or on a host, by the exploration of certain kinds of data through monitoring. Such activities may be initiated from external intruder or from internal misuse. According to the monitored system, IDS could be categorized into [Song 2007, Sundaram 2002, Crothers 2003, and Kazienko & Piotr 2004]:

- Network-based IDS: is an independent platform that monitors the network backbones and look for attack scenarios by analyzing, examining, and monitoring network traffic data. Network Intrusion Detection Systems (NIDS) gain access to network traffic by connecting to a hub, network switch configured for port mirroring, or network tap. The NIDS reassemble and analyze all network packets that reach the network interface card. They do not only deal with packets going to a specific host - since all the machines in a network segment benefit from the protection of the NIDS. Network-based IDS can also be installed on active network elements, for example on router.
- Host-based IDS: reside on a particular computer and tries to detect malicious activity and provide protection for a specific computer system by monitoring the operating and file systems for signs of intrusion. This can be done through an agent placed on that host to identify intrusions by analyzing system calls, application logs, file-system modifications (binaries, password files) and other host activities and state.
- Hybrid of HIDS and NIDS, Host agent data is combined with network information to form a comprehensive view of the network. the main reason for introducing such hybrid IDS is the need to work online with encrypted networks and their data destined to the single host (only the source and destination can see decrypted network traffic).

The fact is that intrusion detection systems are not organs of what regulations deter more control and monitor, alarm any detect process will determine the intruder and where breach occurred, when and what the response depends on the design of the system. In addition, the alarm does not provide system security itself; it only to indicate that some sort of potentially malicious activity is being attempted.

2.2 Classification of IDS

ID is a network security tool that concerned with the detection of illegitimate actions. This network security tool uses one of two main techniques [Song 2007, Crothers 2003, and Kazienko & Piotr 2004]:

- Anomaly detection explores issues in ID associated with deviations from normal system or user behavior. It is based on the assumption that the characteristics of attacks are significantly different from normal behavior. Anomaly detection is capable of detecting unknown attacks or variants of known attacks if such attacks significantly change the monitored characteristics of the system. And deviations of normal usage of programs regardless of whether the source is a privileged internal user or an unauthorized external user. The disadvantage of the anomaly detections approach is that well-known attacks may not be detected, particularly if they fit the established profile of the user. Another drawback of many anomaly detection approaches is that a malicious user who knows that he or she is begin profiled can change the profile slowly over time to essentially train the anomaly detection system to learn the attacker's malicious behavior as normal.
- The second employs Misuse (Signature detection) refers to known attacks that exploit the known vulnerabilities of the system to discriminate between anomaly or attack patterns (signatures) and known ID signatures. The main disadvantage of misuse detection approaches is that they will detect only the attacks for which they are trained to detect (i.e. not capable of detecting novel or unknown attacks).

The IDS can operate as standalone, centralized application or integrated applications that create a distributed system. One may categorize IDSs in terms of behavior i.e., they may be Passive (those that simply generate alerts and log network packets). They may also be active which means that they detect and respond to attacks, attempt to patch software holes before getting hacked or act proactively by logging out potential intruders, or blocking services.
IDSs can run on either a continuous or periodic feed of information (Real-Time IDS and Interval-base IDS respectively) and hence they use two different ID approaches. Audit trail analysis is the prevalent method used by periodically operated systems. In contrast, the IDS deployable in real-time environments are designed for online monitoring and analyzing system events and user actions.
With on the fly processing, an ID performs verification of system events. Generally, a stream of network packets is constantly monitored. With this type of processing, ID uses the knowledge of current activities over the network to sense possible attack attempts (it does not look for successful attacks in the past). Figure (1.2) shows the classification of IDS from different point of views:

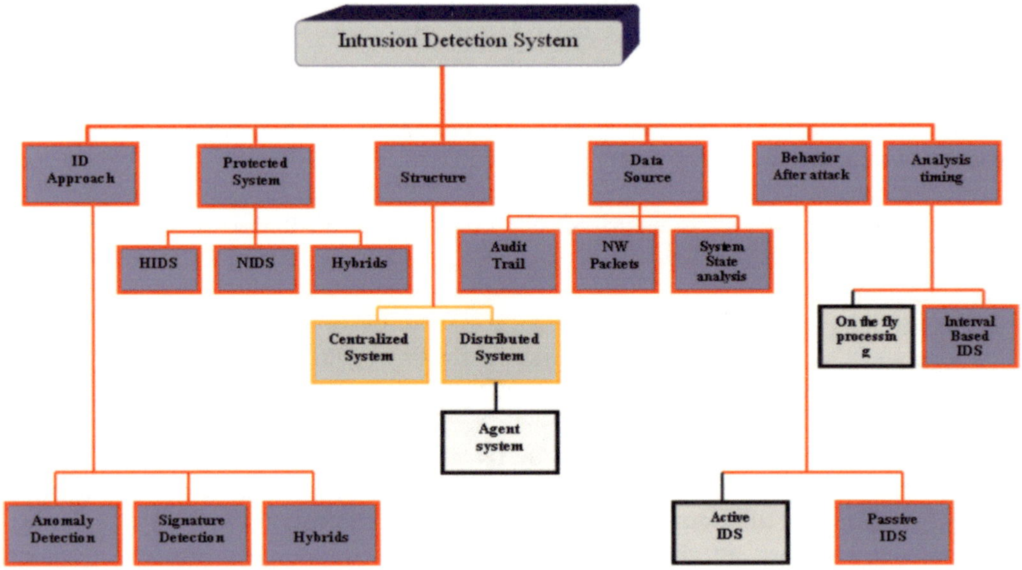

Fig. 1.2. The classification of IDS from six different points of views

3. Problem definition

Recently, the problem of computer systems intrusions grows and intruders become intelligent and flexible agents. The reason is that, new automated hacking tools appear every day, and these tools, along with various system vulnerability information, are easily available on the web. This problem can be solved by using appropriate software which is designed to detect and prevent intrusions.
Intrusion detection (ID) is an appealing concept since the current techniques used in computer security are not able to cope with dynamic and increasingly complex nature of computer systems and their security. The intrusion detector learning task is to build a predictive model (i.e. a classifier) capable of distinguishing between "bad" connection,

called intrusion or attack, and "good" normal connections depending on special attributes (*features*) that are collected from *the packet header* and *audit trail* files (behavior during the connection). Such classifiers could be built using different approaches (statistical approaches, genetic algorithms, fuzzy systems, or neural networks).

To evaluate any intrusion detection system, dataset collected by Defense Advanced Research Project Agency is used. This dataset is a version of the 1999 DARPA intrusion detection evaluation data set prepared and managed by MIT Lincoln Labs. In this data set, 41 attributes that describe the different features of the corresponding connection (22 of these features describe the connection itself and 19 of them describe the properties of connections to the same host in last two seconds). The value of the connection is labeled either as an attack with one specific packet header and the data payload.

There are 39 different attack types presented and falls exactly into one of the following four categories [Salvatore and et al 2000]:

1. Probing (surveillance and other probing): Probing is a class of attack where an attacker scans a network to gather information or find known vulnerabilities.
2. DOS (denial-of-service): it is a class of attack where an attacker makes a computing or memory resource too busy or too full handles legitimate requests thus denying legitimate users access to a machine.
3. U2R (User to root): unauthorized access to local super user (root) privileges exploits. It is a class of attacks where an attacker starts out with access to a normal user account on the system and is able to exploit vulnerability to gain root access to the system.
4. R2L (A remote to local): unauthorized access from a remote machine. It is a class of attack where an attacker sends packets to a machine over a network, then exploits the machine's vulnerability to illegally gain local access as a user.

Another problem, current intrusion detection systems (IDS) examine all data features to detect intrusion or misuse patterns, use all the feature adds extra burden on the system, and extra features can increase computation time, and can impact the accuracy of IDS. Therefore, it is important to reduce number of features (attributes) that would be used to train the classifier. One of the major problems is to select the proper attributes (from the total 41 attribute in dataset) that have the best discrimination ability (between normal and attack connections). It is also important to choose the suitable classifier with high classification rate.

4. Objectives

One way to detect illegitimate use in network system is through monitoring unusual user activity by using IDS. Different methods used to build intrusion detection system (such as statistical, genetic, fuzzy genetic, neural networks etc). This chapter aims to study the classification ability of feed-forward neural network with actual data and feed-forward neural network with fuzzified data and compare their results from distinguishing accuracy point of view. Also, try to reduce the 41 attributes since some of these features will not affect the classification accuracy (or even may negatively affect it) at which their values are the same in different attack types or normal one. The main goal of this chapter is to improve classification rate of the discrimination ability (i.e. discriminate attacks from normal behavior).

In additional, most of the previous studies focused on classification of records in one of the two general classes-normal and attack, this chapter aim's to solve a multi-class problem at which the type of attack is also detected by the suggested intrusion detector. Using the reduced data sets, 5-class classifier is built (normal data belongs to class 5, probe belongs to class 1, denial of service belongs to class 2, user to super user belongs to class 3, remote to local belongs to class 4). The dataset is partitioned into 3 different parts (validation part, training part, and testing part). The evaluation of the system accuracy will depend on the testing results.

5. Artificial Neural Network

The idea of Artificial Neural Network (ANN) came from the idea of working human brain; the first step toward artificial neural networks came in 1943 when Warren McCulloch, a neurophysiologist, and a young mathematician, Walter Pitts, wrote a paper on how neurons might work. Think scientists in a way which can simulate the process, which occur in the human mind, and came to the knowledge of Neural Network, which falls under science artificial intelligence, so as to make computers intelligent devices, they can gain knowledge of the same way that acquires the rights of knowledge, they control the way weights during the learning. In addition, on the structural side large number of highly interconnected processing elements (neurons) working together. The neuron is the basic information processing unit of a Neural Network (NN); it consists of: A set of links, describing the neuron inputs, with weights W1, W2, ...,Wm, An adder function (linear combiner) for computing the weighted sum of the inputs (real numbers):

$$U_j = \sum_{i=1}^{p} W j_i x_i \qquad (1)$$

And an activation function (squashing function) for limiting the amplitude of the neuron output.

$$\text{Tan-Sigmoid function} = 2/\ (1+\exp(-2*n))-1 \qquad (2)$$

In addition, there is extra weight value considered which is corresponding to the constant bias (extra input). The bias is an external parameter of the neuron; it can be modeled by adding an extra input. Figure (1.3) shows the neuron and bias, while Figure (1.4) shows the biological neuron:

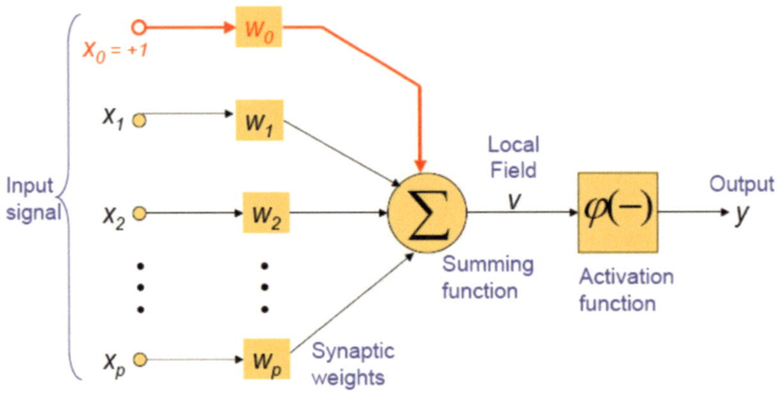

Fig. 1.3. The artificial neuron

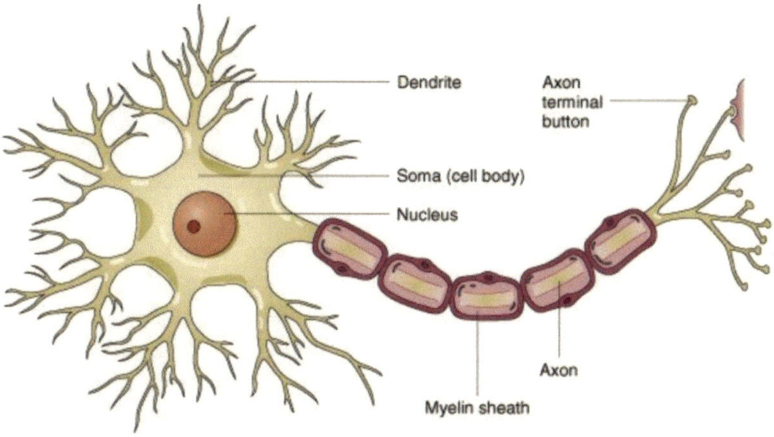

Fig. 1.4. Biological neuron

5.1 Classification of Neural Network

Neural networks can be classified into dynamic and static categories. Static (Feed-forward) networks have no feedback elements and contain no delays; the output is calculated directly from the input through feed-forward connections. The training of static networks was discussed in Backpropagation. In dynamic networks, the output depends not only on the current input to the network, but also on the current or previous inputs, outputs, or states of the network. You saw some linear dynamic networks in Linear Filters.

Dynamic networks can also be divided into two categories: those that have only feed-forward connections, and those that have feedback, or recurrent, connections.

Generally classified neural networks on the basis of either training (learning) or architectures. There are two approaches to training-supervised and unsupervised. Supervised training involves a mechanism of providing the network with the desired output either by manually "distinguish" the network's performance or by providing the desired outputs with the inputs. Unsupervised training is where the network has to make sense of the inputs without outside help. Therefore more, we have three main classes of network architectures:

- - Single-layer Perceptron (SLP).
- - Multi-layer Perceptron (MLP).
- - Recurrent (Feedback).

5.1.1 Supervised training

In supervised training, both the inputs and the outputs are provided. The network then processes the inputs and compares its resulting outputs against the desired outputs, because in fact we will have two of the output of one of the actual and one is required (desired). Errors are then propagated back through the system, causing the system to adjust the weights which control the network. This process occurs over and over as the weights are continually tweaked. The set of data which enables the training is called the "training set." During the training of a network the same set of data is processed many times as the connection weights are ever refined. The problems are resolved such as classification, recognition, diagnostic and regression. In addition to that the model such as perceptron, adaline, feed-forward and radial basis function.

5.1.2 Unsupervised training

The other type of training is called unsupervised training. In unsupervised training, the network is provided with inputs but not with desired outputs. The system itself must then decide what features it will use to group the input data. This is often referred to as self-organization or adaption. The problems are resolved such as clustering and content addressable memory. In addition, the model such as Hopfield networks and self organizing maps.

5.1.3 Single-layer Perceptron (SLP)

This reflects structural one of the oldest structures in neural networks, which consists of one layer of neurons on the basis that the computational input layer does not undertake any operations of arithmetic. Associated with each neuron layer of input layer of all neuron in the output layer (fully connected), the figure (1.5) below shows the single- layer networks:

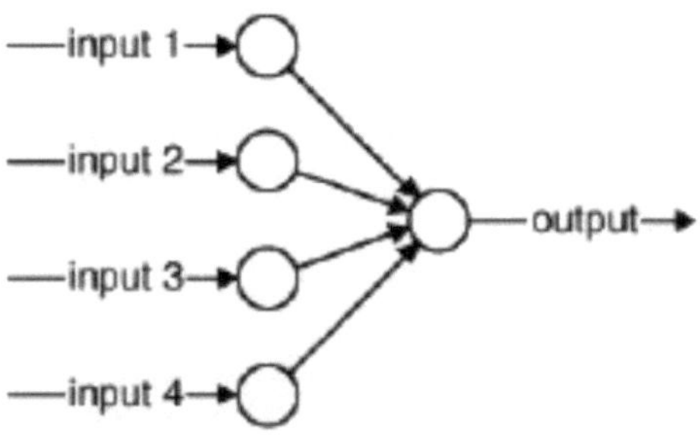

Fig. 1.5. A single-layer linear model

5.1.4 Multi-layer Perceptron (MLP)

There is input layer and the output layer, in addition to the many hidden layers. If the lines of communication between cells of the input layers moving towards the introduction hidden layers and then output layer then called these structures structure Feed-forward (feed-forward Architecture). This in addition to Single-layer Perceptron (SLP), the figure (1.6) below shows the multi - layer networks:

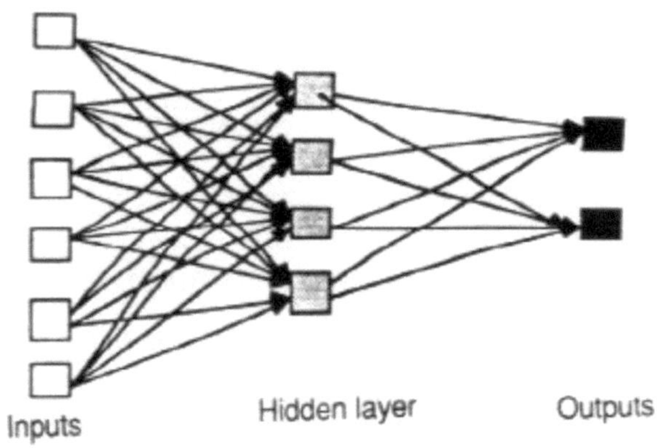

Fig. 1.6. A multi - layer liner model

5.1.5 Recurrent (Feedback)

Recurrent networks: can be unstable, or oscillate, or exhibit chaotic behavior e.g., given some input values, can take a long time to compute stable output and learning is made more difficult. However, can implement more complex agent designs and can model systems with state the Figure (1.7) below shows recurrent networks:

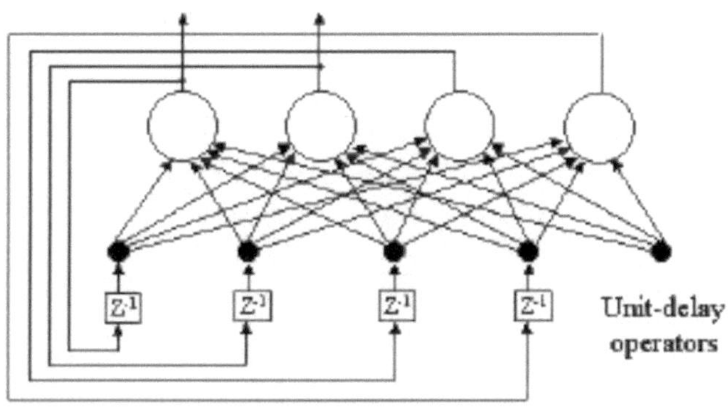

Fig. 1.7. A recurrent network with hidden neurons

5.2 Major components of an artificial neuron

This section describes the seven major components which make up an artificial neuron. These components are valid whether the neuron is used for input, output, or is in one of the hidden layers:

a. Weighting Factors: A neuron usually receives many simultaneous inputs. Each input has its own relative weight which gives the input the impact that it needs on the processing element's summation function. These weights perform the same type of function as do the varying synaptic strengths of biological neurons. In both cases, some inputs are made more important than others so that they have a greater effect on the processing element as they combine to produce a neural response.
b. Summation Function: The first step in a processing element's operation is to compute the weighted sum of all of the inputs. Mathematically, the inputs and the corresponding weights are vectors which can be represented as (i1, i2 . . . in) and (w1, w2 . . . wn). The total input signal is the dot, or inner, product of these two vectors.
c. Transfer Function: The result of the summation function, almost always the weighted sum, is transformed to a working output through an algorithmic process known as the transfer function. In the transfer function the summation total can be compared with some threshold to determine the neural output. If the sum is greater than the threshold value, the processing element generates a signal. If the sum of the input and weight products is less than the threshold, no signal (or some inhibitory signal) is generated. Both types of responses are significant. In addition, the threshold, or transfer function is generally non-linear. Linear (straight-line) functions are limited because the output is simply proportional to the input. Linear functions are not very useful. The Figure (1.8) below shows the activation function
d. Scaling and Limiting: After the processing element's transfer function, the result can pass through additional processes which scale and limit. This scaling simply multiplies a scale factor times the transfer value, and then adds an offset.

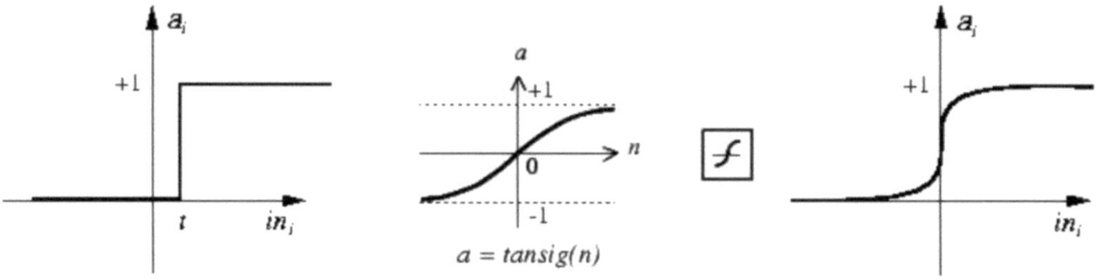

(a) Step function (b) Tan Sigmoid (c) Sigmoid function

Fig. 1.8. sample transfer functions

e. Output Function (Competition): Each processing element is allowed one output signal which may output to hundreds of other neurons. This is just like the biological neuron, where there are many inputs and only one output action. Normally, the output is directly equivalent to the transfer function's result.
f. Error Function and Back-Propagated Value: In most learning networks the difference between the current output and the desired output is calculated. This raw error is then transformed by the error function to match particular network architecture.
g. Learning Function: The purpose of the learning function is to modify the variable connection weights on the inputs of each processing element according to some neural based algorithm. This process of changing the weights of the input connections to achieve some desired result can also be called the adaption function, as well as the learning mode.

5.3 Feed-forward Neural Network: Backpropagation (BP):

Most popular training method for neural networks, the generalized delta rule [Rum86], also known as Backpropagation algorithm which is explained here briefly for feed-forward Neural Network (NN). The explanation here is intended to give an outline of the process involved in Backpropagation algorithm. The (NN) explained here contains three layers. These are input, hidden, and output layer. During the training phase, the training data is fed into to the input layer. The data is propagated to the hidden layer and then to the output layer. This is called the forward pass of the Backpropagation algorithm. In forward pass, each node in hidden layer gets input from all the nodes from input layer, which are multiplied with appropriate weights and then summed. The output of the hidden node is the nonlinear transformation of this resulting sum. Similarly each node in output layer gets input from all the nodes of the hidden layer, which are multiplied with appropriate weights and then summed. The output of this node is the non-linear transformation of the resulting sum. The output values of the output layer are compared with the target output values. The target output values are used to teach network. The error between actual output values and target output values is calculated and propagated back toward hidden layer. This is called the backward pass of the Backpropagation algorithm. The error is used to update the connection strengths between nodes, i.e. weight matrices between input-hidden layers and hidden-output layers are updated. During the testing phase, no learning takes place i.e., weight matrices are not changed. Each test vector is fed into the input layer. The feed-forward of the testing data is similar to the feed-forward of the training data. Backpropagation architecture was developed in the early 1970s by several independent sources (Werbor; Parker; Rumelhart, Hinton and Williams). There are many laws (algorithms) used to implement the adaptive feedback required to adjust the weights during training. The most common technique is backward-error propagation, more commonly known as back propagation. The Backpropagation algorithm searches for weight values that minimize the total error of the network over the set of training examples (training set). Backpropagation consists of the repeated application of the following two passes:

- Forward pass: in this step the network is activated on one example and the error of (each neuron of) the output layer is computed.
- Backward pass: in this step the network error is used for updating the weights (credit assignment problem).

Therefore, starting at the output layer, the error is propagated backwards through the network, layer by layer. This is done by recursively computing the local gradient of each neuron. Here, a simple example shows the work of Backpropagation algorithm, uses supervised training, if the output is not correct, the weight are adjusted according to the formula:

$$W_{new} = W_{old} + \alpha \text{ (desired - output) * input.} \quad (3)$$

α is the learning rate, assume $\alpha = 1$.
Assume output threshold = 1.2.
Figure (1.9) shows the neural network:

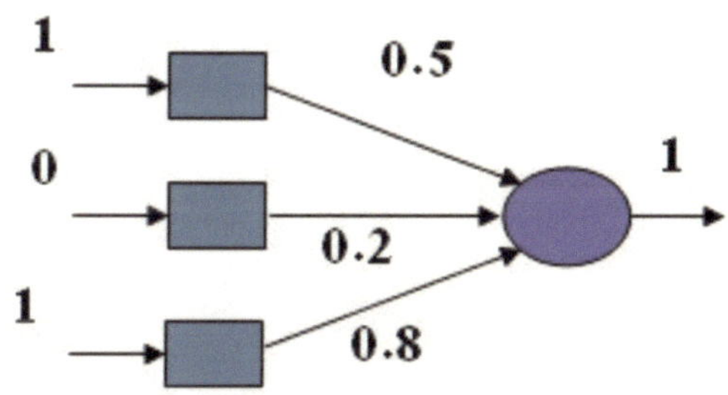

Fig. 1.9. sample neural network

To apply the above:

$= 1 * 0.5 + 0.2 * 0 + 1 * 0.8$
$= 1.3$
$1.3 > 1.2$

Then adjust the weight:

$W_{1new} = 0.5 + 1 * (0 - 1) *1 = - 0.5$
$W_{2new} = 0.2 + 1 * (0 - 1) *0 = 0.2$

$W_{3new} = 0.8 + 1 * (0 - 1) *1 = - 0.2$
$= 1 *(- 0.5) + 0.2 * 0 + 1 * (- 0.2)$
$= (- 0.5) + (- 0.2)$
$= - 0.7$ ➡ $- 0.7 < 1.2$

Threshold, this is the edge and identify the value in the neural network.

6. Crisp set and Fuzzy set

Fuzzy logic (FL) was introduced by Dr. Lotfi Zadeh in the 1960 as a means to model the uncertainty of natural language [Zadeh 1965]. There are many motivation that encouraged scientists to develop the science of fuzzy logic or crisp logic, with the development of computer and software have the desire to reinvent or programmable systems can deal with inaccurate information along the lines of human, but this problem was born as the computer can not deal only with specific and accurate information, and has resulted in this trend known as expert systems or artificial intelligence. Knowledge of fuzzy logic is one of the theories through which they could build such systems. We can say in general that fuzzy logic as the fuzzy logic and fuzzy set. Fuzzy Logic (FL) is a multi valued logic, that allows middle values to be defined between conventional evaluations like true/false, yes/no, high/low, etc, this concept is sufficient for many areas of applications, but it can easily be seen, that it lacks in flexibility for some applications like classification of remotely sensed data analysis, with the fuzzy logic use the rule. In addition drawbacks of crisp set the membership function of crisp logic fails to distinguish between members of the same set, Figure (1.10) below shows the process:

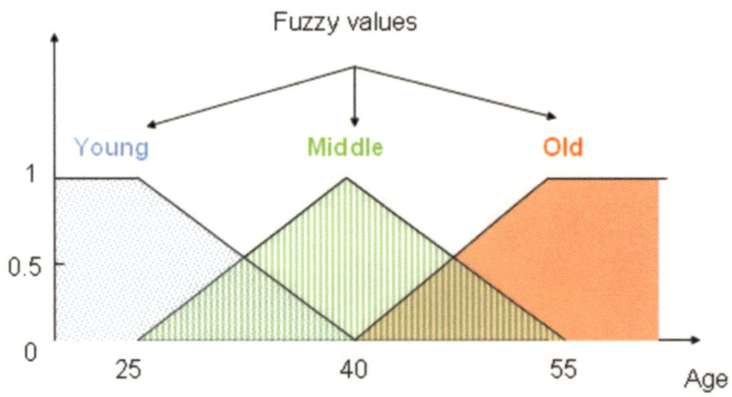

Fig. 1.10. the fuzzy logic process

We can note from Figure (1.10) the meaning of the Fuzzification scales and maps input variables to fuzzy sets, but the Defuzzification convert fuzzy output values to control signals. While in fuzzy sets an object can partially be in a set, the membership degree takes values between 0 and 1, 1 mean entirely in the set, 0 means entirely not in the set, other values mean partially in the set. The fuzzy sets are in the range [0.0, 1.0], with 0.0 representing absolute falseness and 1.0 representing absolute truth. This does not deal with rule but deal with the membership degree, we will deal with only fuzzy set, we will fuzzy the data only. Fuzzy set play an important role in recognizing dangerous events and reducing false alarms level [Yao and et al 2002]. Interest from the use the fuzzy set if the dataset are huge and complex (overlapping), the Fuzzification resolve this overlap. The fuzzy set deals with a linguistic variable associate's words or sentences with a measure of belief functions, also called membership function (use the natural language). The set of values that it can take is called term set, the figure (1.11) shows simple example of membership relation of age.

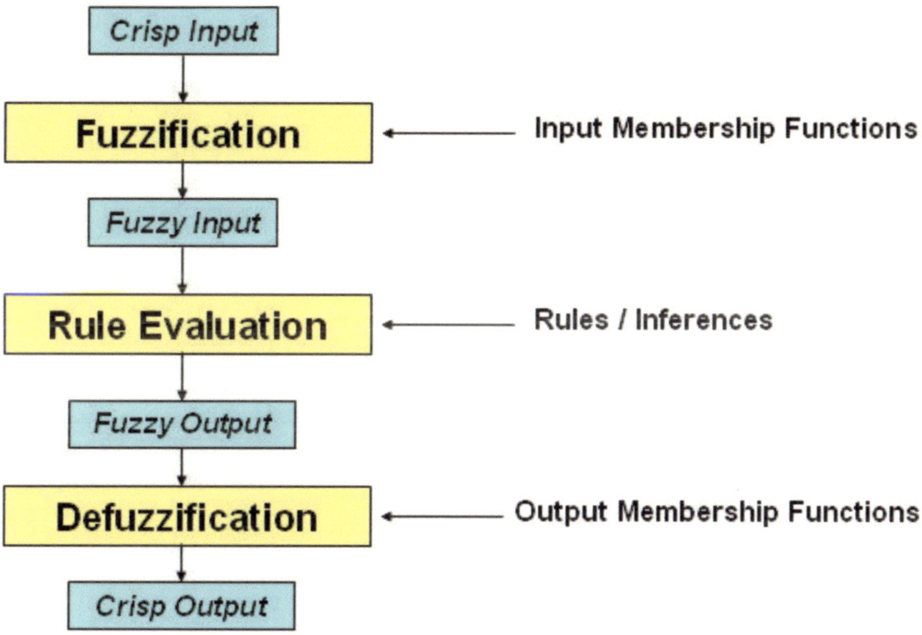

Fig. 1.11. Membership function

Through example, we can note the degree of affiliation of each and every one. Each value in the set is a fuzzy variable defined over a base variable.

7. Architecture of the Artificial Neural Networks

This part concerned with the explanation of the structural Artificial Neural Networks (ANN) used in this chapter, types and components have been clarified in the previous pages. In fact, in this work we used one type of neural network namely (feed-forward neural network), but with two different architectures, one trained with nonfuzzified dataset and other for the fuzzified data.

7.1 Artificial Neural Networks used with non-fuzzified data

In general we know that the feed-forward neural networks consists of three layers, these are input, hidden, and output layers. In this chapter, the feed-forward neural networks

(Backpropagation) are used. Input layer consists of twelve neurons (input) as equal features that have been selected from KDD dataset based on previous studies [Chebrolu and et al 2005]. The process of determining the number of hidden layers of each network is by using the concept (Trail and Error). Is to identify a certain number of layers and number of neurons per layer, therefore, different nets are trained and examining the network performance. Then choose the best network architecture. In this chapter, the hidden layer consists of 20 neurons. In addition to output layer consists of five neurons, this will be four of the intrusion (Probing, Dos, U2R, and R2L) and is one of the outputs is normal. In addition to the parameters used in this feed-forward Neural Network (NN) such as:

- TrainParam.epochs = 500; Epoch number (Batch, Sequential) – improve the result and condition stop.
- TrainParam.lr = 0.000001; learn rate, value to update weight – improve the result.
- TrainParam.goal = 0000; condition stop.
- TrainParam.min_grad=0.0000000001; value change in min_grad–improve the result.
- Threshold if the value is zero or less than zero is equal (-1), otherwise i.e. if the value more than zero is equal (1).

This is the type of neural network discussed briefly in previous pages: the units each perform a biased weighted sum of their inputs and pass this activation level through a transfer function to produce their output, and the units are arranged in a layered feed-forward topology. An activation function used to transform the activation level of a unit (neuron) into an output signal. The Backpropagation algorithm uses an activation function. In this chapter, Tan-Sigmoid transfer function (tansig) is used, like the logistic function, except that output lies in the range (-1, +1). Often performs better than the logistic function because of its symmetry. Ideal for customization of multilayer perceptrons, particularly the hidden layers, Figure (1.12) below shows the Tan-Sigmoid function:

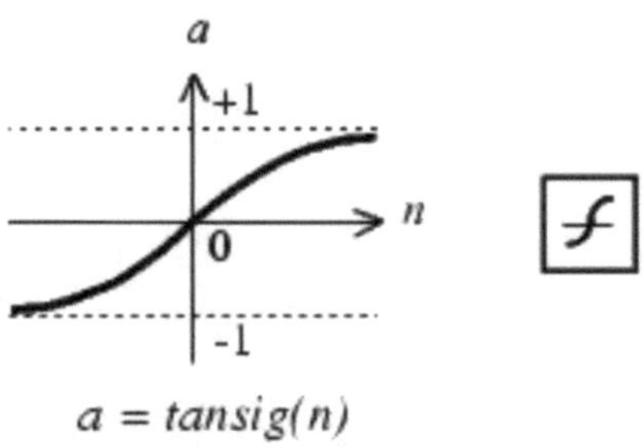

Fig. 1.12. Tan-sigmoid transfer function

Figure (1.13) shows the structure feed-forward neural network of that.

7.2 Artificial Neural Networks used with fuzzified data

In this type of feed-forward neural networks with fuzzified data, the input layer consists from sixty neurons, because of the membership, each value in the previous network will be represented with five values, the hidden layer consists of seven neurons. In addition to output layer consists of five neurons. In addition, the network will use the previous parameters and use the Backpropagation algorithm with the same transfer function. Figure (1.14) below shows the structure of the feed-forward neural network:

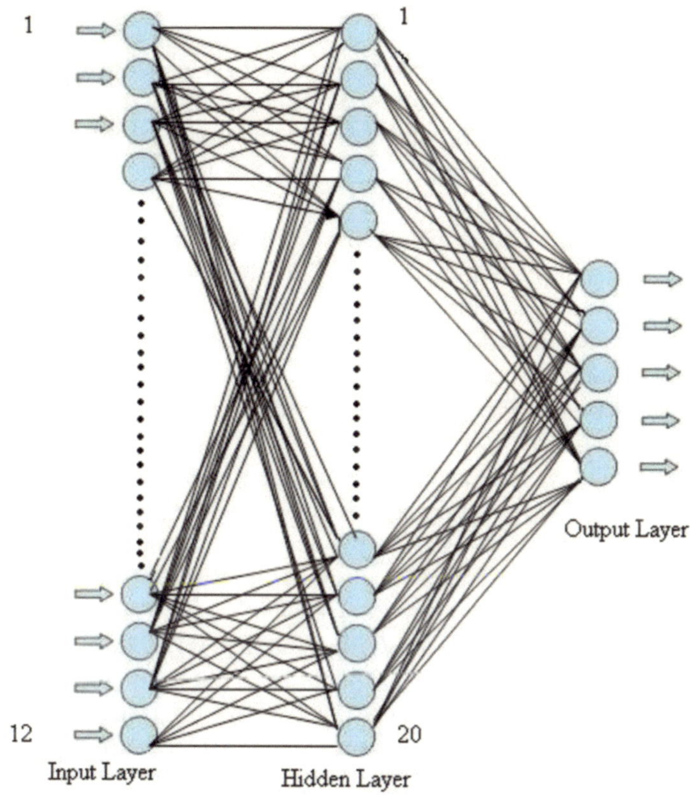

Fig. 1.13. Structure the neural network with normal data

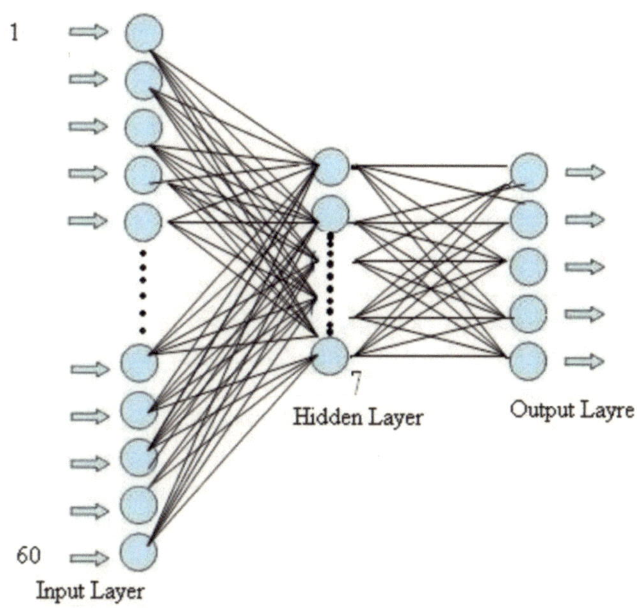

Fig. 1.14. Structure the neural network with Fuzzification data

8. Conclusions

The main contribution of the present chapter is to achieve a classification model with high intrusion detection accuracy and mainly with low false negative. This was done through the design of a classification process for the problem using neural network and neural network with Fuzzification data for the detection of various types of attacks.
From the given results, the following substantial remarks were obtained:

1. The neural networks were able to produce good detectors that give a good estimation of the amount of difference from the normal. This shows that it is possible to apply the suggested classifiers to detect anomalies on real network traffic data.
2. Two classifiers were suggested (Neural Network, Neural Network with Fuzzification data) with best classification accuracy 95.9303 % and 97.4890 % respectively. The suggested neural network with Fuzzification data is more efficient and meets the contribution of this chapter.
3. During the training process it was found that changing the size of the normal training data set with respect to the size of the attack data set (same percentages of the two data set or different percentages) did not affect the obtained classification.
4. Both anomaly detection and misuse detection are supported by the system. This was obvious from the ability of the designed NN (with fuzzified data) of giving approximately the same recognition ability (97.0038%) when tested with whole data set (311029) connection record) not only the trained set (30000 connection record) at which the testing result was (97.2700%). This shows that the designed net gives the ability to respond to anomalies and not only to signatures of known attacks.

The result of training and testing the neural network with Fuzzification data highly reduces the false negative alarms (to 0.804 %) compared with the NN trained with non fuzzified data set (the false negative rate was (1.9943 %) and that the false negative alarms only caused by R2L attack for fuzzified data set, while for non fuzzified data set caused by Prob, DOS, R2L.

9. Future work

1. Built an OCON (one class one neural) for each attack and study its ability to detected attacks and reduce the false alarms.
2. In this chapter, we used 12 features to classify connection records, as future work try to study the most suitable feature for each type of normal and attack, for example, in the normal use the feature number (3,11,21,40), in the probing use (1,3,12,18,20,21,23,26), in the Dos use (1,8,10,11,16,17,20,21,23,28,29,31), in the U2R use (11,14,17,28,29,32,36,38), and R2l use (1,3,11,12,18,20,22,25,38). This could be done with OCON structure
3. Another improvement of the specific intrusion system developed is the use of real-time intrusion detection, because such a system can catch a range of intrusion like viruses, Trojan horses, and masquerading before these attacks have time to do extensive damage to a system.
4. Design a classifier depending on the idea of data mining and compare its behavior with this chapter work.

10. References

[1] [Axe99] Stefan Axelsson, "Research in Intrusion -Detection System: A Survey ", Department of Computer Engineering, Chalmers University of Technology, Sweden. 1999, pp.1-25.

[2] [Bac01] Rebecca Bace & Peter Mell, "Intrusion Detection Systems", Released by National Institute of Standards and Technology (NIST), 2001 last accessed in 29-7-2007,pp,5-55. http://www.21cfrpart11.com/files/library/goverment/intrusion_detection_systems_0201 _draft PDF.

[3] [Che05] Chebrolu S, Abraham A, Thomas JP." Feature detection and ensemble design of intrusion detection systems". Compute Secur; 24:, 2005, pp.295–307.

[4] [Cro03] Tim Crothers, "Implementing Intrusion Detection Systems", Willey Publishing, 2003.

[5] [Den87] Dorothy E. Denning, "An Intrusion-Detection Model", IEEE Transactions on Software Engineering, Vol.SE-13.No.2, February 1987, pp.222-232.

[6] [Kem02] R. A. Kemmerer and G. Vigna, "Intrusion detection: a brief history and overview", Computer, vol. 35, no. 4, 2002, pp. 27–30.

[7] [Kim02] Jung won Kim, "Integrating Artificial Immune Algorithms for Intrusion Detection", Dissertation in University of London, 2002, pp,1-5.

[8] [Kum95] Sandeep Kumar, "Classification and Detection of Computer Intrusions", A PHD Dissertation to the Faculty of Purdue University, August 1995, pp.49-51.

[9] [Mal02] By Saadat Malik," Network Security Principles and Practices", chapter 14, November 15, 2002.

[10] [Myk94] Mykerjee B., Heberlein L. T., & Levitt K. N., " Network Intrusion Detection", IEEE Network, Vol.8, No.3, 1994, pp. 26-14.

[11] [Por92] Porras, P. A., "STAT: A State Transition Analysis Tools for Intrusion Detection", MSc Thesis, Department of Computer Science, University of California Santa Barbara, 1992, pp.15-20.

[12] [Pri97] Katherine E. Price. "Host-based misuse detection and conventional operating system 'audit data collection ", A thesis Submitted to the Faculty of Purdue University, December 1997, pp. 6- 8.

[13] [Kaz04] Przemyslaw Kazienko & Piotr Dorosz,"Intrusion Detection Systems (IDS) part2- Classification; method; techniques", 2004, Web, last access day: 28-july-2007, http://www.windowsecurity.com/articles/IDS-part2-classification-methods-techniques.html.

[14] [Sto00] Salvatore J. Stolfo, Wei Fan, Wenke Lee, Andreas Prodromidis, & Philip K. Chan, "Cost-based modeling for Fraud and Intrusion Detection: Results from the JAM Project", 2000, http://www1.cs.columbia.edu/jam/recent-project-papers.html, last access day 28-july-2007, pp.1-15.

[15] [Sun02] Aurobindo Sundaram, "An Introduction to Detection ", ACM'c First Electronic Publication 2002.

[16] [Tao07] Tao Song, "Formal Reasoning about Intrusion Detection Systems", a dissertation submitted in partial satisfaction of the requirements for the degree of

doctor of philosophy in computer science in the office of graduate studies of the university of California, 2007.
[17] [Yao02] J.T Yao, S.L. Zhao, L.V. Saxton,"A study on Fuzzy Intrusion Detection", Department of computer science, University of Regina. Saskatchewan, Canada S4S 0A2, 2002.
[18] [Zad65] L.A. Zadeh, Fuzzy Sets, "Information and Control", 8(31965), pp.338-353, 1965.

8

Hybrid Intrusion Detection Systems (HIDS) using Fuzzy Logic

Bharanidharan Shanmugam and Norbik Bashah Idris
Advanced Informatics School (AIS),
Universiti Teknologi Malaysia International Campus,
Kuala Lumpur
Malaysia

1. Introduction

The rapid growth of the computers that are interconnected, the crime rate has also increased and the ways to mitigate those crimes has become the important problem now. In the entire globe, organizations, higher learning institutions and governments are completely dependent on the computer networks which plays a major role in their daily operations. Hence the necessity for protecting those networked systems has also increased. Cyber crimes like compromised server, phishing and sabotage of privacy information has increased in the recent past. It need not be a massive intrusion, instead a single intrusion can result in loss of highly privileged and important data. Intusion behaviour can be classified based on different attack types. Smart intruders will not attack using a single attack, instead, they will perform the attack by combining few different attack types to deceive the detection system at the gateway. As a countermeasure, computational intelligence can be applied to the intrusion detection systems to realize the attacks, alert the administrator about the form and severity, and also to take any predetermined or adaptive measures dissuade the intrusion.

2. Need for hybrid IDS systems

This section introduces a classification (Debar *et al.*, 1999) of intrusion detection systems that highlights the current research status. This classification defines families of intrusion detection systems according to their properties. There are four different types (Figure 1) of intrusion detection available based on the past (Axelsson, 1998; Richard and Giovanni, 2002) and current researches (Scarfone and Peter, 2007; Sabahi and Movaghar, 2008). The following paragraphs explain the types in detail. Principally, an IDS is concerned with the detection of hostile actions. The intrusion detection approaches can be classified into anomaly based and signature based which any network security tools are mostly using (Ozgur *et al.,* 2005). One more classification can be made by considering the source of data used for intrusion detection. The taxonomy can be given based on the information derived from a single host (named as Host based IDS (HIDS)) and the information derived from complete segment of the network that is being monitored (named as Network based IDS (NIDS).

Any IDS can be categorized upon its operation as standalone or centralized applications that create a distributed system. Standalone systems will be working individually without any agents but centralized applications work with autonomous agents that are capable of taking preemptive and reactive measures.

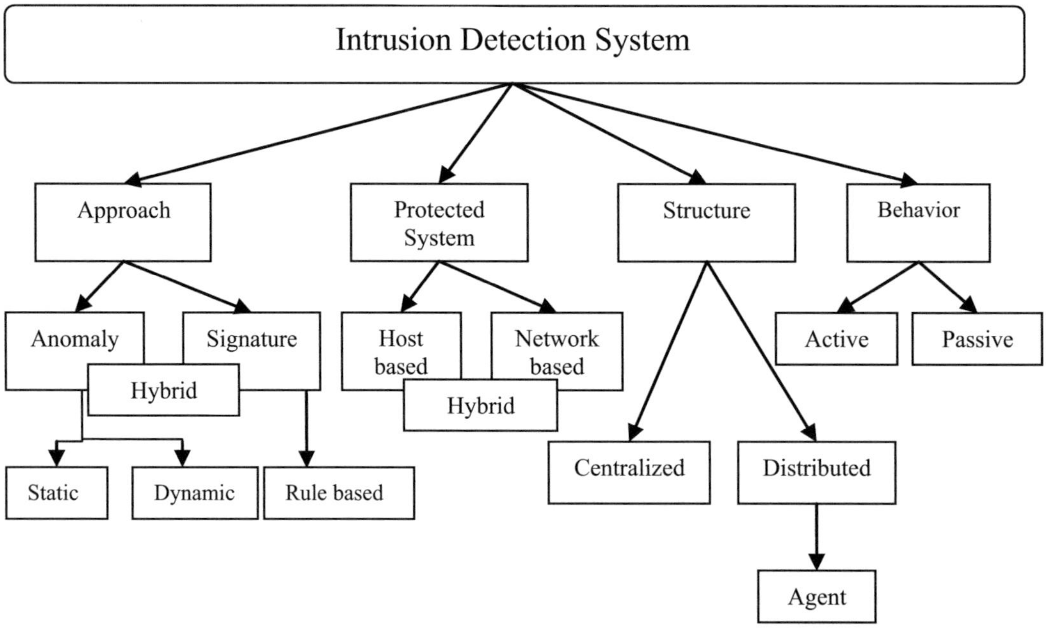

Fig. 1. Classification of intrusion detection systems

An IDS is categorized as behavior-based system, when it uses information about the normal behavior of the system it monitors. Behavior on detection describes the response of the IDS after the detection of attacks. It can be divided into active or passive based on the attack response. These two types of intrusion detection systems differ significantly from each other, but complements one another well. The architecture of host-based is completely dependent on agent-based, which means that a software agent resides on each of the hosts, and will be governed by the main system. In addition, more efficient host-based intrusion detection systems are capable of monitoring and collecting system audit trails in real time as well as on a scheduled basis, thus distributing both CPU utilization and network overhead and providing for a flexible means of security administration. It would be advantageous in IDS implementation to completely integrate the NIDS, su ch that it would filter alerts in a identical manner to HIDS and can be controlled from teh same centralized location. In conclusion, highly secure environment should require both NIDS and HIDS to be implemented for not only providing a complete defence against dynamic attacks but also to effectively and effecintly monitor, respond and detected the computer/network misuse against threats and malicious activities.

3. Different aritificial intelligence approaches in HIDS

Artificial Intelligence (AI) techniques play a vital role by reducing the data used for detection and also classifying the data according to the needs and it is applied in both techniques (misuse detection and anomaly detection). AI techniques have been used to automate the intrusion detection process; which includes neural networks, fuzzy inference systems, evolutionary computation, machine learning, support vector machines, etc. The following sections will give an overall view (Table 1) about some of the Artificial Intelligence (AI) techniques applied for intrusion detection.

3.1 Artificial neural networks (ANN)

An Artificial Neural Network (ANN) consists of a collection of processing units called as neurons, which are highly interconnected. They have the ability to learn-by-example and also via generalizing from limited, noisy, and complete data too. Neural Networks can be distinguished into two types based on its architecture (Wu and Banzhaf, 2009):

1. **Supervised training algorithms**, where in the learning phase, the network learns the desired output for a given input or pattern. The well known architecture of supervised neural network is the Multi-Level Perception (MLP).
2. **Unsupervised training algorithms**, where in the learning phase, the network learns without specifying any desired output. Self-Organizing Maps (SOM) are popular among unsupervised training algorithms. A SOM tries to find a topological mapping from the input space to clusters.

Lippman and Cunningham (1999) and Ryan *et al.*, (1998) created keyword count based IDS with neural networks. Researchers (Ghosh *et al.*, 1999) created a neural network to analyze program behavior profiles instead of user behavior profiles. Cannady (1998), developed a network-based neural network detection system in which packet-level network data was retrieved from a database and then classified according to nine packet characteristics and presented to a neural network. Self-Organizing Maps (SOMs) have also been used as anomaly intrusion detectors (Girardin and Brodbeck, 1998). SOM was used to cluster and then graphically display the network data for the user to determine which clusters contained attacks. Applications of ANN in intrusion detection can be found in Cansian *et al.*, (1997). However, on contrary to neural networks, self-organizing maps do not provide a descriptive model which explains a particular detection decision.

3.2 Genetic algorithms

Genetic Algorithm for Simplified Security Audit Trials Analysis (GASSATA) proposed by the Me (1998), introduced genetic algorithm for misuse intrusion detection. GASSATA constructed a two dimensional matrix. One axis of the matrix specifies different attacks already known. The other axis represents different kinds of events derived from audit trails. Therefore this matrix actually represents the patterns of intrusions. Given an audit record being monitored which includes information about the number of occurrences of every event; this method will apply genetic algorithms to find the potential attacks appearing in the audit record. However, the assumption that the attacks are dependent only on events in this method will restrict its generality. There are two steps involved in genetic algorithm, one is coding a solution to the problem with a string of bits, and the other is finding a fitness function to test each individual of the population against evaluation criteria. Me (1998) used a standard GA, while Dass used a micro-GA in order reduce the time overhead normally associated with GA. Diaz-Gomez and Hougen (2005) corrected the fitness definition (Me, 1998) used after a detailed analysis and mathematical justification (Diaz-Gomez and Hougen, 2006). The detection rate can be high and false alarm can be low if the fitness function is well designed. The disadvantage is that it cannot locate the attack in audit trails (Zorana *et al.,* 2009) and it cannot detect novel attacks as it requires more domain specific knowledge (Li, 2006). Genetic based intrusion detection has no ability to detect multiple simultaneous attacks (Suhail *et al.,* 2008) and this detection approach meets computation complexity problems. A novel approach proposed by addresses the problem of detecting masquerading, a security attack in which an intruder assumes the identity of a legitimate user. The approach uses the techniques used in bioinformatics for a pair-wise sequence alignments to compare the monitored session with past user behavior. The algorithm uses a semi-global alignment and a unique scoring system to measure similarity between a sequence of commands produced by a potential intruder and the user signature, which is a sequence of commands collected from a legitimate user. Even though a novel method was proposed, false positive rate is somewhat a lackluster.

3.3 Immune system approach

The Human Immune System (HIS) (Somayaji *et al.,* 1997) protects the body against damage from extremely large number of harmful bacteria and viruses, termed pathogens. It does this largely without prior knowledge of the structure of these pathogens. This property, along with the distributed, self-organized and light weighted nature of the mechanisms by which it achieves this protection, has in recent years made it the focus of increased interest within the computer science and intrusion detection communities. The AIS described by Kephart (1994) is one of the earliest attempts of applying HIS mechanisms to intrusion detection. The paper focuses on automatic detection of computer viruses and worms. They utilized fuzzy matching techniques based on the existing signatures. Aickelin *et al.,* (2003) discussed the application of danger theory to intrusion detection and the possibility of combining research from wet and computer labs in a theoretical paper. Sarafijanovic and Boudec (2003) developed an immune based system to detect malfunctioning nodes in a ad-hoc networks. They use Dynamic Source Routing (DSR) protocol to create a series of data sets. A detailed review of the AIS applied to intrusion can be found in (Kim, 2003).

3.4 Fuzzy logic

Fuzzy logic starts and builds on a set of user-supplied human language rules. The fuzzy systems convert these rules to their mathematical equivalents. This simplifies the job of the system designer and the computer, and results in much more accurate representations of the way systems behave in the real world. Additional benefits of fuzzy logic include its simplicity and its flexibility. Fuzzy logic can handle problems with imprecise and incomplete data, and it can model nonlinear functions of arbitrary complexity. Fuzzy logic techniques have been employed in the computer security field since the early 90's (Hosmer, 1993). Its ability to model complex systems made it a valid alternative, in the computer security field, to analyze continuous sources of data and even unknown or imprecise processes (Hosmer, 1993). Fuzzy logic has also demonstrated potential in the intrusion detection field when compared to systems using strict signature matching or classic pattern deviation detection. Bridges (Bridges and Vaughn, 2000), states the concept of security itself is fuzzy. In other words, the concept of fuzziness helps to smooth out the abrupt separation of normal behavior from abnormal behavior. That is, a given data point falling outside/inside a defined "normal interval", will be considered anomalous/normal to the same degree regardless of its distance from/within the interval. Fuzzy logic has a capability to represent imprecise forms of reasoning in areas where firm decisions have to be made in indefinite environments like intrusion detection.

The model suggested in (Dokas *et al.*, 2002) building rare class prediction models for identifying known intrusions and their variations and anomaly/outlier detection schemes for detecting novel attacks whose nature is unknown. The latest in fuzzy is to use the Markov model. As suggested in (Xu *et al.*, 2004) a Window Markov model is proposed, the next state in the window equal evaluation to be the next state of time t, so they create Fuzzy window Markov model. As discussed, researchers propose a technique to generate fuzzy classifiers using genetic algorithms that can detect anomalies and some specific intrusions. The main idea is to evolve two rules, one for the normal class and other for the abnormal class using a profile data set with information related to the computer network during the normal behavior and during intrusive (abnormal) behavior.

3.5 Integrating fuzzy logic with datamining

Data mining techniques have been commonly used to extract patterns from sets of data. Although association rules can be mined from audit data for anomaly detection, the mined rules are at the data level. Many quantitative features are involved in intrusion detection. As per previous researches (Lunt *et al.*, 1992; Varun *et al.*, 2009) IDES classifies the statistical measures into four types: ordinal measures, categorical measures, binary categorical measures and linear categorical measures. Both ordinal measures and linear categorical measures are quantitative. SRIs EMERALD (Lunt *et al.*, 1989) also divides the network traffic statistical measures into four classes: categorical measures, continuous measures, intensity measures and event distribution measures. Example for continuous measures is the connection duration and intensity measure is the number of packets during a unit of time.

The fuzzy sets provide a smooth transition between member and non-member of a set; therefore, there are fewer boundary elements being excluded. An alternative solution using fuzzy sets, introduced by Kuok (Kuok *et al.*, 2001) to categorize quantitative variables, offered smooth transitions from one fuzzy set to another. Classification has been repeatedly applied to the problem of intrusion detection either to classify events into separate attack categories (e.g., the 1999 KDD Cup Competition) or to characterize normal use of a network service.

In our research work, the greatest need was to reduce the amount of data needed for processing and the false alarm rate. We are primarily seeking to improve the performance of an existing system rather than trying to replace current intrusion detection methods with a data mining approach. While current signature-based intrusion detection methods have limitations as stated in the previous section, they do still provide important services and this required us to determine how data mining could be used in a complementary way to existing measures and improves it.

4. Different hybrid IDS

To the best of our knowledge there are few research work and papers that have been published in the area of Network Security, particularly in the area of hybrid intrusion detection. But the work of integrating misuse and anomaly detection is very rare. Based on the objective set for our research, Table 1 summarizes the closely related work, with the method used and the findings by the respective researchers for each research work selected.

Researcher and Model	Method	Findings
Lee *et al.*, 2001 IIDS	Classification based anomaly detection	It uses inductive rule generation to generate rules for important, yet infrequent events
Dickerson and Dickerson (2000) FIRE	Classification based anomaly detection	It generates fuzzy sets for every observed feature which are in turn used to define fuzzy rules to detect individual attacks
Barbara *et al.*, 2001 ADAM	Association rules and classification based anomaly detection	It performs anomaly detection to filter out most of the normal traffic, then it uses a classification technique to determine the exact nature of the remaining activity
Zhang and Zulkernine (2006)	-	The outlier detection provided by the random forests algorithm is utilized to detect unknown intrusions
Tajbakhsh *et al.*, 2006; Tajbakhsh, *et al.*, 2009	Association based classification	The proposed method has proved the ability to handle more categorical attributes and the efficiency to classify large data sets especially for IDS.
Kai *et al.*, 2007 HIDS	Association rules	This hybrid system combines the advantages of low false-positive rate of signature-based intrusion detection system (IDS) and the ability of anomaly detection system (ADS) to detect novel unknown attacks.
Jianhui *et al.*, 2008	Prefix tree rule mining	Authors proposed a new rule mining algorithm base prefix tree (PTBA), which compress the fuzzy pattern candidate set and frequent set through constructing a tree structure, thus it can save the memory cost of fuzzy pattern candidate and frequent set.

Table 1. Different hybrid IDS

Lee *et al.* (2001) used a classification algorithm called RIPPER to update the rules used by Network Flight Recorder (NFR), a commercial real-time network-monitoring tool. Manganaris *et al.*, (2000) used association rules from Intelligent Miner to reduce false alarms generated by NetRanger's sensors. MITRE used HOMER (Heuristic for Obvious Mapping Episode Recognition) and BART (Back End Analysis and Review if Tagging) along with clustering analysis for detection. (Lee *et al.*, 1999) proposed an association rule-based data mining approach for anomaly detection where raw data was converted into ASCII network packet information, which in turn was converted into connection-level information. These connection level records contained connection features like service, duration, etc. Association rules were then applied to this data to create models to detect intrusions. They utilized Common Intrusion Detection Framework (CIDF) to extract the audit data, which is used to build the models, and also to push the signatrues for "novel" attacks ensuring the faster response time for attack detection.

The primary advantage of CIDF is, it is capable of including heterogeneous intrusion detection and response components to share the information and resources in a distributed environments for faster attack detection. The method proposed by Lee *et al.,* (2001) extracts fuzzy classification rules from numerical data, applying a heuristic learning procedure. The learning procedure initially classifies the input space into non-overlapping activation rectangles corresponding to different output intervals. In this sense, our work is similar to that of (Lee *et al.*, 2001; Manganaris *et al.*, 2000 and MITRE).There are no overlapping and inhibition areas. However, the disadvantage listed is, the high false positive rates which is the primary scaling of all the IDS.

Researchers (Dickerson and Dickerson, 2000) developed the Fuzzy Intrusion Recognition Engine (FIRE) (Figure 2) using fuzzy sets and fuzzy rules. FIRE produces fuzzy sets based on a simple data mining technique by processing the network input data. Then the fuzzy rules are defined by the fuzzy sets to detect attacks. FIRE relies on attack specific as they do not establish any model that represents the current state of the system. On the other hand, FIRE detection is based on the fuzzy logic rules that was created, and applies it to the testing audit data for attack classifications. The authors recorded port scan and probes attacks can be detected highly by using this method. But, the primary disadvantage as noted by authors is the labor intensive rule generation process.

In another work, (Barbará *et al.*, 2001) describes Audit Data Analysis and Mining (ADAM) (Figure 3), a real-time anomaly detection system that uses a module to classify the suspicious events into false alarms or real attacks. Customized profiles were built using data mining techniques, and then the classification of observed events are classified into either as attacks or as false alarms. ADAM uses a method that combined association rules along with mining and classification techniques. ADAM builds a "normal" database consists of frequent itemsets by using data that is attack free during the training phase.

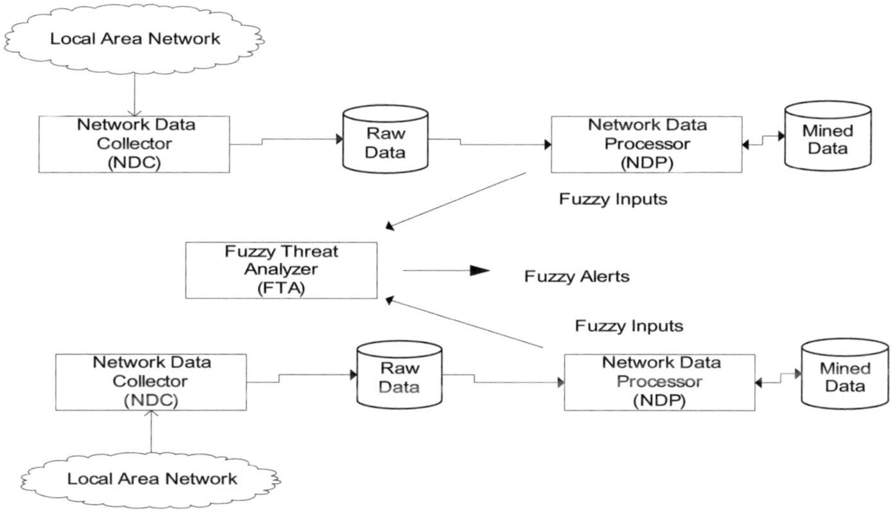

Fig. 2. Fuzzy Intrusion Recognition Engine (FIRE) (Dickerson and Dickerson, 2000)

During the testing (or detection) phase it runs a sliding windoe algorithm to find the frequent itemsets in the last few connections and then compares with the normal item set repository which has already been created. With the remaining item sets which have been flagged as suspicious, ADAM uses a classifier that was trained to classify the known attacks, unknown or a false alarm. Association rules play a major role in gathering necessary data (knowledge) about the nature of audit data. The major drawback is that new type attacks rules need to be given by the external security officer i.e. it does not automate rule generation process and more number of components prevents it from working fast.

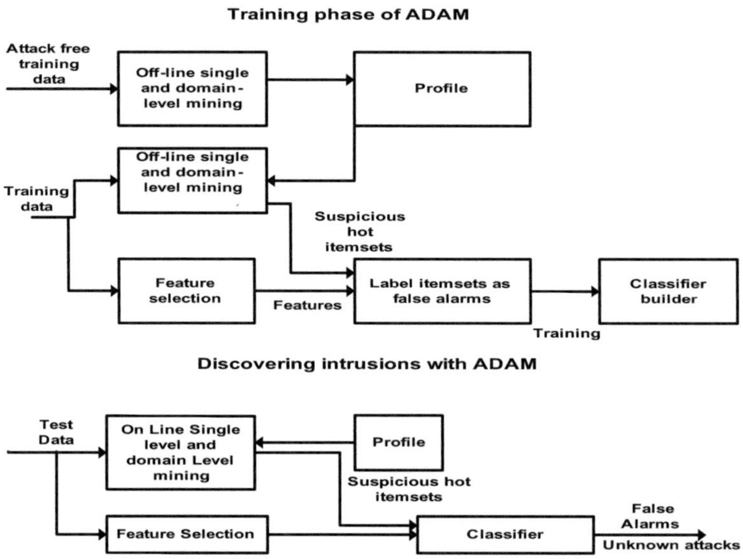

Fig. 3. Training and discovery phases of ADAM (Barbará *et al.*, 2001)

Zhang and Zulkernine (2006) detects known intrusions were detected by signature detection module by implementing Random forest algorithm (Breiman, 2001). In the following step, the outlier detection that was produced by random forests algorithm was utilized to detect new or unknown intrusion attempts. Approaches that use both signature detection and anomaly detection produces two set of reports recording the intrusive activities provided they have a correlation component which will analyze and produce perfect results.

Researchers (Tajbakhsh *et al.*, 2006; Tajbakhsh *et al.*, 2009) use association based classification methods (Figure 5) to classify normal and abnormal attacks based on the compatibility threshold. The proposed system consists of training phase and detection phase. In training phase authors use FCM clustering algorithm to define fuzzy membership functions and use hyper edge concept for item / feature reduction. Once rules are defined, then the knowledge base is used in the training phase to match and alert for testing data. FCM an extension of K-means suffer from a basic limitation, i.e. using pair wise similarity between objects and cluster centroids for membership assignment, thereby lacking the ability to capture nonlinear relationships. Since this limitation is not considered by the researchers, there by limiting the system itself in capturing slightly deviated attacks. Next, the system was tested with only 10% of corrected data set from DARPA, which is considered not effective because it is observed (Su-Yun and Ester, 2008) that there is a difference in detection rate and false positive rates, compared to testing with complete data set and sampling 10% of test data. Also not to forget, that most of the researchers are benchmarked after testing the whole data set and moreover the authors have note mentioned what testing data they used as there are about few weeks of available test data.

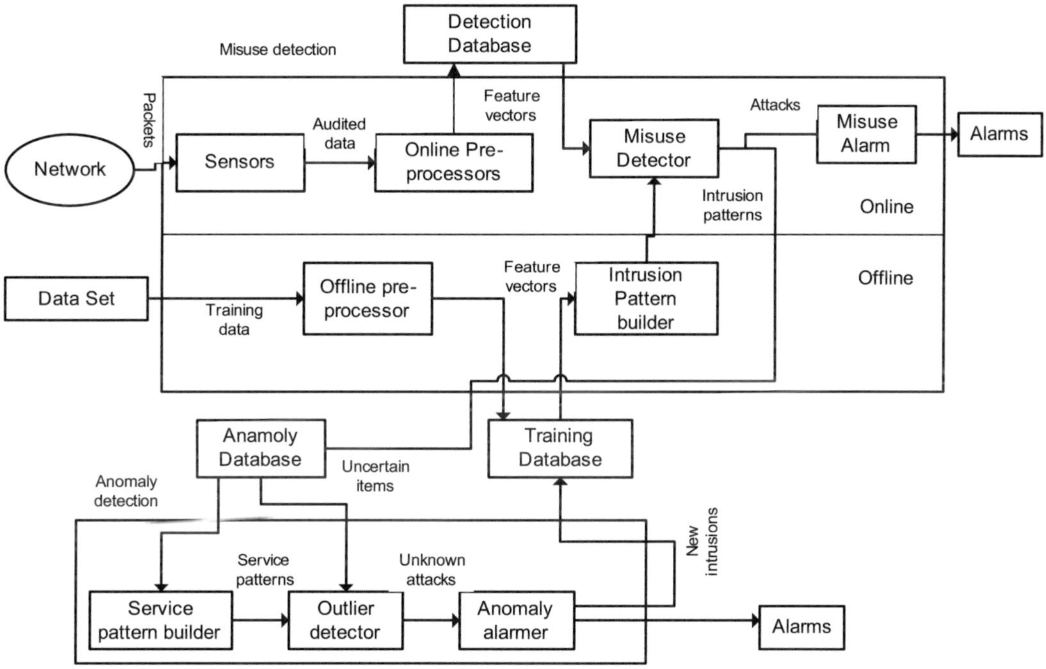

Fig. 4. Misuse and anomaly detection components (Zhang and Zulkernine, 2006)

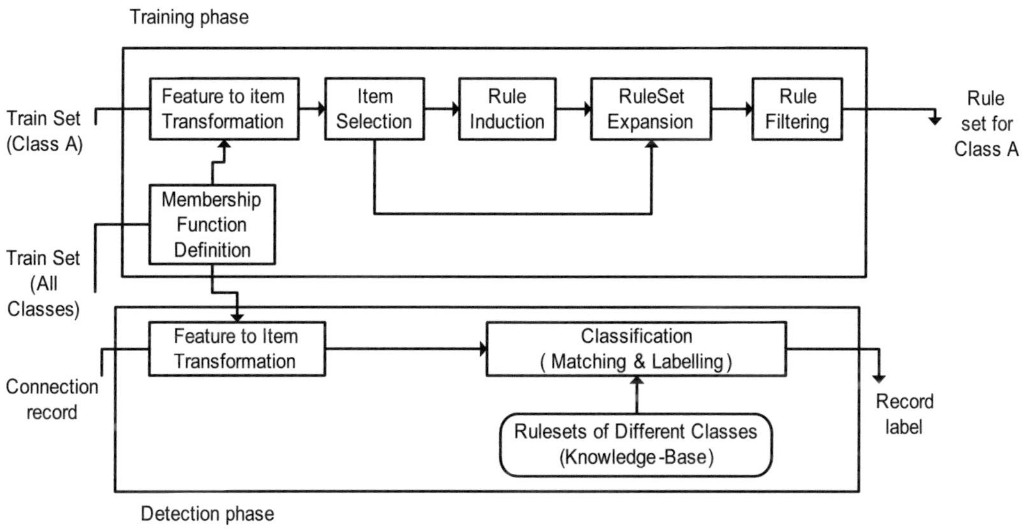

Fig. 5. Block diagram for IDS framework (Tajbakhsh *et al.*, 2009)

The research work (Kai *et al.*, 2007) paper reports the design principles and evaluation results of a new experimental Hybrid Intrusion Detection System (HIDS). This hybrid system combines the advantages of low false-positive rate of signature-based intrusion detection system (IDS) and the ability of Anomaly Detection System (ADS) to detect novel unknown attacks. By mining anomalous traffic episodes from Internet connections, the authors build an ADS that detects anomalies beyond the capabilities of signature-based systems. A weighted signature generation scheme is developed to integrate ADS with SNORT by extracting signatures from anomalies detected. HIDS extracts signatures from the output of ADS and adds them into the SNORT signature database for fast and accurate intrusion detection. The test results of HIDS scheme over real-life Internet trace data mixed with 10 days of Massachusetts Institute of Technology/Lincoln Laboratory (MIT/LL) attack data set (Lippmann *et al.*, 2000), the experimental results showed a 60 percent detection rate of the HIDS, compared with 30 percent and 22 percent in using the SNORT and Bro systems, respectively. This sharp increase in detection rate is obtained with less than 3 percent false alarms. The signatures generated by ADS upgrade the SNORT performance by 33 percent. The HIDS approach proves the vitality of detecting intrusions and anomalies, simultaneously, by automated data mining and signature generation over Internet connection episodes. But, this system is lacking in a major aspect of detection rate, as stated earlier detection rate should be high (some what near to 90%), according to the HIDS, if more than 30% of the attacks are left unnoticed, then the purpose of IDS is getting defeated making it easier for intruders to take control over the protecting networks.
In this research (Jianhui *et al.*, 2008), an intrusion detection model base on fuzzy sets is presented to avoid the sharp boundary problem in rules mining. Considering Apriori algorithm is time-consuming as well as space-consuming; moreover, we propose a new rule mining algorithm base prefix tree (PTBA). PTBA algorithm (Borgelt, 2005) compress the fuzzy pattern candidate set and frequent set through constructing a tree structure, thus it can save the memory cost of fuzzy pattern candidate and frequent set. This characteristic provides a better mining tragedy: if the support degree of a certain node is smaller than the threshold value of support (minsup), the pattern of this node is non-frequent, and then the whole sub-trees whose root node is this node are non-frequent. This characteristic avoids combination explosion and improve mining efficiency prominently. Experiments prove that capability and efficiency of IDS model is obviously improved but, the authors have not addressed the weight supplied on each tree, if the tree goes further down and moreover false positive rate was not recorded and the test data was 10% sampled data of DARPA data set.

5. Proposed hybrid IDS

Our aim is to design and develop an Hybrid Intrusion Detection System (HIDS) that would be more accurate, low in false alarms, Intelligent by using fuzzy mechanisms, not easily deceived by small variations, capable of sniffing and detecting real time packets. The data processor and classifier component summarizes and tabulates the data into carefully selected categories because the amount of data and meta-data associated with network traffic is large. Prior to data analysis, attributes representing relevant features of the input packets must be established. Once the attributes of relevance have been defined, data processor and classifier is employed to compute control variables. Data processor is responsible for accepting raw packet data and produce records for each group as specified by the control variables.

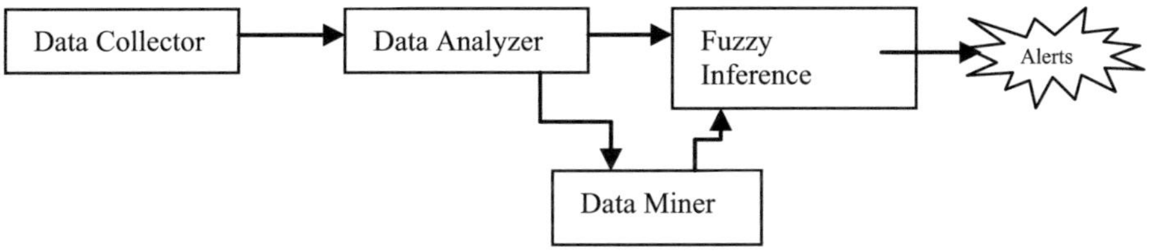

Fig. 6. Overall view of proposed Hybrid IDS

Data mining algorithm by Kuok *et al.,* (1999) is modified and implemented (Shanmugm and Idris 2009)to produce a set of association rules. These rules are expressed as a logic implication with antecedent and consequence. The systems work in two different modes, first being the learning mode and the second being the detection mode. Prior to any data analysis, attributes representing relevant features of the input data (packets) must be established for any IDS. In complex domains like security, attribute selection may play a crucial role. Attributes are represented by names that will be used as linguistic variables by the Data Miner and the Fuzzy Inference Engine and is implemented using the attribute selection algorithm as explained as folows:

Step 1. Initialize the queue S with example set values and the attribute set values.
Step 2. The following steps from 3 until step 7 is performed while CARD(R) is less than the maxsize provided or if the size of the stack is not null.
Step 3. Create a set value which consists of the queue value with maximum support and is a subset of the queue value.
Step 4. Information gain is computed using the formula.
Step 5. Select the attributes with maximum info gain values
Step 6. If the attribute value does not belong to the subset R then
Step 6a. The subset R is the common values of R along with the attributes
Step 7. Following steps are performed for every t_k with their terms of attributes
Step 7a. Example set of terms forms a set based on the examples or the attribute values equals that t_k.

Decision trees are powerful tools in classification and prediction of larger dataset. The attractiveness lies in the formation of rules that is easier for human understanding and the direct usage of those rules with the existing database tools. In majority of the applications especially security, the accuracy of the data classification plays a vital role. In order to define information gain precisely, we need to define a measure commonly used in information theory, called entropy, that characterizes the (im)purity of an arbitrary collection of examples. Given a set S, containing only positive and negative samples with their corresponding labels. The expected information need to classify the DARPA sample is calculated by :

$$I(S_c) = \sum_{i=1}^{c} - p_i \log_2 p_i$$

Where s = total number of samples
c = total classes
$p_i = s_i / s$

For our experiments a feature F with values (f_1,f_2,....f_w) are divided into *w* training sub sets (s_1,s_2,....s_w) where Sj is the subset which holds the value fj for F. Entropy of the selected feature is

$$E(F) = \sum_{j=1}^{c} \frac{S_{1j} + ... + S_{cj}}{S} * I(s_{ij}.....s_{cj})$$

More precisely, the information gain, Gain (F) of an attribute A, relative to a collection of examples S, is defined as

$$\text{Gain (F)} = I(s_1,s_2,....s_c) - E(F)$$

Table 2 shows the information gain calculated for all the attributes based on the equation explained above.

Rank	Information Gain	Feature	Rank	Information Gain	Feature
1	0.988292114	E	13	0.673576388	V
2	0.985914569	C	14	0.671545707	AM
3	0.970739369	J	15	0.662169667	AN
4	0.895566287	AH	16	0.637824522	AO
5	0.844695164	AJ	17	0.591035993	W
6	0.826015494	F	18	0.543491709	AA
7	0.774897786	AI	19	0.516671516	AC
8	0.767343313	AG	20	0.476343726	AF
9	0.767053827	AK	21	0.439147285	L
10	0.724208609	M	22	0.427774836	X
11	0.703067734	A	23	0.391083691	K
12	0.692155232	B	24	0.359009856	D

Table 2. Information gain for DARPA features

6. Implementation results and discussion

To implement and prove the proposed method we used Java 2.0 programming language as our support and implementation tool for IDS. Any research work should be verified with some form of experiment using data. Specifically in the field of Intrusion Detection, testing plays a vital role. To fulfill the above requirements and also to obtain proof of our concept, we tested our system with two sets of data first with DARPA dataset and second, with online data captured inside UTM Citycampus.

Until the year 1998 intrusion detection research has lacked a corpus of data that could serve as the basis for system development, improvement and evaluation. To meet that need, DARPA developed a corpus of data for the DARPA 1998 off-line intrusion detection evaluation, using a network and scripted actors to loosely model the network traffic measured between a US Air Force base and the internet. The latest dataset was added with few more attacks that reflect more real-time data. More details about the 1999 DARPA evaluation data set can be found in Appendix A. For experimental purpose a subset of 1999 DARPA data was used to test the prototype system. A quick glance at the 1999 DARPA dataset, shows it contains 3 weeks of training data and two weeks of testing data. First and third week data do not contain any attack and this was used as training data for anomaly intrusion detection. Second week contains all types of attacks so this was used for creating attack profiles. We used two weeks of test data for our testing. The prototype was developed using Java programming language. The developed prototype was tested in Pentium 4 2.40 GHz machine with 1 GB RAM. Both testing and real-time data capturing were carried out in the same platform.

The primary aim in our work is to find the relevant attributes with maximum information gain. Table 3 shows the different set of attributes considered for difference classes of attacks ranked accordingly by information gain algorithm. The first attribute found by the attribute selection algorithm, as expected, was ICMP with 0.836 information gain. This is the value with maximum information gain. As a result, the root node of the decision tree is associated with this attribute i.e. root node will carry ICMP.

Types	**Ranking of Features**
NORMAL	AH,E,J,AJ,C,F,A,W,B,M,AC,AK,AF,AG,AI,AN,AA,AM,MO
DOS	AH,E,J,C,AI,AJ
PROBE	E,C,AJ,J,F,AH,B,AG,AI,AK,V,AM,AO,M,AC,AN,AK,W,AF,AA,G,H,L,P,X, AD,AE
U2R	C,J,E,AJ,AM,M,F,AH,AG,AF,AC,AN,AA,V,A,W,L,D
R2L	F,C,J,AH,AJ,AI,AG,AK,F,A,L,M,V,AA,AO,X,AC,AN,W,AM,AF,D,AE
ALL	E,C,J,AH,AJ,F,AI,AG,AK,M,A,B,V,AM,AN,AO,W,AA,AC,AE,AF,L,X,K,D

Table 3. Ranking of attributes for four classes of attacks

The majority of the positive and negative examples will be obviously associated with the ABOVE branch rather than the AVERAGE and BELOW branches. The examples associated with ABOVE were then used for the second iteration, selecting TCP as the most relevant attribute with an information gain of 0.064 and the majority of the training examples in the AVERAGE branch. The third and final iteration selected the FIN attribute with an information gain of 0.00056. This attribute represents tcp packets with the fin flag set. In other words, the attributes ICMP, TCP and FIN are most relevant in this case and are selected to describe the input data in the data mining algorithm.

The aim of this test is to find out the attack type "smurf". This attack is new to 1999 DARPA data set. The following table describes the attack signature and the description of "smurf"

Attack	**Description**	**Signature**
Smurf	In the *smurf* attack, attackers use ICMP echo request packets directed to IP broadcast addresses from remote locations to create a denial-of-service attack	There is a large number of 'echo replies' being sent to a particular victim machine from many different places, but no 'echo requests' originating from the victim machine.

Table 4. Attack description and signature for smurf

This type of attack detection also required the counter to reach a larger percentage. Hence the threshold was set at 0.6 i.e. the rule must have a firing strength below 0.6 to increase the graph value. Figure 6 shows the firing strength of the rules against the testing data. For the records from 300 to 500, the firing strength fell to zero and suddenly it shot up to 1 i.e. an increase by 100%. So this sudden rise indicated an attack.

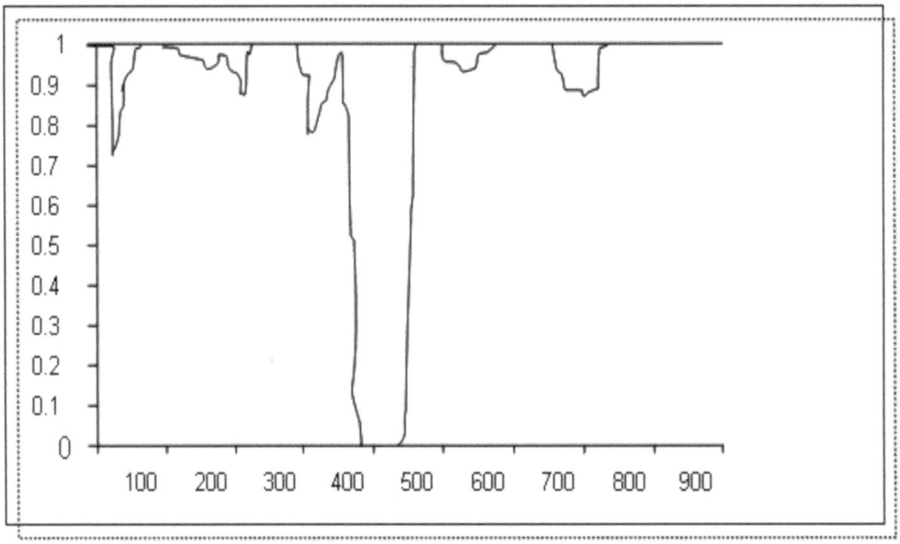

Fig. 7. Consolidated firing strength for rules to detect smurf attack

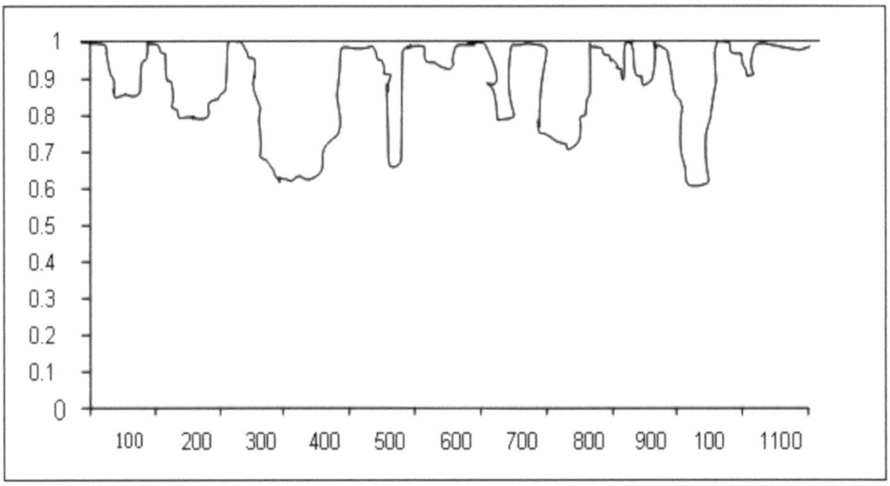

Fig. 8. Consolidated firing strength for real time data

To prove that the system can also work online, the prototype was tested with online data captured in UTM Citycampus. As networking packets constituted huge amount of data, we will however discuss only a small amount of the test data. Here the anomaly detection profiles were based on the DARPA data set. It constituted a clear data i.e. data without any attacks. The data was captured using our own sniffing tool which was written using the Java language. The packages for packet capturing were widely available on the Internet. The data was collected on different days and at different time as follows.

Day 1 : Feb 20th starting from 10.00 a.m. to 6 p.m.
Day 2 : Feb 22nd starting from 10.00 a.m. to 2.00 p.m.

The amount of data collected on the above mentioned days was about 1.76 GB. The collected data was processed and tested with the IIDS. The following graph represents the testing for 20 minutes on day 2 i.e. from 11.30 a.m. to 11.50 a.m.

In the above figure, the firing strengths for most of the records were near to 1. So, there was not much change, which indicated that the prototype did not detect any attack during the testing period. The consolidated results for all four attack types are shown in Table 6.12. The overall analysis and benchmarking of our prototype against others is as shown in Table 6.14. The performance table shows that the detection rate is comparatively higher than all other systems. The false positive rate is also low in comparison to the values obtained from other models.

It was interesting to note that during the experimental stage U2R attacks performance was relatively less, this was because the attacks were distributed across the entire test data. More interesting and important was the fact that the prototype was able to detect the "yaga" attack which occurred during Week 5 day 5. This attack was new and moreover it was not available in the training data set. The proposed prototype was able to detect another new attack, "sechole" which occurred during week 4 day 2. In most cases U2R attack detection performance was always low because of its distribution of attacks and also multiple connections are involved which need more features to be selected.

Attack Types	Detection %	False positive %
R2L	92.1	10.7
PROBE	98.4	1.8
DOS	94.77	5.5
U2R	69.6	6.7
Average	88.71	6.1

Table 5. Consolidated result for all the four attack types

The R2L attack performance was satisfactory because the prototype was able to detect most of the attacks with high detection rate and with low false positives. The system was able to detect new attacks like net cat, net bus and ncftp, which do not occur in the training data. The total false positive rate seems to be larger but since it has more number of attack instances the value also had increased simultaneously. In the future, we will try to bring down the false positives rate by at least to 0.5%.

During the research, the IIDS were able to detect arppoison, a new type of attack with a high detection rate nearing 95% and with a low false positive < 1%. We were able to achieve 100% detection rate for smurf attacks. These performance shows (Table 6.14) that our system is better in detecting certain types of attacks fully. Some of the researchers mentioned in our earlier chapters use only 10% of the KDD training data. Using such a small amount of training dataset is questionable because the dataset is idealistically simple and moreover 98% of the training data contains "smurf" and "neptune" class. However, for content based attacks which is based on the payload, depending on a feature that is irrelevant with content may lead to false positives.

In a more recent work (Su *et al.*, 2009) have applied fuzzy-association rules using incremental mining. The major advantages cited by the authors are the ability of the system

to create a learning data set based on the real time data and to handle real time network traffic. Even though it has the ability to handle real time systems, the research has not addressed the query frequencies as apriori algorithm will generate huge number of candidates. Using incremental data mining will also lead to increase in the number of queries to the rule databases since the rules are checked every two minutes, which could be a bottle neck especially when the system goes online. However, another limitation (Su *et al* 2009) did not mention is the storage requirements for the huge amount of rules produced by the aprirori algorithm based on the online traffic. This limitation was well handled in (Shanmugam and Idris 2009) and has solved the storage and query frequencies. This was however acknowledged by (Hossain Mahmood *et al.,* 2003) who concluded that the incremental mining approach has some advantages, but the application to intrusion detection need to be explored further as it depends on the various aspects like algorithm selected, training and testing data used etc.
We were not able to produce the detection rate, false positives or any other values for real-time data because there is no any universal benchmarking methods available.
Our experimental results are summarized in the below table (Table 6.14) for different attributes. We selected the features by calculating the detection rate for each feature and deleting it one by one. We have not discussed the values due to space restrictions. By the above method we were able to select the appropriate features using the information gain algorithm. Table 8 gives the comparison of using all 41 features against selected 24 features by our proposed method. This clearly reveals the fact that all the features are not important and the selected features had played an important role in improving the overall performance. Initial FIRE (Dickerson and Dickerson, 2000) tests were performed on production local area networks in the College of Engineering at Iowa State University. Using the fuzzy rules, FIRE able to detect nine distinct TCP port scans and separate ICMP (ping) scans of hosts on the network potentially malicious attackers from outside the local network domain. Additionally, it was able to detect non-malicious port scans launched against the system from the local domain. The system also triggered HIGH alerts when seldom seen types of network traffic were observed, in agreement with the Fuzzy Rules used. The system reported a high false positive rate (10.6%) with an average detection rate (79.2%). ADAM (Barbara *et al* 2001) was aimed to detect intrusions of the type Denial of Service (DOS) and Probe attacks (although ADAM can discover other types of intrusions as well).
The overall detection rate recorded was about 84% with a very high false positive rate of 14%.ADAM is a test bed to research which data mining techniques are appropriate for intrusion detection. In spite of the furious activity in intrusion detection, the problem of false alarms and missed attacks (false positives and negatives) is still prevalent.

Features	Detection %	FP %
All features (41)	77.21	9.23
Selected features (24)	88.71	6.1

Table 6. Different feature selection

The experimental results (Thombini *et al* 2004) shows that the approach drastically reduces the amount of false positives and unqualified events. The proposed model clearly addresses the problem of false positives and the anomaly and signature can be updated as and when needed. The system was tested against HTTP traffic for its effectiveness and the comparison was made against capture traffic on their own and not on DARPA dataset. The proposed

hybrid system (Zhang and Zulkernine (2006)) combines the advantages of these two detection approaches. Besides, the misuse detection can remove known intrusions from datasets, so the performance of the anomaly detection can be improved by applying the misuse detection first. The experimental results (Detection rate of about 86%) show that the proposed hybrid approach can achieve high detection rate with low false positive rate, and can detect novel intrusions. However, some intrusions that are very similar with each other cannot be detected by the anomaly detection. That is a limitation of the outlier detection provided by the random forests algorithm.
By combining the anomaly detection method (Tajbakhsh, A., *et al.* 2006; Tajbakhsh, *et al*,. 2009) with misuse detection method, the false positive error rate in the proposed anomaly detection method is kept as low as in misuse detection scenario. There is a remarkable decrease in the detection rate of the known attacks in the anomaly detection scenario. And in the case of unseen attacks the anomaly scenario performs better than the misuse approach. This is actually the most important advantage of combining both the methods. This method is somewhat near to IIDS detection rate and false positive rate. In the weighted signature generation approach (Kai *et al.*, 2007), only the most frequent patterns of detected anomalies are characterized as signatures. By further eliminating nondiscriminative patterns, the generated signatures are quite specific to anomalies detected. Therefore, the newly generated signatures have quite low false alarm rates. The proposed HIDS results in a detection rate of 60 percent, and False alarm rates are maintained about 3 percent. Alerts from intrusions and anomalies detected need to be correlated to result in an even smaller overhead in the detection process.

Group Name	Detection rate %	False positive %
Lee *et al.*, 2001 IIDS	78	12.2
Dickerson and Dickerson (2000) FIRE **	79.2	10.6
Barbara *et al.*, 2001 ADAM	84	14
Zhang and Zulkernine (2006)	86	NA
Tajbakhsh *et al.*, 2006; Tajbakhsh *et al.*, 2009	85.5	6.9
Kai *et al.*, 2007 HIDS	60	30
Jianhui *et al.*, 2008	94	NA
IIDS	88.71	6.1

Table 7. Comparison with other selected models

In this work (Jianhui *et al.*, 2008), the model of intrusion detection based on fuzzy sets is suggested and experiment results showed its accuracy and capability. In the process of rules mining, however, we found the select of membership function depended excessively upon the expert knowledge, which necessarily causes the deviation between results and experiment conclusion. The authors need to focus on how to obtain an optimal membership function with minimum overhead. In the experiment (Gongxing and Yimin, 2009), authors collect the audit data of users' 7 day's normal operations as training data so as to get the user's behaviors. In this system, misuse detection can detect the attack attempt well, but due to no intrusion rule of impersonation attack and legal user attack in the misuse detection rule base, the two attacks can not be detected. Combined with the characteristics of misuse detection and anomaly detection, designs and realizes a new type of intrusion detection system with adaptive ability and applies the Apriori algorithm based on Trie tree to the database intrusion detection system to improve the generation efficiency of rule base.

7. Conclusions and future directions

In the recent years, IDS have slowly changed from host based application to a distributed systems that involves a variety of operating systems. The challenges that lie ahead of us for intrusion detection system, particularly for hybrid systems are huge. First, is the inability to reduce the number of false positives that prevents from intrusion detection systems being deployed widespread. As reported (Varun, 2009), the intrusion detection systems crash because of its in-ability to withstand the heavy load of false alarms. Second, the time take to process the huge amount of data is mounting, a process to reduce the time taken should be considered. Third, there is a lack of standard evaluation dataset that can simulate the real time network environments. The existing evaluation data set DARPA/Lincoln labs are a decade old and they are currently being used to evaluate any intrusion detection systems. There is a need to create a new data set, where it could be used to evaluate the intrusion detection systems for the dynamic topologies. Finally, our system crashed, as it could not withstand the traffic for more than three weeks without restarting, and that issue has to be sorted out using a high-end hardware and systematically re-tuned source code.

8. References

Aickelin, U., P. Bentley, et al. (2003). Danger theory: The link between ais and ids. *Proceedings of Second International Conference on Artificial Immune Systems (ICARIS-03)*,147-155.

Aly El-Semary, Janica Edmonds, et al. (2006). Applying Data Mining of Fuzzy Association rules to Network Intrusion Detection. *Proceedings of IEEE workshop on Information Assurance*,100-107.

Axelsson, S. (1998). Research in intrusion-detection systems: a survey. Goteborg, Sweden,, Department of Computer Engineering, Chalmers University of Technology.

Barbará, D., J. Couto, et al. (2001). ADAM: a testbed for exploring the use of data mining in intrusion detection. *ACM SIGMOD* 30(Special):pp. 15-24

Breiman, L. (2001). Random forests. *Machine Learning* 45(-):pp. 5-32

Bridges, S. M. and R. B. Vaughn (2000). Fuzzy data mining and genetic algorithms applied to intrusion detection. *Proceedings of National Information Systems Security Conference* Baltimore.

Cannady, J. (1999). Artificial Neural Networks for Misuse Detection. *Proceedings of National Information Systems Security Conference*,443-456, Arlington.

Cansian A, M., Moreira E, et al. (1997). Network intrusion detection using neural networks. *Proceedings of International conference on computational intelligence and multimedia applications ICCMA*.

Debar, H., M. Dacier, et al. (1998). A workbech for Intrusion detection systems. *IBM Zurich Research Laboratory*:pp.

Diaz-Gomez. and D. F. Hougen (2005). Analysis and mathematical justification of a fitness function used in an intrusion detection system. *Proceedings of Genetic and Evolutionary Computation Conference*,1591-1592, ACM.

Dickerson, J. E. and J. A. Dickerson (2000). Fuzzy Network Profiling for Intrusion Detection. *Proceedings of 19th International Conference of the North American Fuzzy Information Processing Society*,301-306, Atlanta.

Dokas, P., L. Ertoz, et al. (2002). Data Mining for Network Intrusion Detection. *Proceedings of National Science Foundation Workshop on Next Generation Data Mining*,21-31.

Girardin, L. and D. Brodbeck (1998). A Visual Approach or Monitoring Logs. *Proceedings of 12th System Administration Conference*,299-308.

Gongxing, W. and H. Yimin (2009). Design of a new Intrusion detection system based on database. *Proceedings of International conference on signal processing systems*,814-817.

Hosmer, H. (1993). Security is fuzzy!: applying the fuzzy logic paradigm to the multipolicy paradigm. *Proceedings of 1992-1993 Workshop on New Security Paradigms*,175-184, Little Compton.

Hossain, M., Bridges Susan M, et al. (2003). Adaptive intrusion detection with data mining. *Proceedings of IEEE Conference on Systems, Man and Cybernetics*,3097-3103.

Jianhui, L., T. HUANG, et al. (2008). A Fast Fuzzy Set Intrusion Detection Model. *Proceedings of 2008 International Symposium on Knowledge Acquisition and Modeling*,601-605, ACM.

Kai, H., C. Min, et al. (2007). Hybrid Intrusion Detection with Weighted Signature Generation over Anomalous Internet Episodes. *IEEE Treansactions on dependable and secure computing* 4(1):pp. 41 55

Kephart. J (1994). A biologically inspired immune system for computers. *Proceedings of Fourth International Workshop on Synthesis and Simulatoin of Living Systems, Artificial Life*,130-139.

Kim, J. (2003). Integrating artificial immune algorithms for intrusion detection. Department of Computer Science. London, University College London: 190.

Kuok, C., A. Fu, et al. (1999). Mining Fuzzy Assocication Rules in Databases. *The ACM SIGMOID Record* 27(1):pp. 41-46

Lee, W. (2001). A Data Mining framework for construction features and models for intrusion detection systems, Columbia University: 200.

Li, W. (2006). Using Genetic Algorithm for Network Intrusion Detection, Department of Computer Science and Engineering, Mississippi State University,: 10.

Lippmann, R. P., D. J. Fried, et al. (2000). Evaluating Intrusion Detection Systems : The 1998 DARPA Offline Intrusion Detection Evaluation. *DARPA Information Survivability Conference and Exposition* 2:pp. 12-26

Lippmann. R. and Cunningham. R. (1999). Improving Intrusion Detection performance using Keyword selection and Neural Networks. *Proceedings of Proceedings of Recent Advances in Intrusion Detection*,223-230, Indiana.

Lunt, T. F. (1993). Detecting Intruders in Computer Systems. *Proceedings of Conference on Auditing and Computer Technology*.

Manganaris, S., M. Christensen, et al. (2000). A data mining analysis of RTID alarms. *Computer Networks* 34(4):pp. 571-577

Me, L. (1998). GASSATA, a Genetic Algorithm as an alternative Tool for Security Audit Trials Analysis. *Proceedings of 1st International workshop on Recent Advances in Intrusion Detection*,11, Belgium.

Mitrokotsa, A., K. Nikos, et al. (2007). Towards an Effective Intrusion Response Engine Combined with Intrusion Detection in Ad Hoc Networks. *Proceedings of The Sixth Annual Mediterranean Ad Hoc Networking WorkShop*,137-145.

Ozgur, D., T. Murat, et al. (2005). An intelligent intrusion detection system (IDS) for anomaly and misuse detection in computer networks. *Expert Systems and Applications* 29(4):pp. 713-722

Richard, K. and V. Giovanni (2002). Intrusion Detection: A Brief History and Overview. Security and Privacy: 27-30.

Ryan. J., Lin. M., et al. (1998). Intrusion Detection with Neural Networks. *Advances in Neural Information Processing Systems* 10:pp.

Sabahi, F. and A. Movaghar (2008). Intrusion Detection: A Survey. *Proceedings of Third International Conference on Systems and Networks Communications*,23-26.

Sarafijanovic, S. and J. Boudec (2003). An artificial immune system approach with secondary response for misbehavior detection in mobile ad-hoc networks., Ecole Polytechnique Federale de Lausanne.

Scarfone, K. and M. Peter (2007). Guide to Intrusion Detection and Prevention Systems, National Institute of Standards and Technology: 127.

Shanmugam, B. and N. B. Idris (2009). Improved Intrusion Detection System Using Fuzzy Logic for Detecting Anamoly and Misuse Type of Attacks, International Conference of Soft Computing and Pattern Recognition, 2009 pp.212-217.

Somayaji, A., H. Steven, et al. (1997). Principles of a Computer Immune System. *Proceedings of New Security Paradigms Workshop*.

Su., M.-Y., G.-J. Yu., et al. (2009). A real time network intrusion detection system for large-scale attacks based on an incremental mining approach. *Computers and Security* 28(5):pp. 301-309

Suhail, O., S. Vaclav, et al. (2008). Using Genetic Algorithm Approach in Intrusion Detection Systems Techniques. *Proceedings of 7th Computer Information Systems and Industrial Management Applications*,300-307.

Su-Yun, W. and Y. Ester (2008). Data mining-based intrusion detection. *Expert Systems with Applications* 36(3):pp. 5605-5612

Tajbakhsh, A., M. Rahmati, et al. (2006). A new classification approach using fuzzy association rules. *Proceedings of 11th International CSI computer conference*,263-270.

Tajbakhsh, A., M. Rahmati, et al. (2009). Intrusion detection using fuzzy association rules. *Applied Soft Computing* 9(2):pp. 462-469

Tombini, E., H. Debar, et al. (2004). A serial combination of anomaly and misuse IDSes applied to HTTP traffic. *Proceedings of 20th Annual Computer Security Applications Conference*,428-437, Arizona.

Varun, C., B. Arindam, et al. (2009). Anomaly Detection - A Survey. *ACM Computing Surveys* 41(3):pp.

Wu.X and W. Banzhaf (2009). The use of computational intelligence in intrusion detection systems: A review. *Applied Soft Computing Journal*:pp. 35

Zhang, J. and M. Zulkernine (2006). A hybrid network intrusion detection technique using random forests. *Proceedings of First International Conference on Availability, Reliability and Security*,262-269., Vienna.

Zorana, B., J. M. Moya., et al. (2009). A Genetic Algorithm-based Solution for Intrusion Detection. *Journal of Information Assurance and Security* 4:pp. 192-199

9

Integral Misuse and Anomaly Detection and Prevention System

Yoseba K. Penya, Igor Ruiz-Agúndez and Pablo G. Bringas
DeustoTech - University of Deusto
Basque Country

1. Introduction

Nowadays hardly anyone will dare to deny the serious security problems that computer networks must cope with. Old-fashioned techniques for isolating the network and providing a secure access control are just impotent to stop the attack flood since the production of code with harmful intentions grows not only in number but in quality as well. Network Intrusion Detection Systems (NIDS) were developed with this scenario in mind.

Historically, the first efficient methodology was *misuse detection*, consisting on recognising malicious behaviours based upon a knowledge base. This technique successes on discovering threads already registered in its database but fails when detecting new, unknown menaces. *Anomaly detection* was specifically designed to address this shortcoming. This kind of techniques model the legitimate usage of the system in order to afterwards notice, evaluate and, if applies, avoid deviations from that normal profile. Still, its efficiency decreases dramatically when handling well-known attacks, specially if compared to misuse detections systems. As the reader may note, both do flop when applied to each other's natural domain.

More in detail, misuse detection is currently the most extended approach for intrusion prevention, mainly due to its efficiency and easy administration. It's philosophy is quite simple: based on a rule base that models a high number of network attacks, the system compares incoming traffic with the registered patterns to identify any of these attacks. Hence, it does not produce any false positive (since it always finds exactly what is registered) but it cannot detect any new threat. Further, any slightly-modified attack will pass unnoticed. And, finally, the knowledge base itself poses one of the biggest problems to misuse detection: as it grows, the time to search on it increases as well and, after some time, it may require too long to be used on real-time.

Anomaly detection systems, on the contrary, start not from malicious but from legitimate behaviour in order to model what it is allowed to do. Any deviation from this conduct will be seen as a potential menace. Unfortunately, this methodology is a two-sided sword since, though it allows to discover new unknown risks, it also produces false positives (i.e. packets or situations marked as attack when they are not). Moreover, anomaly detection presents a constant throughput since its knowledge base does not grow uncontrollably but gets *adapted* to new situations or behaviours. Again, an advantage is also source of problems because it is theoretically possible to make use of this continuous learning to little by little modify the knowledge so it ends seeing attacks as proper traffic (in NIDS jargon, this phenomenon is known as *session creeping*). This is, its knowledge tends to be unstable. Finally, anomaly detection, unlike misuse, demands high maintenance efforts (and costs). In sum, both alternatives present notable disadvantages that demand a new approach for network intrusion prevention.

In previous works (Bringas & Penya, 2008; Penya & Bringas, 2008b), we presented the first methodology to seamlessly integrate anomaly and misuse detection within one single system, giving a proper simultaneous response to either kind of attacks, unknown and well-known ones. This system uses a Bayesian Network that analyses incoming network packets learning to distinguish dangerous from harmless traffic. Moreover, we evaluate it against well-known and new attacks showing how it outperforms a well-established industrial NIDS.

Nevertheless, the training process of the Bayesian network is the Achilles' heel of this approach. Basically, that phase is devoted to create a knowledge representation model combining misuse and anomaly-based data that will be used later on and it may become intractable very fast in some extreme situations. Against this drawback, we propose the use of expert knowledge to enhance and optimise the design of the NIDS, shortening subsequently the training process. This expert knowledge is represented as a set of hypotheses that must be verified to justify their utility. In this way, we have tested our approach with several samples of data showing that all the hypotheses assumed were true and, therefore, that the proposed methodology to trim down the design and training processes yields an optimal Bayesian network for Intrusion Detection.

Finally, there are a number of problems and difficulties that arose in the integration process that we solved as well; this work will also describe them as well. In summary, this article presents a comprehensive survey of our work integrating misuse and anomaly prevention detection in one single system (Bringas & Penya, 2008; Penya & Bringas, 2008b; Bringas & Penya, 2009; Penya & Bringas, 2008a; Ruiz-Agundez et al., 2010).

The rest of the article is organised as follows. In section 2, we introduce the general architecture of the system to depict the big picture. In section 3, we detail the Bayesian Network, including its entire obtaining process. In section 4, we discuss the results obtained. In section 5, we present the hypotheses assumed and demonstrate them true. Section 6 is devoted to explain problems experimented and the solution adopted, and, finally, section 7 concludes and draws the avenues of future works.

2. Architecture

The internal design of ESIDE-Depian, our integrated anomaly and misuse detector system is principally determined by its dual nature. Being both a misuse and anomaly detection system requires answering to sometimes clashing needs and demands. This is, it must be able to simultaneously offer efficient response against both well-known and zero-day attacks. In order to ease the way to this goal, ESIDE-Depian has been conceived and deployed in a modular way that allows decomposing of the problem into several smaller units. Thereby, Snort[1] (a rule-based state of the art Misuse Detection System, see (Roesch, 1999), has been integrated to improve the training procedure to increase the accuracy of ESIDE-Depian. Following a strategy proven successful in this area, (Alipio et al., 2003), the reasoning engine we present here is composed of a number of Bayesian experts working over a common knowledge representation model.

The Bayesian experts must cover all possible areas where a menace may rise. In this way, there are 5 Bayesian experts in ESIDE-Depian, as follows: 3 of them deal with packet headers of TCP, UDP, ICMP and IP network protocols, the so-called TCP-IP, UDP-IP and ICMP-IP

[1] Available at http://www.snort.org/

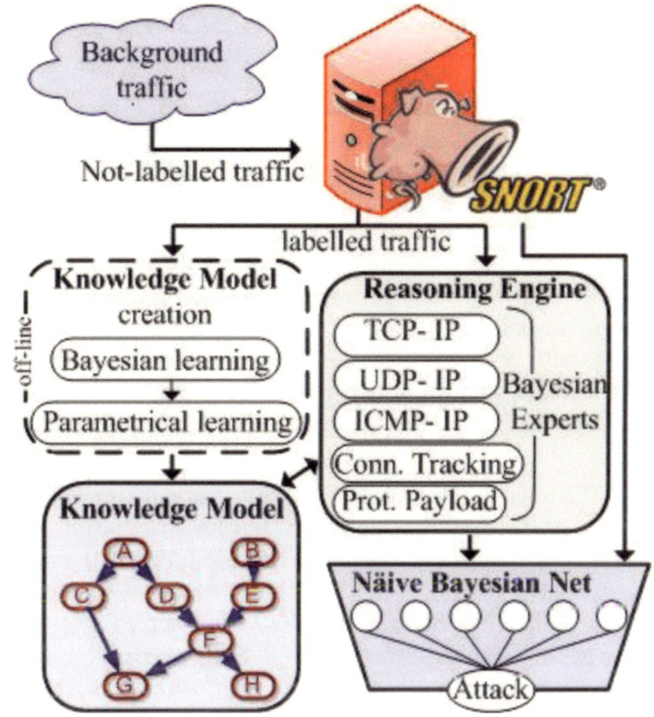

Fig. 1. ESIDE-Depian general architecture

expert modules. A further one, the Connection Tracking Expert, analyses potential temporal dependencies between TCP network events and, finally, the Protocol Payload Expert in charge of the packet payload analysis. In order to obtain the knowledge representation model, each expert carries out separately a Snort-driven supervised learning process on its expertise area. Therefore, the final knowledge representation model is the sum of the individual ones obtained by each expert. Fig. 1 shows the general ESIDE-Depian architecture.

3. Bayesian-network-based IDS

The obtaining of the knowledge representation model in an automated manner can be achieved in an unsupervised or supervised way. Typically, unsupervised learning approaches don't have into consideration expert knowledge about well-known attacks. They achieve their own decisions based on several mathematical representations of distance between observations from the target system, revealing themselves as ideal for performing Anomaly Detection. On the other hand, supervised learning models do use expert knowledge in their making of decisions, in the line of Misuse Detection paradigm, but usually present high-cost administrative requirements. Thus, both approaches present important advantages and several shortcomings. Being both ESIDE-Depian, it is necessary to set a balanced solution that enables to manage in an uniform way both kinds of knowledge. Therefore, ESIDE-Depian uses not only Snort information gathering capabilities, but also Snort's decision-based network traffic labelling. Thereby, the learning processes inside ESIDE-Depian can be considered as automatically-supervised Bayesian learning, divided into the following phases. Please note that this sequence only applies for the standard generation process followed by the Packet Header Parameter Analysis experts, (i.e. the TCP-IP, UDP-IP and ICMP-IP expert modules):

- *Traffic sample obtaining*: First we need to establish the information source in order to gather the sample. This set usually includes normal traffic (typically gathered from the network by sniffing, ARP-poisoning or so), as well as malicious traffic generated by the well-known arsenal of hacking tools such as (Metasploit, 2006), etc. Subsequently, the Snort Intrusion Detection System embedded in ESIDE-Depian adds labelling information regarding the legitimacy or malice of the network packets. Specifically, Snort's main decision about a packet is added to the set of detection parameters, receiving the name of attack variable. In this way, it is possible to obtain a complete sample of evidences, including, in the formal aspect of the sample, both protocol fields and also Snort labelling information. Therefore, it combines knowledge about normal behaviour and also knowledge about well-known attacks, or, in other words, information necessary for Misuse Detection and for Anomaly Detection.
- *Structural Learning*: The next step is devoted to define the operational model ESIDE-Depian should work within. With this goal in mind, we have to provide logical support for knowledge extracted from network traffic information. Packet parameters need to be related into a Bayesian structure of nodes and edges, in order to ease the later conclusion inference over this mentioned structure. In particular, the PC-Algorithm (Spirtes et al., 2001) is used here to achieve the structure of causal and/or correlative relationships among given variables from data. In other words, the PC-Algorithm uses the traffic sample data to define the Bayesian model, representing the whole set of dependence and independence relationships among detection parameters. Due to its high requirements in terms of computational and temporal resources, this phase is usually performed off-line.
- *Parametric Learning*: The knowledge representation model fixed so far is a qualitative one. Therefore, the following step is to apply parametric learning in order to obtain the quantitative model representing the strength of the collection of previously learned relationships, before the exploitation phase began. Specifically, ESIDE-Depian implements maximum likelihood estimate (Murphy, 2001) to achieve this goal. This method completes the Bayesian model obtained in the previous step by defining the quantitative description of the set of edges between parameters. This is, structural learning finds the structure of probability distribution functions among detection parameters, and parametric learning fills this structure with proper conditional probability values. The high complexity of this phase suggests a deeper description, that is accomplished in section 3.
- *Bayesian Inference*: Next, every packet capture from the target communication infrastructure needs one value for the posterior probability of a badness variable, (i.e. the Snort label), given the set of observable packet detection parameters. So, we need an inference engine based on Bayesian evidence propagation. More accurately, we use the Lauritzen and Spiegelhalter method for conclusion inference over junction trees, provided it is slightly more efficient than any other in terms of response time (Castillo et al., 1997). Thereby, already working in real time, incoming packets are analysed by this method (with the basis of observable detection parameters obtained from each network packet) to define the later probability of the attack variable. The continuous probability value produced here represents the certainty that an evidence is good or bad. Generally, a threshold based alarm mechanism can be added in order to get a balance between false positive and negative rates, depending on the context.

- *Adaptation*: Normally, the system operation does not keep a static on-going way, but usually presents more or less important deviations as a result of service installation or reconfiguration, deployment of new equipment, and so on. In order to keep the knowledge representation model updated with potential variations in the normal behaviour of the target system, ESIDE-Depian uses the general sequential/incremental maximum likelihood estimates (Murphy, 2001) (in a continuous or periodical way) in order to achieve continuous adaptation of the model to potential changes in the normal behaviour of traffic.

3.1 Connection tracking and payload analysis Bayesian experts knowledge representation model generation

The Connection Tracking expert attends to potential temporal influence among network events within TCP-based protocols (Estevez-Tapiador et al., 2003), and, therefore, it requires a structure that allows to include the concept of time (predecessor, successor) in its model. Similarly, the Payload Analysis expert, devoted to packet payload analysis, needs to model state transitions among symbols and tokens in the payload (following the strategy proposed in (Kruegel & Vigna, 2003). Usually, Markov models are used in such contexts due to their capability to represent problems based on stochastic state transitions. Nevertheless, the Bayesian concept is even more suited since it not only includes representation of time (in an inherent manner), but also provides generalisation of the classical Markov models adding features for complex characterisation of states. Specifically, the Dynamic Bayesian Network (DBN) concept is commonly recognised as a superset of Hidden Markov Models (Ghahramani, 1998), and, among other capabilities, it can represent dependence and independence relationships between parameters within one common state (i.e. in the traditional static Bayesian style), and also within different chronological states.

Thus, ESIDE-Depian implements a fixed two-node DBN structure to emulate the Markov-Chain Model (with at least the same representational power and also the possibility to be extended in the future with further features) because full-exploded use of Bayesian concepts can remove several restrictions of Markov-based designs. For instance, it is not necessary to establish the first-instance structural learning process used by the packet header analysis experts since the structure is clear in beforehand.

Moreover, according to (Estevez-Tapiador et al., 2003) and (Kruegel & Vigna, 2003), the introduction of an artificial parameter may ease this kind of analysis. Respectively, the Connection Tracking expert defines an artificial detection parameter, named TCP-h-flags (which is based on an arithmetical combination of TCP header flags) and the Payload Analysis expert uses the symbol and token (in fact, there are two Payload Analysis experts: one for token analysis and another for symbol analysis).

Finally, traffic behaviour (and so TCP flags temporal transition patterns) as well as payload protocol lexical and syntactical patterns may differ substantially depending on the sort of service provided from each specific equipment (i.e. from each different IP address and from each specific TCP destination port). To this end, ESIDE-Depian uses a multi-instance schema, with several Dynamic Bayesian Networks, one for each combination of TCP destination address and port. Afterwards, in the exploitation phase, Bayesian inference can be performed from real-time incoming network packets. In this case, the a-priori fixed structure suggests the application of the expectation and maximisation algorithm (Murphy, 2001), in order to calculate not the posterior probability of attack, but the probability which a single packet fits the learned model with.

3.2 Naive Bayesian network of the expert modules

Having different Bayesian modules is a two-fold strategy. On the one hand, the more specific expertise of each module allows them to deliver more accurate verdicts but, on the other hand, there must be a way to solve possible conflicting decisions. In other words, a unique measure must emerge from the diverse judgements.

To this end, ESIDE-Depian presents a two-tiered schema where the first layer is composed of the results from the expert modules and the second layer includes only one class parameter: the most conservative response among those provided by Snort and the expert modules community (i.e. in order to prioritises the absence of false negatives in front of false positives). Thus, both layers form, in fact, a Naive Bayesian Network (as shown in Fig. 1 and Fig. 2).

Such a Naive classifier (Castillo et al., 1997) has been proposed sometimes in Network Intrusion Detection, mostly for Anomaly Detection. This approach provides a good balance between representative power and performance, and also affords interesting flexibility capabilities which allow, for instance, ESIDE-Depian's dynamical enabling and disabling of expert modules, in order to support heavy load conditions derived e.g. from denial of service attacks.

Now, Naive Bayesian Network parameters should have a discrete nature which, depending on the expert, could not be the case. To remove this problem, ESIDE-Depian allows the using of the aforementioned set of administratively-configured threshold conditioning functions.

Finally, the structure of the Naive Bayesian Network model is fixed in beforehand, assuming the existence of conditional independence hypothesis among every possible cause and the standing of dependency edges between these causes and the effect or class. Therefore, here is also not necessary to take into consideration any structural learning process for it; only sequential parametric learning must be performed, while the expert modules produce their packet classifying verdicts during their respective parametric learning stages.

Once this step is accomplished, the inference of unified conclusions and the sequential adaptation of knowledge can be provided in the same way mentioned before. Fig. 2 details the individual knowledge models and how do they fit to conform the general one.

3.3 The structural learning challenge

As it was outlined before, Structural Learning allows modelling in a completely automated way the set of dependence and independence relationships that can exist between the different detection parameters. Nevertheless, in situations that have a large volume of evidences and detection parameters with many different possible states, the aforementioned PC Algorithm (as well as similar alternative methods) presents very high computational requirements. Moreover, depending on the inner complexity of the set of relationships, those requirements can grow even more. Therefore, the complexity depends entirely on the nature of data, rendering it unpredictable so far. In this way, this task may be sometimes too resource-demanding for small and medium computing platforms. Against this background, we have developed a method that splits the traffic sample horizontally in order to reduce the complexity the structural learning process. This method is detailed next.

First of all, please note that the different structural learning methods commonly use a significance parameter in order to define in a flexible manner the strength that a dependence relationship needs in fact to be considered as a definitive one in the Bayesian Network. Thus, this significance parameter can be used to relativise the concept of equality required in the independence tests implemented inside the learning algorithms; in particular, inside the PC Algorithm. On the one hand, a high significance value produces a higher number

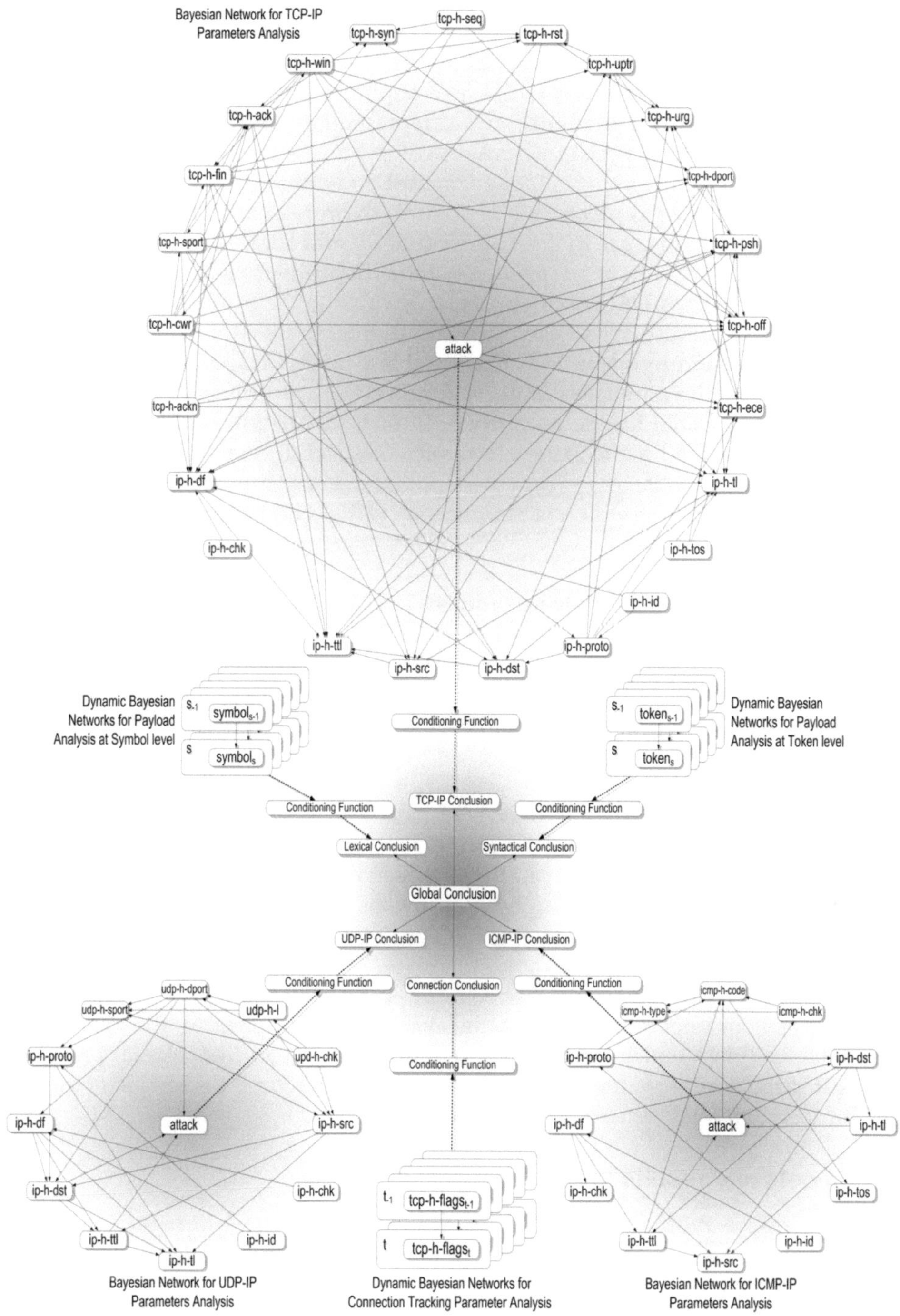

Fig. 2. ESIDE-Depian general architecture

of connections in the Bayesian model, with an increase on the degree of representativeness but also with larger requirements in terms of main memory and computational power and the possibility that overfitting occurs. On the other hand, a low significance value usually produces a sparse Bayesian Network, with lower requirements but also less semantic power. Therefore, in order to achieve a trade-off between representativeness and throughput, we have implemented the expansion of the structural learning process through multiple significance levels. More accurately, we have used the seven most representative magnitude-orders.

Once the expansion process is planned, it is possible to proceed with the structural learning process itself, applied in this case to the TCP-IP, UDP-IP and ICMP-IP protocols, which were defined a priori as a set of working dependence and independence hypotheses based on each different RFC. It is also possible to apply the PC Algorithm to the entire traffic sample in order to verify the accuracy of these hypotheses. In our case, this process was estimated to long 3,591 hours (150 days) of continuous learning. Thus, and also considering that this is a generalised problem, we propose the parallelisation of the collection of learning processes, depending on the equipment available for the researcher. In fact, this parallelisation, performed over 60 computers at the same time managed to reduce the overall time to 59.85 nominal hours. Finally, one instance of the PC Algorithm was applied to every fragment, for each of the four data-sets, and with the seven different significance values, 1197 partial Bayesian structures were obtained at this point.

3.4 Partial Bayesian structures unifying process

The collection of partial Bayesian structures obtained in the previous phase must be unified into an unique Bayesian Network that gives a full representation of the application domain. With this purpose, we defined a statistical measure based on the frequency of apparition in the set of partial structures of each dependence relationship between every two detection parameters.

In this way, it is possible to calculate one single Bayesian structure, for each of the 7 significance levels and for each of the 4 data sets, remaining only 28 partial structures from the initial 1197. The next step will achieve the definitive unifying. To this end, we use the average value for each of the edges between variables, which allows us to reach the desired balance between representativeness and throughput by means of the subsequent selective addition to the Bayesian model of those edges above a specific and configurable (depending on the application domain) significance threshold.

Still, both the horizontal splitting of the traffic sample and also the significance-based expansion present an important problem: the cycles that can appear in the Bayesian model obtained after unifying, which render the model invalid. An additional step prevents such cycles by using the average value obtained before as a criteria for the selection of the weakest edge in the cycle, which is the one to be deleted.

4. Experiments and results

In order to measure the performance of ESIDE-Depian, we have designed two different kinds of experiments. In the first group, the network suffers well-known attacks (i.e. Misuse Detection) and, in the second group, zero-day attacks (i.e. Anomaly Detection), putting each aspect of the double nature of ESIDE-Depian to the test. In both cases, the system was fed with a simulation of network traffic comprising more than 700.000 network packets that were sniffed during one-hour capture from a University network. The first experiment (corresponding to Misuse Detection) aimed to compare Snort and the Packet

Indicator	TCP	UDP	ICMP
Analysed net packets	699.568	5.130	1.432
Snort's hits	38	0	450
ESIDE-Depian's hits	38	0	450
Anomalous packets	600	2	45
False negatives	0	0	0
Potential false positives	0,08%	0,03%	3,14%

Table 1. Bayesian expert modules for TCP, UDP and ICMP header analysis results.

Header Parameters Analysis experts. To this end, Snort's rule-set-based knowledge was used as the main reference for the labelling process, instantiated through Sneeze Snort-stimulator (Roesch, 1999). The sample analysed was a mixture of normal and poisoned traffic. Table 1 details the results of this experiment.

As it can be seen, the three experts achieved a 100% rate of hitting success. Anyway, such results are not surprising, since ESIDE-Depian integrates Snort's knowledge and if Snort is able to detect an attack, ESIDE-Depian should do so. Nevertheless, not only the number of hits is important; the number of anomalous packets detected reflects the level of integration between the anomaly and the misuse detection part of ESIDE-Depian. In fact, the latter can be highlighted as the most important achievement of ESIDE-Depian: detecting unusual packets preserving the misuse detection advantages at the same time. Concerning potential false rates, it is possible to observe that very good rates are reached for TCP and UDP protocols (according to the values defined in (Crothers, 2002) to be not human-operator-exhausting), but not so good for ICMP. Table 1 shows, however, a significant bias in the number of attacks introduced in the ICMP traffic sample (above 30%), and labelled as so by Snort; thus, it is not strange the slightly excessive rate of anomalous packets detected here by ESIDE-Depian.

In the second experiment (also corresponding to misuse detection), the goal was to test the other expert modules (Connection Tracking and Payload Analysis). With this objective in mind, a set of attacks against a representation of popular services were fired through several hacking tools such as (Metasploit, 2006). The outcome of this test is summarised in Table 2.

Indicator	Conn. Tracking	Payload Analysis (Symbol)	Payload Analysis (Token)
Analysed net packets	226.428	2.676	2.676
Attacks in sample	29	139	19
ESIDE Depian hits	29	139	19
Anomalous net packets	0	0	3
False negatives	0	0	0
Pot. false positives	0%	0%	0,11%

Table 2. Bayesian expert modules for TCP, UDP and ICMP header analysis results.

Protocol	Artificial Network Anomaly	Snort	ESIDE-Depian
TCP	packit -nnn -s 10.12.206.2 -d 10.10.10.100 -F SFP -D 1023	x	√
TCP	packit nnn -s 10.12.206.2 -d 10.10.10.100 -F SAF	x	√
UDP	packit -t udp -s 127.0.0.1 -d 10.10.10.2 -o 0x10 -n 1 -T ttl -S 13352 -D 21763	x	√
UDP	packit -t udp -s 127.0.0.1 -d 10.10.10.2 -o 0x50 -n 0 -T ttl -S 13352 -D 21763	x	√
ICMP	packit -i eth0 -t icmp -K 17 -C 0 -d 10.10.10.2	x	√

Table 3. Example of Zero-day attacks detected by ESIDE-Depian and not by Snort.

As we see, ESIDE-Depian prevailed in all cases with a 0% rate of false negatives and a 100% of hitting rate success. Still, not only Snort's knowledge and normal traffic behaviour absorption was tested; the third experiment intended to assess ESIDE-Depian's performance with zero-day attacks. With this idea in mind, a sample of artificial anomalies (Lee et al., 2001) was prepared with Snort's rule set as basis and crafted (by means of the tool Packit) with slight variations aiming to avoid Snort's detection (i.e. Zero-day attacks unnoticeable for misuse detection systems). Some of these attacks are detailed next in Table 3.
Note that overcoming of Snort's expert knowledge only has sense in those expert modules using this knowledge. This is, in protocol header specialised modules, because the semantics of Snort's labelling does not fit the morphology of payload and dynamic nature parameters.

5. Optimal knowledge base design

As we have shown, ESIDE-Depian is able to simultaneously offer efficient response against both well-known and zero-day attacks. In order to ease the way to this goal, our system has been conceived and deployed in a modular way that allows decomposing of the problem into several smaller units (see section 2). Still, the design and training process of the Bayesian network (BN) demanded huge computational efforts that prevented it from being applied in the real world. Against this background, in this section we present a methodology to enhance the design of the BN (and, thus, shorten the training process) by using expert knowledge. This strategy has been previously used in data mining classifiers (Sinha & Zhao, 2008), for normalizing and binning gene expression data in BN (Helman et al., 2004) or for generalized partition testing via Bayes linear methods (Coolen et al., 2001).
As already introduced in section 3, Bayesian networks require two learning steps to be ready to infer results. The first one is the *structural learning* process that obtains the probability distribution table associated to each variable. The second one is the *parametric learning* process that refines the initial graph. Finally, the system uses a Naive Bayesian network to unify the different experts providing an excellent balance between knowledge representation capacity and performance. It assumes the existence of *conditional independence* hypotheses within every possible cause and the standing of dependency edges between these causes and the effect or class applicable to this problem domain. These hypotheses are the representation of the experts knowledge that tunes the Bayesian network design and training, creating the optimal

network.

5.1 Establishing the hypothesis of dependence and independence

Due to the fact the structural learning methods are able to infer by themselves the relations of dependence and independence of the structure, expert knowledge can refine the resulting model and, hence, the exploitation of the Bayesian network is done in the most efficient way. In this way, we use hypothesis of dependence and independence to refine our knowledge representation model. In particular, the hypotheses are based on the specific issues of four network protocols (IP, ICMP, TCP and UDP). The expert knowledge is based on the following six hypotheses of dependence and independence:

Hypothesis 1: Dependence between TCP and IP. The set of the detection parameters of the TCP protocol is dependent of the set of the detection parameters of the IP, and vice versa.

Hypothesis 2: Dependence between UDP and IP. The set of the detection parameters of the UDP protocol is dependent of the set of the detection parameters of the IP, and vice versa.

Hypothesis 3: Dependence between ICMP and IP. The set of the detection parameters of the ICMP protocol is dependent of the set of the detection parameters of the IP, and vice versa.

Hypothesis 4: Independence between TCP and UDP. The set of the detection parameters of the TCP protocol is dependent of the set of the detection parameters of the UDP, and vice versa.

Hypothesis 5: Independence between TCP and ICMP. The set of the detection parameters of the TCP protocol is independent of the set of the detection parameters of the ICMP, and vice versa.

Hypothesis 6: Independence between UDP and ICMP. The set of the detection parameters of the UDP protocol is independent of the set of the detection parameters of the ICMP, and vice versa.

These hypotheses are supported by the respective set of *Request For Comments (RFC)* of each protocol. An empirical demonstration of the hypotheses is done demonstrating that the knowledge representation model generated from them can be successfully used in the reasoning engine.
Besides, the heterogeneity of the detection parameters headers (information used by the protocols), and data (information used by the users) themselves implies a different formalization for each case. The analysis model is static (based on Bayesian networks) in the case of the head parameters and dynamic (based on Dynamic Bayesian networks) in the case of data parameters. The first group forms an information entity and it is, therefore, susceptible of being used directly in the process of analysis. On the other hand, the second group represents a variable flow of information entities in both lexical and a syntactic levels that requires a specific analysis. Considering all this, another hypothesis is pointed out:

Hypothesis 7: Independence between head and data fields. The set of detection parameters corresponding to the head fields of IP, ICMP, TCP and UDP protocols is independent from the data fields of the corresponding protocols, and vice versa.

Finally, there is an additional aspect to consider. Since for this experiment only one time step is considered, it is not possible to have the second evidence required by the dynamic model. Please note that when more temporal steps are added this restriction disappears.

Hypothesis 8: Independence between static and dynamic parameters. In the case of one temporal step Dynamic Bayesian networks, the set of detection parameters used in the static analysis methods are independent from those used in the dynamic analysis methods, and vice versa.

The specification of the previous hypotheses of dependence and independence defines separated working areas, in which different analysis methods will be applied depending on the type of the detection parameter.
On one hand, we have the head parameters of all the protocols that can be treated in a homogeneous way. These cases can be introduced straightforward into the structural learning process. On the other hand, each protocol data has its own properties and therefore has to be resolved in an independent way. In the case of dynamic parameters, multiple evidences are required, and hence, they will have an independent treatment too.

5.2 Validation of the hypotheses

In order to assess the validity of the work hypothesis described in the previous section, we have performed different kinds of experiments. We start our experiments from the knowledge representation model made up of different Bayesian networks that form the reasoning engine. From then on, and considering the hypotheses of dependence and independence, we analyse the obtained results of the structural learning process. As the results confirm the hypotheses of dependence and independence, the *RFC* specifications of each protocol are ratified. Finally, a knowledge representation model based on the different Bayesian networks can be built.
Taking that into account, and with the objective of minimising the possible appearance of noise in the results that could affect the final conclusions about the hypothesis, we have set a threshold value. Above this threshold value a link between two variables will not be representative. According to our methodology, two protocols will be independent *if and only if* there are no representative relations between the set of parameters of either of them. The hypotheses of dependence and independence are proved to be true:

- **Hypothesis 1: Dependence between TCP and IP.** Table 4 shows the relations between the parameters of TCP and IP, verifying that there are many significant links between the corresponding detection parameters of each protocol, in both ways. Therefore, there are variables of the TCP protocol Bayesian network that depend on variables of the IP protocol, and vice versa. Hence, the hypothesis of dependence between TCP and IP is confirmed.

- **Hypothesis 2: Dependence between UDP and IP.** Equally, as table 5 show the data of the experiment points out the relation between the head parameters of the UDP and IP protocols. There are enough significant links between the detection parameters of both protocols, in both ways. Therefore, there are variables of the UDP protocol in the Bayesian network that depend on variables of the IP protocol, and vice versa. Hence, the hypothesis of dependence between UDP and IP is also confirmed.

- **Hypothesis 3: Dependence between ICMP and IP.** Table 6 show the case of ICMP and IP protocols, the data of the experiment points out the relation between the head parameters of both protocols. There are enough significant links between the detection parameters, in both ways. Therefore, there are variables of the ICMP protocol in the Bayesian network that depend on variables of the IP protocol, and vice versa. Hence, the hypothesis of dependence between ICMP and IP is confirmed similarly.

child\parent	ip-h-dst	ip-h-src	ip-h-proto	ip-h-tll	ip-h-df	ip-h-tl	ip-h-tos
tcp-h-uptr	-	-	15,61	-	-	-	-
tcp-h-win	2,40	2,09	-	2,89	4,46	-	13,55
tcp-h-cwr	-	0,49	-	-	-	31,32	-
tcp-h-ece	-	-	11,08	-	-	-	2,33
tcp-h-psh	-	-	6,63	0,71	-	-	1,38
tcp-h-urg	-	-	12,43	-	-	-	-
tcp-h-ack	-	-	-	-	-	-	2,17
tcp-h-rst	-	-	1,31	1,08	1,92	-	-
tcp-h-syn	0,71	-	-	-	1,79	-	-
tcp-h-fin	-	-	-	1,02	-	-	-
tcp-h-off	-	-	-	1,98	-	-	28,74
tcp-h-ackn	-	-	-	-	-	-	-
tcp-h-seq	-	-	-	-	1,74	-	-
tcp-h-dport	3,84	1,08	-	-	-	9,04	-
tcp-h-sport	8,01	3,57	-	-	-	8,40	-

Table 4. Frequency of links appearance in the Bayesian network for relations of dependence of IP parameters over TCP parameters

- **Hypothesis 4: Independence between TCP and UDP.** Table 7 show the hypothesis of independence between TCP and UDP, the data of the experiment points out the independence between the detection parameters of both protocols, in none of both ways. There are not enough significant links between the detection parameters, in none of both ways. Therefore, there are not variables of the TCP protocol that depend on the variables of the UDP protocol, and vice versa. Hence, the hypothesis of independence between TCP and UDP is also verified.

- **Hypothesis 5: Independence between TCP and ICMP.** Similarly, table 8 shows that the data of the experiment points out the independence between the detection parameters of TCP and ICMP protocols, in any way. There are not enough significant links between the detection parameters, in any way. Therefore, there are not variables of the TCP protocol that depend on the variables of the ICMP protocol, and vice versa. Hence, the hypothesis of independence between TCP and ICMP is also proved.

child\parent	udp-h-chk	udp-h-l	udp-h-dport	udp-h-sport
ip-h-dst	-	-	1,61	-
ip-h-src	9,65	1,02	3,88	1,79
ip-h-proto	-	-	2,04	3,65
ip-h-tll	-	-	-	-
ip-h-df	-	-	1,02	-
ip-h-id	-	-	-	-
ip-h-tl	-	-	-	-
ip-h-tos	-	-	-	-
ip-h-hl	-	-	-	-

Table 5. Frequency of links appearance in the Bayesian network for relations of dependence of UDP parameters over IP parameters

child\parent	icmp-hchk	icmp-hcode	icmp-htype
ip-h-dst	-	-	-
ip-h-src	-	-	-
ip-h-proto	-	2,90	-
ip-h-tll	-	-	-
ip-h-df	-	-	-
ip-h-id	-	-	-
ip-h-tl	-	-	-
ip-h-tos	-	8,94	-
ip-h-hl	-	-	-

Table 6. Frequency of links appearance in the Bayesian network for relations of dependence of ICMP parameters over IP parameters

- **Hypothesis 6: Independence between UDP and ICMP.** Finally, in table 9 and table 10, the data of the experiment points out the independence between the detection parameters of UDP and ICMP protocols, in anyway. There are not enough significant links between the detection parameters, in none of both ways. Therefore, there are not variables of the UDP protocol that depend on the variables of the ICMP protocol, and vice versa. Hence, the hypothesis of independence between UDP and ICMP is also verified.

The validity of the hypotheses 7 and 8 is already proved by their set out. This is, the set of detection parameters corresponding to the head fields of IP, ICMP, TCP and UDP protocols is independent from the data fields of the corresponding protocols, and vice versa. In the case of one temporal step dynamic BN, the set of detection parameters used in the static analysis methods are independent from those used in the dynamic analysis methods, and vice versa. Since the results confirm the hypothesis of dependence and independence, the RFC specifications of each protocol are ratified. Therefore, a knowledge representation model

child\parent	udp-hchk	udp-h-l	udp-h-dport	udp-h-sport
tcp-h-uptr	0,49	-	2,86	-
tcp-h-win	-	-	-	-
tcp-h-cwr	-	-	-	-
tcp-h-ece	0,59	-	2,63	1,79
tcp-h-psh	-	1,79	1,79	0,59
tcp-h-urg	1,02	-	1,57	4,11
tcp-h-ack	-	-	-	-
tcp-h-rst	-	-	-	1,79
tcp-h-syn	-	-	-	-
tcp-h-fin	-	-	-	-
tcp-h-off	-	-	-	-
tcp-h-ackn	-	-	-	-
tcp-h-seq	-	-	-	-
tcp-h-dport	-	-	-	-
tcp-h-sport	-	-	-	-

Table 7. Frequency of links appearance in the Bayesian network for relations of dependence of UDP parameters over TCP parameters

child\parent	icmp-hchk	icmp-hcode	icmp-htype
tcp-h-uptr	-	2,86	-
tcp-h-win	-	-	-
tcp-h-cwr	-	-	-
tcp-h-ece	-	-	-
tcp-h-psh	-	0,59	-
tcp-h-urg	-	3,52	-
tcp-h-ack	-	-	-
tcp-h-rst	-	-	-
tcp-h-syn	-	-	-
tcp-h-fin	-	0,49	-
tcp-h-off	-	-	-
tcp-h-ackn	-	-	-
tcp-h-seq	-	-	-
tcp-h-dport	-	-	-
tcp-h-sport	-	-	-

Table 8. Frequency of links appearance in the Bayesian network for relations of dependence of ICMP parameters over TCP parameters

based on the different Bayesian networks can be built, decreasing in this way the complexity of the design of the BN and minimising its training process.

6. Problems and solutions

This section gives account of the main problems that emerged during the design and test phase. More accurately, they were:

- **Integration of Snort**: The first difficulty we faced was to find an effective way of integrating Snort in the system. Our first attempt placed the verdict of Snort at the same level as those of the Bayesian experts in the Naive classifier. This strategy failed to capture the real possibilities of Bayesian networks since it simply added the information generated by Snort at the end of the process, more as a graft than a real integrated part of the model. The key aspect in this situation was letting the Bayesian network absorb Snort's knowledge to be able to actually replace it. Therefore, in the next prototype we recast the role of Snort as a kind of advisor, both in training and in working time. In this way, the Bayesian experts use Snort's opinion on the badness of incoming packets in the learning procedure and afterwards and manage to exceed Snort's knowledge (Penya & Bringas, 2008b).
- **Different parameter nature**: The next challenge consisted on the different nature of the parameters that ESIDE-Depian has to control. Whereas TCP, UDP and ICMP are static and

child\parent	icmp-h-chk	icmp-h-code	icmp-h-type
udp-h-chk	-	-	-
udp-h-l	-	-	-
udp-h-dport	-	-	-
udp-h-sport	-	-	-

Table 9. Frequency of links appearance in the Bayesian network for relations of dependence of ICMP parameters over UDP parameters

child\parent	udp-h-chk	udp-h-l	udp-h-dport	udp-h-sport
icmp-h-chk	-	-	-	-
icmp-h-code	-	-	-	-
icmp-h-type	-	-	-	-

Table 10. Frequency of links appearance in the Bayesian network for relations of dependence of UDP parameters over ICMP parameters

refer exclusively to one packet (more accurately to its header), the connection tracking and payload analysis experts are dynamic and require the introduction of the time notion. In this way, the connection tracking expert checks if packets belong to an organised sequence of an attack, so time is needed to represent predecessor and successor events. Similarly, the payload analysis expert must model state transitions between symbols and tokens that appear on it. Thus, in the same way that different tests had to be performed (see (Penya & Bringas, 2008b), we had to prepare an special traffic sample tailored to the kind of traffic those expert should focus to inspect.

- **Disparity between good and bad traffic amount**: Another problem to tackle was the composition of the traffic sample used to train the first group of experts (TCP, UDP, ICMP). In order to help the acquisition of the initial reference knowledge in the training phase, the BN is fed with a traffic sample basically based on the attack-detection rules battery provided by Snort. Therefore, the training acquaints the BN with either kind of traffic simultaneously, *good* and *bad*. Still, due to the disparity in the amount of packets belonging to one or another, traces containing attacks have to be fed several times (in the so-called *presentation cycles*) in order to let the BN learn to evaluate them properly. In this way, the TCP expert required 2943 presentation cycles, the UDP expert 2 and the ICMP expert also 2. The high number of presentation cycles required by the TCP-IP expert to grasp the initial reference knowledge is due to the very high good/bad traffic ratio, much lower in the cases of UDP and ICMP.
- **Task parallelisation**: Bayesian networks require many computational resources. Thus, some of the tasks to be performed were designed in a parallel way to accelerate it. For instance, the structural learning was devoted concurrently in 60 computers. In this way, the traffic sample (about 900.000 packets) was divided in blocks of 10.000 of packets that were processed with the PC-Algorithm (see section 3). Moreover, already on real-time, each expert was placed in a different machine not only to divide the amount of resources consumed but also to prevent from having a single point of failure.
- **False positives and false negatives**: Finally, we coped with a usual problem related to anomaly detection systems: false positives (i.e. packets marked as potentially dangerous when they are harmless). In fact, minimising false positives is one of the pending challenges of this approach. Nevertheless, the double nature of ESIDE-Depian as anomaly and misuse detector reduces the presence of false positives to a minimum (Penya & Bringas, 2008b). False negatives, on the contrary, did threaten the system and, in this way, in the experiments accomplished in ESIDE-Depian, security was prioritized above comfort, so quantitative alarm-thresholds were set upon the production of the minimum false negatives, in spite of the false positive rates. It is possible to find application domains, e.g. anti-virus software, in which false positive numbers are the target to be optimized, in order not to saturate the final user or the system administrator. Also in these cases ESIDE-Depian is able to manage the detection problem, simply by the specific setting-up of the mentioned thresholds.

7. Conclusions and future works

Network Intrusion Detection Systems monitor local networks to separate legitimate from dangerous behaviours. According to their capabilities and goals, NIDS are divided into Misuse Detection Systems (which aim to detect well-known attacks) and Anomaly Detection Systems (which aim to detect zero-day attacks). So far, no system to our knowledge combines advantages of both without any of their disadvantages. Moreover, the use of historical data for analysis or sequential adaptation is usually ignored, missing in this way the possibility of anticipating the behaviour of the target system.

Our system addresses both needs. We present here an approach integrating Snort as Misuse detector trainer so the Bayesian Network of five experts is able to react against both Misuse and Anomalies. The Bayesian Experts are devoted to the analysis of different network protocol aspects and obtain the common knowledge model by means of separated Snort-driven automated learning process. A naive Bayesian network integrates the results of the experts, all the partial verdicts achieved by them. Since ESIDE-Depian has passed the experiments brilliantly, it is possible to conclude that ESIDE-Depian using of Bayesian Networking concepts allows to confirm an excellent basis for paradigm unifying Network Intrusion Detection, providing not only stable Misuse Detection but also effective Anomaly Detection capabilities, with only one flexible knowledge representation model and a well-proofed inference and adaptation bunch of methods.

Moreover, we have accurately studied how to create a model of knowledge representation. First of all, we obtained a representative data sample. Second, we defined how many temporal steps we were going to use for our experiment. Third, we established the hypothesis according to the expert knowledge. Fourth, we planned the process of structural learning and performed it. After this step, we obtained statistical metrics from the partial Bayesian networks. These partial fragments were unified and adapted before verifying the hypotheses of dependence and independence. Finally, we obtained the optimal structural definition of the knowledge representation model on which we performed parametric learning. According to this experiment, we have proved the validity of the hypotheses and obtained the optimal BN for Network Intrusion Detection Systems. This knowledge model is currently being used as the expert system of our own IDS architecture.

It is worth mentioning that the integration of misuse and anomaly was very challenging and we had to cope with the following problems. First of all, the most effective placement for Snort within the model. Then, the composition of these training samples posed also a problem, since the ratio between good and bad traffic was too low. Furthermore, is very resource demanding and, finally, integrating misuse and anomaly simultaneously prevented it from presenting a high rate of false negatives, which is a typical inconvenience of anomaly detectors, but, still, we had to cope with the problem of false negatives.

Future work will focus on the so-called *data-aging* problem. The constant feeding of upcoming data issues poses a new challenge to the Bayesian network: it extends and enhances its knowledge base but, in parallel, information about these new traffic has too less importance compared to older ones, and therefore, predictions about new packets are not as exact as they should be. Therefore, further work will be concentrated on how to extrapolate the techniques developed to the very special case we deal here with. Furthermore, we will research on the use of expert knowledge for Bayesian networks modelling over different domains beyond the Intrusion Detection and the creation of a formal metric. This metric will measure the impact of the use of expert knowledge in the model creation time and the final performance of a Bayesian network.

8. References

Alipio, P., Carvalho, P. & Neves, J. (2003). *Using CLIPS to Detect Network Intrusion*, Vol. 2902/2003, Springer-Verlag.

Bringas, P. G. & Penya, Y. (2008). Bayesian-networks-based misuse and anomalies detection system, *Proceedings of the 10th International Conference on Enterprise Information Systems (ICEIS)*, pp. 12–16.

Bringas, P. G. & Penya, Y. (2009). Next-generation misuse and anomaly prevention system, *in* J. Filipe & J. Cordeiro (eds), *LNBIP 19 (Lecture Notes in Business Information Processing)*, Springer-Verlag, Heidelberg Berlin, pp. 117–129.

Castillo, E., Gutierrez, J. M. & Hadi, A. S. (1997). *Expert Systems and Probabilistic Network Models*, Springer-Verlag.

Coolen, F., Goldstein, M. & Munro, M. (2001). Generalized partition testing via Bayes linear methods, *INFORMATION AND SOFTWARE TECHNOLOGY* 43(13): 783–793.

Crothers, T. (2002). *Implementing Intrusion Detection Systems: A Hands-On Guide for Securing the Network*, John Whiley & Sons Inc.

Estevez-Tapiador, J., Garcia-Teodoro, P. & Diaz-Verdejo, J. (2003). Stochastic protocol modeling for anomaly based network intrusion detection, *Proceedings of the first IEEE International Workshop on Information Assurance*, pp. 3–12.

Ghahramani, Z. (1998). *Learning Dynamic Bayesian Networks*, Vol. 1387, Springer-Verlag.

Helman, P., Veroff, R., Atlas, S. & Willman, C. (2004). A Bayesian network classification methodology for gene expression data, *JOURNAL OF COMPUTATIONAL BIOLOGY* 11(4): 581–615.

Kruegel, C. & Vigna, G. (2003). Anomaly detection of web-based attacks, *Proceedings of the 10th ACM Conference on Computer and Communications Security*, pp. 251–261.

Lee, W., Stolfo, S., Chan, P., Eskin, E., Fan, W., Miller, M., Hershkop, S. & Zhang., J. (2001). Real time data mining-based intrusion detection, *Proceedings of the second DARPA Information Survivability Conference and Exposition*, pp. 85–100.

Metasploit (2006). Exploit research. Available at http://www.metasploit.org/.

Murphy, K. (2001). An introduction to graphical models, *Technical report*, Intel Research, Intel Corporation.

Penya, Y. & Bringas, P. G. (2008a). Experiences on designing an integral intrusion detection system, *Flexible Database and Information System Technology Workshop (FlexDBIST), at the DEXA-08 International Conference on Database and Expert Systems Applications*, pp. 675–679.

Penya, Y. & Bringas, P. G. (2008b). Integrating network misuse and anomaly prevention, *Proceedings of the 6th IEEE International Conference on Industrial Informatics (INDIN'08)*, pp. 586–591.

Roesch, M. (1999). SNORT: Lightweight intrusion detection for networks, *Proceedings of LISA99: 13th Systems Administration Conference*, pp. 229–238.

Ruiz-Agundez, I., Penya, Y. & Bringas, P. (2010). Expert knowledge for optimal bayesian network-based intrusion detection, *Proceedings of the 3rd International Conference on Human System Interaction (HSI 2010)*, pp. 444–451.

Sinha, A. R. & Zhao, H. (2008). Incorporating domain knowledge into data mining classifiers: An application in indirect lending, *DECISION SUPPORT SYSTEMS* 46(1): 287–299.

Spirtes, P., Glymour, C. & Scheines, R. (2001). *Causation, Prediction, and Search, Second Edition (Adaptive Computation and Machine Learning)*, The MIT Press.

10

Correlation Analysis Between Honeypot Data and IDS Alerts Using One-class SVM

Jungsuk Song[1], Hiroki Takakura[2], Yasuo Okabe[3] and Yongjin Kwon[4]

[1]*National Institute of Information and Communications Technology (NICT)*

[2]*Information Technology Center, Nagoya University*

[3]*Academic Center for Computing and Media Studies, Kyoto University*

[4]*Information and Telecom. Eng., Korea Aerospace University*

[1,2,3]*Japan*

[4]*Korea*

1. Introduction

With the rapid development and proliferation of the Internet infrastructure and local networks, more and more security threats, *e.g.*, distributed denial of service (DDoS), computer viruses, Internet worms, trojan horses, sywares, adwares and bots, for computer systems and networks are also constantly emerging as well as evolving. There have been many efforts on fighting against these security threats in the last decade, which include cryptography, firewalls and intrusion detection systems (IDSs), etc. Especially, IDS(Base & Mell, 2001; Denning, 1987) is becoming increasingly significant to maintain high-level network security and to defend our crucial computer systems and networks from malicious attackers(Allen et al., 2000).

There are mainly two kinds of intrusion detection methods: misuse detection and anomaly detection. IDSs based on misuse detection method monitor network traffic to detect invalid incoming and/or outgoing accesses using predefined attack signatures(Bro, 2010; Snort, 2010). If they find any intrusion or suspicious activities which include the patterns of predefined signatures, they raise the corresponding alerts. In anomaly detection based IDSs, on the other hand, they use normal patterns to detect abnormal activities from observed data. They attempt to identify deviations from predefined normal patterns, and if such activities are observed over the network, then they are regarded as potential attacks. The former has capability to detect well-known attacks with a relatively high accuracy than that of the latter, but they have a fatal limitation in that they are unable to detect unforeseen attacks, *i.e.*, 0-day attacks, which are not included in the set of predefined signatures. While IDSs based on anomaly detection method have the potential capability of detecting unknown attacks, because their activities are different from normal ones.

During the last decade, many machine learning and data mining techniques have been applied to IDSs, so that their performance was significantly improved as well as they could be constructed with low cost and effort. Particularly, *unsupervised* anomaly detection techniques(Eskin et al., 2002; Guan et al., 2003; Laskov et al., 2004; Leung & Leckie, 2005; Li et al., 2003; Oldmeadow et al., 2004; Portnoy et al., 2001; Song et al., 2008a; 2009; Wang & Megalooikonomou, 2005) have received remarkable attention, because they are able to construct intrusion detection models without using any labeled training data (*i.e.*, with instances preclassified as being an attack or not) in an automated manner, and they also have intrinsic ability to detect 0-day attacks. Furthermore, considering labeled data or purely normal data cannot be obtained easily in practice, it is better to focus on applying unsupervised anomaly detection techniques to the construction of IDSs than supervised ones. Existing unsupervised anomaly detection techniques have been applied to mainly two types of data sources: raw traffic data and IDS alerts. In the case of approaches based on raw traffic data, they have a strong point compared with another that it is possible to detect all of cyber attacks which are being happened over our networks theoretically, while there is also a fatal problem in that they trigger an unmanageable amount of alerts. In fact, by some estimates, more than thousands of alerts are raised everyday(Manganaris et al., 2000), and about 99% of them is false positive(Julisch, 2003). This situation makes analyst impossible to inspect all of them in time and to identify which alerts are more dangerous. As a result, it is very difficult that IDS operators discover unknown and critical attacks from IDS alerts even if they contain such attacks.

Due to this impracticability of approaches based on raw traffic data, during the last few years, a lot of researchers have focused on mitigation of the amount of false alerts and detection of cyber attacks by analyzing IDS alerts(Bass, 2000; Clifton & Gengo, 2000; Giacinto et al., 2005; Manganaris et al., 2000; Treinen & Thurimella, 2006; Yu & Frincke, 2004; Zurutuza & Uribeetxeberria, 2004). Especially, by analyzing IDS alerts, it is possible to reveal invisible intrusions from them(Song et al., 2007; 2008b), because skillful attackers devise diverse artifice to hide their activities from recent security devices such as IDS, which leads to different combination and/or frequency of alerts from those of well-known attack activities. For example, attackers sometimes try to make IDSs trigger a large amount of alerts intentionally by sending well-crafted packets which have no malicious codes, but they are designed to match some signatures which are defined to detect an outdated attack. In this case, IDS operators are apt to misjudge such events as false positives or unimportant attacks. After that, real attacks are started to the targeted vulnerability because these attacks are no longer considered as suspect activities by IDS operators. Therefore, it is possible to identify something new activities by analyzing patterns of the tricked IDS alerts. Although those approaches based on IDS alerts have a shortcoming that they are only able to detect limited intrusions which could be observed from the IDS alerts, they enable us to discover hidden attacks which are undetectable in raw traffic data and to make the analysis task of IDS alerts more easy.

Considering the above two approaches (*i.e.*, those based on raw traffic data and IDS alerts) have advantages and disadvantage to each other, a hybrid approach for carrying out the correlation analysis between them is essential. In this chapter, we conduct correlation analysis between raw traffic data and IDS alerts using one-class SVM(Li et al., 2003; Schölkopf et al., 2001), focusing on evaluation of *unsupervised anomaly detection*, which is one of the most general and powerful unsupervised machine learning technique.

To this end, we first collected raw traffic data from our honeypots deployed in Kyoto University(Song et al., 2008c), and we extracted 14 statistical features(Benchmark Data, 2010; Song et al., 2009) from them. We also obtained IDS alerts that were recorded by Snort (ver. 4.9.1.4)(Snort, 2010) deployed in front of our honeypots. Snort is an open source network intrusion prevention and detection system (IDS/IPS) developed by Sourcefire(Sourcefire, 2010). Similar to honeypot data, we extracted 7 statistical features from IDS alerts(Song et al., 2008b). We then applied one-class SVM to two data sources, honeypot data and IDS alerts, and consequently obtained two intrusion detection models. With the two intrusion detection models, we investigated what each model detected from our evaluation data and carried out correlation analysis between the intrusions detected from them. Our experimental results for correlation analysis show that it is more useful and practical to integrate the detection results obtained from the two intrusion detection models.

The rest of this chapter is organized as follows. In Section 2, we give a brief description for one-class SVM and previous approaches based on raw traffic data and IDS alerts. In Section 3, we describe our experimental environment and benchmark data (*i.e.*, honeypot data and IDS alerts). In Section 4, we present experimental results obtained from each of two benchmark data and our correlation analysis elicited by combining them. Finally, we present concluding remarks and suggestions for future work in Section 5.

2. Related work

2.1 Intrusion detection using raw traffic data

The earlier methods for intrusion detection were based on intrusion detection rules, i.e., signatures, that are manually constructed by human experts(Sebring et al., 1988). However, since the amount of audit data increases rapidly, their methods consume huge amounts of cost and time to construct the signatures. In addition, these systems can detect only attacks that have been modeled beforehand. In order to cope with the problems, many researchers have applied data mining and machine learning techniques to intrusion detection(Amor et al., 2004; Bridges & Luo, 2000; Lee et al., 1998; 1999). However, there is also a problem that construction of intrusion detection models requires labeled training data, i.e., the data must be pre-classified as attack or not. In general, labeled data can not be obtained readily in real environment since it is very hard to guarantee that there are no intrusions when we are collecting network traffic. A survey of these methods is given in (Warrender et al., 1999).

Over the past few years, several studies to solving these problems have been made on anomaly detection using unsupervised learning techniques, called unsupervised anomaly detection, which are able to detect previously "unseen" attacks and do not require the labeled training data used in the training stage(Denning, 1987; Javitz & Valdes, 1993). A clustering method for detecting intrusions was first presented in (Portnoy et al., 2001), without being given any information about classifications of the training data. In (Eskin et al., 2002) Eskin, et al. presented a geometric framework for unsupervised intrusion detection. They evaluated their methods over both network records and system call traces, and showed that their algorithms were able to detect intrusions over the unlabeled data. In (Guan et al., 2003) Guan, et al. proposed a K-means based clustering algorithm, named Y-means, for intrusion detection. Y-means can overcome two shortcomings of the K-means: number of clusters dependency and degeneracy. In (Oldmeadow et al., 2004) Oldmeadow, et al. presented a solution that can automatically accommodate non-stationary traffic distributions, and demonstrated the effectiveness of feature weighting to improve detection accuracy against certain types of attack. In (Laskov et al., 2004) Laskov, et al. proposed a quarter-sphere SVM that is one variant of one-class SVM, with moderate success. In (Leung & Leckie, 2005) Leung, et al. proposed a new density-based and grid-based clustering algorithm, called fpMAFIA, that is suitable for unsupervised anomaly detection. In (Wang & Megalooikonomou, 2005) Wang, et al. proposed a new clustering algorithm, FCC, for intrusion detection based on the concept of fuzzy connectedness. In (Song et al., 2008a), Song, et al. proposed a K-means based clustering algorithm for intrusion detection. The proposed algorithm improves the detection accuracy and reduce the false positive rate by overcoming shortcomings of the K-means in intrusion detection. Also, Song, et al. proposed a new anomaly detection method based on clustering and multiple one-class SVM in order to improve the detection rate while maintaining a low false positive rate(Song et al., 2009).

2.2 Intrusion detection using IDS alerts

As IDS has played a central role as an appliance to effectively defend our crucial computer systems or networks, large organization and companies have deployed different models of IDS from different vendors. Nevertheless, there is a fatal weakness that they trigger an unmanageable amount of alerts. Inspecting thousands of alerts per day and sensor(Manganaris et al., 2000) is not feasible, specially if 99% of them are false positives(Julisch, 2003). Due to this impracticability, during the last few years a lot of researches have been proposed to reduce the amount of false alerts, by studying the cause of these false positives, creating a higher level view or scenario of the attacks, and finally providing a coherent response to attacks understanding the relationship between different alerts(Zurutuza & Uribeetxeberria, 2004).

T. Bass firstly introduced data fusion techniques in military applications for improving performance of next-generation IDS(Bass, 2000). In (Manganaris et al., 2000) Manganaris, et al. analyzed the alerts gathered by real-time intrusion detection systems by using data mining, and characterized the "normal" stream of alerts. In (Clifton & Gengo, 2000) Clifton, et al. also used data mining techniques to identify sequences of alerts that likely result from normal behavior, and then filtered out false positives from original alerts based on them. Yu, et al. proposed a framework for alert correlation and understanding in intrusion detection system. Their experimental results show that their method can reduce false positives and negatives, and provide better understanding of the intrusion progress by introducing confidence scores(Yu & Frincke, 2004). Giacinto, et al. performed alert clustering which produces unified description of attacks from multiple alerts to attain a high-level description of threats(Giacinto et al., 2005). In (Treinen & Thurimella, 2006) Treinen, et al. used meta-alarms to identify known attack patterns in alarm streams, and used association rule mining to shorten the training time.

As mentioned above, a number of approaches have been suggested to effectively manage IDS alerts, but their researches have been limited to reduction in the amount of IDS alerts mainly. However, since unusual behavior of intruders to evade modern well-managed security systems, in many cases it can be identified by analyzing IDS alerts. In (Song et al., 2007), Song, et al. suggested a data mining technique in order to extract unknown activities from IDS alerts. Also, Song, el al. proposed a generalized feature extraction scheme to detect serious and unknown cyber attacks in that new 7 features were extracted by using only the basic 6 features of IDS alerts; detection time, source address and port, destination address and port, and signature name(Song et al., 2008b).

3. Overview

Figure 1 shows the overall architecture of our correlation analysis. In our approach, we first collected traffic data from three different types of networks, *i.e.*, the original campus network of Kyoto University, QGPOP network and IPv6 network. QGPOP network is being provided by Kyushu GigaPOP Project(QGPOP, 2010) which aims to build a dedicated R&D Internet over Kyushu region in parallel with commodity Internet, focusing on Internet's end-to-end principle and new features like IPv6, multicasting, and Mobile IP. We also deployed Snort (ver. 4.9.1.4)(Snort, 2010) at the perimeter of the above three networks and stored IDS alerts recorded by it into our dedicated DB system. In order to decoy attackers into our networks, we deployed many types of honeypots in the internal network and we stored the traffic data observed on the honeypots into our dedicated DB system. We then construct two benchmark data from honeypot data and IDS alerts described in Sections 4.1 and 4.2. Finally, we apply two benchmark data to one-class SVM, respectively, evaluate their performance and carry out the correlation analysis between them.

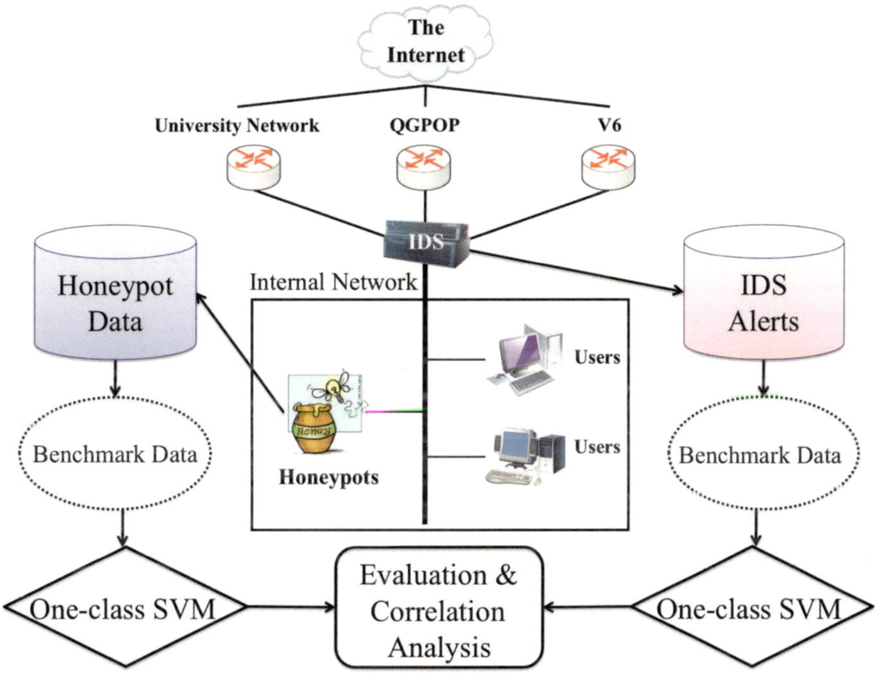

Fig. 1. The overall architecture of our correlation analysis.

4. Benchmark data

4.1 Honeypot data

In intrusion detection field, KDD Cup 1999 dataset(KDD Cup 99', 1999) has been used for a long time as benchmark data for evaluating performance of IDSs. However, there is a fatal drawback in that KDD Cup 1999 dataset is unable to reflect current network situations and latest attack trends, because it was generated by simulation over the virtual network more than 10 years ago, and thus its attack types are greatly old-fashioned. In spite of this drawback, researchers have used it as their evaluation data, because it is quite difficult to get high-quality evaluation data due to privacy and competitive issues: many organizations scarcely share their data with other institutions and researchers. To make matters worse, labeling traffic data as either normal or intrusion requires enormous amount of time for many human experts, even if real traffic data is available.

In order to provide more practical and useful evaluation results, it is needed to carry out our experiments using real traffic data. In (Song et al., 2008c), we deployed several types of honeypots over the 5 different networks which are inside and outside of Kyoto University: 1 class A and 4 class B networks. For example, there are some Windows base honeypots (*e.g.* with Windows XP with SP2, full patched Window XP, Windows XP without any patch,

Windows Vista), and Symantec honeypot with Solaris, network printer, home appliance, *e.g.*, TV, Video Recorder and so on. In addition to traditional honeypots which only receive attacks, we deployed proactive systems which access to malicious web servers and join real botnets to get various types of commands. We collected all traffic data to/from our honeypots, and observed that most of them consist of attack data. In fact, for the collected traffic data, we carried out a deep inspection for every connection if there was a buffer overflow attack or not. In order to identify a shellcode and an exploit code from traffic data, we used the dedicated detection software(Ashula, 2010). We also used IDS alerts obtained from Snort (ver. 4.9.1.4)(Snort, 2010) and malware information obtained from ClamAV(Clamav, 2010) as extra information for inspecting traffic data. By using these diverse information, we thoroughly inspected the collected traffic data, and identified what happened on the networks.

In spite of our effort for inspecting real attacks on the campus networks, there is still a possibility that unidentified attacks are being contained in the honeypot traffic data. However, in our investigation, we observed that most of honeypot traffic data captured in our honeypots are composed of attack data and there were few unidentified traffic data. Therefore, all the original honeypot traffic data are regarded as attack data in our benchmark data, because performance of one-class SVM is almost unaffected by a small amount of unidentified attack data or they can be treated as just noisy data.

On the other hand, since the most of the honeypot traffic data consist of attack data, we should prepare a large amount of normal data in order to evaluate performance of one-class SVM effectively. In order to generate normal traffic data, we deployed a mail server on the same network with honetpots, and regarded its traffic data as normal data. The mail server was also operated with several communication protocols, *e.g.*, ssh, http and https, for its management and also received various attacks. Although all of these activities were included with the traffic data, they do not affect to performance of machine learning techniques considered in our experiments due to their small amount.

4.1.1 Extracting 14 statistical features

Among the 41 original features of KDD Cup 99 data set, we have extracted only 14 significant and essential features (*e.g.*, Figure 3) from traffic data (*e.g.*, Figure 2) of honeypots and a mail server, and we used 13 continuous features excluding one categorical feature (*i.e.*, "flag") for our evaluation data. The reason why we extracted only the 14 statistical features is that among the original 41 features of the KDD Cup 99 dataset(KDD Cup 99', 1999) there exist substantially redundant and insignificant features. Our benchmark data is open to the public at (Benchmark Data, 2010). Visit our web site for more detail.

1. **Duration**: the length (number of seconds) of the connection
2. **Service**: the connection's service type, e.g., http, telnet, etc
3. **Source bytes**: the number of data bytes sent by the source IP address
4. **Destination bytes**: the number of data bytes sent by the destination IP address
5. **Count**: the number of connections whose source IP address and destination IP address are the same to those of the current connection in the past two seconds.
6. **Same_srv_rate**: % of connections to the same service in Count feature
7. **Serror_rate**: % of connections that have "SYN" errors in Count feature
8. **Srv_serror_rate**: % of connections that have "SYN" errors in Srv_count(the number of connections whose service type is the same to that of the current connection in the past two seconds) feature

1, 2010-07-1 00:00:00, 0.00, 10.*. *.12, 192. *. *.24, 8, 3836, 25, tcp, 0, 0, RSTOS
2, 2010-07-1 00:00:02, 0.00, 10. *. *.128, 192. *. *.248, 49, 12317, 17216, udp, 20, 0, S0
3, 2010-07-1 00:00:03, 0.00, 10. *. *.87, 192. *. *.105, 25, 2648, 445, tcp, 0, 0, S0
4, 2010-07-1 00:00:03, 0.00, 10. *. *.39, 192. *. *.78, 25, 3817, 445, tcp, 0, 0, S0
5, 2010-07-1 00:00:04, 7.00, 10.*.*.32, 192. *. *.24, 8, 17831, 25, tcp, 307, 946, RSTO
6, 2010-07-1 00:00:04, 7.45, 10.*.*.62, 192. *. *.24, 8, 21990, 25, tcp, 320, 959, RSTO
7, 2010-07-1 00:00:04, 8.29, 10.*.*.13, 192. *. *.24, 8, 4400, 25, tcp, 1050, 3185, RSTO
8, 2010-07-1 00:00:04, 0.00, 10.*.*.53, 192. *. *.58, 25, 2931, 445, tcp, 0, 0, S0
9, 2010-07-1 00:00:05, 0.00, 10.*.*.17, 192. *. *.94, 25, 64024, 445, tcp, 0, 0, S0
10, 2010-07-1 00:00:05, 0.00, 10.*.*.22, 192. *. *.123, 25, 3564, 445, tcp, 0, 0, S0

Fig. 2. Example of session data.

1, 6.38, 8, 284.00, 789.00, 8.00, 0.88, 0.12, 0.00, 1.00, 99.00, 0.00, 0.00, 0.00, S0
2, 0.00, 25, 0.00, 0.00, 0.00, 0.00, 0.00, 1.00, 0.00, 0.00, 0.00, 0.00, 0.00, S1
3, 13.69, 8, 4524.00, 648.00, 5.00, 1.00, 0.00, 0.00, 0.00, 99.00, 0.00, 0.00, 0.00, SF
4, 0.00, 25, 0.00, 0.00, 0.00, 0.00, 0.00, 1.00, 0.00, 1.00, 0.00, 0.00, 1.00, REJ
5, 6.43, 8, 386.00, 1198.00, 7.00, 1.00, 0.00, 0.00, 0.00, 99.00, 0.00, 0.00, 0.00, S2
6, 0.00, 25, 0.00, 0.00, 0.00, 0.00, 0.00, 1.00, 1.00, 1.00, 1.00, 1.00, 1.00, S3
7, 10.45, 8, 479.00, 613.00, 4.00, 1.00, 0.00, 0.00, 0.00, 99.00, 0.00, 0.00, 0.00, RSTOS0
8, 2.93, 8, 458.00, 600.00, 5.00, 1.00, 0.00, 0.00, 0.00, 99.00, 0.00, 0.00, 0.00, RSTRH
9, 0.00, 25, 0.00, 0.00, 0.00, 0.00, 0.00, 0.83, 1.00, 1.00, 1.00, 1.00, 1.00, SH
10, 0.00, 25, 0.00, 0.00, 0.00, 0.00, 0.00, 0.86, 0.00, 1.00, 0.00, 0.00, 1.00, SHR

Fig. 3. Example of 14 statistical features.

9. **Dst_host_count**: among the past 100 connections whose destination IP address is the same to that of the current connection, the number of connections whose source IP address is also the same to that of the current connection.
10. **Dst_host_srv_count**: among the past 100 connections whose destination IP address is the same to that of the current connection, the number of connections whose service type is also the same to that of the current connection
11. **Dst_host_same_src_port_rate**: % of connections whose source port is the same to that of the current connection in Dst_host_count feature
12. **Dst_host_serror_rate**: % of connections that have "SYN" errors in Dst_host _count feature
13. **Dst_host_srv_serror_rate**: % of connections that "SYN" errors in Dst_host_ srv_count feature
14. **Flag**: the state of the connection at the time the summary was written (which is usually when the connection terminated). The different states are summarized in the below section.

4.1.2 Example of session data and their 14 statistical features

Figures 2 and 3 show examples of session data captured in our honeypots and their 14 statistical features, respectively. Note that we sanitized source and destination IP addresses because of secrecy of communication. 192.x.x.x indicates sanitized internal IP address and 10.x.x.x indicate sanitized external IP address. In Figure 2, each row indicates one session data, and it consists of 12 columns: ID, time, duration, source IP address, destination IP address, service type (*e.g.*, 8 represents HTTP), source port number, destination port number, protocol, source bytes, destination bytes, flag.

Feature name	Value
Duration	6.38 seconds
Service	8 (*i.e.*, HTTP)
Source bytes	284 bytes
Destination bytes	789 bytes
Count	8
Same_srv_rate	88%
Serror_rate	12 %
Srv_serror_rate	0%
Dst_host_count	1
Dst_host_srv_count	99
Dst_host_same_src_port_rate	0%
Dst_host_serror_rate	0%
Dst_host_srv_serror_rate	0%
Flag	S0

Table 1. Values of 14 statistical features in line 1.

In Figure 3, each row indicates one session data, and it consists of 15 columns, *i.e.*, one ID and 14 statistical features. For example, Table 1 shows the values of the 14 statistical features in line 1.

4.2 IDS alerts

In our previous work, we introduced a feature extraction scheme so that one can detect 0-day attack from IDS alerts(Song et al., 2007). In the feature extraction scheme, it uses "Incident ID" feature among the original features of IDS alerts that were recorded by SNS7160 IDS system(SNS7160, 2010). The Incident ID feature indicates a group of IDS alerts that are considered as correlated attack by SNS7160 IDS system. Hence, if two alerts contain the same Incident ID, then they become members of the same group. However, there is a problem that not all vendors provide the Incident ID feature in their IDS product. Furthermore, even if it provided, its building mechanism is different from each other.

On the other hand, in recent years, many organizations (*e.g.*, ISAC(REN-ISAC, 2010; TELECOM-ISAC, 2010)) are getting started to share their security information with others in order to improve network security. However, these organizations deploy various types of security devices such as IDSs, firewalls and so on. In addition, if we force them to utilize the same product, its weakness causes signs of many 0-day attacks invisible. Because of this, we need to devise a mechanism to integrate their information effectively. However, if we utilize only the common features of IDS such as IP address, port, detection time and so on, it is not enough to extract useful information from them. In order to satisfy these requirements, in (Song et al., 2008b) we extracted 7 statistical features (see subsection 4.2.1) using only the basic 6 features of IDS alerts: detection time, source address and port, destination address and port, and signature name.

To obtain IDS alerts, we used Snort (ver. 4.9.1.4)(Snort, 2010) that is actually deployed at perimeter of Kyoto University. Snort is charged with protecting 2 class B and 4 class C networks. If Snort observes a suspicious session on the networks, it triggers a corresponding alert according to its detection engine. Note that we have obtained IDS alerts that were triggered by SNS7160 IDS system on our experimental network described in Figure 1 since 2006, and we have started to deploy Snort into our network since 2010. Thus, it is possible to extract the 7 statistical features from both IDS alerts (*i.e.*, Snort and SNS7160 IDS), because the 7 statistical features can be extracted from only the basic 6 features. Since Snort is a free software, we use its alerts as our evaluation data in this chapter.

4.2.1 Extracting 7 statistical features

From the IDS alerts of Snort, we extracted the 7 statistical features (Figures 4) from each alert (Figures 5). Note that the following features refer to the last N alerts whose source address and destination port number are the same to the current alert.

1. **NUM_SAME_SA_DA_DP**
   Among N alerts, the number of alerts whose destination address is the same to the current alert. We define them as n alerts.
2. **RATE_DIFF_ALERT_SAME_SA_DA_DP**
   Rate of the number of alerts whose alert types are different from the current alert to n.
3. **TIME_STDDEV_SAME_SA_DA_DP**
   Standard deviation of the time intervals between each instance of n alerts including the current alert.
4. **NUM_SAME_SA_DP_DIFF_DA**
   Among N alerts, the number of alerts whose destination address is different from the current alert; it becomes $(N - n)$.
5. **RATE_DIFF_ALERT_SAME_SA_DP_DIFF_DA**
   Rate of the number of alerts whose alert types are different from the current alert to $(N - n)$.
6. **TIME_STDDEV_SAME_SA_DP_DIFF_DA**
   Standard deviation of the time intervals between each instance of $(N - n)$ alerts including the current alert.
7. **RATE_REVERSE_SP_SAME_SA_DP**
   Rate of the number of the alerts whose source port is the same or larger than that of the current alert to N.

NUM_SAME_SA_DA_DP and NUM_SAME_SA_DP_DIFF_DA features represent that an attacker tries to exploit just one victim host and a lot of victim hosts, respectively. RATE_DIFF_ALERT_SAME_SA_DA_DP and RATE_DIFF_ALERT_SAME_SA_DP_DIFF_DA features indicate that if there is happening a real attack on the network, it sometimes raises several different kinds of IDS alerts. TIME_STDDEV_SAME_SA_DA_DP and TIME_STDDEV_SAME_SA_DP_DIFF_DA features are based on the fact that in the case of real attacks, since the time intervals between each alert triggered by IDS are very long and unpredictable, the values of these features will increase. RATE_REVERSE_SP_SAME_SA_DP feature means that if several successive sessions are made from a certain host, their source port numbers also increase automatically. Note that the values of the above 7 features have '0', if the number of the corresponding IDS alerts does not exceed N.

2, 35403, 1285453100, 567, 1, 11, 29, 3, 192.*.*.24, 10.*.*.120, 25, 59687, 6
2, 35404, 1285453100, 567, 1, 11, 29, 3, 192.*.*.24, 10.*.*.254, 25, 36165, 6
2, 35405, 1285453103, 1325, 1, 7, 15, 1, 10.*.*.60, 192.*.*.103, 54850, 22, 6
2, 32361, 1285453105, 567, 1, 11, 29, 3, 192.*.*.24, 10.*.*.23, 25, 41484, 6
2, 32362, 1285453105, 567, 1, 11, 29, 3, 192.*.*.24, 10.*.*.215, 25, 4768, 6
1, 3333, 1285453109, 2189, 1, 7, 25, 2, 192.*.*.254, 10.*.*.13, 0, 0, 103
2, 32363, 1285453110, 567, 1, 11, 29, 3, 192.*.*.24, 10.*.*.248, 25, 11245, 6
2, 29117, 1285453111, 1325, 1, 7, 15, 1, 10.*.*.229, 192.*.*.35, 37414, 22, 6
2, 35406, 1285453111, 1325, 1, 7, 15, 1, 10.*.*.229, 192.*.*.24, 58670, 22, 6
1, 2307, 1285453113, 1384, 1, 12, 30, 2, 192.*.*.23, 10.*.*.250, 1900, 1900, 17

Fig. 4. Examples of IDS Alerts

sensor_ID	Identification of each IDS
event_ID	Identification of each event
event_sec	UNIX time when the corresponding event was detected
sig_ID	Identification of each signature
gen_ID	Identification of each detection engine
rev	Revision of each signature
class	Attack types
priority	severity of each alert (1: high, 2: medium, 3: low)
src_address	source address (sanitized)
dst_address	destination address (sanitized)
src_port	source port number
dst_port	destination port number
ip_protocol	TCP, UDP, ICMP and so on

Table 2. Description of each column in IDS alerts.

1, 100.00, 0.67, 80.26, 0.00, 0.00, 0.00, 0.92, 20041
2, 0.00, 0.00, 0.00, 0.00, 0.00, 0.00, 0.00, 4128
3, 0.00, 0.00, 0.00, 0.00, 0.00, 0.00, 0.00, 13251
4, 100.00, 0.67, 62.62, 0.00, 0.00, 0.00, 0.91, 20501
5, 100.00, 0.67, 63.86, 0.00, 0.00, 0.00, 0.93, 49901
6, 0.00, 0.00, 0.00, 0.00, 0.00, 0.00, 0.00, 4138
7, 100.00, 0.00, 12.54, 0.00, 0.00, 0.00, 1.00, 19171
8, 0.00, 0.00, 0.00, 0.00, 0.00, 0.00, 0.00, 5671
9, 100.00, 0.67, 116.47, 0.00, 0.00, 0.00, 0.96, 20501
10, 100.00, 0.67, 122.14, 0.00, 0.00, 0.00, 0.95, 49901

Fig. 5. Example of the extracted 7 statistical features

4.2.2 Example of IDS alerts and their 7 statistical features

Figures 4 and 5 show examples of the alerts recorded by Snort and their 7 statistical features, respectively. Similar to the honeypot data, we sanitized source and destination IP addresses. 192.x.x.x indicates sanitized internal IP address and 10.x.x.x indicate sanitized external IP address. In Figure 4, each row indicates one alert, and it consists of 13 columns. The meaning of each column is described in Table 2.

Feature name	Value
NUM_SAME_SA_DA_DP	100
RATE_DIFF_ALERT_SAME_SA_DA_DP	67%
TIME_STDDEV_SAME_SA_DA_DP	80.26
NUM_SAME_SA_DP_DIFF_DA	0
RATE_DIFF_ALERT_SAME_SA_DP_DIFF_DA	0%
TIME_STDDEV_SAME_SA_DP_DIFF_DA	0%
RATE_REVERSE_SP_SAME_SA_DP	92%

Table 3. Values of 7 statistical features.

In Figure 5 each row indicates one alert, and it consists of 9 columns, *i.e.,*, one ID, 7 statistical features and alert type. For example, Table 3 shows the values of the 7 statistical features in line 1 in that we set N to 100. Note that 8th column represents identification of each alert.

5. One-class SVM

In our correlation analysis, we apply one-class SVM to two types of benchmark data, *i.e.*, honeypot data and IDS alerts, in order to detect cyber attacks from them. Support Vector Machines(SVM)(Vapnik, 1995; 1998) have received great interest and have been one of the most developed machine learning techniques. Some reasons why SVM has been succeeded in many applied applications are their good theoretical properties in generalization and convergence(Cristianini & Shawe-Taylor, 2000). Another reason is their excellent performance in some hard problems(Dumais et al., 1998; Osuna et al., 1997).
One-class SVM(Schölkopf et al., 2001) is one of the extension of the binary SVM(Vapnik, 1995; 1998), which is based on unsupervised learning paradigms. Given the unlabeled l data points, $\{x_1, \ldots x_l\}$ where $x_i \in R^n$; one-class SVM is to map the data points x_i into the feature space by using some non-linear mapping $\Phi(x_i)$, and to find a hypersphere which contains most of the data points in the feature space. Figure 6 shows the geometry of the hypersphere where it is formulated with the center c and the radius R in the feature space. Therefore, in intrusion detection field, the data points that belong to the outside of the hypersphere can be regarded as anomalies(*i.e.*. potential cyber attacks) because there are a few attacks in traffic data and IDS alerts, and most of them are usual false positives.
Mathematically, the problem of searching such a hypersphere is formulated as follows:

$$\begin{aligned} &\min_{R\in\Re,\xi\in\Re^l,c\in\mathcal{F}} \quad R^2 + \frac{1}{vl}\sum_{i=1}^{l}\xi_i, \\ &\textbf{subject to}: ||\Phi(x_i) - c|| \leq R^2 + \xi_i, \\ &\xi_i \geq 0, i = 1, \ldots, l. \end{aligned} \tag{1}$$

The non-negative slack variables ξ_i allow that some points belong to the "wrong" side of the hypersphere. Also, the parameter $v \in [0, 1]$ determines the trade off between the radius of the hypersphere (*i.e.*, its size) and the number of the data points that belong to the hypersphere. When v is small, more data are put into the hypersphere. When v is larger, its size decreases. Since the center c belongs to the possibly high-dimensional feature space, it is difficult to solve the primal problem (1) directly. Instead of the primal problem (1), it is possible to the primal

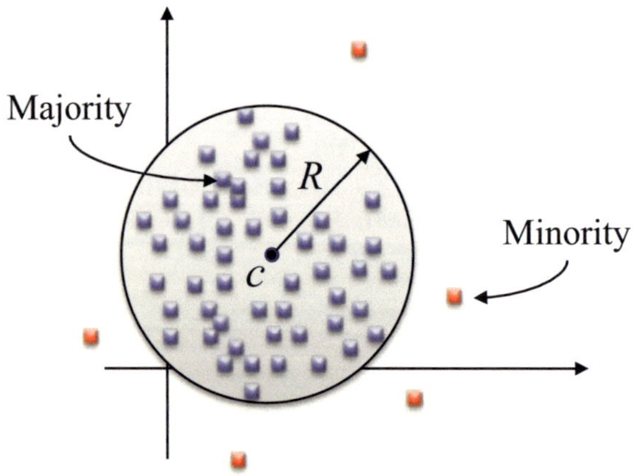

Fig. 6. The geometry of the sphere formulation of one-class SVM.

problem by its dual form with kernel functions, $k(x,y)$:

$$\begin{aligned} \min_{\alpha \in \Re^l} \ & \sum_{i,j=1}^{l} \alpha_i \alpha_j k(x_i, x_j) - \sum_{i=1}^{l} \alpha_i k(x_i, x_i) \\ & \textbf{subject to} : \sum_{i=1}^{l} \alpha_i = 1, \\ & 0 \le \alpha_i \le \frac{1}{vl}, i = 1, \ldots, l. \end{aligned} \tag{2}$$

If we find a hypersphere from the training data, we can classify the testing data as either normal or attack using the hypersphere. In this classification, the following decision function, whether point x in the testing data is normal(*i.e.*, inside of the hypersphere), is used:

$$\begin{aligned} f(x) = \textbf{sgn}\Bigg(R^2 - & \sum_{i,j=1}^{l} \alpha_i \alpha_j k(x_i, x_j) \\ & + 2\sum_{i} \alpha_i k(x_i, x) - k(x,x) \Bigg). \end{aligned} \tag{3}$$

The points with $f(x) = -1$ are considered to be anomalies because this means that they exist outside of the hypersphere. Otherwise they are considered to be normal, because they are members of the hypersphere. In our correlation analysis, we used LIBSVM library(Chang & Lin, 2001) to carry out the experiments with one-class SVM.

6. Experimental results and their analysis

6.1 Preprocessing and data preparation

In our experiments, we used the traffic data and IDS alerts of a day (Jul. 3rd, 2010) as our training data and they have contained 496,090 session data and 35,195 IDS alerts, respectively. Also, in the case of the traffic data, the ratio of attack data occupied 80% of the original traffic data. In case of real network, however, there are a few attack data or really dangerous attack data in its traffic data. Because of this, we adjusted the ratio of attack data to 1% and consequently we obtained 115,509 session data that were randomly and fairly selected from the original training data and regarded them as our training data. On the other hand, we regarded the original IDS alerts as our training data, because in IDS alerts, our goal is just to identify more serious and dangerous attacks from them. As the testing data, we used the traffic data and the IDS alerts of 4 days: Jul. 5th, 12th, 25th and 29th, 2010.

6.2 Evaluation process

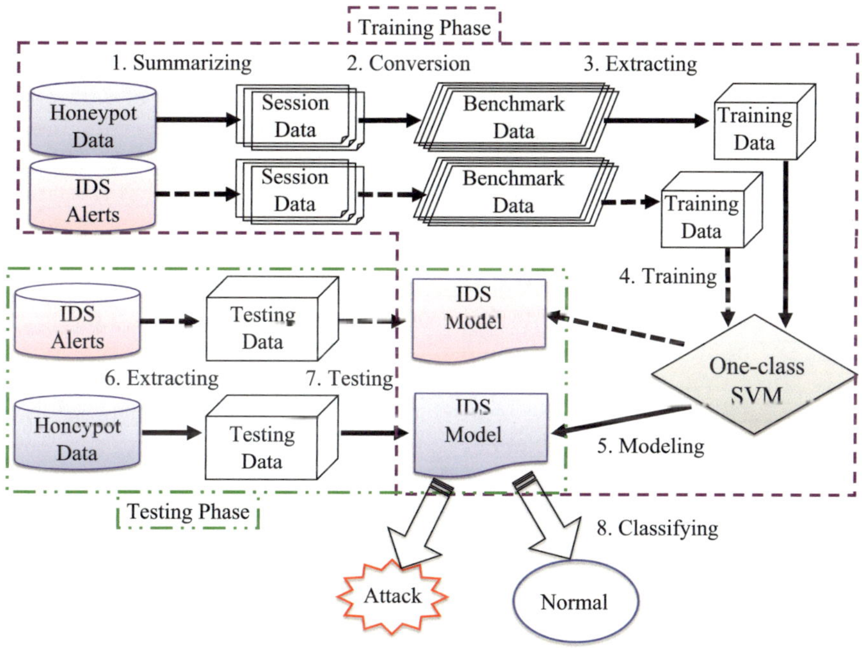

Fig. 7. The overall process of the training and testing phases.

Figure 7 shows the overall process of correlation analysis between two types of evaluation data: honeypot data and IDS alerts. The evaluation process is composed of two phases: training phase and testing phase. The training phase is summarized as follows.

1. **Summarizing**: summarize collected raw traffic data and IDS alerts in session data as described in subsections 4.1.2 and 4.2.2. Especially, in the case of honeypot data, we used BroBro (2010) for this summarizing process.
2. **Conversion**: convert summarized session data of traffic data and IDS alerts into connection records which consist of 14 statistical features and 7 statistical features as described in subsections 4.1.1 and 4.2.1, respectively.
3. **Extracting**: build the training data from converted two types of connection records: honeypot data and IDS alerts. Note that the ratio of attack data to normal data is 1% in the training data of honeypot data and we set the parameter N, which is described in subsection 4.2.1, to 100.
4. **Training and Modeling**: apply two types of benchmark data to one-class SVM, and thus we obtain two IDS models.

In the testing phase, we applied the two processes, *i.e.*, 6 and 7 in Figure 7, which are the same to those of the training phase to the traffic data and IDS alerts of 4 days, and consequently obtained two types of connection records with 14 statistical features and 7 statistical features. After that, we fed two types of connection records of the testing data into the corresponding IDS model which was built in the training phase, and then we evaluated each IDS model according to their detection results.

6.3 Analysis results of honeypot data

In our experiments, we first evaluated performance of one-class SVM using honeypot data. In our performance evaluation, we varied the parameter, v, of one-class SVM. The parameter v represents the ratio of data points which are located outside of the hypersphere discovered by one-class SVM. In other words, if v is smaller (or larger), then number of data points which are inside the hypersphere increases (or decreases). Figure 8 shows the evaluation results of one-class SVM where we set the value of parameter v to 0.1% $\sim$ 10%. In Figure 8, x-axis indicates the values of the parameter v and y-axis indicates the detection rate and the false positive rate of one-class SVM. In our investigation, we observed that the optimized value of the parameter was 6% $\sim$ 10% for each testing data. Table 4 shows the best detection rate and the false positive rate. From Table 4, we can see that there are too many false positives: the number of false positives in four testing data is 7,833, 5,512, 74,463 and 6,772, even if the detection rate is around 90%. Note that in real traffic data, the number of false positives will be extremely larger than that of our honeypot data, because the ratio of attack data in our testing data was about 80%. In other words, since it is obvious that there are much more normal data in real traffic data, the number of false positives will also increase according to the amount of normal data. Therefore, it is needed to minimize those false positives so that network operators can identify more serious and dangerous attacks effectively.

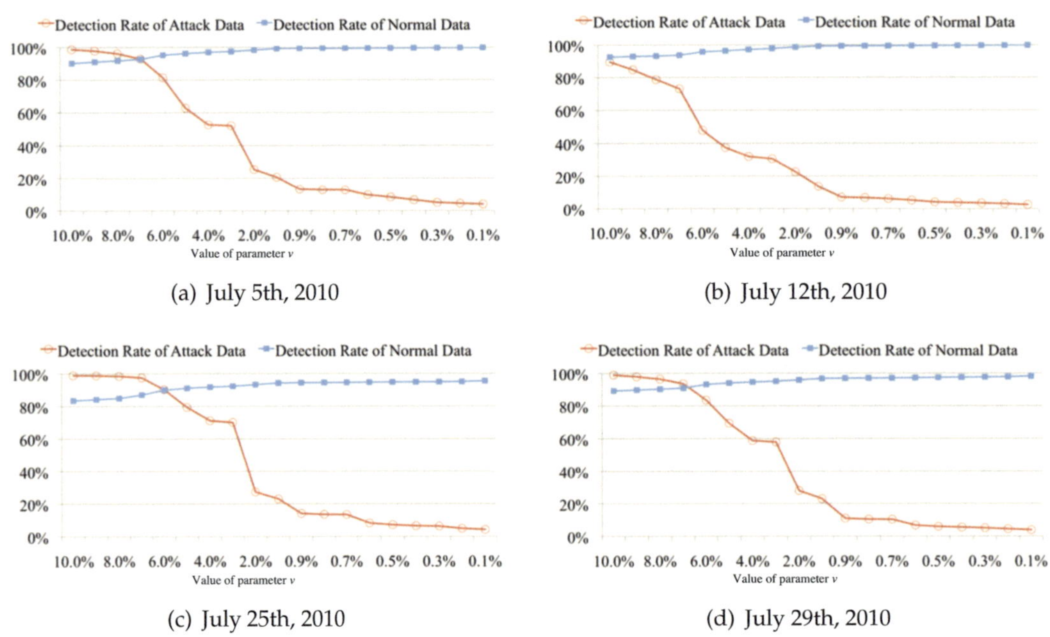

(a) July 5th, 2010

(b) July 12th, 2010

(c) July 25th, 2010

(d) July 29th, 2010

Fig. 8. Performance of one-class SVM by honeypot data.

Date	v	True positive rate	False positive rate
Jul. 5th, 2010	7%	92.91% (316,134/340,235)	7.33% (7,833/106,983)
Jul. 12th, 2010	10%	89.39% (340,180/380,541)	7.41% (5,512/74,436)
Jul. 25th, 2010	6%	90.19% (268,881/298,124)	10.01% (11,653/116,496)
Jul. 29th, 2010	7%	93.54% (200,408/214,247)	9.10% (6,772/74,451)

Table 4. Best true positive rate and false positive rate.

6.4 Analysis results of IDS alerts

In this experiment, we evaluated performance of one-class SVM using IDS alerts. Since there is no label information, we cannot obtain ROC curve(Lippmann, 2000) like Figure 8. However, as mentioned in Section 1, it is possible to reveal unknown attacks by identifying unusual patterns of IDS alerts, even if most of them are false positives(Julisch, 2003), and we demonstrated it in our previous research(Song et al., 2007; 2008b). Therefore, in our evaluation, we call the IDS alerts detected by one-class SVM as "dubious" alerts, and the others as "trivial" alerts.

In our experiments, we first investigated how many real attack data and real normal data are included in the dubious alerts. Figure 9 shows the classification results. In Figure 9, x-axis indicates the values of the parameter v and y-axis indicates the number of real attack data and normal data which belong to the dubious alerts. From Figure 9, we can observe that the number of attack data and normal data has the similar distribution: if the number of attack data increases, the number of normal data also increases.

In general, there is a few attacks (less than 100 attacks in many cases) which are serious and dangerous on the certain organization network. From viewpoint of this, it could be said that the optimized value of the parameter v is 0.1%, because the number of the dubious alerts which were detected by one-class SVM is smallest. In fact, Table 5 shows the number of real attack data and normal data when v was 0.1%. However, it is obvious that we need to improve performance of one-class SVM, because there still exist some trivial alerts.

Date	v	Number of real attack data	Number of real normal data
Jul. 5th, 2010	0.1%	92	16
Jul. 12th, 2010	0.1%	195	15
Jul. 25th, 2010	0.1%	365	96
Jul. 29th, 2010	0.1%	308	7

Table 5. Number of real attack data and normal data when v is 0.1%.

6.5 Results of correlation analysis

In order to demonstrate the effectiveness and the necessity of correlation analysis between traffic data and IDS alerts, we conducted the following two experiments. Figure 10 shows the overall process of our correlation analysis. Firstly, we investigated the number of session data ('C' marked in Table 6) that are real attacks in the honeypot data and are not members of the IDS alerts (①). From Table 6, it is obvious that there are lots of real attacks which were not observed in the IDS alerts. For example, in the case of the testing data of Jul. 5th, 2010, it contained 447,217 session data which consist of 340,235 attack data and 106,983 normal data, and among 340,235 attack data, 323,559 attack data were not identified in the IDS alerts. This means that it is essential to analyze traffic data and it is not enough to analyze only the IDS alerts.

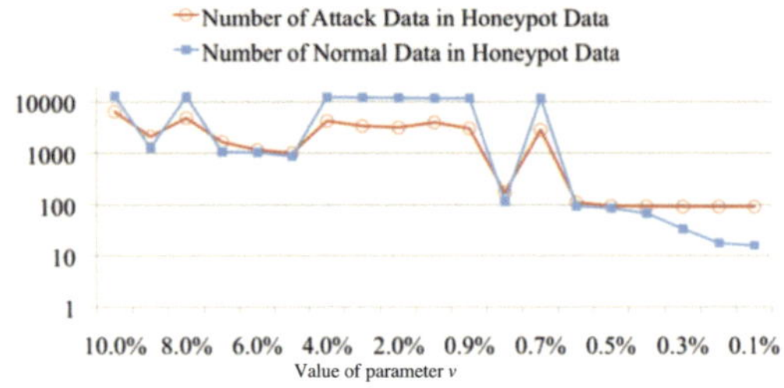

(a) July 5th, 2010

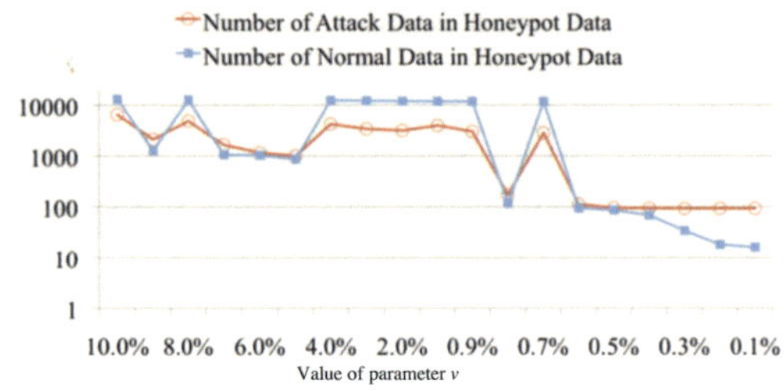

(b) July 12th, 2010

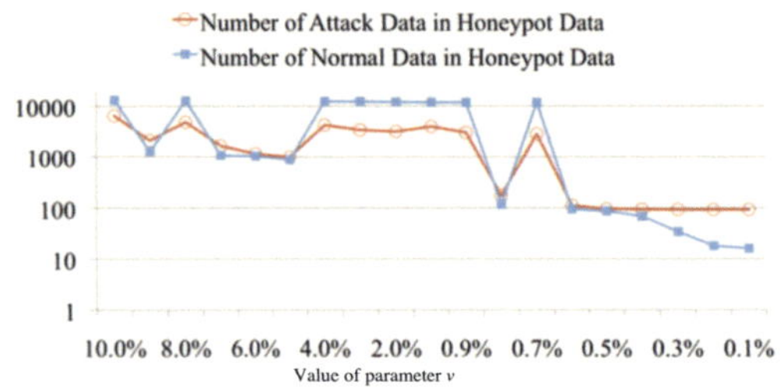

(c) July 25th, 2010

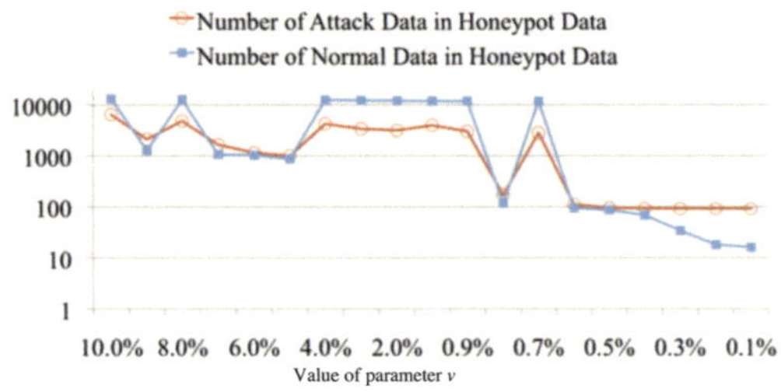

(d) July 29th, 2010

Fig. 9. Performance of one-class SVM by IDS alerts.

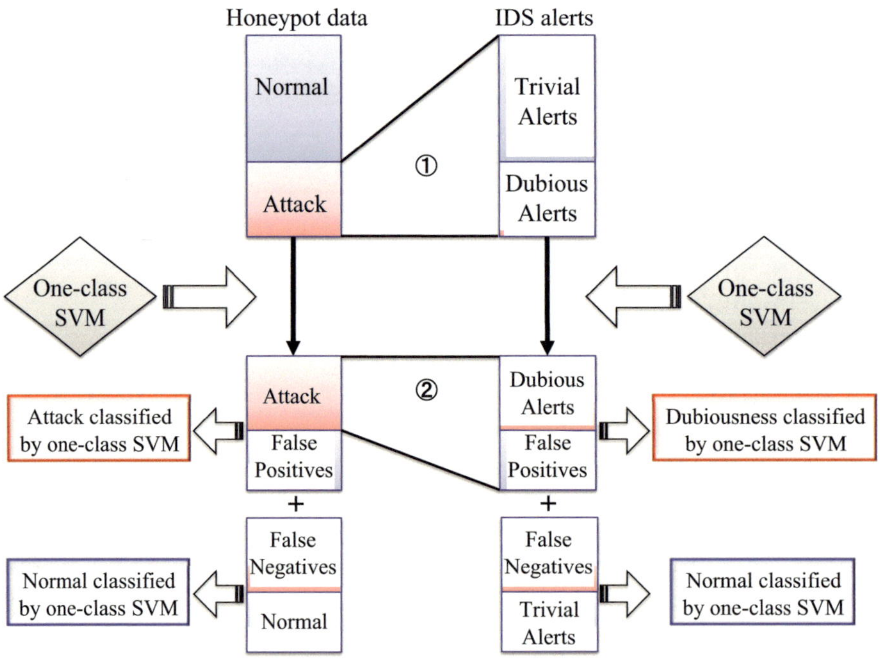

Fig. 10. The overall process of correlation analysis.

Secondly, we compared the real attacks detected from the honeypot data with the dubious alerts (②). In this experiment, we first counted the number of attack data ('D' marked in

Date	Total number of session data	Total number of attack data	C
Jul. 5th, 2010	447,218	340,235	323,559
Jul. 12th, 2010	454,977	380,541	363,831
Jul. 25th, 2010	414,620	298,124	272,938
Jul. 29th, 2010	288,698	214,247	200,311

Table 6. Results of correlation analysis between the original honeypot data and the original IDS alerts.

Table 7) which were detected from the two benchmark data at the same time. From Table 7, we can see that among 108 dubious alerts which were detected from the original IDS alerts, only 40 alerts were also observed from the real attacks detected from the honeypot data. This means that if we analyze only traffic data, it is unable to detect 68 real attacks which could be detected by analyzing the IDS alerts. After all, those results show that we need to analyze not only traffic data, but also IDS alerts, and to carry out correlation analysis between them so that network operators are able to identify more serious and dangerous cyber attack effectively.

Date	v	Number of the dubious alerts	D
Jul. 5th, 2010	7%	108	40

Table 7. Results of correlation analysis between the real attacks detected from the honeypot data and attack data detected from the IDS alerts.

7. Conclusion

In this chapter, we have carried out correlation analysis between honeypot data and IDS alerts. To this end, we first collected raw traffic data from our honeypots(Song et al., 2008c), and we extracted 14 statistical features(Benchmark Data, 2010; Song et al., 2009) from them as described in subsection 4.1. We also captured IDS alerts that were recorded by Snort (ver. 4.9.1.4)(Snort, 2010) deployed in front of our honeypots. Similar to honeypot data, we extracted 7 statistical features from IDS alerts(Song et al., 2008b) as described in subsection 4.2. We then applied one-class SVM to two benchmark data, *i.e.*, honeypot data and IDS alerts, and consequently obtained two intrusion detection models. With the two intrusion detection models, we evaluated each benchmark data, conducted correlation analysis between two benchmark data. Our experimental results show that it is more useful and practical to integrate the detection results obtained from the two intrusion detection models.

8. References

Allen, J.; Christie, A. & Fithen, W., (2000). State of the Practice of Intrusion Detection Technologies, Technical Report, CMU/SEI-99-TR-028, 2000.

Amor, N. B.; Benferhat, S. & Elouedi, Z., (2004). Naive Bayes vs decision trees in intrusion detection systems, *Proc. 2004 ACM Symp. on Applied Computing*, pp. 420-424, 2004.

Ashula, (2010). URL: *http://www.secure-ware.com/contents/product/ashula.html*

Base, R. & Mell, P., (2001). Intrusion Detection Systems, *NIST Special Publications*, November, 2001, SP 800-31.

Bass, T., (2000). Intrusion detection systems and multisensor data fusion, *Communications of the ACM*, ACM Press, pp. 99-105, New York, NY, USA, 2000.

Benchmark Data, (2010). URL: *http://www.takakura.com/Kyoto_data/*

Luo, J. & Bridges, S. M., (2000). Mining fuzzy association rules and fuzzy frequency episodes for intrusion detection, *International Journal of Intelligent Systems*, pp. 687-703, 2000.

Bro, (2010). URL: *http://www.bro-ids.org/*

Chang, C.-C. & Lin, C.-J., (2001). Libsvm: a library for support vector machines, URL: *http://www.csie.ntu.edu.tw/ cjlin/libsvm*

Clamav, (2010). URL: *http://www.clamav.net/*

Clifton, C. & Gengo, G., (2000). Developing custom intrusion detection filters using data mining, *21st Century Military Communications Conference Proceedings(MILCOM2000)*, Vol. 1, pp. 440-443, Los Angeles, California, USA, 2000.

Cristianini, N., & Shawe-Taylor, J., (2000). An introduction to support vector machines, *Cam bridge University Press*, 2000.

Denning, D. E., (1987). An intrusion detection model, *IEEE Transactions on Software Engineering*, 1987, SE-13:222-232.

Dumais, S.; Platt, J.; Heckerman, D. & Sahami, M., (1998). Inductive learning algorithms and representations for text categorization, *7th International Conference on Information and Knowledge Management, ACM-CIKM98*, pp.148-155, 1998.

Eskin, E.; Arnold, A.; Prerau, M.; Portnoy, L. & Stolfo, S., (2002). A Geometric Framework for Unsupervised Anomaly Detection : Intrusion Detection in Unlabeled Data, In *Applications of Data Mining in Computer Security*, 2002.

Giacinto, G.; Perdisci, R. & Roli, F., (2005). Alarm Clustering for Intrusion Detection Systems in Computer Networks, *MLDM 2005*, LNAI 3587, pp. 184-193, 2005.

Guan, Y.; Ghorbani, A. & Belacel, N., (2003). Y-means : A Clustering Method for Intrusion Detection, In *IEEE Canadian Conference on Electrical and Computer Engineering, Proceedings*, 2003.

Javitz, H. S. & Valdes, A., (1993). The NIDES statistical component: description and justification, *Technical Report, Computer Science Laboratory, SRI International*, 1993.

Julisch, K., (2003). Clustering Intrusion Detection Alarms to Support Root Cause Analysis, *ACM Transactions on Information and System Security* 6(4), ACM Press, pp. 443-471, 2003.

KDD Cup 99' dataset, (1999). The third international knowledge discovery and data mining tools competition dataset KDD99-Cup URL: *http://kdd.ics.uc i.edu/databases/kddcup99/kddcup99.html*

Laskov, P.; Schäfer, C. & Kotenko, I., (2004). Intrusion detection in unlabeled data with quarter-sphere support vector machines, In: *Proc. DIMVA*, pp. 71-82, 2004.

Lee, W.; Stolfo, S. J. & Mok, K.W., (1998). Mining audit data to build intrusion detection models, *Proc. Int. Conf. Knowledge Discovery and Data Mining (KDD'98)*, pp.66-72, 1998.

Lee, W.; Stolfo, S. J. & Mok, K.W., (1998). A data mining framework for building intrusion detection model, *Proceedings of the IEEE Symposium on Security and Privacy*, pp.120-132, 1999.

Leung, K. & Leckie, C., (2005). Unsupervised Anomaly Detection in Network Intrusion Detection Using Clusters, *ACSC2005*, 2005.

Li, K.L.; Huang, H.K.; Tian, S.F. & Xu, W., (2003). Improving one-class SVM for anomaly detection, *International Conference on Machine Learning and Cybernetics*, Vol. 5, pp. 3077-3081, 2003.

Lippmann, R.P., (2000). Evaluating Intrusion Detection Systems: the 1998 DARPA Off-Line Intrusion Detection Evaluation, *Proceedings of the 2000 DARPA Information Survivability Conference and Exposition*, Vol. 2.

Manganaris, S.; Christensen, M.; Zerkle, D. & Hermiz, K., (2000). A Data Mining Analysis of RTID Alarms, *Computer Networks: The International Journal of Computer and Telecommunications Networking*, Vol. 34, No. 4, pp. 571-577, 2000.

Oldmeadow, J.; Ravinutala, S. & Leckie, C., (2004). Adaptive Clustering for Network Intrusion Detection, In *Proceedings of the Third International Pacific Asia Conference on Knowledge Discovery and Data Mining*, 2004.

Osuna, E.; Freund, R. & Girosi, F., (1997). Training support vector machines: an application to face detection, *International Conference on Computer Vision and Pattern Recognition(CVPR97)*, pp.30-136, 1997.

Portnoy, L.; Eskin, E. & Stolfo, S., (2001). Intrusion Detection with Unlabeled Data Using Clustering, In *Proceedings of ACM CSS Workshop on Data Mining Applied to Security*, 2001.

QGPOP, (2010). URL: *http://www.qgpop.net/en/*

REN-ISAC, (2010). URL: *http://www.ren isac.net/*

Schölkopf, B.; Platt, J.; Shawe-Taylor, J.; Smola, A. & Williamson, R., (2001). Estimating the support of a high-dimensional distribution, *Neural Computation*, 13(7):1443-1471, 2001.

Sebring, M. M.; Shellhouse, E.; Hanna, M. E. & Whitehurst, R. A., (1988). Expert systems in intrusion detection: A case study, *Proceedings of the 11th National Computer Security Conference*, pp.74-81, Baltimore, Maryland, October, 1988.

Snort, (2010). URL: *http://www.snort.org/*

SNS7160 IDS System, (2010). Symantec network security 7100 series

Sourcefire, (2010). URL: *http://www.sourcefire.com/*

Song, J.; Ohba, H.; Takakura, H.; Okabe, Y. & Kwon, Y., (2007). A Comprehensive Approach to Detect Unknown Attacks via Intrusion Detection Alerts, *ASIAN2007 Focusing on Computer and Network Security*, LNCS 4846, pp. 247-253, Doha Qatar, December 2007.

Song, J.; Ohira, K.; Takakura, H.; Okabe, Y. & Kwon, Y., (2008a). A Clustering Method for Improving Performance of Anomaly-based Intrusion Detection System, *IEICE Transactions on Information and Communication System Security*, Vol.E91-D, No.5, pp.1282-1291, May. 2008.

Song, J.; Takakura, H. & Kwon, Y., (2008b). A Generalized Feature Extraction Scheme to Detect 0-Day Attacks via IDS Alerts, *The 2008 International Symposium on Applications and the Internet(SAINT2008)*, The IEEE CS Press, 28 July - 1 Aug. 2008.

Song, J.; Takakura, H. & Okabe, Y., (2008c). Cooperation of intelligent honeypots to detect unknown malicious codes, *WOMBAT Workshop on Information Security Threat Data Exchange (WISTDE 2008)*, The IEEE CS Press, April, 2008.

Song, J.; Takakura, H.; Okabe, Y. & Kwon, Y., (2009). Unsupervised Anomaly Detection Based on Clustering and Multiple One-class SVM, *IEICE Transactions on Communications*, Vol. E92-B, No. 06, pp.1981-1990, Jun. 2009.

TELECOM-ISAC, (2010). URL: *https://www.telecom isac.jp/index.html* (Japanes only)

Treinen, J. J. & Thurimella, R., (2006). A Framework for the Application of Association Rule Mining in Large Intrusion Detection Infrastructures, *RAID 2006*, LNCS 4219, pp. 1-18, 2006.

Yu, D. & Frincke, D., (2004). A Novel Framework for Alert Correlation and Understanding, *ACNS 2004*, LNCS 3089, pp. 452-466, 2004.

Vapnik, V., (1995). The nature of statistical learning theory, *Springer Verlag*, New York, 1995.

Vapnik, V., (1998). Statistical Learning Theory, *Wiley*, New York, 1998.

Wang, Q. & Megalooikonomou, V., (2005). A Clustering Algorithm for Intrusion Detection, In *SPIE Conference on Data Mining, Intrusion Detection, Information Assurance, and Data Networks Security*, 2005.

Warrender, C.; Forrest, S. & Pearlmutter, B., (1999). Detecting intrusions using system calls: alternative data models, *1999 IEEE Symposium on Security and Privacy*, pp. 133-145, IEEE Computer Society, 1999.

Zurutuza, U. & Uribeetxeberria, R., (2004). Intrusion Detection Alarm Correlation: A Survey, In *Proceedings of the IADAT International Conference on Telecommunications and Computer Networks*, 1-3 December, 2004.

Part 4

IDS Dedicated Mobile Networks – Design, Detection, Protection and Solutions

11

A Survey on new Threats and Countermeasures on Emerging Networks

Jacques Saraydayran[1], Fatiha Benali[2] and Luc Paffumi[1]
[1]*LogLogic R&D*
[2]*INSA de Lyon*
France

1. Introduction

Companies business is more and more influenced by the rapid evolution of technologies. Indeed, companies mostly rely on computers for their business processes, for instance to keep tracks of stocks, to automate orders, and to store business secrets. From the electronic mail and web sites to the electronic commerce or online banking, all types of electronic services are widely used by everyone nowadays; very soon most of daily tasks will be done through the Internet. Many companies have become interdependent on their business, and dependent on each other infrastructures. New users have emerged such as mobile users (who can be employees, partners, customers). Therefore, access to computer systems is no longer physically limited.

Initially, computer systems were designed for environments and purposes completely different than today's ones. Indeed, a lot of systems were designed for small research labs where people worked in a trusted environment and thus had few need of authentication or encryption mechanism. An example of such a system is the Internet Protocol (IP). Even if those problems are known, it is often difficult to make changes in systems, in particular in those used by a great number of people around the world. Current systems still have vulnerabilities in design, implementation and configuration that may be used by outsiders to penetrate systems, or by legitimate users to misusing their privileges. New threats emerged with new vulnerabilities: increase in amount of anomalous and malicious traffic on the Internet, destructive worms, virus that spread quickly, large coordinated attacks against organizations such as distributed denial-of-service attacks, and even small attacks are very frequent due to free availability of attacking tools. Threats are increasing both in number, severity, sophistication and impact. Attacks can cause serious damages such as loss of income, time, intellectual property, reputation, sensitive information and a disruption of critical operations within an organization.

In this context, security has been raised to an important level due to increased threats, as well as legislation and compliance requirements. The security is become necessary to protect our vulnerable society. First attentions were focused on protecting information systems and data from accidental or intentional unauthorized accesses, disclosure, modification, or destruction. The consequences of these mechanisms can range from degraded or disrupted service to customers to corporate failure. Today, traditional security mechanisms cannot completely address those threats and need to be improved with new intrusion detection mechanisms.

Intrusion detection covers both methods and tools to detect intrusions performed by both outsiders and insiders.

In various contexts such military communication services, on-demand service on mobile computer/PDA, emergence disaster coordinating efforts, the apparition of new needs highlights weaknesses of standard network architectures. New emerging networks grew up aiming at providing network communication between distributed mobile transmitters (probes, computer, mobile phone, PDA). Such networks, called Mobile Ad-hoc NETworks (MANET) consist of autonomous systems that are composed of a variety of mobile hosts. These hosts form a temporary network without any fixed architecture. A MANET provides new characteristics such as dynamic topology without any fixed architecture and entails some constraints (limited resources and physical architecture).

The success of the MANET networks increases due to its properties and new available services. Nevertheless, the success of such a network was followed by the emergence of a large amount of new threats. The characteristics of MANET networks imply new weaknesses and vulnerabilities. For example, the routing protocol is one of the most sensitive parts of a MANET network. Due to its configuration, the establishment of the network topology and the routing service is built through nodes collaboration. This collaboration is an opportunity for malicious nodes and attackers.

This chapter provides a survey of recent threats and attacks existing on MANET networks. In a first part, we will provide a description of new threats coming from on demand services and applications. This description include the presentation of attack classifications in the intrusion detection field and select some that fit with MANETs requirements. To counter such attacks, security mechanisms based on node collaboration and reputation are discussed and compared in a second part. Finally, the MANET threats and security are discussed in a last part.

2. Attacks and security breaches on MANET

As information systems become more and more important to our everyday lives, it is necessary to protect them from being compromised. In the information systems context, intrusions refer to any unauthorized access or malicious use of information resources.

2.1 General attacks

There are numerous network-based attacks that can be found in both wired and wireless network, this first part sums up the main ones.

- IP Spoofing
  The attacker uses the IP address of another machine to be "hidden" and exploit weak authentication methods. If the target machines rely on the IP address to authenticate (e.g. source IP address access lists), IP spoofing can give an attacker access to systems he should not have access to. Additionally, IP spoofing can make it very difficult to apprehend an attacker because logs will contain decoy addresses instead of real ones.
- Session hijack
  The attack consists in stealing network connections by kicking off the legitimate user or sharing a login. This type of attack is used against services with persistent login sessions, such as Telnet, rlogin, or FTP. For any of these services, an attacker can hijack a session and cause a great amount of damage. The connection between two hosts is monitored to observe the TCP sequence number of the packet. The attacker guesses the appropriate

sequence numbers and spoofs one of the participants address, taking over the conversation with the other participant.

- Denial-of-service (DoS)
  DoS attacks are among the most common exploits available today. As their name implies, a denial-of-service attack prevents (legitimate) users from being able to use a service. By bringing down critical servers, these attacks could also present a real physical threat to life. An attacker can cause the denial of service by flooding a system with bogus traffic. The technical result of a denial of service can range from applications sending wrong results to machines being down. Malformed Packet Attacks can be used to make DoS by generated badly formatted packets. Many vendor product implementations do not take into account all variations of user entries or packet types. If the software handles such errors poorly, the system may crash when receiving such packets. A classic example of this type of attack involves sending IP fragments to a system that overlap with each other. Some unpatched Windows and Linux systems will crash when they encounter such packets.
- Buffer overflow
  Buffer overflows attacks consists in injecting data into a program (e.g. in web page form) to run malicious code. They can be used by an attacker to take control of a remote system or by local malicious users to elevate their privileges. This exploits weak parameters verifications. If user input length is not examined by the code, a particular variable on the stack may exceed the memory allocated to it on the stack, overwriting all variables and even the return address for where execution should resume after the function is complete. Therefore, with very carefully constructed code, the attacker can actually enter information as a user into a program that consists of executable code and a new return address. Such attack allows an attacker to break out of the application code, and access any system components with the permissions of the broken program. If the broken program is running with superuser privileges, the attacker has taken over the machine with a buffer overflow.

2.2 Attacks on MANET

Security problematics on wired networks have been deeply studied. Many MANETs characteristics make it harder to secure such environment and new threats appeared on such networks. Those characteristics can be classified into 3 categories:

- Hardware: Node mobility, wireless medium, resources consumption,
- Communication: Distributed administration, variable topology,
- Software: On demand service, Reputation based applications.

Such MANET-specific attributes entails the appearance of new attacks that were classified and described in different papers. The following section describes the most know attacks. Due to the need of cooperation for network topology building, communication and services, distribution, new types of threats appears on MANET.

2.2.1 Hardware MANET attacks

One of the main MANETs properties is the wireless communication mode. Such communication mode has the advantage to allow network components to move easily without losing connection. Nevertheless wireless communications and mobility are very exposed to the following attacks.

- Eavesdropping
  This attack consists in sniffing the wireless medium to collect messages exchanged between

different nodes. This is a very simple attack as the wireless medium is shared by everyone in the MANET. If no cipher mechanism is used, the attacker can directly have access to the information exchanged. In case ciphering is used, many techniques allow attacker to uncipher weakly encrypted messages.

- Physical access to mobile components
  Mobile devices are smaller and smaller and are widely transported. Unlike laptops, PDAs and mobile phones (smartphones) are seldom securely locked and/or ciphered. If they are stolen, the attacker can, most of the time, easily take control of the device and steal information. In the worst cases, the attacker can enter a MANET thanks to the credentials left in the device.
- Wireless communication DoS
  Due to the wireless characteristics, all nodes belonging to a MANET receive all messages exchanged within their range. By injecting a huge amount of traffic close to the different machines, a denial of service can be triggered. Nodes having few computing capabilities will not be able to handle all traffic and could either crash or miss important messages.
- Signal jamming
  An attacker injects in the wireless medium some noise. The increased noise floor entails a degraded signal-to-noise ratio which prevents legitimate users to handle messages correctly.

2.2.2 Protocol MANET attacks

These types of attacks mainly target the routing features (discovery, forwarding, etc.) of the different nodes in the network. As there is no "routers" (devices dedicated to routing) in MANETs, the routing mechanisms are one of the most critical services of the MANETs.

- Wormhole attack Ilyas & Dorf (2003)
  This attack consists in collecting packets in a part of the MANET and sending them to another location, which generates a "tunnel". This latter is referred to as a wormhole. Legitimate nodes will miss information. This can especially generate wrong routing tables (if the original destination node does not receive updated routing information) on different nodes (see blackhole attack) or redirection of useful information to illegitimate users.
- Blackhole attack Baadache & Belmehdi (2010)
  In this attack, the attacker drops some of the received messages that should be forwarded. In a first step, the malicious node gives wrong routes to its neighbors. By doing this, legitimate nodes will send messages to malicious nodes that will drop all or part of the messages. Most of the time, only part of the messages is not forwarded to avoid suspicion of neighbors (that could monitor the traffic).
- Byzantine attack Awerbuch et al. (2002)
  Such an attack represents an attacker aiming at disturbing the overall network communication. The malicious node generates wrong routing information to create, for instance, loops, wrong paths which entail delays or packet drops.
- Routing table poisoning
  A malicious node sends erroneous routing updates to legitimate nodes or modifies correct route update packets. The legitimate nodes then use non-optimal routes and/or can generate network congestion.

- Routing table overflow
  Legitimate nodes in the network are sent route updates to non-existing nodes in order to generate an overflow of the routing tables and prevent the creation of entries corresponding to new routes to correct nodes. This attack is more effective on proactive routing protocols than on reactive ones.
- Malicious broken-links report
  The malicious nodes inform legitimate users that some links are broken whereas they are not. This attack affects route maintaining protocols or route discovering protocols.
- Rushing attack Hu et al. (2003b)
  Two malicious nodes take advantage of the tunnel generated by a wormhole attack. In certain cases, the "tunneled" packets will reach the destination before the normal route. Such a result characterizes the rushing attack.
- Resource consumption attack
  Malicious nodes inject wrong and extra information in the network. Such actions reduce the bandwidth available for "normal" activities and make them perform extra (unnecessary) actions. Consequently, that makes local resources (such as battery) decreasing quickly.
- Location disclosure attack
  This is a kind of information leak attack. Attackers gather information regarding the network topology (locations, routing information, etc.). This information is then used to build attack scenarios.

2.2.3 Software MANET attacks

On MANET nodes are most of the time resource limited. To reach some services, nodes need to ask service to neighbors. Such mechanisms are mainly based on node reputation for the service provider selection.

- Application proving fishing
  One of the characteristics of MANETs is their decentralized architecture. Applications can be run by any node on the network. The benefit of such architecture is its resilience to failures. However, a malicious node can take advantage and run fake applications. It then sends messages to their neighbors indicating that they run the application. Combined with previously presented attacks (e.g. wormhole), the malicious node can prevent other nodes to be aware of the correct location of the legitimate application and avoid any suspicion,
- Reputation Attack
  In some MANETs, in order to prevent the previous type of attacks, a trust mechanism has been designed: each node assigns a trust level to the other nodes of the network. This level is based on their direct and indirect relationships. By degrading the other legitimate nodes trust level, a malicious node can create a denial of service and/or a denial of participation in all or part of the communications. This is called a repudiation attack.

2.3 Attacks classification

Security countermeasures which are going to provide the essential tools to develop security defenses and improve the overall security outcomes, require a deep understanding of the threats. The overall tools used to protect the IS emphasize the complexity of collaborating all these tools and mapping the security threats through classification categories. Managing information security has to deal with the heterogeneity of data generated by the monitoring products. In follows, we discuss several research works that classify security threats.

There is a high number of attack classifications proposed in intrusion detection research. Four approaches were used to describe attacks: list of terms, taxonomies, ontologies and attacks language. The easiest classification is a list of single terms Cohen (1997), covering various aspects of attacks, the number of terms differs from author to author. Other authors have created categories to group many terms under a common definition. Cheswick and Bellovin classify attacks into seven categories Cheswick & Bellovin (1994). Stallings classification Stallings (1995) is based on the action, the model focuses on transiting data and defines four categories of attacks: interruption, interception, modification and fabrication. Cohen Cohen (1995) groups attacks into categories that describe the result of an attack. Some works developed categories based on empirical data, each one uses an events corpus generated in a specific environment. Neumann and Parker Neumann & Parker (1989) works were based on a corpus of 3000 incidents collected for 20 years; they created nine classes according to attacking techniques. Terms tend not to be mutually exclusive; this type of classification cannot provide a classification scheme that avoids ambiguity.

To avoid these drawbacks, a lot of taxonomies were developed to describe attacks. Neumann Neumann (1994) extended the classification in Neumann & Parker (1989) by adding the exploited vulnerabilities and the impact of the attack. Lindqvist and Jonson Lindqvist & Jonsson (1997) presented a classification based on the Neumann classification Neumann & Parker (1989). They proposed *intrusion results* and *intrusion techniques* as dimensions for classification. John Howard presented in Howard (April 1997) a process-driven taxonomy of computer and network attacks in five dimensions: *attackers, tools, access, results* and *objectives*. John Howard worked on the incidents of the Computer Emergency Response Team (CERT). Howard extends this work in Howard & Longstaff (1998) by refining some of the dimensions. Representing attacks by taxonomies is an improvement compared with the list of terms: individual attacks are described with an enriched semantics, but taxonomies fail to meet mutual exclusion requirements, some of the categories may overlap. However, the ambiguity problem still exists with the refined taxonomy.

Undercoffer and al Undercoffer et al. (2003) describe attacks by an ontology. It is a new effort for describing attacks in intrusion detection field by sharing the knowledge about intrusions in distributed IDS environment. Initially, they developed a taxonomy defined by *the target, means, consequences of an attack* and *the attacker*. The taxonomy was extended to an ontology, by defining the various classes, their attributes and their relations based on an examination of 4000 alerts. The authors have built correlation decisions based on the knowledge that exists in the modeling. The developed ontology represents the data model for the triggered information by IDSs.

Attack languages are proposed by several authors to detect intrusions. These languages are used to describe the presence of attacks in a suitable format. These languages are classified into six distinct categories Eckmann et al. (2002): *Exploit languages, event languages, detection languages, correlation languages, reporting languages* and *response languages*. The correlation languages are currently the interest of several researchers in the intrusion detection community. They specify relations between attacks to identify numerous attacks against the system. These languages have different characteristics but are suitable for intrusion detection in a particular environment. Language models are based on the models that are used for describing alerts or events semantics. They do not model the semantics of events but they implicitly use taxonomies of attacks in their modeling.

All the researches quoted above only give a partial vision of the monitored system, they were focused on the conceptualization of attacks or incidents, which is due to the consideration of

a single type of monitoring product, the IDS.
It is important to mention the efforts done to realize a data model for information security. The first attempts were undertaken by the American agency - Defense Advanced Research Projects Agency (DARPA), which has created the Common Intrusion Detection Framework (CIDF) Staniford-Chen & Schnackenberg (1998). The objective of the CIDF is to develop protocols and applications so that intrusion detection research projects can share information. Work on CIDF was stopped in 1999 and this format was not implemented by any product. Some ideas introduced in the CIDF have encouraged the creation of a work group called Intrusion Detection Working Group (IDWG) at Internet Engineering Task Force (IETF) co-directed by the former coordinators of CIDF. IETF have proposed the Intrusion Detection Message Exchange Format (IDMEF) Curry & Debar (2007) as a way to set a standard representation for intrusion alerts. The effort of the IDMEF is centered on alert syntax representation. In the implementations of IDSs, each IDS chooses the name of the attack, different IDSs can give different names to the same attack. As a result, similar information can be tagged differently and handled as two different alerts (IDMEF became a standard format with the RFC 4765 Curry & Debar (2007)).
There is no previous work reported in the literature about specific attack classifications in Wireless Sensor Networks (WSN). Partial solutions exist that allows checking the security of the WSN against a some type of attacks Perrig et al. (2002). Recent work in Padmavathi & Shanmugapriya (2009) have classified attacks basically into two categories; active attacks and passive attacks. Under each category, a list of attacks and their definition that widely happen on WSN are presented. No classification scheme or rule were presented to avoid ambiguity.
Even if it is not specific to MANETs, an interesting attack classification was proposed in Paulauskas & Garsva (2006). Authors suggest to characterize attacks around 14 attributes: the objective of the attack(1), the effect type produce by the attack(2), the OSI layer involved (3), the targeted Operating System (4), the location of the attacker (5), the attacker target location (6) and the attacked service (7), attack concentration (8) (e.g. target one packet or several packets), need of feedback (9) (e.g. sniffing attack do not need feedback), the initial attack conditions (10), the impact type (11), the number of attack sources (13) and connection quantity (14) (figure 1). Detailing number of attack parameters, this approach is an effective way to classify and define attacks.

2.4 MANET attacks classification mapping

As presented in the previous section, MANETs, in a security point of view, are very interesting and offer various challenges. Not only are they vulnerable to generic threats but as well to wireless specific ones. To better understand them and find the best solutions to faces those attacks, classifications - presented above - were used. The attack classification of Paulauskas & Garsva (2006) allows clearly defining attacks and classifying them. We propose to map the 14 features defined in their paper with the MANET attacks defined in 2.2 (figure 2).
First of all, all MANET attacks share common features:

- *Target Location* (6): in MANET each node collaborates with unknown node to build a network. Each targeted object is located on individual node. Despite the entire network could be affected the target object is still located on locate system (6.1) for each participant.
- *Attack Execution Initial Condition* (10): all described attacks are focused on ad hoc network. The initial condition for these attacks is that the targeted object (10.1) runs dynamic ad hoc routing protocol and wireless communications.
- *Connection quantity* (14): described attacks always used single connection (14.1) attack type.

1 Objective		2 Effect Type		3 ISO		4 OS		5 Attacker Location	
1.1	Super-User privilege gain	2.1	Executable code detection	3.1	Physical	4.1	Windows	5.1	Inside Local Segment
1.2	User Privilege gain	2.2	Trojan" horse, virus	3.2	Data Link	4.2	Linux	5.2	Between Segment
1.3	Denial of Service	2.3	Web application executable code detection	3.3	Network	4.3	Solaris	5.3	Physical Access
1.4	Information integrity violation	2.4	Unauthorized proxy server use	3.4	Transport	4.4	BSD	5.4	System User Privilege
1.5	Information or Resource Confidentiality violation	2.5	Buffer overflow	3.5	Session	4.5	MacOs	5.5	System Admin Privilege
1.6	Malicious code execution	2.6	Probe or scan	3.6	Presentation	4.6	Other		
1.7	Security policy violation	2.7	Nonstandard protocol use	3.7	Application				
		2.8	Nonstandard port use						
		2.9	Masquerading as another host						
		2.10	False object insertion						

6 Targeted Location		7 Targeted Service		8 Attack Concentration		9 FeedBack		10 Initial Condition	
6.1	Local System	7.1	Web(http)	8.1	Atomic	9.1	With Feedback	10.1	On attack request
6.2	Local Network	7.2	File Transfert(FTP,SMB,CIFS)	8.2	Fragmented	9.2	Without Feedback	10.1	On specified attack object
6.3	Global Network	7.3	Mail(SMTP,POP3,IMAP)					10.2	Unconditional
6.4	Wireless Network	7.4	Network Control (SNMP)						
6.5	P2P Network	7.5	Domain Name (DNS)						
		7.6	Remote Control(telnet,ssh,RDP)						
		7.7	Host Configuration (DHCP)						
		7.8	Dynamic Routing (RIP,OSPF,BGP,....)						
		7.9	Encryption(SSL)						
		7.10	Other						

11 Impact Type		12 Attack automation		13 Attack source		14 Connection	
11.1	active	12.1	Automatic	13.1	One vs one	14.1	Single
11.2	passive	12.2	Semi-Automatic	13.2	Many vs one	14.2	Multiple
		12.3	Manual	13.3	One vs many		

Fig. 1. Attack Taxonomy Paulauskas & Garsva (2006)

The feature *Operating System* (4) is not mandatory for MANET attack. In fact all attacks depend on the specifics routing protocol and not a specific Operating System.
The attack objective of MANET attacks are mostly focused on the *DoS* (1.3) on the routing protocol and produce a *non standard protocol use* (2.7). Some others attacks (Eavesdropping,Physical access to mobile components,Location disclosure attack) attempt to gathering information (1.5) working as *probe or scan* (2.6).
Three types of ISO layers are targeted:

- The *Physical* (3.1) layer inducing two types of attacker location: a *Physical Access* (5.3) to the MANET component itself and *Inside Local Segments* (5.2) location meaning that attacker is in the radio range of the targeted component,
- The *Network* layer (3.3) implying that the attacker is at least *Between Segments* (5.2),
- The *Application* layer (3.7) concerning the Reputation attack.

Targeted Service mainly differs from hardware attack to protocol attacks. Protocol attacks target the collaborative *routing service* (7.8) whereas Hardware attack disturbs physical communication or physically access to data (*other* 7.10). Software attack differs also from Protocol attacks by targeted "'service provider"' mechanism (*other* 7.10).
Finally, all considered attacks are active by interacting directly with the MANET components (*active* 11.1). Only Eavesdropping and Location disclosure use only received information (*passive* 11.2). MANET attacks are complex and need to exchange several information to produce the expected effect (attack *fragmented* 8.2 except Physical Access). With the help of context aware definition MANET attacks could be automated(*Semi-Automatic* 12.2). Only the Physical Access attacks involve manual actions of the attacker.

	1	Objective	2	Effect Type	3	ISO	5	Attacker Location	7	Targeted Service	9	Feedback	8	Attack Concentration	11	Impact Type	12	Attack automation
Eavesdropping	1.5	Information or Resource Confidentiality violation	2.6	Probe or scan	3.1	Physical	5.1	Inside Local Segment	7.10	Other	9.2	Without feedback	8.2	Fragmented	11.2	passive	12.2	Semi-Automatic
Physical access to mobile components	1.5	Information or Resource Confidentiality violation	2.6	Probe or scan	3.1	Physical	5.3	Physical Access	7.10	Other	9.1	With feedback	8.1	Atomic	11.1	active	12.3	Manual
Wireless communication DoS	1.3	DoS	2.7	Nonstandard protocol use	3.1	Physical	5.1	Inside Local Segment	7.10	Other	9.2	Without feedback	8.2	Fragmented	11.1	active	12.2	Semi-Automatic
Signal jamming	1.3	DoS	2.7	Nonstandard protocol use	3.1	Physical	5.1	Inside Local Segment	7.10	Other	9.2	Without feedback	8.2	Fragmented	11.1	active	12.2	Semi-Automatic
Wormhole attack	1.3	DoS	2.7	Nonstandard protocol use	3.3	Network	5.2	Between segments	7.8	Dynamic Routing (RIP,OSPF,BGP,..)	9.1	With feedback	8.2	Fragmented	11.1	active	12.2	Semi-Automatic
Blackhole attack	1.3	DoS	2.7	Nonstandard protocol use	3.3	Network	5.2	Between segments	7.3	Dynamic Routing (RIP,OSPF,BGP,..)	9.2	Without feedback	8.2	Fragmented	11.1	active	12.2	Semi-Automatic
Byzantine attack	1.3	DoS	2.7	Nonstandard protocol use	3.3	Network	5.2	Between segments	7.3	Dynamic Routing (RIP,OSPF,BGP,..)	9.1	With feedback	8.2	Fragmented	11.1	active	12.2	Semi-Automatic
Routing table poisoning	1.3	DoS	2.7	Nonstandard protocol use	3.3	Network	5.2	Between segments	7.8	Dynamic Routing (RIP,OSPF,BGP,..)	9.1	With feedback	8.2	Fragmented	11.1	active	12.2	Semi-Automatic
Routing table overflow	1.3	DoS	2.5	Buffer overflow	3.3	Network	5.2	Between segments	7.8	Dynamic Routing (RIP,OSPF,BGP,..)	9.1	With feedback	8.2	Fragmented	11.1	active	12.2	Semi-Automatic
Malicious broken-links report	1.3	DoS	2.7	Nonstandard protocol use	3.3	Network	5.2	Between segments	7.8	Dynamic Routing (RIP,OSPF,BGP,..)	9.1	With feedback	8.2	Fragmented	11.1	active	12.2	Semi-Automatic
Rushing attack	1.3	DoS	2.7	Nonstandard protocol use	3.3	Network	5.2	Between segments	7.8	Dynamic Routing (RIP,OSPF,BGP,..)	9.1	With feedback	8.2	Fragmented	11.1	active	12.2	Semi-Automatic
Resource consumption attack	1.3	DoS	2.7	Nonstandard protocol use	3.3	Network	5.2	Between segments	7.8	Dynamic Routing (RIP,OSPF,BGP,..)	9.1	With feedback	8.2	Fragmented	11.1	active	12.2	Semi-Automatic
Location disclosure attack	1.5	Information or Resource Confidentiality violation	2.6	Probe or scan	3.3	Network	5.2	Between segments	7.8	Dynamic Routing (RIP,OSPF,BGP,..)	9.1	With feedback	8.2	Fragmented	11.2	passive	12.2	Semi-Automatic
Reputation Attack	1.3	DoS	2.7	Nonstandard protocol use	3.7	Application	5.2	Between segments	7.10	Other	9.1	With feedback	8.2	Fragmented	11.1	active	12.2	Semi-Automatic

Fig. 2. MANET Attack Taxonomy Mapping

3. Countermeasure and security achievements on MANET

The section 2.2 describes and defines attack opportunity on MANET. Despite lots of attack vectors on wireless communications, collaborative routing protocol and collaborative services providing, emerging security solutions and protocols exist and preserve MANET from such threads. In this section, the different counter measures mechanisms are presented and compared allowing showing the current available thread countermeasures.

3.1 Security challenges

Securing company data, activities and communications become an open challenge and especially nowadays where collaboration and on demand services grow up. As introduced in 1, the appearance of new needs involved the emergence of new vulnerabilities and cyber criminality organizations. The first step to deal with this threat is to understand what security means in our company/organization context. All risk management procedures (*COBIT* (2007),*ISO 27000 series* (2005)]) are organized around the following fundamental security indicators Bing Wu (2006):

- **Confidentiality** is to keep information available only for authorized entities (users, applications, nodes). All unauthorized entities cannot read, manipulate, execute or gather information coming from the system. E.g. invoices can only be read by users of the sales/accounting entity.
- **Integrity** ensures that transmitted/stored/used information is not altered or destroyed by any illegal manipulation. E.g. an email sent is not modified until it reaches its destination.
- **Availability** ensures that services can be used at any moment and provide the expected results. Any service (application, networks, hardware) is kept available to legitimate entities. Most of the time, DoS attacks target availability of systems.
- **Accountability** ensures that any entity that performs an action can be made responsible for its actions. This entails the use of authentication mechanisms. Access control allowing only authorized users, network flows or packets can be viewed as a sub-property of authentication.
- **Non-repudiation** defines the fact that entities making an action cannot claim that they did not perform this action. E.g. a user who digitally signed an email cannot deny that he has not sent this email.

3.2 Countermeasure and security tools definition

Countermeasures, which can be procedures and security tools, aim at ensuring that one or several Security Indicators linked to an object are preserved. To define a security tool we will address the following six questions:

- **Why** is the security tool used for? Which type of security indicators is targeted by the security tool?
- **What** types of services are protected by the security tool?
- **When** is the security tool active? When does the security tool operate to reach its objective?
- **Where** is the security tool active? What is the monitoring perimeter?
- **Who** is responsible for the security tool? What is his objective?
- **How** does the security tool work to reach its objective?

Several security tool properties have been described in literature to classify those tools in different families (Debar et al. (1999)). In this section, we propose a set of attributes responding to the questions listed above. They are firstly presented and then described. The security indicators are used to define the **Why** attribute. The **What** is defined by the OSI Layer attribute defining the targeted services. The **When** question is covered by the Time Frame attribute. The Scope attribute (area monitored by the tool) defines the **Where**. The person responsible for the the security tool (**Who**) is expressed in the Security tools attribute called purpose. Finally the Internal Architecture attribute determines the **How**.

- **OSI Layer** : Several approaches classified security breaches and attacks Paulauskas & Garsva (2006). ISO layer appears as a starting point to know which service is protected by the security tool. This attribute "localizes" the action of the security tool. The Open System Interconnection (OSI) layer ISO-IEC (1994) is composed of the well known seven layers:
  - Physical layer is composed of all hardware or physical processes. This layer defined the electrical and physical specifications for devices. Physical layer security tools can be biometrics door mechanisms, digital lock as well as channel radio selection.
  - Data Link layer aims at providing communication with direct neighbor in Wan network or in nodes on a same segment in LAN. Intrusion Detection system monitoring ARP address and preventing ARP attack or MAC address spoofing securing the Data link Layer.
  - Network is responsible for all data transition between network segments inside a LAN/MAN/WAN. This layer aims at defining packet path and network topology. Varieties of security tools operating at this level. Tools like Intrusion Detection System, Secure routing protocol or virtual Private Network can be quoted.
  - Transport layer manages end-to-end communication. This is the upper layer where error correction is managed. Transport Layer Security protocol (RFC 2246) is one of the most important ways to secure the transport layer.
  - Session layer aims at synchronizing communications and managing transactions. This consists, for instance, in correcting errors by restoring past known states.
  - Presentation layer ensures the application data encoding. This layer converts data between manipulated applicative data and byte chain forwarded by the network.
  - Application layer manages all communications and data of applications and services. Most of security tools cover the session, the presentation and the application layers. Anti-viruses are well known security tools ensuring the good behavior of applications.
- **Protect purpose** : the security indicators (Confidentiality, Integrity, Availability, Accountability, Non-repudiation) that should be ensured but the security tools are referred to as protect purpose.
- **Scope** : Security tools operate at different locations of the Information System. Four perimeters have been identified from the Host (specific coverage) to the Whole System (extended coverage).
  - Single Component : security tools aims at protecting a single host. Antiviruses or personal Firewalls focus their work on single network components.

  - Network Area: security tools protect components of a delimited network zone. Located on network segments, Network Intrusion Detection Systems are especially designed to detect malicious network activities. Firewalls become also key security points in the protection of LANs or DeMilitarized Zones (DMZ).
  - Overall IS: the security tool intends to protect the entire company or organism Information System. We can quote Distributed IDS, protecting all IS components or Public Key Infrastructure allowing communication privacy in the IS.
  - Communication: security tools aiming at ensuring a security indicator such as confidentiality or availability are often embedded inside communication protocol. Secure Routing protocol (ad hoc secure routing protocol) ensuring the whole system secure behavior is an example.
- **Purpose** : Bing Wu (2006) defines two families of security tools classified according to their manager's purposes.
  - Preventive: all security tools aiming at avoiding attacks or malicious activities by assuring authentication or encryption form the first line of defense in the IS. Cryptographic protocols, secure routing protocols, physical authentication mechanisms (PIN code) are examples of such preventive mechanisms.
  - Reactive security tools form the second line of defense ensuring the detection and reaction against attacks. IDS, antiviruses are part of this second line of defense.
- **Internal Architecture** defines how the tool's modules work and its behavior. It also specifies the internal communication.
  - Standalone architecture means that the security tool is isolated and makes decision alone. Configuration files and security policies are directly loaded on a single component. Most of firewalls are classified in this category using its own knowledge of the environment.
  - Central architecture defines security tool collecting information through probes and making decisions on a central computation point. Security Event Management systems (LogLogic SEM, Prelude) use distributed agents to collect information. The set of data are then analyzed on a central component.
  - Hierarchical architecture describes security tool that uses distributed components. Each component holds an analysis function block aims at making a local decision (Zheng Zhang & Ucles (2001), S. Staniford-Chen & Zerkle (1996)). Several levels can be implemented, each one managing the lower level.
  - Collaborative architecture provides communication between distributed security components. Decision is not computed on a central component but coming from the exchanged experience between each security component. Such architecture allows achieving a Security objective with the help of the others entities. Local decision is improved with the enrichment neighbors information and global decision can be made to improve the global system security Martin Rehak (2008).
  - Protocol architecture defines security tools embedded in global system behavior. The success of such system is based on predefined policy respected by each component in the network. PKI architectures hold cryptographic rules and best practices. Any entity wanting to benefit from such security mechanism needs to respect protocol to be able to exchange information.

- **Time frame** attribute is used to identify the security tool protection period. It describes when the security tool operates.
  - Real-Time processes are running all the time by, they do not have to be triggered to be active. Mechanisms such as encryption are a good example.
  - On demand processes are only called whenever they are needed. For instance, forensics T. Duval & Roger (2004), vulnerability scanners (Nessus, Qualys) and backup systems are on demand systems.

3.3 Security tools parameters representation

To easily compare Security tools, we provide a security tool parameters graphical representation allowing to link parameters together. Two different panels are used. The first panel represents a list of protection purposes. This list displays an overview of the security indicators covered by presented security tools. A second panel is composed of a radar chart representing the other security parameters defined in section 3.2. The parameters are organized as follow.

On the left part of the graph, the Time Frame and Purpose parameters are listed. This side of the graph represents the reactivity of the security tools. Real-time (Time Frame) and reactive (Purpose) security tools parameters are more reactive than on-demand (Time Frame) and preventive (Purpose) security tool.

On the right part of the graph, the scope and internal architecture parameters expresses the global coverage of the security tool. Communication (Scope) and protocol (Internal Architecture) security tool parameter have got a wider coverage than Single component (scope) and standalone (Internal Architecture).

The top branch is the layer parameter. This parameter is transversal to the others.

3.4 Security tool attributes allocates: samples

This section shows how the Security tools parameters representation allows comparing different security tools. We will take as examples a Certificate and a Firewall.

3.4.1 Certificate security tool

Certificates are built to prove the Identity of its owner. Different objects are held by the certificate such as user or component identities (Name, Group,...), public key of the certificate owner, digital signature of the Certificate Authority (CA) who delivered the certificate. Certificate can be used to ensuring the authentication its owner, using the asymmetric encryption mechanism certificate can guaranty non-repudiation and integrity of messages sent (digital signature of the owner), confidentiality of exchanges (encryption with public key). The certificate is defined by the following attributes:

- Layer (What): Application layer, PKI guaranties confidentiality, integrity, non-repudiation from the network communication to the application used. In case of the sending an email, digital signature, ensures the integrity of the message sent during the computation of the mail application, the "transformation" of the presentation/session layer and during the message transport (transport/network/data Link/Physical layers).
- Protect Purpose (Why): Confidentiality, Integrity, Authentication and Non-Repudiation.
- Time Frame (When): On-Demand, the certificate properties used would be done on the demand of the application.

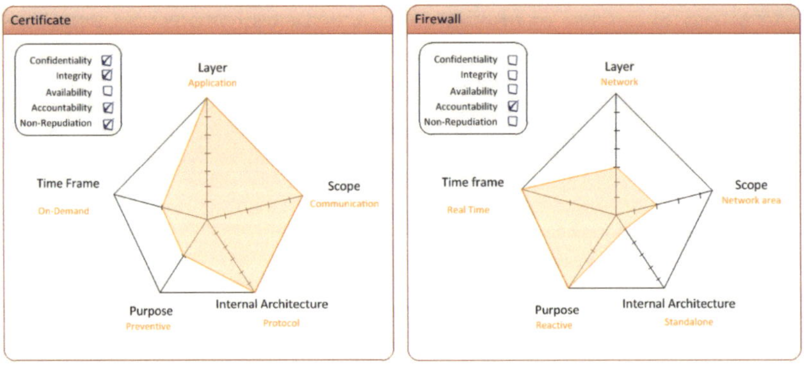

Fig. 3. Firewall Security Attribute Definition

- Scope (Where): Overall IS, the application of the certificate properties are available on the all the Information System.
- Purpose (Who): Preventive System, the security indicators covers by certificate prevents information from information disclosure and unauthorized modifications.
- Internal Architecture (How): Protocol, the deployment of certificates is realized via a Public Key Infrastructure. Any used components of the Information System needs to know How certificates and asymmetric encryption work to apply the security properties.

3.4.2 Firewall security tool

Firewall system aims at blocking all unauthorized network flows both from public network to the internal system and from internal system to the public network. the firewall is defined by the following attributes (figure 3)

- Layer (What): Network, Firewalls operated at the network level by analyzing network flows and apply authorized flows rules. Some firewalls operate at higher levels acting like proxies.
- Protect Purpose (Why): Authentication, Firewall guaranties an access control of the incoming network traffic.
- Time Frame (When): Real time, each incoming network flow is analyzed and dropped if needed.
- Scope (Where): Network area, Firewall guaranties the protection of defined networks area. In case of a company composed of several sites, several firewalls would be used, each one to protect one site.
- Purpose (Who): Reactive, the firewall allows blocking unauthorized communication by dropping network packet.
- Internal Architecture (How): Standalone, a firewall is an autonomous system, making decision only with its internal rules.

The figure 3 shows the representation of the 2 security tools. As displayed, certificate cover a larger security perimeter than the firewall but is less reactive.

3.5 MANET counter-measures definition

Some recent papers provide interesting surveys of different countermeasures on MANETs Ngadi et al. (2008), Satria Mandala & Abdullah (2006). Some papers provide security

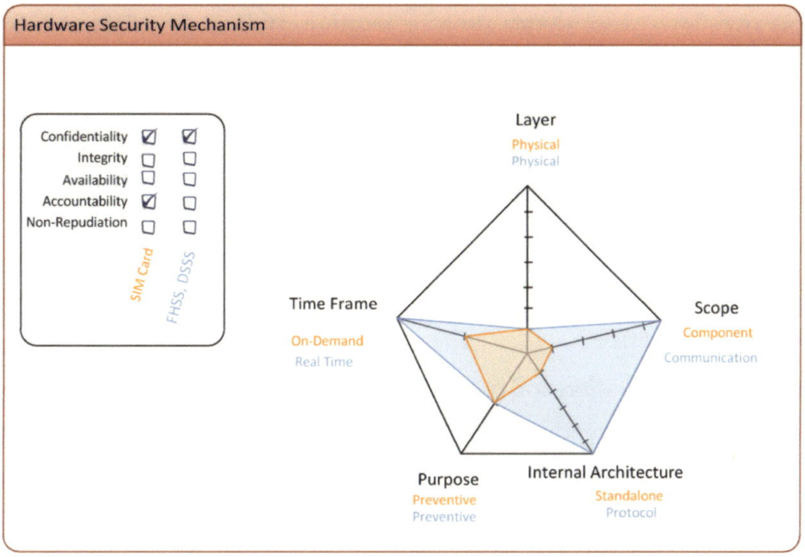

Fig. 4. Hardware Security Mechanism Attributes

mechanisms classified by OSI layer Bing Wu (2006). In this section, security tools are organized around the previously defined categories: hardware security mechanisms, protocol security mechanism, software security mechanism.

3.5.1 Hardware security mechanism

MANETs are composed of a set of mobile components. Mobile components can be smart phone, laptop, PDA, probes. Such component can hold physical protection against unauthorized use. Common mechanism like SIM cards rely on a PIN code to access to the component. More sophisticated approaches use biometrics mechanisms (fingerprint, Iris identification), token or smart card for components authentication. The security attributes definition of SIM cards are displayed in blue in the figure 4.
Moreover, wireless MANET communications can be intercepted by anyone monitoring Radio Frequency spectrum. As explained before, MANET communications can be jammed or interfered, creating loses of data integrity or denial of service. FHSS Stallings (2002) modulates the signal with radio frequency series avoiding signal discovering or jamming. DSSS Stallings (2002) is another solution by modulating each bit of the communication with a "spreading code". The spreading code spreads the signal across a wider frequency band in proportion to the number of bit used. Such technique shares similar security attributes but covers different security goals (displayed in orange in the figure 4).

3.5.2 Protocol security mechanism

Communication protocol recommendation:
The 802.11 IEEE (2007) norm provides recommendation to secure communication in wireless environments. Encryption protocols such as WEP, WPA are specified to ensure confidentiality between wireless communications.
Routing security protocol:
As defined in section 1, collaboration between mobile components is used to route information across the network. This collaboration can lead to attacks such as Black Hole, Worm hole,

Routing table overflow, Sleep deprivation or location disclosure. Main efforts have been made to secure MANET routing protocol. Khan (2004) provide a survey of major types of secure routing protocol. Secure Routing Protocol (SRP) Papadimitratos et al. (2006) secures the MANET systems against the network topology discovering. SRP is a secure variant of the Dynamic Source Routing (DSR) Johnson & Broch (2001). It uses symmetric-key authentication (MACs) between the source and the target nodes. There is only end-to-end authentication. The route is sent to the trust destinations and the replies travel through the same route. This routing protocol avoids black whole attack.

Packet Leashes Hu et al. (2003a) is keeping constraints on packet in a Temporal or Geographical way. In the case of the Geographical constraints, the following information can be computed and kept:

- Where in location information and loosely synchronized clocks is used to create a leash,
- The distance between the sender and receiver is calculated nodes velocity and timestamps.

Packet Leashes avoids wormhole and can be used in addition to other routing protocol.

Secure Efficient Ad hoc Distance Vector Routing Protocol SEAD Hu et al. (2002) is a distance vector routing protocol extending the Destination Sequences Distance Vector routing protocol (DSDV) in which was added One way Hash Chain mechanism. In DSDV each node maintains routing information for all known destinations. Instead of asymmetric cryptographic operations, SEAD uses efficient one-way hash function to prevent sequence number and hop count from being modified by malicious nodes. SEAD uses the one-way hash function to authenticate the metric and the sequence number of a routing table. The receiver of the routing information authenticates also the sender. SEAD is robust against multiple uncoordinated attackers creating incorrect routing states but failed against the wormhole attack.

Ariadne is an on demand routing protocol Hu et al. (2005). This on demand routing protocol assumes the fact that a sending node attempts to discover a route to a destination only when it has a need to send data to that destination. In the Ariadne protocol routing messages are authenticated with 3 available schema shared secrets between each pair of nodes, Time-delayed broadcast authentication TESLA Perrig et al. (2002) and digital signatures. The route management, for its part, is done by the DSR protocol.

If the shared secret is used; each node forwarding a request includes a MAC computed with the key it shares with the target. Then, this MAC is included in a MAC list, analogous to the node list in a normal request packet. Finally, the destination checks the authentication for each hop and sent the route to the source.

If the TESLA authentication is used; each node forwarding a request includes a MAC computed using a TESLA key. The target checks TESLA security condition for each hop, then authenticates the reply message to avoid modification. Each intermediate node buffers packet until it can disclose its TESLA key, then includes key in the reply. At the end the source verifies each nodes key and MAC.

The digital signature can be used with the help of a PKI infrastructure. Each mobile component holds a certificate, each route message can be sign with the private key of the message owner. This type of authentication requires the use of effective PKI on MANET (virtual Certificate Authority Zhou & Haas (1999), certificate chaining Hubaux et al. (2001) and hybrid method Yi & Kravets (2004)). Ariadne avoids wormhole attacks.

The Authentication Routing for Ad hoc Networks (ARAN) Mahmoud et al. (2005) is an on-demand routing protocol using public key cryptography to avoid any routes modification. The ARAN protocol is used mainly on open infrastructure where network nodes can interact

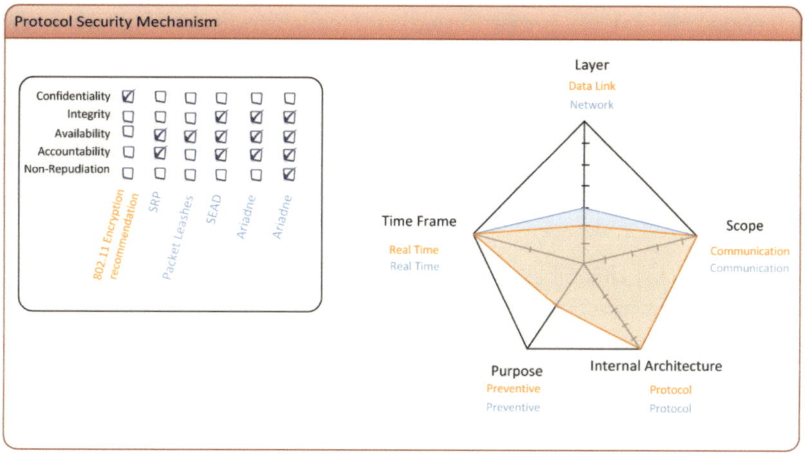

Fig. 5. Protocol Security Mechanism Attributes

with a fixed PKI infrastructure. ARAN protocol guaranties message authentication, integrity and non repudiation.

3.5.3 Software security mechanism

According to Satria Mandala & Abdullah (2006) MANET networks are more vulnerable than conventional networks due to their cooperative algorithms, lacks of centralized monitoring, management point and lack of clear line of defense. Intrusion Detection can be viewed as a second line of defense in MANET networks ensuring a complementary defense to preventive technique like secure routing and encryption mechanism. Intrusion Detection Systems are mainly classified into Host Intrusion detection System (HIDS) and Network Intrusion Detection System (NIDS). HIDS are in charge of the security of a single component. Verifying authorized and usage system activity (login Activity Monitoring, System Call activity Eskin et al. (2001) or incoming Network activity), HIDS detection intrusion through intrusion signature base or anomaly detection. NIDS monitors network flow (network sessions, packets content and structure Sourcefire (1998). They also sometimes compute network trends Paul Barford & Ron (2002)) located at strategic network points such as network entries (frontend or backend firewall locations) and network concentrators (switches). NIDS also use signature based and anomaly detection techniques. As MANETs are completely decentralized and do not have a fixed network infrastructure, NIDS, as known is wired network, cannot be considered in such network. HIDS are in charge of securing the local component network activity with the collaboration of other members. In this section we follow the baseline of Ngadi et al. (2008) to present some Intrusion Detection System References in MANET. The authors provide a summary of such techniques in a table comparing these research achievements on MANET IDS (figure 6).
In the Intrusion detection (ID) and Response System Zhang et al. (2003) each node holds an IDS in charge of the local component monitoring. In this approach, the monitoring is focused on user and system activities and communication activities. If an anomaly is detected, the IDS system launches a local response. If the IDS is not able to launch itself a response, collaboration with neighbors is requested to launch a global reaction. Moreover, if the local system comes in an indecisiveness state, the other nodes' help is requested to make the decision.
The Local Intrusion Detection System (LIDS) Albers et al. (2002) uses mobile agents for

intrusion detection. Based on a distributed and collaborative architecture, two types of messages are exchanged between LIDS nodes: intrusion alerts resulting of a local detection and data logs coming from the local monitoring information. When local LIDS detect an anomaly, if evidences are insufficient, local LIDS can ask neighbors for additional information. In case of an intrusion detection (both anomaly and misuse detection are supported), the local LIDS launches a response and informs the other nodes in the network. As soon as the intrusion alert is received by another node, this one launches an adequate response to prevent itself from the detected attack.
Kachirski & Guha (2003) describes a Multisensor Intrusion Detection System where each nodes hold the following function.

- Monitoring function is in charge of detecting User-Level, System Level and Packet level intrusion,
- Decision function aims at identifying anomalies as intrusion and selecting countermeasure actions,
- Action function ensures the local execution of the countermeasure actions.

In such IDS method, some nodes are selected to monitor networks activity and make global decisions. Such nodes receive alert reports from all nodes in charged. Each node is associated to a threat level defining if the node is compromised or not. When a threat level is exceeded in the global decision, an order is sent to all nodes to launch a specific action against the compromised node.
A Dynamic intrusion detection hierarchy Sterne et al. (2005) provides an approach similar to Kachirski & Guha (2003). Nodes in the network are distinguished in "cluster head" nodes in charge of "cluster leaf" nodes. Each node aims at monitoring, logging, analyzing, responding and reporting to cluster heads. Head cluster nodes are in charge of additional tasks such as gathering received data (fusion), filtering data, high level intrusion detection. The main point of the Sterne et al. (2005) is its capability of cascading different cluster head nodes levels. This property allows the IDS architecture to be scalable.
Zone Based IDS (ZIDS) Sun et al. (2003) try to solve the alert aggregation issue. Assuming the fact that, in collaborative environments, security mechanisms can be flooded by security alert,

Author(s)	Name Specific	Architecture	Addressed Attacks type			Data Source	Technique detection	Routing protocol	Environm ents	Contribution
			Au-then-tica-tion	Routing (black hole, etc)	Sel-fish					
Zhang and Lee, Y. Huang	None	Distributed and collaborative	No	Yes (misrouting, packet dropping)	No	Audit trail (event log processing)	Anomaly	AODV, DSR, DSDV	Simulation	IDS agent for collaboration detection
P. Albers, O. Camp	LIDS	Distributed and collaborative	No	No	No	Audit trail (event log processing)	Misuse, anomaly	Not identified	Simulation	Local IDS mobile agent for intrusion detection model
Kachirski and Guha	None	Hierarchical architecture	No	No	No	Audit trail (event log processing)	Anomaly	Not identified	Simulation	Hierarchical IDS using mobile agent
Sterne et al.	None	Hierarchical architecture	No	No	No	Audit trail (event log processing)	Misuse, Anomaly	Not identified	Simulation	Dynamic intrusion detection hierarchy model
B. Sun, K.Wu, and U. W. Pooch	ZBIDS	Distributed and collaborative	No	Yes (Disruption attacks)	No	Audit trail (event log processing)	Anomaly	DSR	Simulation	Routing protocol protection from disruption

Fig. 6. Comparison researches achievement on the MANET IDS Ngadi et al. (2008)

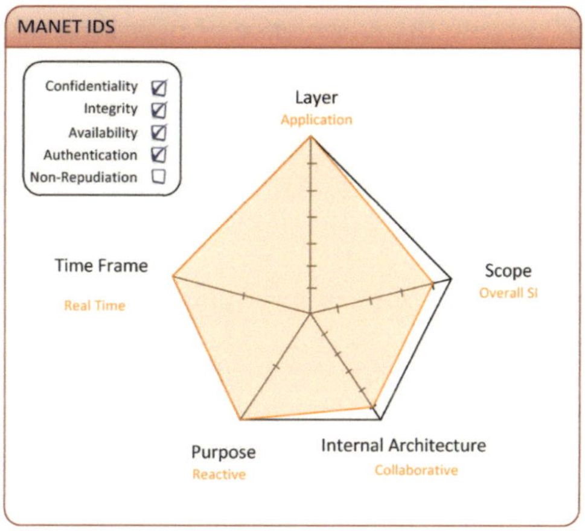

Fig. 7. Software Security Mechanism

the authors suggest the presence of alert concentration points gathering similar security alerts. The scalability issue is also targeted. By providing a non-overlapping zone-based framework, ZIDS selects a set of zones of a suitable size. When an intrusion is detected by a node, the alert message is broadcasted to all nodes of the current zone. Nodes in the same zone simply forward the received alerts. Nodes belonging to inter-zone (belonging to 2 different zones) receiving such alerts would aggregate and correlate alerts before generating alarms in the second zone.
All MANET IDS needs cooperation to prevent network and nodes from malicious activities. This collaboration is made through a collaborative architecture. MANET IDS mainly provide higher layers protection, detecting and responding when signatures or anomalies are detected on monitored users and application logs. MANET IDS share similar security attributes: preventing system against vulnerability exploit on data confidentiality and integrity, system authentication and then node availability (figure 7).

4. Conclusion / discussion

In this paper, we provide a survey of current attacks and countermeasures on MANETs. The main MANET properties imply a routing protocol collaboration and reputation mechanisms to share services. Such collaboration creates new types of attacks. Most of these attacks intent to disable the routing protocol (section 2). Threats on MANETs range from the wireless communication DoS to the service providing disturbing and fishing. Numbers of new attacks target the MANET properties such as radio communication medium, protocol collaboration and application collaboration. Mapping MANET attacks to the attack classification of Paulauskas & Garsva (2006) allows us to better clarify MANET attack properties and to easily compare MANET and non-MANET attacks. The classification allows also the attacks comparison and can help selecting the appropriate countermeasures. A survey of current security tools on MANET has been done in the second part of our document. This survey distinguishes the countermeasures available on hardware, protocol and software parts of MANETs. By providing 6 security tools properties (Protect purpose, OSI Layer, Time Frame, Purpose, Internal Architecture, Scope), these security tools can be classified and compared. Moreover, with the help of a graphical representation, the scope and purpose of security tools are highlighted allow a quick comparison.

As described in the paper, despite the emergence of new attacks, several security tools are available to protect MANETs. Nevertheless, the best security mechanisms imply, most of the time, strong requirements (deployed PKI) or consume lots of resources. Attacks on security tools themselves appear; they use the collaboration as attack vector. The reputation of collaborative nodes involved in a security mechanism becomes one of the best solutions to prevent evasion and security tool DoS. In this collaboration context, to guarantee of a security level, the main requirements are that there are more legitimate nodes than malicious nodes in the network. A virus propagation or false information divulgation can quickly disturb the entire network.

Despite great security challenges, the apparition of more and more equipments communicating together and the need of always and anywhere available services enforce the MANET growth. Nevertheless, services providing growth faster than security solutions.

5. Acknowledgment

The authors would like to thank LogLogic for its support and for allowing them to work on innovative security monitoring projects.

6. References

Albers, P., Camp, O., Percher, J.-M., Jouga, B., Mé, L. & Puttini, R. S. (2002). Security in ad hoc networks: a general intrusion detection architecture enhancing trust based approaches, *Wireless Information Systems*, pp. 1–12.

Awerbuch, B., Holmer, D., Nita-Rotaru, C. & Rubens, H. (2002). An on-demand secure routing protocol resilient to byzantine failures, *WiSE '02: Proceedings of the 1st ACM workshop on Wireless security*, ACM, New York, NY, USA, pp. 21–30.

Baadache, A. & Belmehdi, A. (2010). Avoiding black hole and cooperative black hole attacks in wireless ad hoc networks, *International Journal of Computer Science and Information Security (IJCSIS)* 7: 10–16.

Bing Wu, Jianmin Chen, J. W. M. C. (2006). A survey on attacks and countermeasures in mobile ad hoc networks, *WIRELESS / MOBILE NETWORK SECURITY* 6: Springer.

Cheswick, W. R. & Bellovin, S. M. (1994). *Firewalls and Internet SecurityRepelling the Wily Hacker*, Addison-Wesley.

COBIT (2007). *Technical report*, The IT Governance Institute (ITGI).

Cohen, F. B. (1995). *Protection and security on the information superhighway*, John Wiley & Sons, Inc., New York, NY, USA.

Cohen, F. B. (1997). Information system attacks: A preliminary classification scheme, *Computers and Security* 16, No. 1: 29–46.

Curry, D. & Debar, H. (2007). Intrusion detection message exchange format. http://www.ietf.org/rfc/rfc4765.txt.

Debar, H., Dacier, M. & Wespi, A. (1999). Towards a taxonomy of intrusion-detection systems, *Comput. Netw.* 31: 805–822.

Eckmann, S. T., Vigna, G. & Kemmerer, R. A. (2002). STATL: an attack language for state-based intrusion detection, *J. Comput. Secur* 10: 71–103.

Eskin, E., Lee, W. & Stolfo, S. J. (2001). Modelling system calls for intrusion detection with dynamic window sizes, *the DARPA Conference and Exposition on Information Survivability. DISCEX '01*.

Howard, J. D. (April 1997). *An Analysis of Security Incidents on the Internet -normalement phd dissertation-*, PhD thesis, Carnegie Mellon University, Pittsburgh, Pennsylvania 15213 USA.

Howard, J. & Longstaff, T. (1998). A common language for computer security incidents, *Sand98-8667*, Sandia International Laboratories.

Hu, Y.-C., Johnson, D. B. & Perrig, A. (2002). Sead: Secure efficient distance vector routing for mobile wireless ad hoc networks, *Mobile Computing Systems and Applications, IEEE Workshop on* 0: 3.

Hu, Y. C., Perrig, A. & Johnson, D. B. (2003a). Packet leashes: a defense against wormhole attacks in wireless networks, *INFOCOM 2003. Twenty-Second Annual Joint Conference of the IEEE Computer and Communications Societies. IEEE*, Vol. 3, pp. 1976–1986.

Hu, Y.-C., Perrig, A. & Johnson, D. B. (2003b). Rushing attacks and defense in wireless ad hoc network routing protocols, *WiSe '03: Proceedings of the 2nd ACM workshop on Wireless security*, ACM, New York, NY, USA, pp. 30–40.

Hu, Y.-C., Perrig, A. & Johnson, D. B. (2005). Ariadne: a secure on-demand routing protocol for ad hoc networks, *Wirel. Netw.* 11: 21–38.

Hubaux, J.-P., Buttyán, L. & Capkun, S. (2001). The quest for security in mobile ad hoc networks, *MobiHoc '01: Proceedings of the 2nd ACM international symposium on Mobile ad hoc networking & computing*, ACM, New York, NY, USA, pp. 146–155.

IEEE (2007). Ieee 802.11: Lan/man wireless lans.

Ilyas, M. & Dorf, R. C. (2003). *The handbook of ad hoc wireless networks*, CRC Press, Inc., Boca Raton, FL, USA.

ISO-IEC (1994). Open systems interconnection (osi) – basic reference model.

ISO 27000 series (2005). *Technical report*, International Organization for Standardization.

Johnson, David B., M. D. A. & Broch, J. (2001). Dsr: the dynamic source routing protocol for multihop wireless ad hoc networks, *Ad hoc networking* 1: 139–172.

Kachirski, O. & Guha, R. (2003). Effective intrusion detection using multiple sensors in wireless ad hoc networks, *HICSS '03: Proceedings of the 36th Annual Hawaii International Conference on System Sciences (HICSS'03) - Track 2*, IEEE Computer Society, Washington, DC, USA, p. 57.1.

Khan, O. A. (2004). A survey of secure routing techniques for manet, National University of Computer and Emerging Sciences, Karachi Campus.

Lindqvist, U. & Jonsson, E. (1997). How to systematically classify computer security intrusions, *In proceeding of the IEEE Symposium on Security and Privacy* 1: 154–163.

Mahmoud, A., Sameh, A. & El Kassas, S. (2005). Authenticated routing for ad hoc networks protocol and misbehaving nodes, *TELE-INFO'05: Proceedings of the 4th WSEAS International Conference on Telecommunications and Informatics*, World Scientific and Engineering Academy and Society (WSEAS), Stevens Point, Wisconsin, USA, pp. 1–5.

Martin Rehak, Michal Pechoucek, P. C. J. N. P. M. (2008). Camnep: Agent-based network intrusion detection system (short paper), *AAMAS'08 (Autonomous Agents and MultiAgent Systems)*.

Neumann, P. G. (1994). *Computer-Related Risks*, Addison-Wesley.

Neumann, P. G. & Parker, D. B. (1989). A summary of computer misuse techniques, *Proceedings of the 12th National Computer Security Conference*, Baltimore, Maryland, pp. 396–407.

Ngadi, M. A., Abdullah, A. H. & Mandala, S. (2008). A survey on manet intrusion detection, *International Journal of Computer Science and Security* 2: 1–11.

Padmavathi, G. & Shanmugapriya, D. (2009). A survey of attacks, security mechanisms and challenges in wireless sensor networks, *IJCSIS International journal of Computer Science and Information Security* 4: 117–125.

Papadimitratos, P., Haas, Z. J. & Hubaux, J.-P. (2006). How to specify and how to prove correctness of secure routing protocols for manet, *BROADNETS*.

Paul Barford, Jeffery Kline, D. P. & Ron, A. (2002). A signal analysis of network traffic anomalies, *IMW '02: Proceedings of the 2nd ACM SIGCOMM Workshop on Internet measurment*, ACM Press, New York, NY, USA, pp. 71–82.

Paulauskas, N. & Garsva, E. (2006). Computer system attack classification, *Electronics and Electrical Engineering* 2: 84–87.

Perrig, A., Canetti, R., Tygar, J. D. & Song, D. (2002). The tesla broadcast authentication protocol, *RSA CryptoBytes* 5: 2002.

S. Staniford-Chen, S. Cheung, R. C. M. D. J. F. J. H. K. L. C. W. R. Y. & Zerkle, D. (1996). Grids – a graph-based intrusion detection system for large networks, *Proceedings of the 19th National Information Systems Security Conference*.

Satria Mandala, M. A. N. & Abdullah, A. H. (2006). A survey on manet intrusion detection, *International Journal of Computer Science and Security (IJCSS)* 2: 1.

Sourcefire (1998). Snort open source network intrusion prevention and detection system, http://www.snort.org/.

Stallings, W. (1995). *Network and internetwork security: principles and practice*, Prentice-Hall, Inc, Upper Saddle River, NJ, USA.

Stallings, W. (2002). Wireless communication and networks,, Pearson Education.

Staniford-Chen, .S, T. B. & Schnackenberg, D. (1998). The common intrusion detection framework (CIDF), *The Information Survivability Workshop (ISW '98)*, CERT Coordination Center, Software Engineering Institute, Orlando, FL.

Sterne, D., Balasubramanyam, P., Carman, D., Wilson, B., Talpade, R., Ko, C., Balupari, R., Tseng, C.-Y., Bowen, T., Levitt, K. & Rowe, J. (2005). A general cooperative intrusion detection architecture for manets, *IWIA '05: Proceedings of the Third IEEE International Workshop on Information Assurance*, IEEE Computer Society, Washington, DC, USA, pp. 57–70.

Sun, B., Wu, K. & Pooch, U. W. (2003). Alert aggregation in mobile ad hoc networks, *WiSe '03: Proceedings of the 2nd ACM workshop on Wireless security*, ACM, New York, NY, USA, pp. 69–78.

T. Duval, B. J. & Roger, L. (2004). Xmeta a bayesian approach for computer forensics, *ACSAC 2004 WIP Session*.

Undercoffer, J. L., Joshi, A. & Pinkston, J. (2003). Modeling computer attacks an ontology for intrusion detections, *in* LNCS-2516 (ed.), *The Sixth International Symposium on Recent Advances in Intrusion Detection*, Springer.

Yi, S. & Kravets, R. H. (2004). Composite key management for ad hoc networks, *Mobile and Ubiquitous Systems: Networking and Services, 2004. MOBIQUITOUS 2004. The First Annual International Conference on*, pp. 52–61.

Zhang, Y., Lee, W. & Huang, Y.-A. (2003). Intrusion detection techniques for mobile wireless networks, *Wirel. Netw.* 9(5): 545–556.

Zheng Zhang, Jun Li, C. M. J. J. & Ucles, J. (2001). Hide: A hierarchical network intrusion detection system using statistical preprocessing and neural network classification, *the 2001 IEEE Workshop on Information Assurance and Security*.

Zhou, L. & Haas, Z. J. (1999). Securing ad hoc networks, *IEEE Network Magazine* 13: 24–30.

12

Designs of a Secure Wireless LAN Access Technique and an Intrusion Detection System for Home Network

Taesub Kim[1], Yikang Kim[1], Byungbog Lee[3],
Seungwan Ryu[2] and Choongho Cho[1]
[1]Department of Computer and Information Science, Korea University,
[2]Department of Information Systems, Chung-Ang University,
[3]Electronics and Telecommunications Research Institute
Korea

1. Introduction

Home network service has been integrated with various communication technologies to help people have a more convenient life. It is expected that wireless LAN (WLAN), Bluetooth, ultra wide band (UWB), and Zigbee will be used in home networks as wireless access technologies to provide various home network services. WLAN study among them is actively making progress. But WLAN communication technologies have a problem in that access points (APs) cannot control the transmission range. This property allows the neighbor or person in the next house to receive the traffic and a malicious intruder to subvert the privacy. Therefore, authentication mechanisms have to be considered so that only an eligible user is authenticated to use the resources of a home network.

IEEE 802.11 working group (WG) specifies an authentication procedure but it provide the only basic mechanism which can't protect the WLAN communications from the ineligible approach. The IEEE 802.11i standardization group is working on an access control based on IEEE 802.1x and air traffic encryption to strengthen WLAN security techniques. In a conventional method, the nonprofessional user finds it very difficult to setup security information inside WLAN stations and APs. However, there are the various user levels of computer knowledge in a home network. Because of this reason the way to setup authentication information should be prepared so it is easy for users who are not computer professionals.

In this research, we propose access control mechanism considering the convenience of users, secure authentication protocol, and the intrusion detection system to support access control mechanism. Section II presents related literatures. In Section III, we propose authentication mechanism and the intrusion detection system for home network. The performance analysis of the proposed security mechanisms is presented in Section IV. Finally Section V concludes the research.

2. Related literatures

2.1 EAP (Extensible Authentication Protocol)

Extensible Authentication Protocol (EAP) is a mechanism that defines a standard message exchange between devices using an agreed upon authentication protocol. EAP is used as one of the base technologies to allow both wired and wireless clients to authentication to network devices. Because the EAP protocol does not require the IP protocol to communicate (it uses the link layer), it can transport messages between devices without the EAP clients requiring an IP Address. EAP is effective in networks that rely on DHCP for their IP addresses - as the client will not be able to retrieve an IP address from the DHCP server until they are authenticated to the network and given a network connection.
EAP by itself cannot be used as an authentication protocol - as it is merely a standard by which to exchange authentication messages between a client and an authentication server. EAP supports a number of authentication protocols to provide security during the authentication process. The security features and encryption strength vary with each EAP authentication protocol allowing companies to choose which EAP authentication protocol makes the most sense for their 802.1X application.
EAP is a method of conducting an authentication conversation between a Client/supplicant, Authenticator and an authentication server.
* Client/Supplicant: The client, or supplicant, is the device that needs to be authenticated. The client supplies the authentication credentials (such as certificate or username and password information) to the authenticator and requests access to the network. The client uses EAP Over LAN (EAPOL) to talk to the authenticator. Examples of clients include workstations (both wired and wireless), PDA's, and wireless Voice Over IP phones.
* Authenticator: The authenticator is the device performing the 802.1X port-level security and it controls access to the network. The authenticator receives the user credentials from the client, passes it onto the authentication server, and performs the necessary block or permit action based on the results from the authentication server. Depending on the EAP authentication protocol negotiated between the client and authentication server, the authenticator relays the necessary messages between the client and authentication server to facilitate the authentication request.
The authenticator can operate in two different modes: it can perform the EAP messaging functions locally and communicate with the authentication server using the RADIUS protocol or it can operate as an EAP pass-through device to allow the authentication server to perform the necessary EAP protocol messaging functions. Examples of authenticators include network switches and routers (wired network application) and wireless access points or wireless gateway switches.
Authentication Server: The authentication server validates the user's credential information from the client and specifies whether or not access is granted. The authentication server also specifies the EAP authentication protocol to be used between the client and itself and may specify optional parameters once access is granted. Optional parameters may be used to authorize access to specific areas of the network using dynamic VLAN or user policies. Examples of authentication servers include RADIUS and Active Directory servers.
It is also an authentication protocol for general purpose. The authentication methods in EAP include message digest 5(MD5), transport layer security (TLS), tunneled TLS (TTLS) and so on. These method protocols have features as follows.

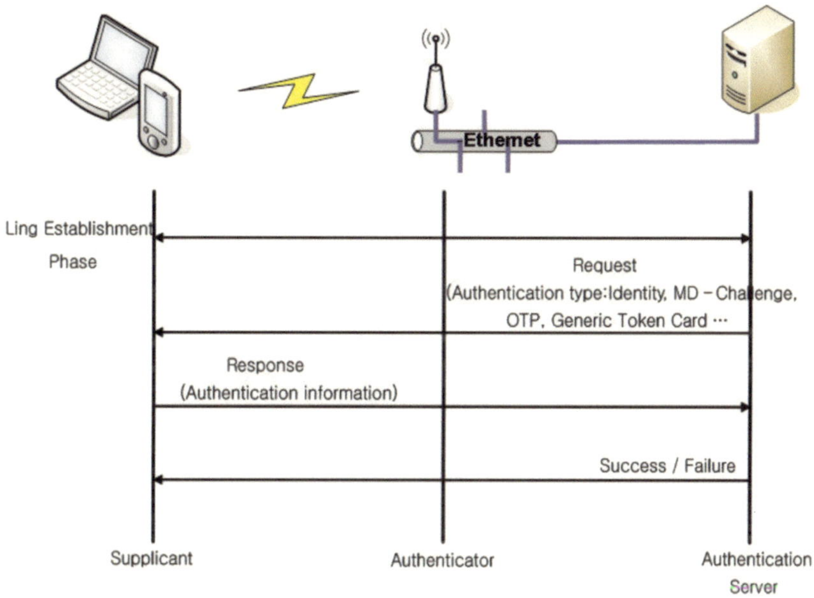

Fig. 1. EAP-based authentication procedure flow

* EAP-MD5: EAP-MD5 is the base security requirement in the EAP standard and uses username and passwords as the authentication credentials. EAP-MD5 protects the message exchange by creating a unique "fingerprint" to digitally sign each packet to ensure that the EAP messages are authentic. EAP-MD5 is very "light weight" and performs its operations very quickly, making it easy to implement and configure. EAP-MD5 does not use any PKI certificates to validate the client or provide strong encryption to protect the authentication messages between the client and the authentication server. This makes the EAP-MD5 authentication protocol susceptible to session hijacking and man-in-the-middle attacks. EAP-MD5 is best suited for EAP message exchanges in wired networks where the EAP client is directly connected to the authenticator and the chances of eavesdropping or message interception is very low. For wireless 802.1X authentication, stronger EAP authentication protocols are used.

* EAP-TLS: EAP-TLS (Transport Level Security) provides strong security by requiring both client and authentication server to be identified and validated through the use of PKI certificates. EAP-TLS provides mutual authentication between the client and the authentication server and is very secure. EAP messages are protected from eavesdropping by a TLS tunnel between the client and the authentication server. The major drawback of EAP-TLS is requirement for PKI certificates on both the clients and the authentication servers - making roll out and maintenance much more complex. EAP-TLS is best suited for installations with existing PKI certificate infrastructures. Wireless 802.1X authentication schemes will typically support EAP-TLS to protect the EAP message exchange. Unlike wired networks, wireless networks send their packets over open air making it much easier to capture and intercept unprotected packets.

* EAP-TTLS: Proposed by Funk and Certicom, EAP-TTLS (Tunneled TLS) is an extension of EAP-TLS and provides the benefits of strong encryption without the complexity of mutual certificates on both the client and authentication server. Like TLS, EAP-TTLS supports mutual authentication but only requires the authentication server to be validated to the

client through a certificate exchange. EAP-TTLS allows the client to authenticate to the authentication server using usernames and passwords and only requires a certificate for the authentication servers. EAP-TTLS simplifies roll out and maintenance and retains strong security and authentication. A TLS tunnel can be used to protect EAP messages and existing user credential services such as Active Directory, RADIUS, and LDAP can be reused for 802.1X authentication. Backward compatibility for other authentication protocols such as PAP, CHAP, MS-CHAP, and MS-CHAP-V2 are also provided by EAP-TTLS. EAP-TTLS is not considered full proof and can be fooled into sending identity credentials if TLS tunnels are not used. EAP-TTLS is best suited for installations that require strong authentication without the use of mutual certificates. Wireless 802.1X authentication schemes will typically support EAP-TTLS.

* PEAP: Protected EAP Protocol (PEAP) is an Internet-Draft that is similar to EAP-TTLS in terms of mutual authentication functionality and is currently being proposed by RSA Security, Cisco and Microsoft as an alternative to EAP-TTLS. PEAP addresses the weaknesses of EAP by:

- protecting user credentials
- securing EAP negotiation
- standardizing key exchanges
- supporting fragmentation and reassembly
- supporting fast reconnects

PEAP allows other EAP authentication protocols to be used and secures the transmission with a TLS encrypted tunnel. It relies on the mature TLS keying method for it's key creation and exchange. The PEAP client authenticates directly with the backend authentication server and the authenticator acts as a pass-through device, which doesn't need to understand the specific EAP authentication protocols. Unlike EAP-TTLS, PEAP doesn't natively support username and password authentication against an existing user database such as LDAP. Vendors are answering this need by creating features to allow this. PEAP is best suited for installations that require strong authentication without the use of mutual certificates. Wireless 802.1X authentication schemes will typically support PEAP.

* Cisco LEAP: Cisco's Lightweight EAP Protocol (LEAP) was developed in November 2000 to address the security issues of wireless networks. LEAP is a form of EAP that requires mutual authentication between the client and the authenticator. The client first authenticates itself to the authenticator and then the authenticator authenticates itself to the client. If both authenticate successfully, a network connection is granted. Unlike EAP-TLS, LEAP is based on username and password schemes and not PKI certificates, simplifying roll out and maintenance. The drawback is that it is proprietary to Cisco and has not been widely adopted by other networking vendors. LEAP is best suited for wireless implementations that support Cisco AP's and LEAP compliant wireless NIC cards.

EAP was originally developed for use with PPP in RFC 2284 and has since been widely deployed with IEEE 802 on both wired and wireless networks. With the growing popularity of wireless networks, securing the authentication process between the client, authenticator, and authentication server have become a high priority. Security concerns that were once benign on wired networks have become challenges and open security holes on wireless networks.

Depending on the EAP authentication protocol used, 802.1X authentication can help solve the following security issues:

- Dictionary Attack: Attacker obtains the challenge and response message exchange from a password authentication session and uses a brute force method to crack the password. 802.1X solves this type of attack with the use of TLS tunnels to protect the username and password exchanges between the client and the authenticator.
- Session Hijack Attack: Attacker obtains the packets passed between the client and the authenticator and recovers the identity information of the client. It forces the "real" client off the network through a form of DoS attack and impersonates the client to continue the conversation with the authenticator. 802.1X's authentication abilities with dynamic session-based keys (with user configurable re-keying) can help encrypt the conversation between the client and authenticator to thwart Hijacking attacks.
- Man-in-the-Middle Attack: Attacker obtains the necessary information from the client and the authenticator and inserts their host between the two. The attacker's host becomes the "middle man" and has access to the packets that are passed between the client and the authenticator. Through 802.1X's authentication and dynamic session-based keys (with user configurable re-keying), the data stream between the client and authenticator is encrypted to prevent Man-in-the-Middle attacks.

To apply these protocols mentioned above to the user's device, the user has to know how to setup these authentication protocols. Accordingly, it needs a simple and easy way to authenticate the home network users. In this research, we consider the home network user who is not familiar with the authentication method. We also discuss how to provide automatic authentication mechanism for the users.

2.2 IEEE 802.1x

IEEE 802.Ix standard specifies how to implement port based access control for IEEE 802 LANs, including wireless LAN. In IEEE 802.1x, the port represents the association between a WLAN station and an AP. Basically IEEE 802.Ix has three entities which are a supplicant, an authenticator, and a backend authentication server. In the context of a wireless LAN, the supplicant is a wireless LAN station, the authenticator is an AP, and the authentication server can be a centralized remote access dial-in user service (RADIUS) server.
802.1X port authentication can be coupled with MAC port security for tighter access control (see Figure 2). With MAC port security enabled, the network port can control access through enforcement of the client's MAC address as well as the user's 802.1X credentials.
The authenticator controls the authorized state of its controlled port depending on the outcome of the authentication processes. Before the supplicant is authenticated, the authenticator uses an uncontrolled port to communicate with the supplicant. The authenticator blocks all traffics except the EAP messages before the supplicant is authenticated. IEEE 802.Ix employs EAP as an authentication framework that can carry many authentication protocols, between the supplicant and the authenticator. The protocol between the authenticator and the authentication server is not specified in the IEEE 802.Ix standard. Instead, IEEE 802.1x provides RADIUS usage guidelines in the Annex.
The advantages of using 802.1X port-based network authentication include:

- Multi-vendor standard framework for securing the network.
- Improves security through session based dynamic keying of encryption keys.
- Standards based message exchange based on EAP.
- Uses open security architecture allowing the addition of newer authentication methods without replacing network equipment.

- Uses industry standard authentication servers (example: RADIUS).
- Centralizes management for network access.
- Uses existing user security information, if necessary.
- Supports both wired and wireless networks.

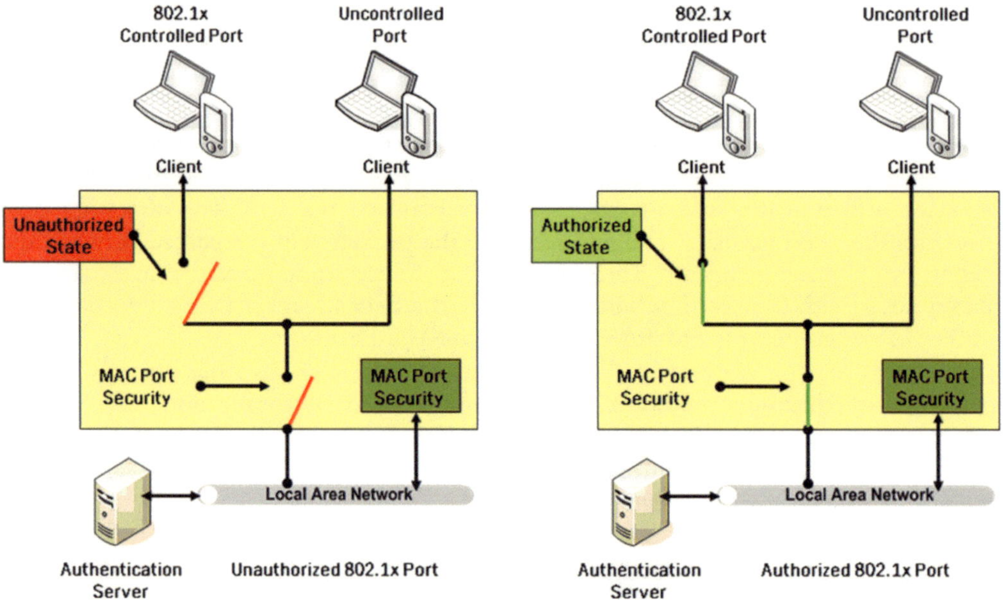

Fig. 2. 802.1x port authentication

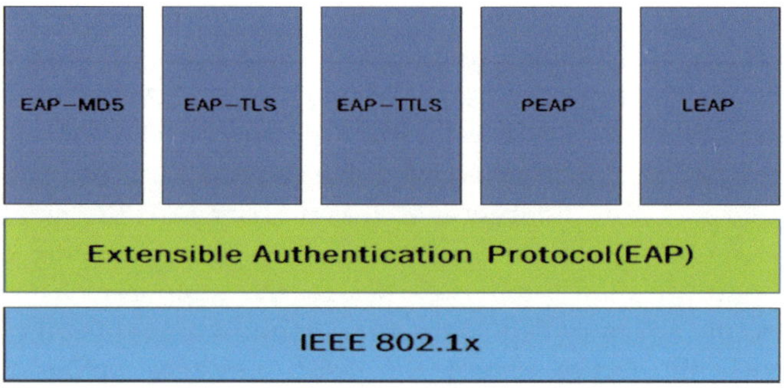

Fig. 3. 802.1x authentication components

2.3 IEEE 802.11i

IEEE 802.11i provides enhanced security in the medium access control (MAC) layer for IEEE 802.11 networks. One of the major missions of IEEE 802.11i is to define a robust security network (RSN). The definition of an RSN according to IEEE 802.11i specification is a security network that only allows the creation of robust security network associations. To provide associations in an RSN, IEEE 802.11i defines authentication, encryption improvements, key management, and key establishment. As shown in Figure. 4, in the first stage, IEEE 802.11i starts with Open System Authentication defined IEEE 802.11. And the WLAN station is authenticated and associated with an AP. At the end of this stage, IEEE 802.1x port remains blocked and no data packets can be exchanged. The second stage consists of IEEE 802.1x authentication which employs extensible authentication protocol (EAP) to authenticate users. A user can surf the Internet after the completion of 4-Way Handshake execution in the third stage.

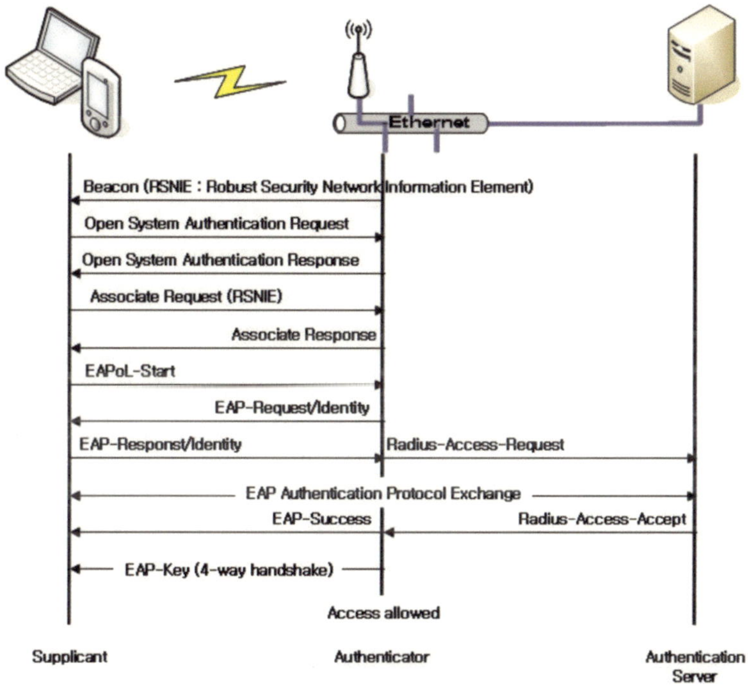

Fig. 4. IEEE 802.11i-based authentication procedure flow

2.4 SNMP (Simple Network Management Protocol)

The SNMP is a management protocol used to manage TCP/IP networks. Nowadays, it is widely used in several commercial networks, since it is a relatively simple protocol, but powerful enough to be used in the management of heterogeneous networks. The SNMP management comprises an agent, a manager and a MIB (Management Information Base), as shown in Figure. 5 The MIB is a database composed of objects that will be managed and/or monitored through the SNMP protocol. A manageable object represents a real resource in the network, such as a rotator, a switch and also the final system resources, like, for example, CPU, memory, etc. Each manageable object has a set of variables of which values can be read or altered by the agents.

The management agent is a software resident in a final system or in some network device about to be managed that collects information from the MIB and send it to the managing process. The latter (NMS - Network Management System) resides in a management station (by acting remotely), or in a local station (by acting in the site) and sends messages to the agent processes in order to read or alter the value of a manageable object. The agents use SNMP primitives to read or change the values of the MIB objects. These are some examples of primitives: get-request, get-response, getnext, set-request and trap.

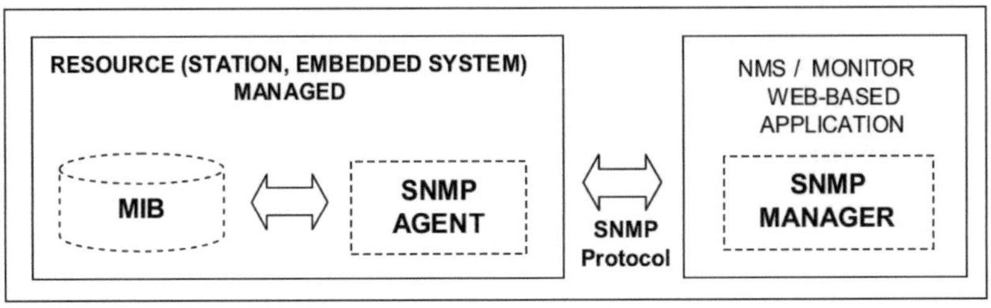

Fig. 5. Relation between components of the SNMP management

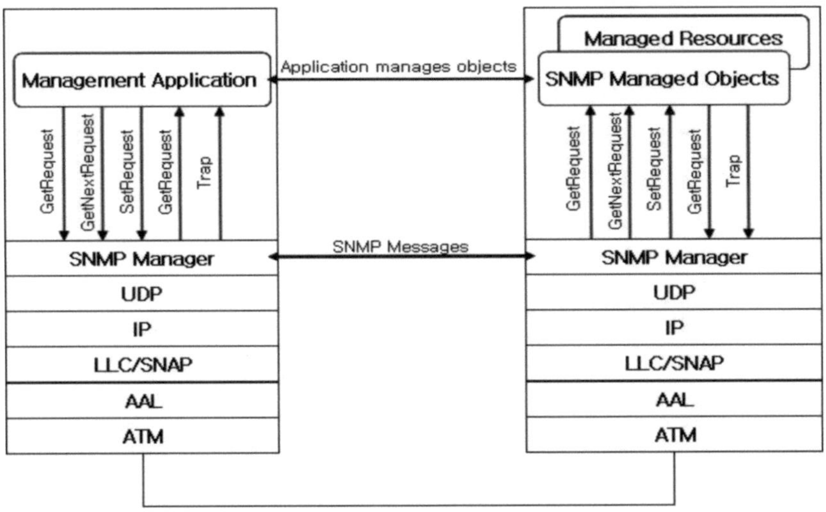

Fig. 6. SNMP management system architecture

3. Design of the security home gateway server

A security home gateway server is proposed to guard the access to the network. The security home gateway server collects and processes security related information from managed devices. It acts as the entry security provider for guarding the proper usage of upper layer application services, such as alarm reporting. Among these network management applications, both type of alarm reporting are of interest in this research. As shown in Figure. 7, this security home gateway server consists of five management units: traffic collection unit, traffic processing unit, authentication unit, policy management unit, and response unit. The gateway also cooperates with an authentication server to guarantee a secure link layer access control. Also to protect intrusion detection the AP must support SNMP agent functions and the security home gateway sever must support SNMP server functions.

Traffic Collection Unit: The unit collects traffic from routers, access points among other devices. The communication information can be obtained by log files, traffic mirror, or by polling SNMP agents on managed devices. The gathered information is passed to traffic processing unit for further classification and computation.

Traffic Processing Unit: This unit processes the data from the traffic collection unit. For example, Data packages are classified according to the type of ICMP, TCP, UDP, SNMP and others. such as IP source and destination addresses. All data are stored in the database associated with timestamps.

Authentication Unit: This unit works together with APs. It is responsible for a port-base access control protocol, as specified in 802.1x. The authentication request, issued by a wireless client, is passed, by AP's forwarding feature, to the RADIUS server for verification. Using the information replied from the RADIUS server, access policy of the requesting client can be determined at AP. The authentication results are passed to behavior analysis unit for further processing.

Policy Management Unit: According to the vulnerabilities and threats we described in last section, there exist certain patterns for each potential security flaw. The characteristics of each attack or abnormal behavior are analyzed and predefined as security policies. Depending upon the management requirement, a policy could also be updated by security configuration management.

Response Unit: The response unit is responsible for notifying the network management server an abnormal behavior or for updating security configuration. Management applications of alarm reporting react upon receiving the messages from response unit correspondingly.

All five management units are integrated together to provide precaution security application services. Specifically, by cooperating with an authentication server, access control in the link layer is provided; by monitoring and analyzing data packages, the security threats prevention can be achieved in IP layer.

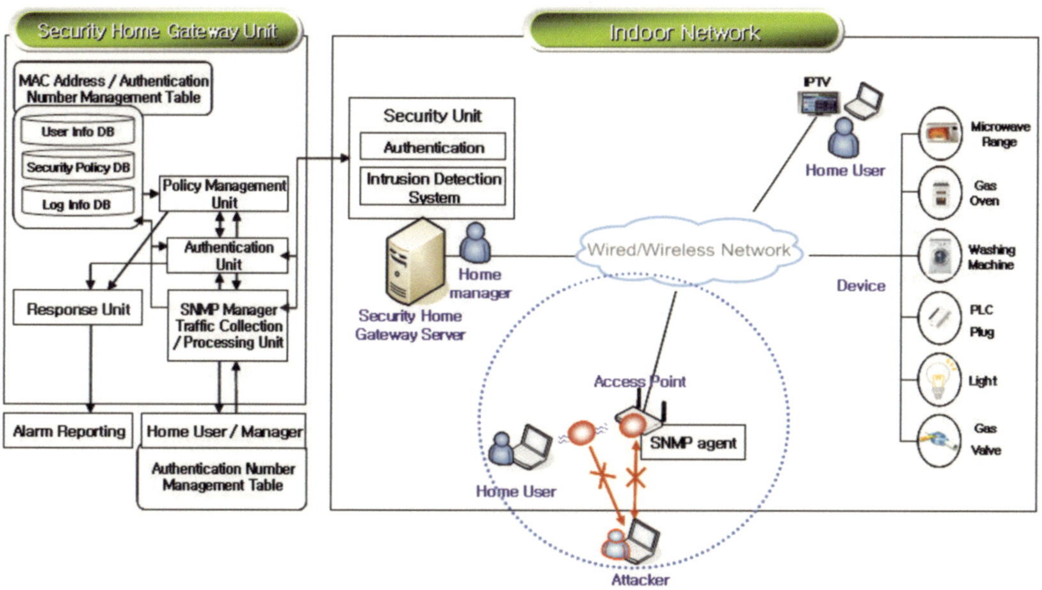

Fig. 7. Security home gateway system server architecture

3.1 The proposed protocol

To support the mentioned scenarios, the authentication protocol requires additional message exchanges including information which is not specified in Standards. Periodic changes may be problems from the viewpoint of users, when the password is changed while a user takes the WLAN station out of home. The WLAN station needs to be authenticated again when the user brings the WLAN station back to home. However the WLAN station can't obtain the authority without user's assistance since the password is already changed. Other devices in home network also are needed to know the new password to keep the authority.

MAC Address	Authentication number
00:00:F0:7A:B1:B7	1
00:00:F1:7A:B4:77	2
00:00:F1:8A:BB:A7	3
...	...

Table 1. The MAC address management table

Authentication Number	Password
1	1234
2	5678
3	9123
...	...

Table 2. The authentication number management table

The proposed protocol solves the problem by adding the authentication number. The authentication number is an index number which corresponds to each password. It is numbered randomly whenever the password is changed. The security home gateway server manages two tables. One is the MAC address management table which records the MAC addresses of the authenticated devices and the authentication number. The other is the authentication number table. When the password is changed, the password and the authentication number are recorded in the authentication table. For example, there is a device which has the MAC address of 00:00:F0:7A:81:B7. After the device is authenticated when the password is 1234, the server records its MAC address with the current authentication number in the MAC address management table as shown in Table 1. Then the server transmits the current authentication number to the device. In this case, the current authentication number is 1. When the password is changed to 5678, as shown in Table 2, the authentication number is also changed to 2 and recorded in the authentication number table. Figure. 8 presents the EAP-TTLS procedure to support the proposed authentication protocol. In this figure, the solid lines represent legitimate message exchanges and the dashed lines indicate supplementary message exchanges. As shown in Figure. 8, the EAP-TTLS procedure by using the authentication number is as follows.

1. The user's WLAN station associates with an AP using open authentication with wired equivalent privacy (WEP) turned off. Then the AP asks for the user's identity
2. The WLAN station transmits an EAP-request message encapsulated in an EAPoL-EAP frame to the AP, which contains the MAC address of the WLAN station.
3. The server is authenticated to the WLAN station using its security certificate and a TLS connection is established between them. The encryption key for the TLS connection will be used for air traffic encryption.

4. Inside the TLS connection (inside box), the exchanged messages are encapsulated into TLS records that are again encapsulated into EAP-request and EAP-response messages. In the existing protocol, the WLAN station informs the AP of a user name and a password. In addition, we propose that the WLAN station sends both the old authentication number and authentication status in the same EAP-Response message. After receiving it, the AP relays it to the server.
5. The server then verifies the old authentication number to determine whether the MAC address and the old authentication number of the WLAN station are the same as the stored data in the MAC address management table.
6. After the old authentication number is authenticated by the WLAN station, the server transmits the new authentication number to the WLAN station through the AP. The WLAN station which received the new authentication number information updates the authentication information for itself. The server will complete the course of authentication by using the password corresponding to the authentication number table. At this point, the authentication method is able to use many protocol. Here, we assume that CHAP is used.
7. The EAP-TTL procedure ends by sending the EAP success message to the WLAN station.

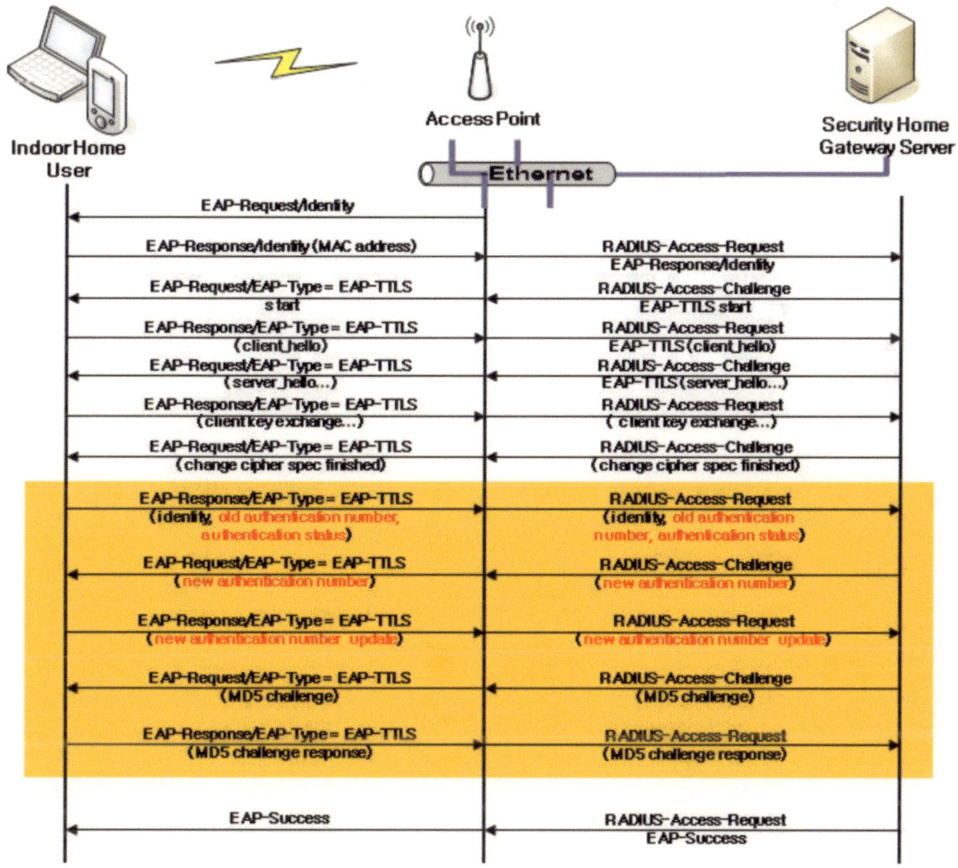

Fig. 8. The proposed protocol flow

In this research, we use the EAP-TTLS protocol since the user name, password and authentication information are protected by the TLS connection. The proposed protocol also can be applied to EAP-MD5, EAP-TLS and other protocols. To inform the new authentication number from the server to the WLAN station, the server sends its authentication number and MAC address together with identity.
The server sends the message that contains authentication information and updates the table. However there is a risk of man-in-the-middle attacks by which the current password and authentication information can be stolen. Hence we suggest that the transmitted information is encrypted by the password like TTLS protocol.

3.2 Packet format

The format of EAP packet is shown in Figure. 9, (a) is the EAP packet format, (b) is the EAP-TLS packet format, and (c) is the proposed packet format

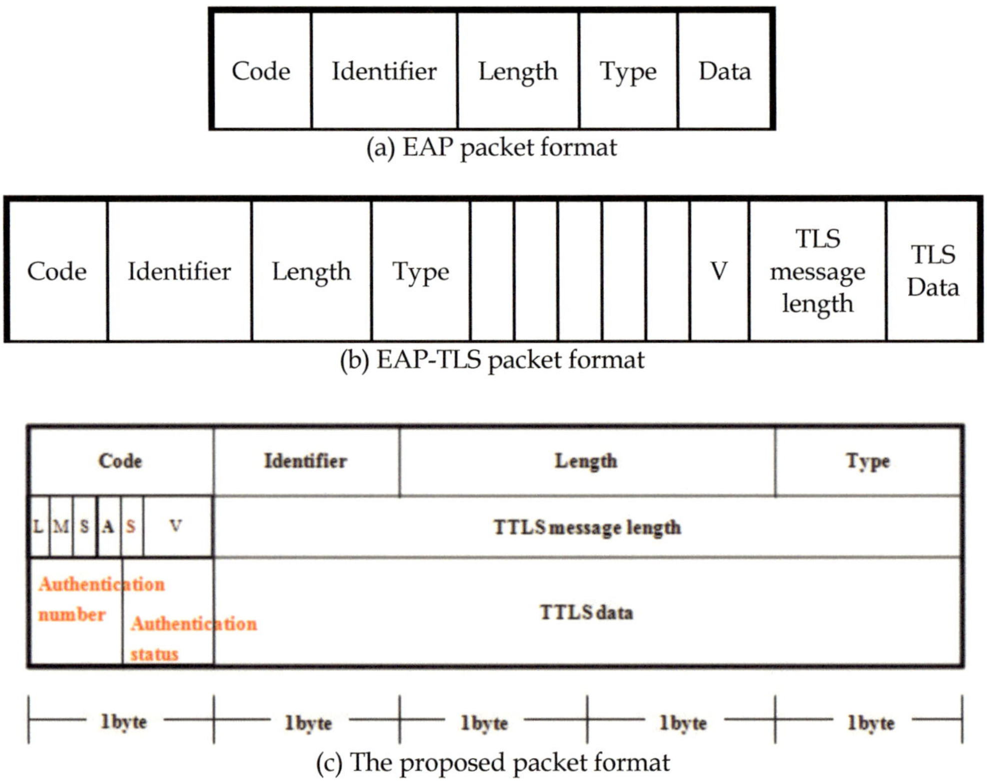

Fig. 9. Packet format

Code is one byte indicating the type of packet; 1 indicates Request, 2 indicates Response, 3 indicates Success and 4 indicates Failure. Identifier is a value in the range 0-255 and it should be incremented for each message transmission. This helps to check which Response goes with which Request. Length is the total number of bytes in the EAP message. The Type field indicates the type of Request or Response. For example, 1 means the identity packet and 13 means the EAP-TLS packet. The Data field is the actual request or response data being sent. The format of the data field is determined by the Code field. If the Code field is 3 or 4 that is a success or a failure, these messages contain no data. In case of EAP-TLS, Data field is divided into more parts as shown in Figure. 9 (b). L, M, S, R, and V are flags which mean the length included, more fragments, start flag, Reserved, and Version number respectively.

For the backward compatibility, the proposed protocol uses the same packet format. In case of the EAP-TTLS protocol, we can use the existing packet format because the packet format for new messages and the additional information is able to use the same format as other messages. We change only the reserved bit with the C bit that means the authentication number is included. If the C bit is set in the EAP message, it means that the message includes the authentication number or the authentication information. But when EAP-MD5 or EAP-TLS is used, the authentication number is added to identity message. The authentication server can't separate the authentication number from the user's identity. Therefore, it needs a new type instead of 1 which means the identity. It can be other number for the Type field. In addition, the Data field can be divided into two parts: the former part is used for the authentication number and the latter part is used for the identity. Additional messages that carry the authentication information are used in the same packet format as EAP-TTLS.

3.3 The proposed intrusion detection system

In the proposed intrusion-detection system, the secure home-gateway server (i.e., SNMP server) identifies whether or not the terminal node is an authenticated MAC address by polling (See Figure. 7). If this MAC address is violated, an alarm message notifies the response unit inside the home. This solves some leakage. Now the user should enroll the MAC address of the AP. Additionally, SNMP can obtain some traffic information (i.e., ICMP, TCP and UDP, etc.). If this traffic quantity is increased beyond a specific threshold, the user may consider it an intentional/unintentional leakage (i.e., an attack of intentional connection or DoS attack). Thus, the response unit warns of the leakage inside the home by giving an alarm message.

4. Security analysis

EAP-MD5 is more vulnerable to unwanted attacks than other authentication methods. One of such attacks is a brute force attack. A brute force attack is a method of defeating a cryptographic scheme by trying a large number of possibilities, for example, exhaustively working through all possible keys in order to decrypt a message. To protect the brute force attack, at least, the password should be changed by every month. The proposed protocol is robust to the brute force attack since it changes the password periodically.

It also helps to detect a replay attack. By using the replay attack, an attacker could pretend to be an authorized user to access a network. For example, an attacker could simply intercept and replay a station's identity and password hash to be authenticated. When a user doesn't use the authentication number, a hacker can receive the challenge message and transmit the response message repeatedly. On the contrary, when the authentication number is used, a hacker also should know it. It is easy to know user's identity. But it is not easy to know the authentication number because it is transmitted under encryption in the previous authentication procedure. Therefore, the server can detect a hacker who uses the authentication number invalid.

In case of the mutual authentication, these security problems will be eliminated. Instead of security, the proposed protocol gives automatic re-authentication under the environment the password is changed.

4.1 Password dictionary attack

A method used to break security systems, specifically password based security systems, in which the attacker systematically tests all possible passwords beginning with words that have a higher possibility of being used, such as names and places. The word dictionary refers to the attacker exhausting all of the words in a dictionary in an attempt to discover the password.

This research proposes authentication scenarios to minimize the process needed by users, a password method which is changed randomly and periodically, and authentication protocols. Also because it added a new parameter, being safe consequently, more it will be able to provide the home network environment which is convenient.

4.2 Replay attack

By using the replay attack, an attacker could pretend to be an authorized user to access a network. For example, an attacker could simply intercept and replay a station's identity and password hash to be authenticated. When a user doesn't use the authentication number, a hacker can receive the challenge message and transmit the response message repeatedly. On the contrary, when the authentication number is used, a hacker also should know it. It is easy to know user's identity. But it is not easy to know the authentication number because it is transmitted under encryption in the previous authentication procedure. Therefore, the server can detect a hacker who uses the authentication number invalid. In our authentication protocol, additional parameters (i.e., old authentication number and authentication status) are padded into challenge response messages, thus protecting from replay attack

4.3 Denial of service and rogue attack

A DoS(Denial of Service) attack is a malicious attempt by a single person or a group of people to cause the victim, site, or node to deny service to its customers. When this attempt derives from a single host of the network, it constitutes a DoS attack. On the other hand, it is also possible that a lot of malicious hosts coordinate to flood the victim with an abundance of attack packets, so that the attack takes place simultaneously from multiple points. This type of attack is called a Distributed DoS, or DDoS attack, exactly an attacker overloads an AP in various ways so that the AP is unable to serve legitimate users. The attacker does not directly benefit but creates a nuisance, and rogue station attack is a rogue station affinitizing itself with an AP. The attacker benefits by becoming a participant in the wireless network and thus gaining the ability to send and receive data.

In our authentication protocol, additional parameters (i.e., old authentication number and authentication status) are padded into challenge response messages, thus protecting from denial of service attack and rogue station attack. Also, this proposed intrusion detection system, If this MAC address is violated, alarm message is notified to response unit inside home. This solves some leakage that user should enroll MAC address of AP. Additionally, SNMP can obtain some traffic information(i.e., ICMP, TCP and UDP etc). If this traffic quantity is increased more than specific threshold, user may consider an intentional/unintentional leakage (i.e., an attack of intentional connection or DoS attack). Thus, response unit alarms the leakage inside home by alarm message.

5. Conclusion

We introduced secure and convenient mechanisms for home network WLAN access. We also proposed the authentication protocol to provide the automatic authentication when the password is changed. The automatic-password change method enables users to use the home network without periodic password changes. Under the threats we considered, the proposed protocol appeared to give a protection against a dictionary attack, a replay attack, a denial of service attack and a rogue station attack. Although the password used before is changed for some reasons, the users do not need to enter the new password or other information again. From the viewpoint of users, the mechanisms applied in the proposed protocol are convenient since users do not need to know the authentication mechanism. Also, it used the SNMP protocol so that the inside home user will be able to perceive an attack.

For the backward compatibility between the authentication methods, we modified the packet format using a reserved bit. The C bit is added for the authentication number and the new type number which indicates not only the user's identity but also the authentication number should be used.

Compared with the current security set up procedure for WLAN, the proposed protocol can provide a simple procedure for WLAN users and protect them from unwanted attacks in home network environment.

6. Acknowledgement

This work was supported by National Research Foundation of Korea Grant funded by the Korean Government(KRF-2007-313-D00503)

7. References

B. Aboba et al. (2004). Extensible Authentication Protocol, *IETF RFC* 3748.

B. Aboba, D. Simon. (1999). PPP EAP TLS Authentication Protocol, *IETF RFC* 2716.

B. Aboba. (1999). PPP EAP TLS Authentication Protocol, *IETF RFC* 2716.

C. He and J. C. Mitchell. Security Analysis and Improvements for IEEE 802.11i, in proc. the *12th Annual Network and Distributed System Security.*

Chih-Mou Shih, Shang-Juh Kao. (2006). Security Gateway for Accessing IPv6 WLAN, *ICIS-COMSAR* 2006, pp83~88.

D. Potter et al. (2002). PPP EAP MS-CHAP-V2 Authentication Protocol, internet draft.

F. Baker. (1997). IP Forwarding Table MIB, RFC 2096.

H. Luo and P. Henry. (2003) A Secure Public Wireless LAN Access Technique That Supports Walk-Up Users, in *proc. GLOBECOM2003*, vol. 22, no. 1, pp. 1415-1419.

IEEE Std 802.11i. Medium Access Control(MAC) security Enhancements, 2004 edition.

IEEE Std 802.1x. Standard for port based Network Access Control, March 2001.

IEEE, LAN/MAN Specific Requirements - Part 11: Wireless Medium Access Control(MAC) and Physical Layer(PHY) Specification: Specification for Robust Security, *IEEE Std* 802.11i/D3.2, Apr. 2003.

J. C. Chen and Y. P. Wang. Extensible Authentication Protocol (EAP) and IEEE 802. lx: *Tutorial and Empirical Experience,* http://wire.cs.nthu.edu.tw/wirelx/.

J.D. Case, M. Fedor, M.L. Schoffstall, J. Davin. (1990). Simple Network Management Protocol(SNMP), RFC 1157.

Ju-A Lee, Jae-Hyun Kim, Jun-Hee Park, Kyung-Duk Moon. (2006). A Secure Wireless LAN Access Technique for Home Network, *VTC* 2006, pp818~822.

K. McCloghrie, Ed. (1996). SNMPv2 Management Information Base for the Internet Protocol using SMIv2, RFC 2011.

K. McCloghrie, Ed. (1996). SNMPv2 Management Information Base for the Transmission Control Protocol using SMIv2, RFC 2012.

K. McCloghrie, Ed. (1996). SNMPv2 Management Information Base for the User Datagram Protocol using SMIv2, RFC 2013.

L. Blunk, j. Vollbrecht. (1998). PPP Extensible Authentication Protocol(EAP), *IETF RFC* 2284.

P. Funk. (2004). EAP Tunneled TLS Authentication Protocol, internet draft.

W. Simpson. (1994). PPP Chanllenge Handshake Authentication Protocol (CHAP), *IETF RFC* 1994.

13

Lightweight Intrusion Detection for Wireless Sensor Networks

Eui-Nam Huh and Tran Hong Hai
Kyung Hee University
Republic of Korea

1. Introduction

Wireless Sensor Networks (WSNs) have grown to become one of the most promising and interesting fields over the past few years. WSNs are wireless networks consisting of distributed sensor nodes which cooperatively monitor physical or environmental conditions. A sensor node is a tiny and simple device with limited computational resources. Sensor nodes are randomly and densely deployed in a sensed environment. WSN is designed to detect events or phenomena, and collect and return sensed data to the user.

WSNs have been used in many applications such as battlefield surveillance, traffic monitoring, health-care, environment monitoring, etc. Some basic features of sensor networks are (Ilyas & Mahgoub, 2005):

- Self-organization
- Short-range broadcast communication and multi-hop routing
- Dense deployment and cooperative sensors
- Frequently changing topology, due to fading and node failures
- Limitations in computational resources, such as energy and memory

The characteristics of wireless infrastructure and characteristics of WSNs cause potential risks of attacks on the network. Numerous studies have attempted to address vulnerabilities in WSNs such as Denial of Service in Sensor Networks (Wood & Stankovic, 2002), Secure Routing in Sensor Networks (Karlof & Wagner, 2003). Current research on security in sensor networks generally focuses on secure routing protocols, key management and prevention techniques for specific attacks (Djenouri et al., 2005).

Although research on security (related to) issues in WSN is productive, the need for a security framework for WSNs still exists.Intrusion Detection System (IDS) is a common prevention mechanism which protects the network from intrusion. In this chapter, we study the problem of intrusion detection in WSNs, and propose a hybrid intrusion detection framework for clustered sensor networks. Our scheme suits the demands and restrictions of the infrastructure and characteristics of WSNs. The analytical analysis and simulation result show that our IDS scheme can detect over 90% of malicious nodes under various attacks, with a high rate of packet collision. Our contribution is as follows:

- A distributed IDS framework for creating, updating and evaluating alert packets in clustered WSNs.

- Detection of common routing problems and attacks in clustered WSNs, based on neighbor knowledge and routing rules.
- Use of a reputation system as the basis of self triggering IDS modules and evaluation of the alert packet from monitor nodes.
- Reduction of alerts using over-hearing to reduce energy consumption in IDS modules.
- High detection rate under burst attacks.

Following this introduction section, the chapter is organized as follows: In the next section, we review and study the problem of application of IDS in WSNs and outline the challenges. Section 3 proposes our security architecture and detection algorithms for WSNs. In section 4, we provide two algorithms to self-trigger and reduce energy consumption in IDS modules. Section 5 provides the simulation and performance analysis. Finally, the chapter ends with a conclusion and future work.

2. Security in wireless sensor networks

2.1 Routing threats

The design of routing protocols in sensor networks never considers security as a primary goal. Routing protocols in sensor networks are simpler and more susceptible to attacks than the other two types of wireless networks: Ad-Hoc and Cellular.

The first serious discussion and analysis on secure routing were performed by (Karlof & Wagner, 2003). They studied multiple types of attacks on routing protocols in detail, and the effects on common routing protocols in WSNs. The assumption is that there are two types of attacks, outside attacks and inside attacks. In this chapter we only examine inside attacks. Outside attacks are prevented by using link layer security mechanisms (Camtepe & Yener, 2005). They propose two types of adversaries, a mote-class adversary and laptop-class adversary. In the mote-class one, the adversary accesses a few sensor nodes with capabilities similar to legitimate nodes. These nodes are tampered with and reprogrammed for an adversary's purpose. In the laptop-class one, the adversary accesses more powerful devices such as a laptop with greater battery power, high CPU processing rate and high-power radio transmitter. In this case, the adversary has more opportunities to deploy attacks on the network. In this section, we review the most common network layer attacks on WSNs and highlight the characteristics of these attacks (Karlof & Wagner, 2003).

Selective forwarding: In a selective forwarding attack, malicious nodes prevent the flow of routing information in sensor networks by refusing to forward or drop the messages traversing them (Karlof & Wagner, 2003). Another aspect of this type of attack is that malicious nodes may forward the messages along an incorrect path, creating inaccurate routing information in the network.

Sinkhole: In a sinkhole attack, the adversary redirects nearly all the traffic from a particular area via a malicious node, creating a metaphorical sinkhole (Karlof & Wagner, 2003). The laptop-class adversary may use higher computational resources and communication power than a legitimate node, to advertise itself as the shortest path to the base-station, or, in our case, the cluster head (CH). A CH aggregates the data of member nodes in a cluster and relays them to another CH or the sink node.

Wormhole: In a wormhole attack, the adversary tunnels messages received in one malicious node and replays them in a different part of the network. The two malicious nodes usually claim that they are merely two hops from the base station. Khalil suggests five modes of wormhole attacks in his paper. Details of these modes are in (Khalil et al., 2005; 2008).

Hello flood attack: Many routing protocols use Hello broadcast messages to announce themselves to their neighbor nodes. The nodes that receive Hello messages assume that source nodes are within range and add source nodes to their neighbor list. The laptop-class adversary can spoof Hello messages with sufficient transmission power to convince a group of nodes that they are its neighbor.
Sybil attack: In this attack, a malicious node can present multiple identities to other nodes in the network. The Sybil attack poses a significant threat to most geographic routing protocols. Sybil attacks are prevented via link layer authentication (Camtepe & Yener, 2005; Sultana et al., 2007). Within the limited scope of this paper, we assume that the Sybil attack is prevented via authentication, so the combination of Sybil with other attacks is not considered in this paper.

2.2 Intrusion detection system in wireless networks

Intrusion Detection System (IDS) is defined as a system that tries to detect and alert of attempted intrusions into a system or a network (Richard Heady, 1990). IDSs are classified into two major approaches: misuse detection and anomaly detection. Each approach has its own unique advantage. The misuse technique has the advantage that it can detect most known attacks in a rule database. But, new attacks require new rules to be constructed and distributed (Roesch, 2002; Paxson, 1999). The anomaly technique has the advantage that it doesn't require any rules and can detect novel attacks. The main disadvantage of anomaly detection is the high false positive rate (Balasubramaniyan et al., 1998; Cuppens & Miège, 2002; Janakiraman et al., 2003). Although IDS is used as a major prevention mechanism in wired networks, it is difficult to apply IDS in wireless networks, because of the vast difference in network characteristics.
Sensor networks inherit all aspects of wireless networks. And, they have their own distinct characteristics that make the design of a security model for sensor networks different from that of Ad Hoc networks. The batteries in sensor networks may not be rechargeable, thus, we cannot recharge or replace the batteries if sensor nodes use excessive computational resources to process the data.
Sensor networks are constrained in resource compared to Ad Hoc and cellular networks (Aboelaze & Aloul, 2005). A typical sensor node such as MICA has an 8 MHz microprocessor, 128 KB program flash memories and 512 KB serial flash memories (Technology, n.d.). WSNs are deployed more densely and randomly in the environment and sensor node failure is likely to happen. So, it is impossible for a sensor node to store the signature data about malicious nodes for the whole network in a manner similar to additional misuse detection. Also, it is very difficult to use traditional anomaly detection methods in WSNs, because sensor nodes cannot monitor all the traffic traversing them and compute anomalous events. These specific characteristics of WSN demand a novel design of the security architecture for such an environment. Though wireless Ad Hoc networks and wireless sensor networks share some common characteristics, and there was development of IDS in a wireless Ad Hoc network (Mishra et al., 2004), R. Roman showed in his paper that they can't be directly applied in WSNs (Roman, 2006). They proposed a novel technique for optimal monitoring of neighbors called spontaneous watchdog, which extends the watchdog monitoring mechanism in (Marti et al., 2000). The problem with this approach is that the author fails to consider the selection of a global agent. Another weakness of this approach is that it does not deal with the collision of packets, which is likely due to the high density of nodes in WSNs. Ilker Onat et al. (2005) proposed an anomaly detection based on security scheme for WSNs. In their method, each

sensor node builds a simple statistical model of its neighbor's behavior, and these statistics are used to detect changes (Onat & Miri, 2005). The system features which analyze anomalies are; the average of received power and packet arrival rate. Their system cannot detect selective forwarding and wormhole attacks, because of their simple statistical features. Soumya et al. (2005) proposed an intrusion detection mechanism based on an ant colonies system (Banerjee et al., 2005). Their basic idea is to identify the affected path of intrusion in the sensor network, by investigating the pheromone concentration. However, they do not specify the detailed solution to routing attacks.

In 2006, Techateerawat P. et al published a paper in which they designed an intrusion framework based on the layout and selection of monitor nodes (Techateerawat & Jennings, 2006). They proposed a voting algorithm for selection of nodes which must trigger their IDS agent. Their approach reduced monitor nodes and energy consumption in networks, but also reduced the probability of detection. Unfortunately, their detection algorithms weren't demonstrated in detail. A recent study of Chong E. L. et al. (2006) developed an intrusion detection scheme that uses a clustering algorithm to build a model of normal traffic behavior. Then, they used this model to detect anomalous traffic patterns (Chong Eik Loo & Palaniswami, 2006). A.P. Silva et al. proposed a decentralized IDS scheme, based on the specification in (da Silva et al., 2005). In these two schemes, every IDS agent functions independently, and can detect signs of intrusion locally, by observing all data received, without collaboration between its neighbors. They tried to apply an anomaly technique based on wired networks for WSNs, so their scheme incurs excessive computational resource consumption in each node.

Afrand Agah et al. applied game theory in order to build a detection framework for denial of service in WSNs. However, their scheme is not specified for routing attacks in WSNs (Agah et al., 2006). There are multiple IDS proposals for WSNs, but many are incomplete or only focus on a specific attack (Wang et al., 2006). Our contribution is based on previous works and involves the creation of a novel, efficient IDSs for WSNs. Furthermore, we propose a simple selection algorithm to trigger IDS modules in particular nodes. Our algorithm minimizes the monitor nodes which must trigger the intrusion detection modules, thus enhancing the network lifetime.

3. A lightweight intrusion detection framework for sensor networks

3.1 Architecture

In sensor networks, multiple routing protocols, power management and data dissemination are designed, in which energy and computational resources are essential designs. Cluster-based routing protocols were developed for sensor networks (LEACH, HEED, PEGASIS, TEEN and APTEEN (Abbasi & Younis, 2007)) to achieve scalability, power savings, data routing redundancy, etc. Routing is usually separated into two phases: the setup phase and the steady phase. In the setup phase, the cluster is organized, and cluster heads are randomly selected and rotated to distribute the energy load among the network. In the steady phase, the cluster heads receive all data in their clusters and send aggregated data to the base station, to reduce the amount of information arriving at the base station.

In our IDS architecture, every node belongs to a single cluster among the clusters which are geographically distributed across the whole network. Our aim is to utilize cluster-based protocols in energy saving, reduced computational resources and data transmission redundancy. In this section, we propose an intrusion framework for information sharing, which utilizes hierarchical architecture to improve intrusion detection capability for all

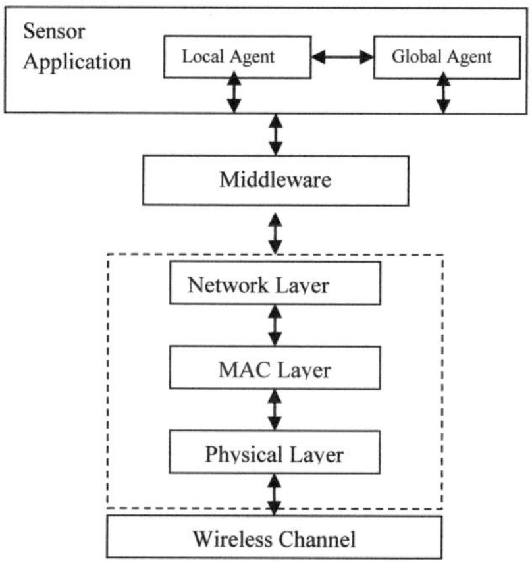

Fig. 1. Intrusion detection agents on sensor protocol's stack

participating nodes. Previous work on the application of IDS for sensor networks was undertaken by R. Roman (Roman, 2006). The author suggested general guidelines for the application of IDS to WSNs, which influenced our work. In addition, our proposed intrusion detection framework is influenced and improved by previous works in (Khalil et al., 2005; da Silva et al., 2005; Hu & Burmester, 2009).

In our scheme, an IDS agent is located in every sensor node. Each sensor node has two intrusion modules, called local IDS agent and global IDS agent. Because of the limited battery life and resources, each agent is only active when it is needed.

Local agent: The local agent module is responsible for monitoring the information sent and received by the sensor. The node stores an internal database, named a blacklist, about specific malicious nodes in network. When the network is initially configured, the sensor nodes lack any knowledge about malicious nodes. After the deployment of WSNs, the signature database is gradually constructed. The entry into the malicious node database is created and propagated to every node by CHs.

Global agent: The global agent is responsible for monitoring the communication of its neighbor nodes. Because of the broadcast nature of wireless networks, every node can receive all packets within its communication range. We use the watchdog monitoring mechanism and pre-defined routing rules with two-hop neighbor knowledge to monitor these packets. If the monitor nodes discover a potential breach of security in their radio range, they create and send an alert to the CHs. Then, the CHs receive the alert and make the decision about a suspicious node. Both agents are implemented in the application layer illustrated in Fig. 1.

3.2 Detection algorithms

We assume that when a sensor node is first deployed in the environmental field, an adversary requires a particular period of time to deploy an attack. This implies that no malicious node appears during the initial stage of sensor node deployment.

The monitor nodes use the watchdog monitoring mechanism and predefined rules with two-hop neighbor knowledge to detect anomalies within their transmission ranges. In watchdog, due to the broadcast nature of wireless networks, monitor nodes receive packets within their radio range. These packets are captured and stored in a buffer which contains information including the packet identification and type, source and destination, etc. Each

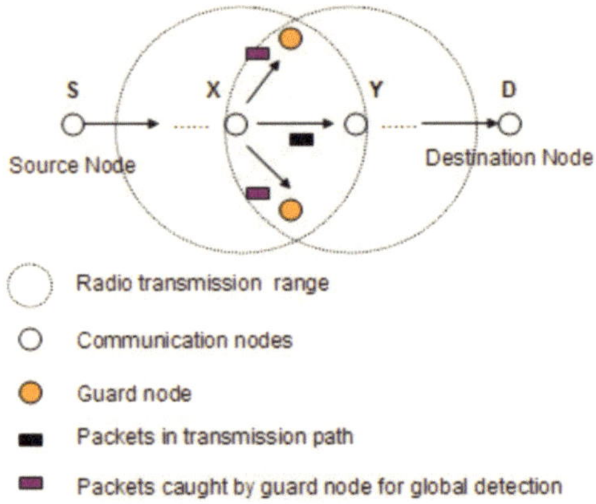

Fig. 2. Monitor node

entry in the buffer is time stamped. This expires after a timeout or after the entry in the buffer is examined by monitor nodes.

Data structure: Sensor nodes maintain two databases: malicious nodes and neighbor knowledge.

Two-hop neighbor knowledge: Two-hop neighbor knowledge is generally used in broadcasting protocols to reduce the number of transmissions, such as Source-based Protocol, Dominant Pruning, etc (Durresi et al., 2005). As we mentioned in Related Work, Issa Khail et al. applied two-hop neighbor knowledge to detect wormhole attacks in WSNs and Ad Hoc networks (Khalil et al., 2005; 2008). We also apply two-hop neighbor knowledge as a component of our detection technique. Unlike the two-phase setup in Khalil's work, we establish our two-hop neighbor list in each sensor node via a single phase, by modifying the Hello packet. When the sensor nodes are initially deployed in the sensing environment, each node must build its direct neighbor list and a list of two-hop neighbors accessible to these one-hop neighbors. To accomplish this, each node broadcasts its Hello message; fields contain information about source node ID, immediate node, and the hop counter is set to two. In the case of the source node, the source node ID and immediate node have the same node ID. When a node receives a two-hop Hello packet, it changes the immediate node as its node ID, decrements the hop count to one and re-broadcasts it. The sensor node receiving this Hello message assigns the immediate node as its direct neighbor, and the source node as its two-hop neighbor. This process is performed once, after the deployment of sensor nodes. We make the assumption that the neighbor node knowledge is secure and confidential within the deployment period.

Malicious node database/ blacklist: This internal database is computed and generated in the CH via the use of anomaly detection in the global detection algorithms of monitor nodes. Once a monitor node discovers an anomalous event within its neighborhood, it creates and sends an alert to its CH. If the malicious counter from a suspicious node stored in a CH crosses a threshold X, the CHs create and propagate a new rule to every sensor node in the cluster. The sensor nodes update the new rule and add the entry to its malicious database. The malicious node is isolated from the cluster and not involved in communication in the network. CH

Source node	Intermediate node	Hop counter	....

Fig. 3. Example of modified HELLO packet

```
Communication Node
Repeat <listen to the packet>
 Check <packet header>
 If {ID = destination node's ID} {
      If Local_Detection(packet)
          Then drop(packet)
      Else receive(packet);
     }
And If (source & destination's ID, 1
hop neighbor)
          Then Global detection (packet)
      Else Drop (packet)
Until No transmission
```

Fig. 4. Algorithm of activating monitor nodes

serves as an intrusion data collection point. The rule must contain the following fields: time of creation, classification (type of alert), and source of the alert (H. Debar & Feinstein, 2005).

Pre-defined routing rules: When the sensor node is initially deployed, there is no entry in its internal malicious node database, except for some predefined, simple rules in the global agent. The global agent uses pre-defined rules and the two-hop neighbors' list to monitor communication in their neighborhood. These rules help monitor nodes detect common problems and specific attacks on routing protocols, based on previous work (da Silva et al., 2005). In our scheme, these rules are adapted to the routing protocols used.

- **Interval rule:** An alert is created by monitor nodes if the period between the receptions of two consecutive packets exceeds the allowed limit.
- **Integrity rule:** The packet payload must be the same along the path on a transmission link.
- **Delay rule:** The delay of a packet from one node must be limited to the timeout period.
- **Radio transmission range rule:** All packets received by a monitor node must originate from among its neighbors or a previous hop; via the estimation of the average receive power (dBm).
- **Neighbor rule:**
  1. The monitor node waits to determine if the destination node forwards the packet along the path to the sink. If not, it sends an alert packet to the CH.
  2. The monitor node waits to detect the packet which was forwarded along the path to the sink. It checks its two-hop neighbor knowledge to determine if the destination node of the forwarded packet is on the right path to the sink. If not, it sends an alert packet to the CHs.

When a sensor node receives a packet from a sensor in the network, if the source node's ID is in its black list then the sensor node uses Local_function() to drop the packet. If both source and destination's node are its one-hop neighbors, it triggers the Global_detection function. The algorithm is illustrated in Fig. 4. The global detection modules use two-hop neighbor knowledge and routing rules to detect anomalies within their transmission ranges. The illustration of Global_function() is represented in Fig. 5.

The CHs are responsible for alert aggregation from monitor nodes and computation. If the number of alerts about a suspicious node crosses the threshold X, the CHs create a rule and propagate it to every node in the cluster. The algorithm is illustrated as follows:

```
Global_detection(packet_i)
{
  If Looking(packet_i_id, buffer)
   then {
     If Check(node's ID, 2 hop neighbor's
         list )
      Or Check(packet_i, predefined-rules)
     then {
              Create(alert);
              Send(alert, cluster_head);
     }
}
```

Fig. 5. Global detection at monitor nodes

By applying our proposed algorithm, following attacks introduced in section 2 are detected easily.

Detection of Selective forwarding: In selective forwarding attacks, the transmission link from node A to node B is monitored by their monitor nodes, for example X, Y, Z. Node X, Y, Z catch and store the packets going out of node A with node B as their next intermediate node. If node B tries to stop or drop these packets, the monitor nodes will create and send an alert to CH. The monitor nodes can also use the predefined rules to check if node B forwards the packet in the right path. If node B tries to send the packets to wrong path by forwarding to an unknown node, the monitor nodes will check their 2 hops neighbor node's list. If the destination node's identification of the forwarded packet is not in node B's neighbor list, the monitor nodes will send an alert to CH. After the packets are forwarded to right path, the entry in the monitor node's intrusion buffer is remove.

Detection of Sinkhole and Hello flood: The common feature between the two attacks is that the malicious node will convince it as the nearest path to base station by using high power transmission. All packets came to node A must be originated from A's neighbor list, the monitor nodes use neighbor's list and predefined signal rule to check if a packet is originated from a far located node.

Detection of Wormhole: Our system can detect four types of wormhole attacks by inherit the advantage of local monitoring mechanism. We use 2 hops neighbor's list and predefined rules to improve the detection of wormhole in clustered WSNs.

```
Cluster head
Repeat
  If Looking (alert, intrusion alert)
  Then {
        Malicious count (node) ++
        If (Malicious count (node) > X)
        Then {
              Create (rule);
              Propagate (rule);
              }
       }
Until No transmission
```

Fig. 6. Alert computation at the cluster-head

4. Optimal triggering of intrusion detection modules

In our scheme and previous work, every node participates in the intrusion detection, so the network lifetime is potentially quickly reduced, because the workload is concentrated in IDS modules. In this section, we provide two algorithms to reduce the energy consumption in IDS modules in WSNs. Current research on intrusion detection and prevention techniques in WSNs are generally built on the assumption of a trusted environment. Unfortunately, sensor nodes are randomly deployed in an unknown, hostile environment, so they cannot be trusted. A disadvantage of cooperative IDS is the detection accuracy of IDSs, because they cannot evaluate alerts from monitor nodes. By using a lightweight trust-based framework as the basis of cooperative IDSs, we can overcome this problem and evaluate alerts from monitor nodes based on their trust values. Evaluation of alerts arriving at CHs makes our IDS scheme more resilient and accurate. We can apply any reputation framework for WSN as an integrated part in our IDS scheme.

4.1 Triggering based on trust priority

Trust is defined as the level of trustworthiness of a particular node. Tv_{xy} is the trust value of node Y calculated by node X. In our schemes, we require each sensor node to maintain a reputation table of its neighbors; the reputation value is a metric of trust. A reputation table is a small database of trust values of direct neighbor nodes, as for example node X.

$$Tv_X = (Tv_{X,1}, Tv_{X,2}, ..., Tv_{X,N}) \tag{1}$$

Where $Tv_{X,i}$ represent the trust value of the ith neighbor node of X. Calculation and update of reputation tables in sensor nodes can be found in (Kaplantzis et al., 2007). Our reputation system is fully adaptive with detection modules, because both schemes are based on an over-hearing mechanism. Each sensor node calculates the average trust of its neighbor nodes with the following equation:

$$E[X] = \frac{\sum_{i=1}^{N} Tv_{X,i}}{N} \tag{2}$$

Where E[X] represents the average trust value of X's neighbor nodes. The trust value is classified by the following mapping function:

$$Mp(Tv_{node}) = \left\{ \begin{array}{c} high - 0.8 \leq Tv_{node} \leq 1 \\ medium - 0.5 \leq Tv_{node} \leq 0.8 \\ uncertain - 0.3 \leq Tv_{node} \leq 0.5 \\ low - 0 \leq Tv_{node} \leq 0.3 \end{array} \right\} \tag{3}$$

After calculating the trust average, the sensor node sets this value according to the mapping function above, to indicate the trust level requirement. Only nodes having a better than average trust value can trigger the global agent for cooperative detection. Each packet includes its own trust requirement (high, medium or uncertain) in its header. Thus, only sensor nodes with a trust value better than the trust requirement can trigger their global agent. However, if a sensor node with a low trust value tries to send a false alert packet to the CHs, the CHs drop the alert packet, and its trust value is reduced for its malicious behavior. In our case, nodes having a low trust value cannot trigger or participate in the intrusion detection.

```
Cluster head
   Repeat
     If  Looking  (alert,  intrusion  alert)
then {
       Case Trust level node of
             'High': MC = MC +λ;
             'Medium': MC = MC +β;
             'Uncertain': MC = MC +δ;
       End Case
   If (Malicious count (node) > X) then {
             Create (rule);
             Propagate (rule);
             }
   }
   Until No transmission
```

Fig. 7. Improved alert computation algorithm at the CHs

4.2 Evaluation of alert packets

The CHs are responsible for alert aggregation and computation. We propose four levels of trust, so we can compute the alert counter in each malicious node, based on trust states of our monitor nodes. The malicious counter is defined as the threshold of malicious activities of a sensor node which cannot be exceeded. If the malicious counter of a sensor node exceeds the threshold, the sensor node is revoked from the cluster and WSNs. We suggest four parameters $(\lambda, \beta, \delta, \varphi)$ associated with four trust levels of a monitor node's incoming alert packet, in our proposed scheme $\lambda = 0$. The equation for computing the alert counter of a malicious node is described as follows:

$$MC_{node} = \beta \sum_{j=1}^{i} i + \delta \sum_{k=1}^{k} j + \varphi \sum_{l=1}^{l} k \tag{4}$$

Where $0 < \beta < \delta < \varphi < 1$ and i, j, k are the number of alert packets with the correlative trust states mentioned above. So, aggregation and computation of alert packets at CHs is improved as Fig. 7 below. By setting the trust-requirement as the average of the trust, we can reduce participation of sensor nodes in the intrusion detection, while providing high trustworthiness of incoming alert packets.

By setting the trust-requirement as the average of the trust, we can reduce participation of sensor nodes in the intrusion detection, while providing high trustworthiness of incoming alert packets.

4.3 Selection algorithm

As mentioned in the previous section, the monitor nodes observe the behavior's packet that pass through them to destination. To minimize the number of nodes activating the intrusion detection modules, our proposed scheme select the nodes which cover as many other nodes as possible. Our main idea is to choose the set of nodes which corporately cover all the nodes in the networks. Our proposed scheme is based only on the neighbor node information built on each node to find these nodes. We also make the assumption that the adversary cannot successfully compromise a node during the short deployment phase. Thus, the neighbor node information sent to sink node is trustful. The selection of monitor nodes is performed by sink node by following process:

At sink node

```
Assign U ={R} / List of nodes in
     networks

Repeat

  For each node i in U

  Find Max N(i) in U

  Put i in stack

  Assign U = U | N(i)

Until U = Null

Send IDS request to nodes in stack
```

Fig. 8. Selection algorithm at sink node

- After deployment, the sensor node builds its direct neighbor node's list and sends it to the sink node.
- The sink node finds the set of nodes which corporately cover all nodes in the network as the chosen monitor nodes. The finding algorithm is explained in detail below.
- The sink node sends the request message to these chosen nodes to require them activating their intrusion detection modules.
- Every message sent by sensor node or sink node is authenticated by using their shared keys.

We consider a network of N sensors as a set of static nodes denotes as and a single sink node denoted as $R = \{n_1, n_2, ..., n_N\}$. To describe selection algorithm, we use the term "sensor" and "node" interchangeably. The communication in the network is always destined toward the sink node . Nodes *i* and *j* are neighbors if they are in its radio range, denoted by an edge (*i j*). Let $N(i) := j|(i,j)$ denote the set of neighbors of node *i* and $N(i)|j$ denote the set without node *j*. Besides, we assume sink node or cluster heads (CHs) can have a greater battery powers, a more capable CPU or a sensitive antenna which can reach to other CHs or the sink node. The sink node search for the set of nodes which corporately cover all nodes in the network based on their neighbor node information received. The algorithm is described in Fig. 8.

4.4 Reduction of alert packets using over-hearing

In some cases of deployment, there are multiple sensor nodes concentrated in a small area. Consequently, if there is malicious activity in a link, multiple alert packets may be transmitted to CHs from different monitor nodes in an instant. Fig. 9 illustrates the case when two monitor nodes X, Z send the same alert packet about a malicious node Y.

The major issue in this case is the redundancy of the transmission of alert packets to CHs, which can cause collisions and waste energy on transmission of the same alert packets. Until now, in a given case, we need a single alert packet sent simultaneously to CHs, for malicious activity. If a single alert packet is sent at the instant malicious activity occurs, we can reduce redundant alert packets, thus reducing energy consumption in monitor nodes. To resolve this problem, we apply an over-hearing mechanism for the Medium Access Control (MAC) layer. Over-hearing is not a new approach. It was initially applied in 802.11 (Bianchi, 2000), where nodes use over-hearing to determine when the channel is free. In (Le et al., 2006), the authors extended S-MAC to event-driven applications, where there are multiple redundant transmissions. The principle of our approach is very simple. When malicious activity occurs in a transmission link, multiple monitor nodes are aware of this malicious activity, and prepare alert packets to send to the CHs. If a monitor node doesn't obtain the medium to send an alert packet, it knows there is a transmission within range. The monitor node buffers the alert packet and over-hears the packets sent within range. If the monitor node detects a neighbor sending the same alert packet, it drops the alert packet in its buffer. Otherwise, the monitor node sends the alert packet until it obtains the medium. Using this method, we can reduce both the number of transmissions and the number of collisions in sending the same alert packets of monitor nodes. The study in (Hill et al., 2000a;b) found that each bit transmitted in WSNs consumes power about equivalent to executing 800-1,000 instructions. Thus, we can minimize the power consumption in detection modules, because communication is more costly than computation in WSNs.

5. Performance analysis

In this section, we analyze and evaluate the proposed detection capability, to determine the performance of our schemes. The probability of detection of an attack, P_D, depends on three factors: number of monitor nodes, probability of a missed detection of a monitor node, and our malicious counter threshold X. We defined K as the number of monitor nodes and P_C as the probability of a collision occurring in a transmission link.
When the number of alerts cross the threshold X, the rule is created and propagated to every sensor nodes by CHs. Therefore, P_D is the probability of more than X nodes in the total of K nodes which send an alert to CH. The event of the probability P_D occurs whenever there is an event which has the probability of more than X nodes sending an alert. Because the events are independent so

$$P_D = P_X + P_{X+1} + ... + P_K \tag{5}$$

The probability of an event that there are X nodes sending alert to CH is:

$$P_X = (1 - P_C)^X {P_C}^{K-X} \tag{6}$$

So the probability detection of an attacker PD can be written as following:

$$P_D = (1 - P_C)^X {P_C}^{K-X} + ... + (1 - P_C)^K {P_C}^{K-K} \tag{7}$$

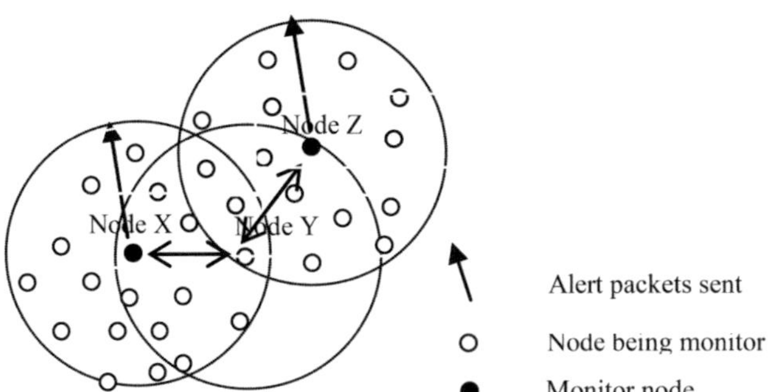

Fig. 9. Illustration of redundancy of alert packets

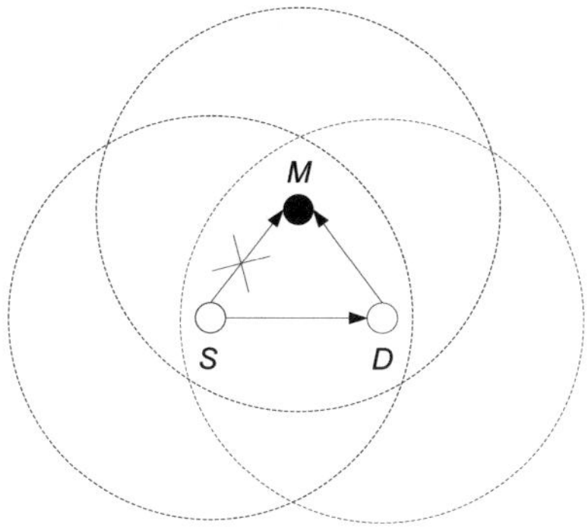

Fig. 10. False positive detection

As the result, when K monitor nodes collaborate in monitoring, the probability detection of an attack is:

$$P_D = \sum_{i=X}^{K} \binom{K}{X} (1 - P_C)^X P_C{}^{K-X} \tag{8}$$

We defined P_F as the probability of a false positive for a legitimate node. A false positive occurs in a link when a monitor node M receives a packet from D, but in its buffer doesn't have any information about the packet from S because of the collision. So the monitor node M may think the node D fabricating the packet instead of forwarding along the path to the destination. The monitor node considers it as a malicious action of the node D. The Fig. 10 illustrates the false positive of a monitor node. The probability of false detection of monitor node M can be found as following steps:

$P_F = P_S + P_D$, where P_S is the probability of a monitor node M which does not receive a packet from S but receive the forwarded packet from D and P_D is the probability of the monitor node M which receive a packet from S but does not receive the forwarded packet from D.

The probability of P_S can be written as following:

$$P_S = P_C{}^2(1 - P_C) \tag{9}$$

The probability of P_D can be written as following:

$$P_D = P_C(1 - P_C)^2 \tag{10}$$

$$\Rightarrow P_F = (1 - P_C)^2 P_C + P_C{}^2(1 - P_C) \tag{11}$$

Similar to equation (8), we have the false probability of monitor nodes:

$$\Leftrightarrow P_{FD} = \sum_{i=X}^{K} \binom{K}{X} (1 - P_F)^X P_F{}^{K-X} \tag{12}$$

With different detection algorithms (in both wired and wireless IDS) there is always a different way to estimate the threshold. There is no way to determine the exactly threshold, just estimate and chose the best threshold based on analytical calculation of the detection algorithms and throughout simulations for the best result. In our model, the threshold is depending on the probability of collision and the average number of monitor nodes in

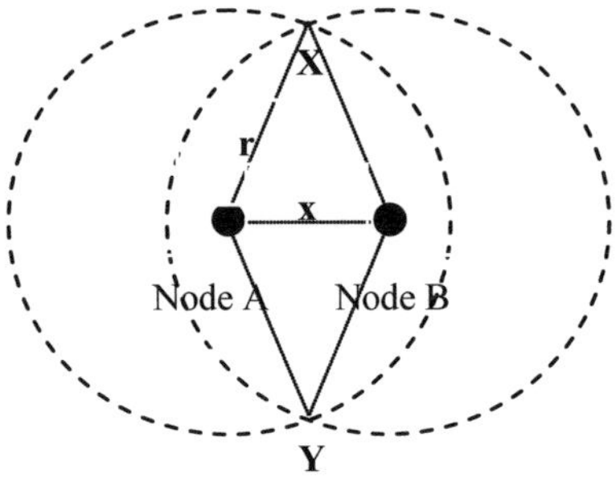

Fig. 11. The radio coverage of two communication nodes

individual transmission link, which we estimate as follow. For any two communication nodes, the average number of monitor nodes for their transmission link is the average number of sensor nodes which reside in their radio range (the Fig. 11).
For any distance x, the radio coverage of two communication nodes is the area of the sectors XAY and XBY minus the area of the rhombus AXBY and is calculated as following:

$$XY(x) = 2r^2\cos^{-1}\left(\frac{x}{2r}\right) - x\sqrt{r^2 - \frac{x^2}{4}} \tag{13}$$

The probability distribution function of x is given by

$$F(x) = P(distance < x) = \frac{x^2}{r^2} \tag{14}$$

So the probability density function is

$$f(x) = F'(x) = \frac{2x}{r^2} \tag{15}$$

The expected area XY is calculated as following:

$$E[XY] = \int_0^r XY(x)f(x)dx \tag{16}$$

$$\Leftrightarrow \int_0^r \left(2r^2\cos^{-1}\left(\frac{x}{2r}\right) - x\sqrt{r^2 - \frac{x^2}{4}}\right)\frac{2x}{r^2}dx \tag{17}$$

$$\Leftrightarrow \left(\pi - \frac{3\sqrt{3}}{4}\right)r^2 = 0.5865r^2 \tag{18}$$

So the average number of monitor nodes for each individual link is given by $[E[XY] \times d$, where d is network density. As shown in Fig. 12, the scheme is effective when the number of monitor nodes is increased. The probability of a missed detection also affects the efficiency of the scheme. However, the probability of detection is close to 1, if the number of monitor nodes exceeds 5, regardless of the high probability of a missed detection. The probability of a false positive, as shown in Fig. 13, indicates that the number of nodes is related to the probability of false detection. Increasing the number of nodes results in an increase in the probability of a collision. We must consider a balance between the number of monitor nodes and the probability of false detection, which suits the requirement of our applications.

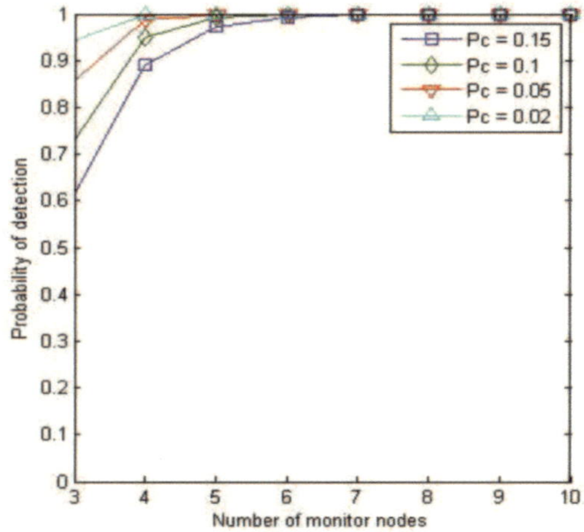

Fig. 12. Detection probability of a malicious node

To evaluate the performance of our proposed detection scheme in realistic sensor applications, we simulate the network with 200 sensor nodes, in a field of 100 meters x 100 meters, using Castalia, a WSNs simulator based on Omnet++ (Castalia Simulator). The parameters used are in accordance with actual sensor network applications and experiments, such as Smart Dust Projcct (2001), Virtual Patrol (2005) (Gui & Mohapatra, 2005). Sensor nodes are deployed in a randomized grid. The simple MAC Carrier Sense is used as the MAC protocol and Simple Tree Routing is used as the routing protocol. The detection algorithms are implemented in the application layer. While handling packets, sensor nodes must call the detection algorithm before forwarding or receiving the data. To simplify algorithms, we assign each sensor node a random trust value. There is no low-trust value during the periods of deployment.

Fig. 14 shows the performance of our scheme with malicious nodes. Castalia also supports packet collision by setting the parameter *SN.WirelessChannel.CollisionModel* (Castalia Simulator). We set sensor nodes to exhibit malicious behavior by increasing their dropped packet ratio, changing the fields of forwarded packets and sending false Hello

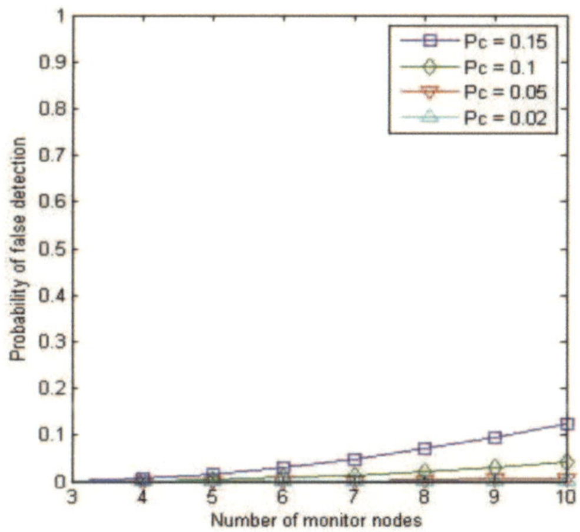

Fig. 13. False detection probability of a malicious node

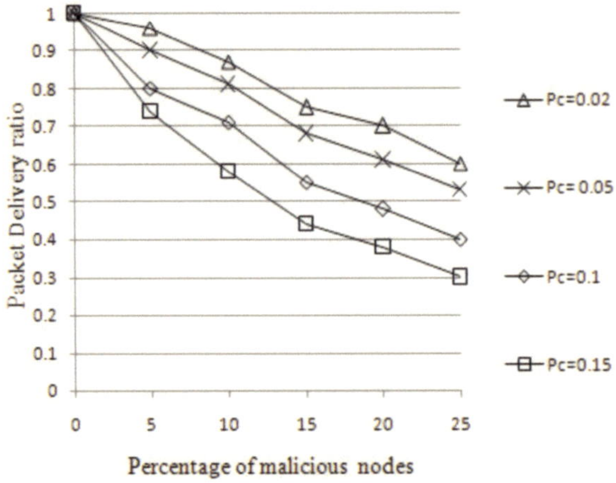

Fig. 14. Packet delivery ratio under attacks

packets with abnormal radio power. This result proves that our scheme yields a good packet delivery ratio under different types of routing attacks. Our simulation investigates the effect of the percentage of malicious nodes on the packet delivery ratio. As the percentage of malicious nodes increases, revoking malicious nodes requires a particular period of time. So, the packet delivery ratio is quickly reduced, if malicious nodes increase.

As shown in Fig. 15, our scheme yields a good detection rate; exceeding 90%; when the collision error is low, 2-5%, and the percentage of malicious nodes is under 5%. An increased collision ratio and malicious nodes cause greater packets loss, so it is difficult to distinguish malicious nodes and lost packets from normal nodes, because of collisions. As the collision error rate increases, misdetection is inevitable. To overcome this problem, we propose a dynamic threshold mechanism to make our scheme more efficient under a high collision rate or dropped packet rate.

Here, we study the energy consumption in detection modules in sensor nodes, in accordance with watchdog-based methods, and our approach with an over-hearing mechanism. Watchdog is used as a selection method of monitor nodes, which was applied in previous detection mechanisms in (Khalil et al., 2005; 2008; Roman,

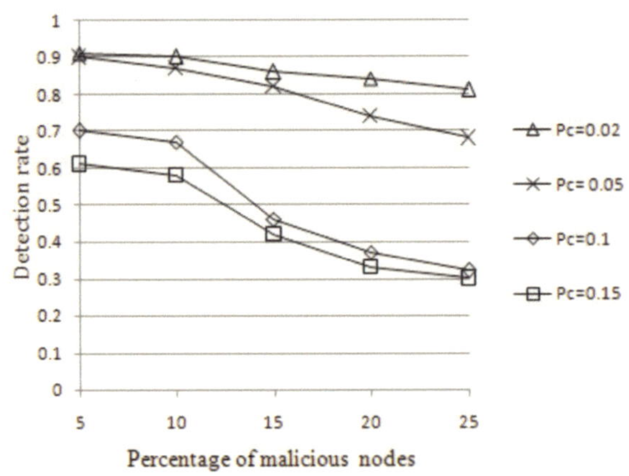

Fig. 15. Detection ratio of malicious nodes

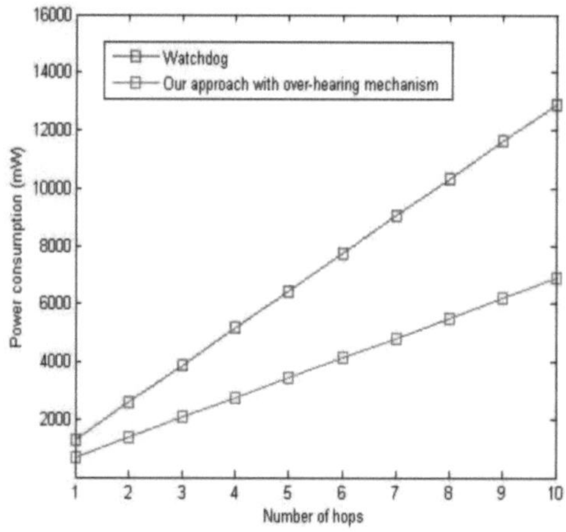

Fig. 16. Power consumption comparison

2006; Chong Eik Loo & Palaniswami, 2006; Hu & Burmester, 2009; Marti et al., 2000; Kaplantzis et al., 2007; Hai et al., 2007). For simplicity, we analyze the energy consumption in monitor nodes in transmission from node A to node B, with n intermediate hops. Using energy consumption models in (Hai et al., 2007; Holger & W, 2005), we obtain the energy consumption of monitor nodes in the transmission link in Fig. 16 with various hops. It is apparent that our scheme has lower energy consumption than the watchdog-based mechanism. We postulate that our scheme reduces energy consumption in monitor nodes, thus enhances the network lifetime. In summary, in Table 1 we review the proposed detection framework compared with other related work on intrusion detection schemes for WSNs.

Onat and Chong's schemes are based on the model of traffic and signal power data for each neighbor node to detect anomalies. In this mechanism, as the number of neighbor nodes and sample data increase, there is substantial consumption of memory and computational resources, which results in delays in detecting attacks. Their schemes are based on previous IDS that are effective for wired networks, but, we postulate it is not currently practical, for WSNs. In Afrand's work (Agah et al., 2006), a detection framework was proposed, based on

IDS framework / **Characteristic**	Our proposed scheme	Onat's scheme	Chong's scheme	Afrand's scheme
Architecture	Distributed & Collaboration	Distributed	Distributed	Distributed
Approach	Major voting, two-hop neighbor knowledge, routing rules	Traffic model & Centralized detection	Traffic model & Centralized detection	Non-cooperative game
Malicious nodes	High (25%)	No detail	No detail	No detail
Accuracy	High	No detail	High	Medium
Attacks	Wormhole, sinkhole, selective forwarding and Hello floods	Sinkhole	Sink hole	Denial of Service
Energy efficient	Yes	No	No	No
Delay	Medium	High	High	Medium
Memory consumption	Medium	High	High	Medium
Complex	Medium	High	High	Medium

Table 1. A review of related works on intrusion detection

non-cooperative games, but the detection algorithms were not shown in detail.

6. Conclusion

In this chapter, we propose a simple, lightweight detection framework for the prevention and detection of common routing attacks in WSNs. Our detection framework was evaluated and it was demonstrated that it was effective, even when the density of the network is high and there is a high probability of collisions in WSNs. In addition, our detection modules involve less energy consumption than techniques proposed in previous works, using an over-hearing mechanism to reduce the transmission of alert packets. In our future work, further research on this topic will be performed, with detailed simulation of different attack scenarios, to test the performance of our proposed algorithm. We expect the result to be available in the near future.

7. References

Abbasi, A. A. & Younis, M. (2007). A survey on clustering algorithms for wireless sensor networks, *Comput. Commun.* 30(14-15): 2826–2841.

Aboelaze, M. & Aloul, F. (2005). Current and future trends in sensor networks: a survey, *Wireless and Optical Communications Networks, 2005. WOCN 2005. Second IFIP International Conference on*, pp. 551 – 555.

Agah, A., Basu, K. & Das, S. K. (2006). Security enforcement in wireless sensor networks: A framework based on non-cooperative games, *Pervasive Mob. Comput.* 2(2): 137–158.

Balasubramaniyan, J. S., Garcia-Fernandez, J. O., Isacoff, D., Spafford, E. & Zamboni, D. (1998). An architecture for intrusion detection using autonomous agents, *ACSAC '98: Proceedings of the 14th Annual Computer Security Applications Conference*, IEEE Computer Society, Washington, DC, USA, p. 13.

Banerjee, S., Grosan, C. & Abraham, A. (2005). Ideas: Intrusion detection based on emotional ants for sensors, *In 5th International Conference on Intelligent Systems, Design and Applications (ISDA-05.*

Bianchi, G. (2000). Performance analysis of the ieee 802.11 distributed coordination function, *Selected Areas in Communications, IEEE Journal on* 18(3): 535 –547.

Camtepe, S. A. & Yener, B. (2005). Key distribution mechanisms for wireless sensor networks: a survey, *Technical report*.

Castalia Simulator *http://castalia.npc.nicta.com.au*.

Chong Eik Loo, Mun Yong Ng, C. L. & Palaniswami, M. (2006). Intrusion detection for routing attacks in sensor networks, *International Journal of Distributed Sensor Networks*, Vol. 2, pp. 313 – 332 Vol. 3.

Cuppens, F. & Miège, A. (2002). Alert correlation in a cooperative intrusion detection framework, *SP '02: Proceedings of the 2002 IEEE Symposium on Security and Privacy*, IEEE Computer Society, Washington, DC, USA, p. 202.

da Silva, A. P. R., Martins, M. H. T., Rocha, B. P. S., Loureiro, A. A. F., Ruiz, L. B. & Wong, H. C. (2005). Decentralized intrusion detection in wireless sensor networks, *Q2SWinet '05: Proceedings of the 1st ACM international workshop on Quality of service & security in wireless and mobile networks*, ACM, New York, NY, USA, pp. 16–23.

Djenouri, D., Khelladi, L. & Badache, A. (2005). A survey of security issues in mobile ad hoc and sensor networks, *Communications Surveys Tutorials, IEEE* 7(4): 2 – 28.

Durresi, A., Member, S., Paruchuri, V. K., Member, S., Iyengar, S. S. & Kannan, R. (2005).

Optimized broadcast protocol for sensor networks, *IEEE Transactions on Computers* 54: 1013–1024.

Gui, C. & Mohapatra, P. (2005). Virtual patrol: a new power conservation design for surveillance using sensor networks, *Information Processing in Sensor Networks, 2005. IPSN 2005. Fourth International Symposium on*, pp. 246 – 253.

H. Debar, D. C. & Feinstein, B. (2005). The intrusion detection message exchange format.

Hai, T. H., Khan, F. & Huh, E.-N. (2007). Hybrid intrusion detection system for wireless sensor networks, *ICCSA'07: Proceedings of the 2007 international conference on Computational science and Its applications*, Springer-Verlag, Berlin, Heidelberg, pp. 383–396.

Hill, J., Szewczyk, R., Woo, A., Hollar, S., Culler, D. & Pister, K. (2000a). System architecture directions for networked sensors, *SIGPLAN Not.* 35(11): 93–104.

Hill, J., Szewczyk, R., Woo, A., Hollar, S., Culler, D. & Pister, K. (2000b). System architecture directions for networked sensors, *SIGARCH Comput. Archit. News* 28(5): 93–104.

Holger, K. & W, W. A. (2005). *Protocols and Architecture for Wireless Sensor Networks - Chapter 2.2*, John Wiley & Son Press.

Hu, J. & Burmester, M. (2009). Cooperation in mobile ad hoc networks, *Guide to Wireless Ad Hoc Networks*, Computer Communications and Networks, Springer London, pp. 1–15. 10.1007/978-1-84800-328-6_3.
http://dx.doi.org/10.1007/978-1-84800-328-6_3

Ilyas, M. & Mahgoub, I. (2005). *Handbook of sensor networks: Compact wireless and wired sensing systems*, CRC Press.

Janakiraman, R., Waldvogel, M. & Zhang, Q. (2003). Indra: a peer-to-peer approach to network intrusion detection and prevention, *Enabling Technologies: Infrastructure for Collaborative Enterprises, 2003. WET ICE 2003. Proceedings. Twelfth IEEE International Workshops on*, pp. 226 – 231.

Kaplantzis, S., Shilton, A., Mani, N. & Sekercioglu, Y. A. (2007). Detecting selective forwarding attacks in wireless sensor networks using support vector machines.

Karlof, C. & Wagner, D. (2003). Secure routing in wireless sensor networks: attacks and countermeasures, *Ad Hoc Networks* 1(2-3): 293 – 315. Sensor Network Protocols and Applications.
http://www.sciencedirect.com /science /article /B7576-499CSFN-7 /2 /ad3f92c2d573d82839cdb5ae91272fd7

Khalil, I., Bagchi, S. & Shroff, N. (2005). Liteworp: a lightweight countermeasure for the wormhole attack in multihop wireless networks, *Dependable Systems and Networks, 2005. DSN 2005. Proceedings. International Conference on*, pp. 612 – 621.

Khalil, I., Bagchi, S. & Shroff, N. B. (2008). Mobiworp: Mitigation of the wormhole attack in mobile multihop wireless networks, *Ad Hoc Netw.* 6(3): 344–362.

Le, H.-C., Guyennet, H. & Zerhouni, N. (2006). Over-hearing for energy efficient in event-driven wireless sensor network, *Mobile Adhoc and Sensor Systems (MASS), 2006 IEEE International Conference on*, pp. 633 –638.

Marti, S., Giuli, T. J., Lai, K. & Baker, M. (2000). Mitigating routing misbehavior in mobile ad hoc networks, *MobiCom '00: Proceedings of the 6th annual international conference on Mobile computing and networking*, ACM, New York, NY, USA, pp. 255–265.

Mishra, A., Nadkarni, K. & Patcha, A. (2004). Intrusion detection in wireless ad hoc networks, *Wireless Communications, IEEE* 11(1): 48 – 60.

Onat, I. & Miri, A. (2005). An intrusion detection system for wireless sensor networks, *Wireless And Mobile Computing, Networking And Communications, 2005. (WiMob'2005), IEEE*

International Conference on, Vol. 3, pp. 253 – 259 Vol. 3.

Paxson, V. (1999). Bro: A system for detecting network intruders in real-time, *Computer Networks*, pp. 2435–2463.

Richard Heady, George Lugar, M. S. A. M. (1990). The architecture of a network level intrusion detection system, *Technical report*, University of New Mexico, Albuquerque, NM.

Roesch, M. (2002). The snort network intrusion detection system. *http://www.snort.org*

Roman, R. (2006). Applying intrusion detection systems to wireless sensor networks, *in CCNC 2006: Proceeding of the 3rd IEEE Consumer Communications and Networking Conference*, pp. 640–644.

Sultana, N., Choi, K.-M. & Huh, E.-N. (2007). Application driven cluster based group key management with identifier in mobile wireless sensor network, *FGCN '07: Proceedings of the Future Generation Communication and Networking*, IEEE Computer Society, Washington, DC, USA, pp. 362–367.

Techateerawat, P. & Jennings, A. (2006). Energy efficiency of intrusion detection systems in wireless sensor networks, *Web Intelligence and Intelligent Agent Technology Workshops, 2006. WI-IAT 2006 Workshops. 2006 IEEE/WIC/ACM International Conference on*, pp. 227 –230.

Technology, C. (n.d.). Mica2, wireless measurement system. *http://www.xbow.com*

Wang, Y., Attebury, G. & Ramamurthy, B. (2006). A survey of security issues in wireless sensor networks, *Communications Surveys Tutorials, IEEE* 8(2): 2 –23.

Wood, A. D. & Stankovic, J. A. (2002). Denial of service in sensor networks, *Computer* 35(10): 54–62.

Part 5

Other Aspects of IDS

An Intrusion Detection Technique Based on Discrete Binary Communication Channels

Ampah[1], N. K., Akujuobi[2], C. M. and Annamalai[3], A.
[1]*Jacobs Engineering Group, Houston, Texas,*
[2]*Alabama State University, Montgomery, Alabama,*
[3]*Prairie View A & M University, Prairie View, Texas*
USA

1. Introduction

Enterprise networks are the main targets for hackers or intruders due to the fact that most financial transactions take place online and the networks also handle vast amounts of data and other resources (Satti & Garner, 2001). Handling transactions online is on the increase everyday because it makes life easier for both the customers as well as the enterprises offering services (Jou et al., 2000; Yau & Xinyu Zhang, 1999; Ko, 2003; Tront & Marchany, 2004). Enterprise networks also have lots of bandwidth, which is very attractive to hackers because they take advantage of that by using those networks as launching pads to attack others (Tront & Marchany, 2004; Janakiraman et al., 2003). It therefore becomes very difficult for the IDSs and IPSs at the receiving end to detect and prevent the attacks or hackers, since the packet header information will indicate legitimate senders. This is the main reason why most IPSs are easily bypassed by hackers (Tront & Marchany, 2004; Paulson, 2002; Weber, 1999). Intrusion prevention, which is a proactive technique, prevents the attacks from entering the network. Unfortunately, some of the attacks still bypass the intrusion prevention systems. Intrusion detection on the other hand, detects attacks only after they have entered the network.

Although attacks are generally assumed to emanate from outside a given network, the most dangerous attacks actually emanate from the network itself. Those are really difficult to detect since most users of the network are assumed to be trusted people. The situation has necessitated drastic research work in the area of network security, especially in the development of intrusion detection and prevention systems intended to detect and prevent all possible attacks on a given network (Akujuobi & Ampah, 2007; Akujuobi et al., 2007a; Akujuobi et al., 2007b; Akujuobi et al., 2007c; Akujuobi & Ampah, 2009). These IDSs use either anomaly or signature-based detection techniques. Anomaly detection techniques detect both known and unknown attacks, but signature-based detection techniques detect only known attacks. The main approaches of anomaly detection techniques are statistical, predictive pattern generation, neural networks, and sequence matching and learning. The main approaches of signature-based detection techniques are expert systems, keystroke monitoring, model-based, state transition analysis, and pattern matching (Biermann et al., 2001). There is no existing IDS or IPS that can detect or prevent all intrusions. For example, configuring a firewall to be 100% foolproof compromises the very service provided by the network. The use of conventional encryption algorithms and system level security techniques have helped to some extent, but not to the levels expected (Fadia, 2006; Leinwand & Conroy, 1996; Stallings, 2003). The following are the five limitations associated with existing IDSs (Satti & Garner, 2001):

1. Use of central analyzer: Whenever the central analyzer is attacked by an intruder the whole system will be without protection, so it becomes a single point of failure (Janakiraman et al., 2003);
2. Limited scalability: Processing all data at a central point limits the size of the entire network that can be monitored and controlled at a time. Data collection in a distributed fashion also causes excessive traffic in the network (Kayacik et al., 2004);
3. Effectiveness: The ability of existing IDSs/IPSs to detect and prevent intrusion is still not clearly established because of high false positive and false negative rates (Chunmei et al., 2004);
4. Efficiency: Quantifying resources like time, power, bandwidth, and storage used by existing IDSs will be a critical success factor (Khoshgoftaar & Abushadi, 2004); and
5. Security: Securing the security data itself from intruders is also a very important limitation to existing IDSs.

It is still an open problem to develop IDSs and IPSs to detect and prevent SNY-flood attacks, Distributed Denial of Service (DDoS) attacks based on SYN-flood attacks, and also eliminate some or all of the limitations of existing IDSs. Although many IDS and IPS techniques have been proposed for securing networks from attacks, problems with SYN-flood attacks and DDoS attacks based on SYN-flood attacks have not been resolved. Also, there is no research work that has attempted to solve the above problems nor have there been attempts to eliminate the majority or all of the five major problems of existing IDSs. Most research works solved only one or two of the major problems. Our approach will resolve the above problems through the following steps:

1. Design an IDS technique based on a well established model (i. e. discrete binary communication Channels), which will be used as a back-up for existing IDS to help eliminate serious attacks like SYN-flood attacks and DDoS attacks based on SYN-flood attacks; and
2. Transmit all security data from the network directly to the central detection point for analysis instead of transmitting them through the network itself.

Step one aims at solving the problems with effectiveness of existing IDSs. Step two aims at solving the problems with efficiency (i. e. saving bandwidth), security (i. e. securing security data from intruders), and limited scalability (i. e. reducing traffic in the network). These are the objectives of our approach.

2. Background

The following major approaches are used to manage network security problems:

i. Intrusion Detection (traditional); and
ii. Intrusion Prevention (proactive).

The basic techniques used by the two approaches are as follows:

i. Signature based detection system (Attack patterns are considered as signatures);
ii. Anomaly detection system (Anything unusual is considered as suspect);
iii. Distributed intrusion detection system (Data is collected and analyzed in a distributed fashion); and

iv. Centralized intrusion detection system (Data is collected in a distributed fashion but analyzed centrally).

The use of intrusion detection and prevention techniques in addition to other authentication techniques has become very necessary in managing enterprise network security. A layer approach is often used since there is no single technique that guarantees absolute security against all attacks on a given network. Very strong authentication techniques will also help prevent attacks from within the network. Depending on where the IDS software is installed, it can be referred to as network based intrusion detection system (NIDS) or host based intrusion detection system (HIDS). NIDS ensures preventive control of a given system, whiles HIDS ensures detective control. The following are some existing NIDS: Internet Security Systems Real Secure, Network Security Wizard Dragon IDS, Symantec Net Prowler, Cisco Systems Net Ranger, Network Flight Recorder Intrusion, Detection Appliance, Network Ice Black Ice Defender, CyberSafe Centrax, and Snort. The following are some existing HIDS: Internet Security Systems Real Secure, Symantec Intruder Alert, CyberSafe Centrax, and Tripwire.

Securing information on data networks and the networks themselves have become very difficult tasks considering the diverse types and number of intrusions being recorded daily. There is a lot of ongoing research work in the area of data network security management to develop techniques to combat intruders because of the financial losses incurred by enterprises due to activities of intruders (Paez & Torres, 2009; Jing-Wen et al., 2009; Kui, 2009; Lixia et al., 2009; Momenzadeh et al., 2009; Jing et al., 2009; Ihn-Han & Olariu, 2009; Cannady, 2009; Changxin & Ke, 2009; Wei et al., 2009). This effort should seriously include securing networks also, and that is exactly what this IDS proves to do. Research work in network security can be categorized into three major areas: intrusion detection systems only; intrusion prevention systems only; and combined intrusion detection and intrusion prevention systems.

2.1 Intrusion detection systems

Intrusion detection, which is a traditional technique, detects attacks only after they have entered the network. The analysis of IDSs in terms of advantages and disadvantages was done in (Vokorokos et al., 2006). This study was purely theoretical and it was proposed to consider different types of IDSs based on attack types, and whether attacks are directed towards a whole network, a sub network or a host. It will finally consider at the implementation stage, the important criterion for determining which layers of the ISO/OSI model will be covered by the IDSs including their ranges of operation. The importance of an automated intrusion response and further proposal on a dynamic intrusion response known as Gnipper vaccine was highlighted in (Zhaoyu & Uppala, 2006). This is a countermeasure, which uses dynamic agents to mitigate denial of service attacks. Although the approach provided an efficient and effective response to an intrusion with very little overhead, future work in this effort will focus on developing an efficient "trust model." A pattern matching NIDS, which consists of four modules: collection module, analysis module, response module and attack rule library was developed in (Zhou et al., 2006).

The system is based on Common Intrusion Detection Framework (CIDF) architecture and mature intrusion detection technology. Although efficient and effective, the system has to include anomaly detection in the future. An intrusion detection engine based on neural networks combined with a protection method, which is based on watermarking techniques, was presented in (Mitrokotsa et al., 2007). This engine exploits two research areas, that is, visual representation and watermarking, which have not been used in mobile ad hoc network (MANET) in the past. The advantages of eSOM and visual representation in achieving intrusion detection were demonstrated. The use of the proposed engine with various routing protocols, for detecting various types of attacks and testing real MANET in the future was emphasized. An approach to combat threats from worms, insiders, and attackers with a toehold was discussed in (Weaver et al., 2007). This was done by exploiting the VLAN capabilities of modern switches to enforce that all LAN communications must traverse and meet the approval of an intrusion detection monitor that operates separately from the switch. Two benefits were realized here: deployment and operation in today's enterprise networks without requiring replacement of existing infrastructure and the use of highly flexible, commodity PCs for LAN monitoring, rather than algorithms embedded in difficult-to-reprogram custom hardware. Further work is required in the development of a mechanism capable of processing WAN traffic and not only LAN traffic as described here.

A novel feature classification scheme for features that can be extracted by sniffing the network was introduced in (Onut & Ghorbani, 2006). It further gives a better understanding for real-time features that can be extracted from packets in order to detect intrusions. Preliminary results are promising for mapping the network features into the network attack domain. Future work will introduce statistical analysis of subsets of features versus specific attacks and attack categories in order to determine the necessary set of features to be analyzed by an IDS/IPS. Research into the question as to whether one can detect attacks without keeping per-flow state was initiated in (Ramana et al., 2007). It suggests that a tradeoff between performance and completeness may not be as Draconian as is commonly thought. Some progress has been made for bandwidth-based and partial completion DoS attacks, and scan-based attacks including worms, but the general problem still remains very difficult. Further work is needed concerning issues of "behavioral aliasing" and "spoofing" in such scalable solutions. An introduction to new evasion methods, presentation of test results for confirming attack outcomes based on server responses, and proposal of a methodology for confirming response validity were discussed in (Chaboya et al., 2006). These methods must be implemented as either analyst guidance or preferably in a NIDS plug-in or similar software solution. Also, these methods lead to the development of payload-size and shell-code-matching filters for Snort. Future work looks promising in reducing both the analyst workload and the risk from evasion attacks.

A framework for internet banking security using multi-layered, feed-forward artificial neural networks was outlined in (Bignell, 2006). Anomaly detection techniques applied for transaction authentication and intrusion detection within internet banking security architectures were utilized. This comprehensive fraud detection model via networks technology has the potential to significantly limit present level of financial fraud experienced with existing fraud prevention techniques. A prototype for this neural network will be developed to quantitatively validate the effectiveness of this machine learning technique. An innovative approach to the design and implementation of a VoIP specific honeypot was presented in (Nassar et al., 2007). Simulation results from using this Session Initiation Protocol (SIP) specific honeypot look promising in relation to the effectiveness of the information gathering tools and the correctness of the inference engine deductions. Attempts to reduce false positive rates generated by cooperative Intrusion Detection Systems (IDSs) in MANETs were discussed in (Otrok et al., 2007). This was done by analyzing the intrusion detected by mobile nodes within a cooperative game theoretic framework. Simulation results provided better results compared to existing methods.

An Incident Response Support System (IRSS) that correlates past and present events in order to classify attacks was introduced in (Capuzzi et al., 2006). This also serves as a preliminary report on a system to support the incident response activities of a security administrator. So far, a prototype has been implemented, but a massive set of experiments in order to evaluate the effectiveness of this system is underway. Plans to investigate new similarity metrics (for response retrieval) and more sophisticated adaptation algorithm will be dealt with in the future. A suit of detection techniques to identify fraudulent usage of mobile telecommunications services by exploiting regularities demonstrated in users' behaviors was presented in (Sun et al., 2007). This leads to the creation of an end user's profile for anomaly detection in wireless networks.

The intrusion detection problem is formulated as a multi-feature two-class pattern classification problem, which applies Bayes Decision Rule to the collected data. Both algorithms can achieve good performance depending on the input parameters as indicated by results from simulation studies. More features need to be considered in the future so as to make the system more general and robust. A fully automated technique for detecting, preventing and reporting SQL Injection Attacks (SQLIAs) incidents was discussed in (Muthuprasanna et al., 2006). Preliminary evaluation results of a prototype developed against various performance metrics affecting web server performance was also provided. Solutions for these critical security issues in web applications ensure easy transition towards next generation web services.

2.2 Intrusion prevention systems

Intrusion prevention, which is a proactive technique, prevents the attacks from entering the network. Unfortunately, some of the attacks still bypass the intrusion prevention systems. A simple methodology for testing dynamic intrusion-prevention systems for McAfee Entercept version 5.0 and the Cisco Security Agent version 4.5 was developed in (Labbe et al., 2006). Although test results showed that neither of the products stood up to their required effectiveness, the Cisco product did better. This test even supports the fact that effectiveness is one of the major problems of existing IDSs and IPSs. A multiple joint prevention technique of information security in Storage Area Networks (SAN) environment was presented in (Zheng-De et al., 2006). Although this technique can greatly improve the ability of preventing intrusion, issues with misreporting of intrusion prevention in IDS and filch of information in SAN need to be considered in future. A novel pattern-matching algorithm, which uses ternary content addressable memory (TCAM) and capable of matching multiple patterns in a single operation was considered in (Weinberg et al., 2006). This system is compatible with Snort's rules syntax, which is the de facto standard for intrusion prevention systems. This Network Intrusion Prevention System (NIPS) presents several advantages over existing NIPS devices.

The necessary and sufficient conditions for the application of Byzantine agreement protocol to the intrusion detection problem were investigated in (Colon Osorio, 2007). This was done by developing a secure architecture and fault-resilient engine (SAFE), which is capable of tolerating such problems. This IPS eliminates some of the common shortcomings of existing IPSs. Both the implementation and evaluation stages are complete and require extra research work in relation to masquerading, distribution and protection of sensitive data, scalability and implementation issues. The link between concepts of the immune system in relation to the Danger Theory and components of operating system (such as application processes and sockets) was investigated in (Krizhanovsky & Marasanov, 2007). Although it is expected to develop intrusion prevention systems out of this link, more work needs to be done for this to be achieved. A framework for protecting against buffer overflow attacks, the oldest and most pervasive attack technique was introduced and discussed in (Piromsopa & Enbody, 2006a). It was used to create an effective, hardware, buffer overflow prevention tool. A formal argument made here was that "a necessary condition for preventing buffer-overflow attacks is the prevention of the integrity of addresses across domains." A further description of how the above statement supports a variety of successful hardware-based methods to prevent buffer overflow attacks was given.

Arbitrary copy, a type of buffer-overflow attack that is capable of bypassing most buffer-overflow solutions was introduced in (Piromsopa & Enbody, 2006b). Work is still ongoing to extend Secure Bit, which is one of the most promising buffer-overflow protection techniques, to protect against buffer-overflow of non-control data. A better solution for Information Security management by designing Preventive Information Security Management (PrISM) aimed at developing and deploying an indigenous Information Security Management System (ISMS) with intrusion prevention capabilities was proposed in (Anwar et al., 2007). This solution is based on reverse engineering of Open Source Security Information Management (OSSIM) system. A new strategy for dealing with the impossible path execution (IPE) and mimicry attack in the N-gram base Host Intrusion Detection System (HIDS) model was introduced in (Bruschi et al., 2007). This is also a novel defensive technique, represented by the obfuscator module, which works in a transparent way and low overhead of 5.9% with the higher accuracy than the state of the art HIDS. Future work will consider using the obfuscator module in order to reduce the false rate and to detect other kinds of IPE attacks.

2.3 Combined intrusion detection and prevention systems

Combined intrusion detection and prevention systems take advantage of both the traditional and proactive approaches with the aim of eliminating some of the limitations of both systems. The use of active traffic splitters on the traffic with the goal of reducing the load on sensors, thereby improving performance in the detection and prevention of intrusion was presented in (Xinidis et al., 2006). Some improvements were made in terms of sensor performance for each of the methods used. The overall cost of the approach was also reasonable. An intelligent agent based intrusion detection and prevention system for mobile ad hoc networks was studied in (Sampathkumar et al., 2007). Although the developed system worked efficiently and detected intrusion at multiple levels, namely, user and packet levels, there is the chance of improving the efficiency in terms of time reduction and effectiveness in terms of increased prediction rate of the system by using training with more instances. A Session Initiation Protocol (SIP) intrusion detection and prevention architecture was implemented as an extension of the very popular open-source software Snort in (Niccolini et al., 2006). The results indicated that the quality of service experienced by clients did not decrease, hence signalling a good basis for further development of more advanced VoIP IDS/IPS solutions. The effective detection of both known and unknown attacks by means of unified real-time analysis of network traffic introduced by ESIDE-DEPIAN based on Bayesian Belief Networks concepts was established in (Bringas, 2007). This is referred to as a unified Intrusion Detection paradigm.

An application-based intrusion detection and intrusion prevention (ID/IP) system coupled with data mining and mobile agent technologies was introduced in (Yee et al., 2006). This hybrid system, consisting of a core engine with data sensor, detector, configuration device and alert and response device as its main components, uses both signature-based and anomaly based mechanisms in detecting and preventing intrusions. It further uses data mining and mobile agent technologies in providing a real-time adaptive and responsive ID and IP systems. An examination of integrated multiple intrusion detection sensors, which seek to minimize the number of incorrect-alarms was designed and implemented in (Beheshti & Wasniowski, 2007). The system was implemented using Open Software whenever possible such as Snort, Honeypot, MySQL, etc. This information fusion based intrusion detection and prevention model, which is a prototype, needs to include database design allowing for more efficient data fusion from multiple sensors.

Proactive screening of the health of a corporate network and performing first aid by systematically monitoring vital signs of mobile devices within the network was outlined in (Ransbottom & Jacoby, 2006). Some of the vital signs to be used to detect and prevent system intrusion were registry content changes, active processes, open ports, power usage thresholds, and power signatures. This system provides a comprehensive overall assessment of a network, which leads to building broader immunities to help maintain the health of any enterprise network. A security model to protect IP Multimedia Subsystem (IMS) Service Delivery Platform (SDP) from different time independent attacks, e. g. SQL injection and media flow attacks was developed in (Sher & Magedanz, 2007). This is an Intrusion Detection and Prevention (IDP) system for detecting and preventing message tempering and media flow attacks for IMS Service Delivery. The performance results at Open IMS Tested Fraunhofer show the processing delay of the IDP as very small. In the next section, we discuss a unified approach to network information security which is the main focus of this chapter.

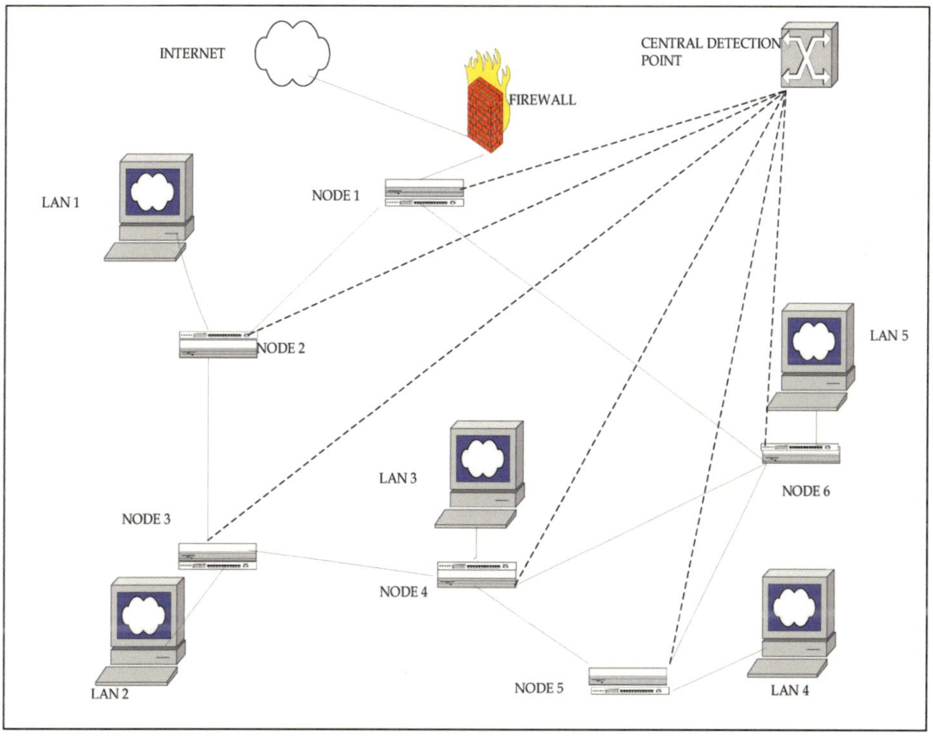

Fig. 1. Implementation scheme for the developed technique

3. The intrusion detection technique

Unlike most existing IPSs/IDSs, which depend on only packet header information or behavior for prevention and detection respectively, this approach goes further to consider using purely quantitative methods for detection and prevention. This new approach employed anomaly detection and host-based detection as its analysis strategy. Only two types of packets were considered by this approach: normal network packet and abnormal packet (i. e. any packet not classified as normal network packet). The classification of the two types of packets could be based on parameters like Hurst parameter, packet arrival rate, inter-arrival time between successive packets, etc., which cannot be easily manipulated by intruders or attackers. This idea is revisited at the implementation stages of this technique. Figure 1 shows how the implementation network looks like. The model for this approach was based on a discrete binary communication channel with detailed analysis of both a priori and a posteriori (conditional) probabilities. The novelty of this approach lies in the fact that no existing IDSs have been modeled as described here.

4. Discrete communication channel

The goal of a discrete communication channel or a discrete memoryless channel (DMC) is to derive an optimum receiver, which minimizes the average probability of message error. The receiver determines, which message m_i was transmitted in order to maximize the probability of correct decision P(C) only after observing the received symbol r_j. Figure 2 describes the whole process.

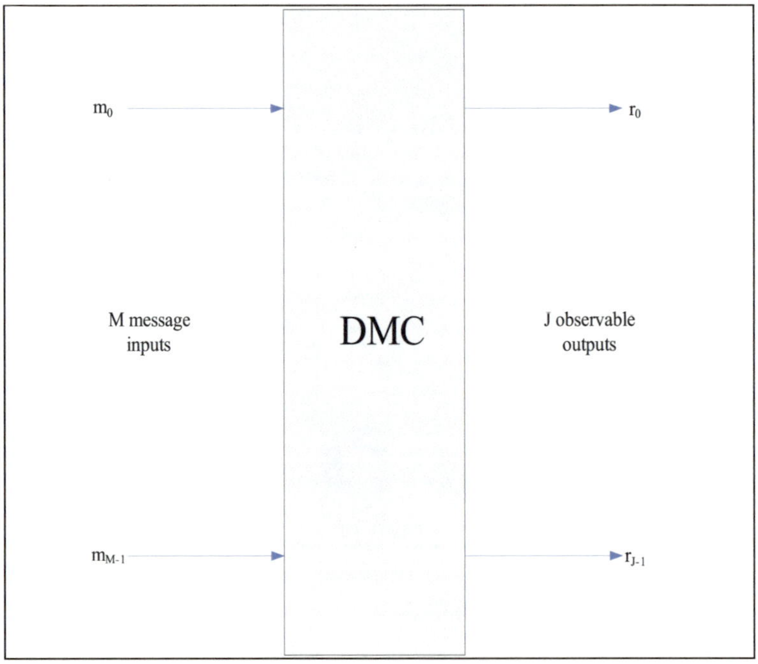

Fig. 2. Discrete memoryless channel

If equation (1) denotes the joint probability of transmitting m_i and receiving r_j, $P(m_i,r_j)$, then, the total probability of receiving r_j, $P(r_j)$, is given by equation (2).

$$P(m_i, r_j) = P(m_i) * P(r_j / m_i) \tag{1}$$

$$P(r_j) = \sum_{k=0}^{m-1} P(m_k, r_j) \tag{2}$$

where,

$P(m_i)$ - The probability of transmitting message m_i;

$P(r_j / m_i)$ - The transitional (conditional) probability of receiving r_j given that m_i was transmitted; and

$P(m_k, r_j)$ - The joint probability of transmitting m_k and receiving r_j.

It is very important to note that $P(m_i)$ depends solely on the message source (i. e. the a priori probability that message m_i was transmitted). From Bayes' rule, the a posteriori (conditional) probability (i. e. comes into play only after receiving symbol r_j) that m_i was transmitted given that r_j was received (or observed), $P(m_i / r_j)$ is given as follows:

$$P(m_i / r_j) = \frac{P(r_j / m_i) * P(m_i)}{P(r_j)} \tag{3}$$

Assuming that $P(m_i / r_j)$ is known, then, the optimum receiver has to map r_j onto mi in order to minimize the probability of error in transmitting message m_l.

If $\hat{m}(r_j)$ denotes the transmitted symbol attributed to observing r_j, then, equation (4) denotes an example of the decision by a receiver that m_9 was transmitted given that r_6 was observed.

$$\hat{m}(r_6) = m_9 \tag{4}$$

Also, the conditional probability of a correct decision given that r_j is observed, $P(\underline{C} / r_j)$ is given by equation (5). This is also equivalent to an a posteriori probability.

$$P(\underline{C} / r_j) = P(\hat{m}(r_j) / r_j) \tag{5}$$

The maximum a posteriori (MAP) decision rule determines the optimum receiver by first maximizing $\hat{m}(r_j)$, which in effect maximizes the conditional probability $P(\hat{m}(r_j) / r_j)$ and finally maximizes $P(\underline{C} / r_j)$. The total probability of a correct decision, $P(\underline{C})$ given that r_j is observed is therefore given as follows:

$$P(\underline{C}) = \sum_{j=0}^{J-1} P(\underline{C} / r_j) * P(r_j) \tag{6}$$

The probability $P(r_j)$ in equation (6) was earlier defined in equation (2). It is a positive term and also independent of the transmitted message. Therefore, it is clear that $P(\underline{C})$ will be maximized only if all terms of $P(\underline{C} / r_j)$ are maximized. The probability of error is given by equation (7) as follows:

$$P(\underline{E}) = 1 - P(\underline{C}) \tag{7}$$

With $P(r_j)$ being independent of the transmitted message, the decision rule reduces to equation (8) if and only if equation (9) holds (Ziemer & Tranter, 2002).

$$P(m_k) * P(r_j / m_k) \geq P(m_i) * P(r_j / m_i) \quad \textit{for all } i. \tag{8}$$

$$\hat{m}(r_j) = m_k \tag{9}$$

5. Modeling technique

The following were the assumptions made for this model:

1. The network was assumed to have only one entry point (sender) and a number of nodes (receivers);
2. It was assumed that a normal packet could be sent into the network, but will be received as an abnormal packet at a given node depending on what happened to it in transit; and
3. The maximum and minimum probabilities (elements) in the 2 x 2 transitional (conditional) probability matrices were assumed to be 0.9 and 0.1 respectively.

This model applied a quantitative approach based on Maximum A Posteriori (MAP) decision rule with the hope of improving the effectiveness of existing IDSs. The network was modeled based on a discrete binary communication channel having two possible input messages and two possible output symbols. It was further assumed to have only one entry point (sender) and a number of nodes (receivers). Finally, all normal operational packets were referred to as normal packets, but any other packets were referred to as abnormal packets. The developed algorithm for this technique initially calculates the a priori probabilities for the normal and abnormal packets both at the sender and receiver ends. These values were further used in finding the threshold probabilities to be compared to the corresponding probabilities of future incoming packets. Figure 3 shows how one channel from the network can be represented. The following describes the developed algorithm.

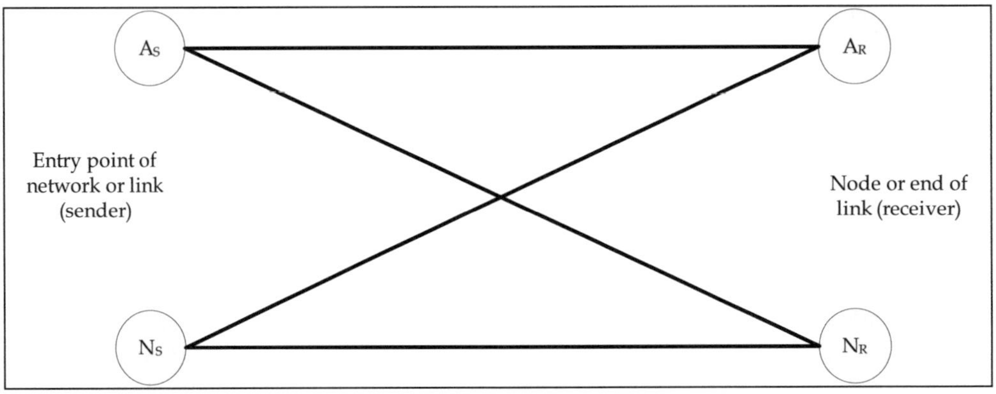

Fig. 3. Discrete binary communication channel for this approach

At Entry Point of Network (*E*):

1. Classify packets as normal and abnormal.
2. Count the number of packets entering the entire network, *E*.
3. Count the number of normal packets entering the entire network, E_N.

4. Count the number of abnormal packets entering the entire network, E_A.
5. Calculate the probability of an abnormal packet entering the entire network, $P(A_S)$.
6. Calculate the probability of a normal packet entering the entire network, $P(N_S)$.

Please note that the "entry point of network (sender)" could also be any node inside the network including the sole entry point of the network, since an attack could be sent from outside the network or from within the network. On the other hand, the "node (receiver)" could be any node inside the network excluding the sole entry point of the network. This implies that every link in the network can be considered as a discrete binary communication channel.

It is assumed that a normal packet can be sent, but received as abnormal depending on what happened to it during the transition. The reverse sounds unrealistic, but possible and that was considered during the simulation studies. The following 2 x 2 matrix describing the transitional (conditional) probabilities in relation to the above figure had to be determined:

$$\begin{bmatrix} P(A_R / A_S) & P(N_R / A_S) \\ P(A_R / N_S) & P(N_R / N_S) \end{bmatrix}$$

Equation (10) calculates the total probability of receiving an abnormal packet at the node.

$$P(A_R) = P(A_R / A_S) * P(A_S) + P(A_R / N_S) * P(N_S) \tag{10}$$

Equation (11) calculates the total probability of receiving a normal packet at the node.

$$P(N_R) = P(N_R / A_S) * P(A_S) + P(N_R / N_S) * P(N_S) \tag{11}$$

Equation (12) calculates the a posteriori (conditional) probability that an abnormal packet was sent given that an abnormal packet was received.

$$P(A_S / A_R) = \frac{P(A_R / A_S) * P(A_S)}{P(A_R)} \tag{12}$$

Equation (13) calculates the a posteriori (conditional) probability that a normal packet was sent given that an abnormal packet was received.

$$P(N_S / A_R) = \frac{P(A_R / N_S) * P(N_S)}{P(A_R)} \tag{13}$$

Equation (14) calculates the a posteriori (conditional) probability that a normal packet was sent given that a normal packet was received.

$$P(N_S / N_R) = \frac{P(N_R / N_S) * P(N_S)}{P(N_R)} \tag{14}$$

Equation (15) calculates the a posteriori (conditional) probability that an abnormal packet was sent given that a normal packet was received.

$$P(A_S / N_R) = \frac{P(N_R / A_S) * P(A_S)}{P(N_R)} \tag{15}$$

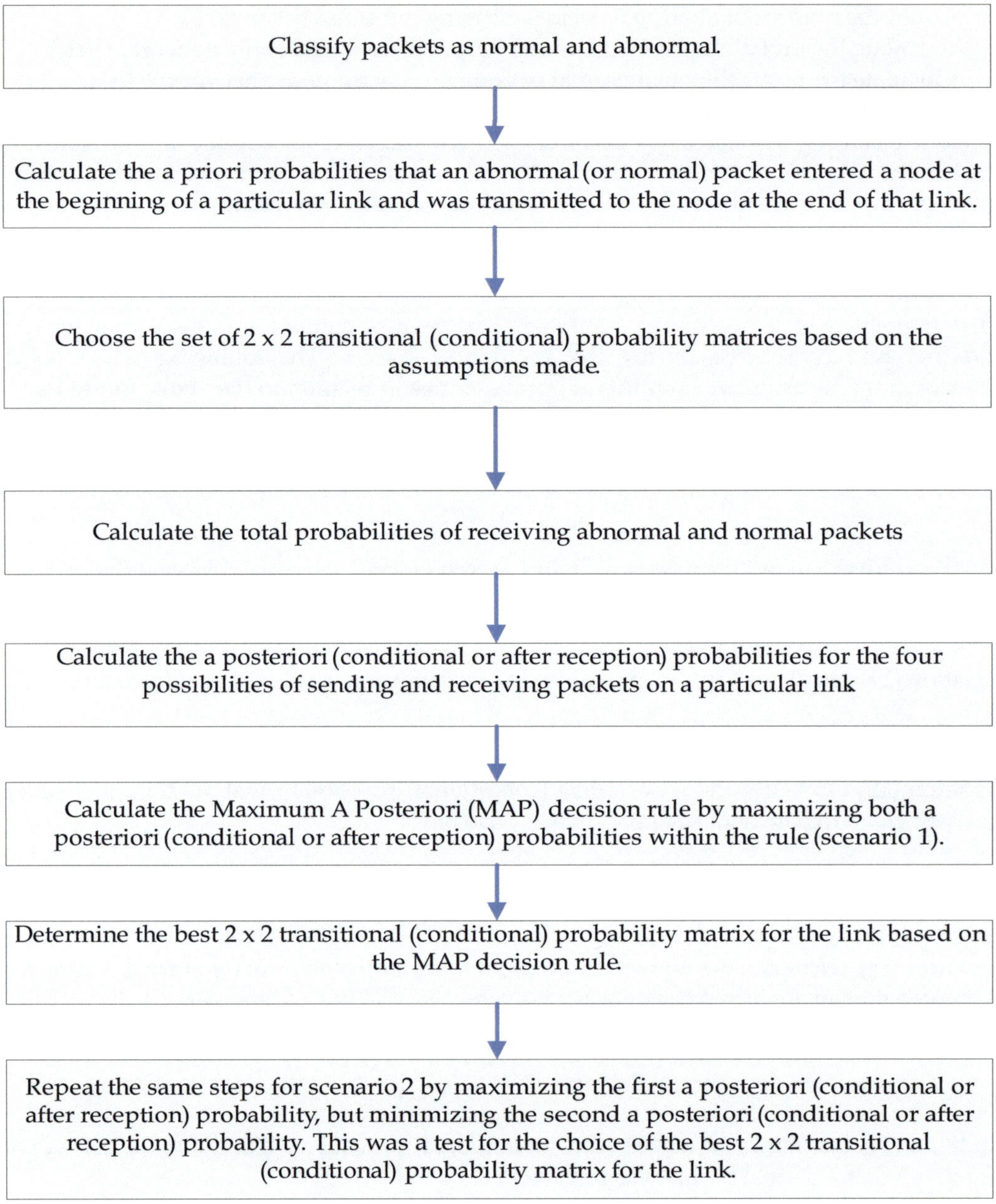

Fig. 4. Algorithm for the developed IDS technique

The MAP decision rule maximizes both the a posteriori (conditional) probability of receiving an abnormal packet and the a posteriori (conditional) probability of receiving a normal packet. This means choosing the higher a posteriori (conditional) probability between $P\ (A_S/A_R)$ and $P\ (N_S/A_R)$ and also choosing the higher a posteriori (conditional) probability between $P\ (A_S/N_R)$ and $P\ (N_S/N_R)$. This rule was considered in the first scenario. A modified version of the MAP decision rule, which placed more weight on the a posteriori (conditional) probability of receiving an abnormal packet, was considered in the second scenario. That modified rule maximized the a posteriori (conditional) probability of receiving an abnormal packet and minimized the a posteriori (conditional) probability of receiving a normal packet. This meant choosing the higher a posteriori (conditional) probability between $P\ (A_S/A_R)$ and $P\ (N_S/A_R)$ and choosing the lower a posteriori (conditional) probability between $P\ (A_S/N_R)$ and $P\ (N_S/N_R)$. The total probability of a correct reception based on equation (6) is given by equation (16) as follows:

$$P(C) = P(C / A_R) * P(A_R) + P(C / N_R) * P(N_R) \tag{16}$$

This probability was further used to determine a threshold value for detecting intrusion or attacks or abnormal packets. Figure 4 describes the algorithm for the developed IDS technique.

6. Simulation studies

MATLAB 7.1 was used for the entire simulation studies. The preliminary results are shown in Table 1. P1 was the same as $P(A_S)$, P18 was the same as $P(\underline{C})$ and each of matrices M(1) to M(13) was the same as the 2 x 2 matrix, which had the transitional (conditional) probabilities as its elements. Various M values were used to describe the channel behavior during the simulation studies. These were the possible channel behaviors used in order to observe the outcomes of the decision rule. They were as follows:
M(1) = [0.1 0.9; 0.1 0.9] - The probability of receiving an abnormal packet given that an abnormal packet was transmitted and the probability of receiving an abnormal packet given that a normal packet was transmitted were kept at the minimum level of 0.1. Also, the probability of receiving a normal packet given that an abnormal packet was transmitted and the probability of receiving a normal packet given that a normal packet was transmitted were kept at the maximum level of 0.9. Please note that the maximum and minimum probabilities were assumed to be 0.9 and 0.1 respectively. Two other intermediary probabilities were considered. They were 0.25 and 0.5. The idea was to consider the channel behavior during extreme and intermediary situations. This was how elements of the various matrices were defined for the simulation studies.

M (2) = [0.5 0.5; 0.5 0.5];	M (3) = [0.9 0.1; 0.9 0.1];	M (4) = [0.9 0.9; 0.9 0.9]
M (5) = [0.9 0.1; 0.5 0.9];	M (6) = [0.9 0.5; 0.1 0.9];	M (7) = [0.9 0.1; 0.1 0.9]
M (8) = [0.9 0.5; 0.5 0.9];	M (9) = [0.9 0.25; 0.25 0.9];	M (10) = [0.9 0.1; 0.25 0.9]
M (11) = [0.9 0.25; 0.1 0.9];	M (12) = [0.9 0.5; 0.25 0.9];	M (13) = [0.9 0.25; 0.5 0.9]

The main reason for going through this random exercise was to determine the best matrix that guaranteed a consistent decision rule (threshold value). Two scenarios were considered in this study. The second scenario was undertaken in order to ascertain the consistency of the chosen matrix presented by the first scenario. Table 1 describes the results obtained from the first scenario. The above results were cross-checked by actually calculating the decision rule (threshold value) when P (A_S) = 0.6, and P (N_S) = 0.4, using M (7) = [0.9 0.1; 0.1 0.9] and comparing the result to what was obtained in Table 1. Both values were the same.

P1 or $P(A_S)$	P18 or $P(C)$ (Decision Rule or Total Probability of a Correct Reception)												
	M(1)	M(2)	M(3)	M(4)	M(5)	M(6)	M(7)	M(8)	M(9)	M(10)	M(11)	M(12)	M(13)
0.9	0.9	0.9	0.9	1.62	0.9	1.26	0.9	1.26	1.04	0.9	1.035	1.26	1.035
0.8	0.8	0.8	0.8	1.44	0.9	1.12	0.9	1.12	0.92	0.9	0.92	1.12	0.92
0.7	0.7	0.7	0.7	1.26	0.9	0.98	0.9	0.98	0.9	0.9	0.9	0.98	0.9
0.6	0.6	0.6	0.6	1.08	0.9	0.9	0.9	0.9	0.9	0.9	0.9	0.9	0.9
0.5	0.5	0.5	0.5	0.9	0.9	0.9	0.9	0.9	0.9	0.9	0.9	0.9	0.9
0.4	0.6	0.6	0.6	1.08	0.9	0.9	0.9	0.9	0.9	0.9	0.9	0.9	0.9
0.3	0.7	0.7	0.7	1.26	0.98	0.9	0.9	0.9	0.9	0.9	0.9	0.9	0.98
0.2	0.8	0.8	0.8	1.44	1.12	0.9	0.9	1.12	0.92	0.92	0.9	0.92	1.12
0.1	0.9	0.9	0.9	1.62	1.26	0.9	0.9	1.26	1.04	1.035	0.9	1.035	1.26

Table 1. Relationship between threshold values and a priori probabilities of abnormal packets (first scenario)

7. Discussion

The discussion here was made separately for each of the two scenarios for the sake of clarity.

7.1 Discussion (scenario 1)

The more realistic matrices out of the thirteen were chosen for further studies. Figure 5 shows the graphs of threshold values and a priori probabilities of abnormal packets for all thirteen "M" matrices. Some of the above matrices were discarded because the probability of receiving a normal packet given that an abnormal packet was transmitted, $P\ (N_R/A_S)$, was considered to be unrealistic so its corresponding value was kept at the minimum of 0.1 throughout the simulation studies. Therefore, all the above matrices with $P\ (N_R/A_S)$ values greater than 0.1 were discarded. This meant that only results from matrices M (3), M (5), M (7), and M (10) were chosen for further analysis. Figure 6 shows the graphs of threshold values and a priori probabilities of abnormal packets for those chosen "M" matrices for scenario 1. From figure 6, it was clear that results from matrices M(5), M(7), and M(10) follow virtually the same trend leaving out those from matrix M(3). From the definition of matrix M(3) (i. e., M(3) = [0.9 0.1; 0.9 0.1]), the probability of receiving an abnormal packet given that a normal packet was transmitted, $P(A_R/N_S)$ was 0.9, which represents an extreme situation, hence lower values for the decision rules or threshold values shown in both Table 1 and figure 6. This left matrices M (5), M (7), and M (10) as the right matrices to consider further. The decision rules or threshold values obtained from using those three matrices were very high (i. e., always greater or equal to 0.9)

Also, considering results from matrices M(5), M(7), and M(10), it is clear that the probability of receiving an abnormal packet given that a normal packet was transmitted, $P(A_R/N_S)$ must always be set between 0.1 and 0.9, but not equal to 0.9 in order to achieve high threshold values. Matrix M (7) stood out to be the best choice because results from matrices M (5) and M (10) had some decision rules or threshold values greater than 1.0, which were unrealistic. All threshold values from using matrix M (7) were lower than 1.0 and consistently 0.9, hence making it a very realistic choice. In other words, no matter the combination of the a priori

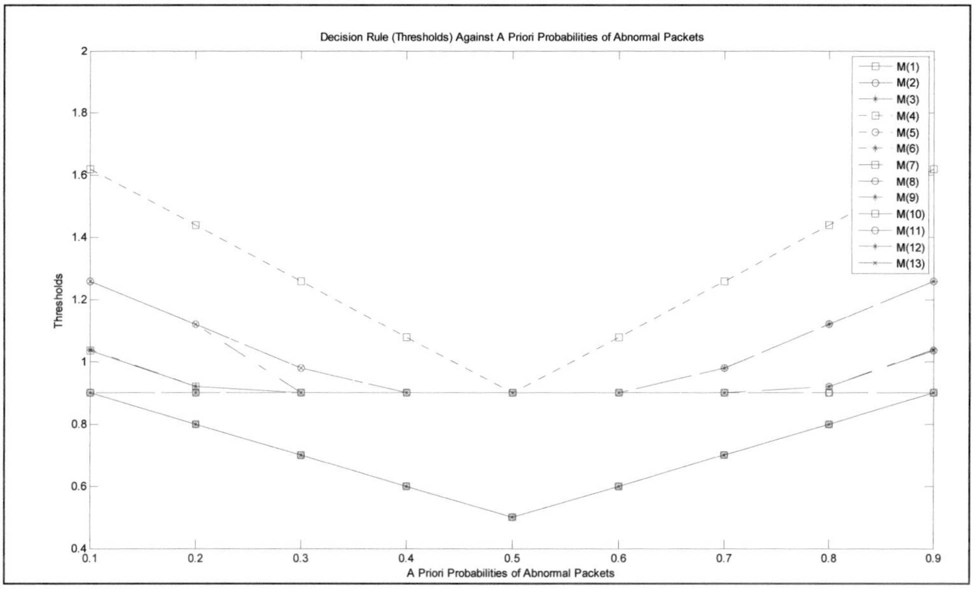

Fig. 5. Graphs of threshold values and a priori probabilities of abnormal packets for all M Matrices

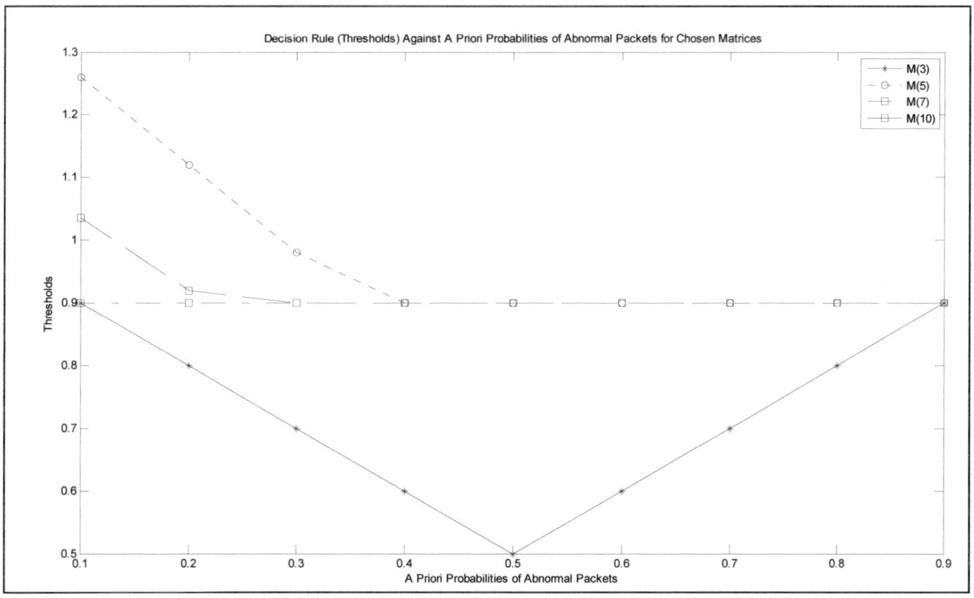

Fig. 6. Graphs of threshold values and a priori probabilities of abnormal packets for the four chosen Matrices (Scenario 1)

probabilities of transmitting abnormal and normal packets, the decision rule would always stay at 0.9, which was high and consistent enough to detect or observe the presence of an abnormal packet at each node. Table 2 shows the results from scenario 2. Those results were again cross-checked by actually calculating the decision rule (threshold value) when $P(A_S)$ =

0.6, and $P(N_S)$ = 0.4, using M (7) = [0.9 0.1; 0.1 0.9] and comparing the result to what was obtained in Table 2. Both results were the same. The difference between this scenario and the first one lies with the decision rule, where the maximum a posteriori (conditional) probability was used in the first part of the rule and the minimum a posteriori (conditional) probability was used in the second part of the rule. In scenario 1 maximum a posteriori (conditional) probabilities were used for both parts of the rule. Figure 7 shows the graphs of threshold values and a priori probabilities of abnormal packets for those chosen "M" matrices for scenario 2.

P1 or $P(A_S)$	P18 or $P(C)$ (Decision Rule or Total Probability of a Correct Reception)												
	M(1)	M(2)	M(3)	M 4)	M(5)	M(6)	M(7)	M(8)	M(9)	M(10)	M (11)	M(12)	M(13)
0.9	0.18	0.5	0.82	0.9	0.9	0.9	0.9	0.9	0.9	0.9	0.9	0.9	0.9
0.8	0.26	0.5	0.74	0.9	0.8	0.9	0.8	0.9	0.9	0.8	0.9	0.9	0.9
0.7	0.34	0.5	0.66	0.9	0.7	0.9	0.7	0.9	0.81	0.7	0.81	0.9	0.81
0.6	0.42	0.5	0.58	0.9	0.6	0.84	0.6	0.84	0.69	0.6	0.69	0.84	0.69
0.5	0.5	0.5	0.5	0.9	0.5	0.7	0.5	0.7	0.58	0.5	0.58	0.7	0.58
0.4	0.42	0.5	0.58	0.9	0.4	0.56	0.4	0.56	0.46	0.4	0.46	0.56	0.46
0.3	0.34	0.5	0.66	0.9	0.38	0.42	0.3	0.5	0.35	0.3	0.35	0.42	0.43
0.2	0.26	0.5	0.74	0.9	0.42	0.28	0.2	0.5	0.25	0.22	0.23	0.3	0.45
0.1	0.18	0.5	0.82	0.9	0.46	0.14	0.1	0.5	0.03	0.24	0.12	0.28	0.48

Table 2. Relationships between threshold values and a priori probabilities of abnormal packets (second scenario)

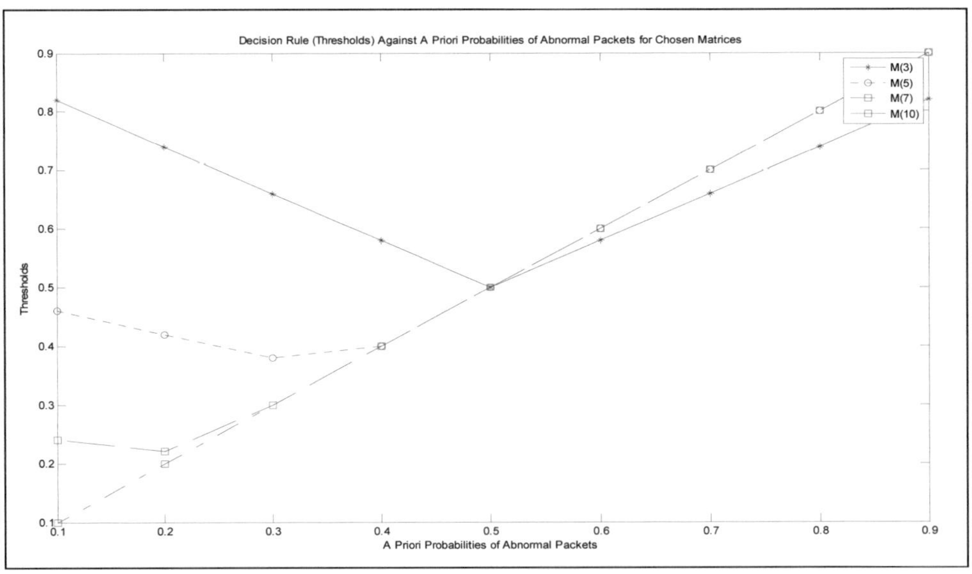

Fig. 7. Graphs of threshold values and a priori probabilities of abnormal packets for the four chosen Matrices (Scenario 2)

7.2 Discussion (scenario 2)

Results from matrices M(3), M(5), M(7), and M(10) were chosen for analysis in this scenario based on the same reasons used in scenario 1 (i. e., $P(N_R/A_S)$ must be equal to 0.1). It was clear from Figure 7 that all the above chosen matrices followed almost the same trend. Only results from matrix M (7) were very consistent and looked most realistic. This outcome further supported the choice of matrix M (7) made in scenario 1.

7.3 Multiresolution techniques

A multiresolution technique is an application of wavelet transform, which decomposes an image and reconstructs it after transmission, with the aim of reproducing the exact image. The decomposition (or decimation) process involves convolving data samples from the image with low pass and high pass wavelet coefficients (i. e. h0 and h1, respectively). This process is also known as sampling. The reconstruction (or interpolation) process involves convolving the received data after decomposition and transmission with the transformed (i. e. reflection in the line y = x or 180° rotation about the origin) low pass and high pass wavelet coefficients. This process is also known as upper-sampling. The high pass portion of the multiresolution technique eliminates any noise associated with the two major processes. The low pass portion of the technique, which contains no noise, is therefore projected further. It contains much of the energy content of the original data samples. Data received from the two portions of the technique are finally summed up to reproduce the original image.

Only the signal processing applications of wavelets was taken advantage of in this research work. In the field of signal analysis, the methods of wavelet transform have wide applications because of their unique merit. One of the important applications is multiresolution technique, which was used to decompose, transmit and reconstruct signals or data from the enterprise network to a Central Detection Point for further analysis. Multiresolution technique simultaneously represents segments of an image or data by multiple scales and further consists of two very important concepts, that is, dilation and translation. Multiresolution Haar transform, which is a multiresolution technique using Haar wavelets coefficients, produces detail information of segments from an image or data as described in (Yung-Da & Paulik, 1996). Transmission of traffic from the network nodes to the central detection point for the technique developed in this research work was done using a one-dimensional, two-stage multiresolution technique. Haar Wavelets was applied here. The effectiveness of multiresolution Haar transform was also taken advantage of in (Piscaglia & Maccq, 1996).

8. Implementation of IDS technique

Implementation of this IDS technique involves two major parts: "set-up inside the network" and "set-up at the central detection point." The following should be the steps under the "set-up inside the network" part:

1. Install a detector (i. e. software on a computer) at each node for classifying packets as normal and abnormal based on parameters like Hurst parameter, packet arrival rate, packet inter-arrival time etc.; and counting both types of packets arriving at that particular node within a given interval; and
2. Install a transmitter at each node for sending the packet count data to the central detection point by multi-resolution technique.

The following should be the steps under the "set-up at the central detection point" part:

1. Install a receiver to receive the packet count data from the network (i. e. at the end of the multi-resolution technique);
2. Consider each link between any two nodes for the entire analysis from here;
3. Calculate all the necessary probabilities for both normal and abnormal packets at the beginning and at the end of each link over a given period of time for further analysis; and
4. Determine the decision rule (or threshold) for each link in the network for further analysis as discussed under the simulation studies above.

9. Conclusion

Based on the discussion under this technique, it was clear that matrix M (7) was the best choice out of the thirteen choices because it showed the strongest consistency under both scenarios. This matrix will therefore be applied at the implementation stage of this work. This approach established a relationship between a priori probabilities of both abnormal and normal packets on one side and threshold values on the other. This relationship will help determine the threshold values at the implementation stage of this work no matter the combination of abnormal and normal a priori probability pairs, due to its consistency.

10. Contributions

Results obtained so far from this IDS technique look promising. This IDS technique seeks to help eliminate the following limitations: limited scalability (i. e. partly by reducing traffic in the network); effectiveness (i. e. reducing false positive and false negative rates); efficiency (i. e. saving bandwidth); and security (i. e. securing security data). It also seeks to counter DDoS attacks based on SYN-flood attacks or distributed attacks in general and also SYN-flood attacks in particular, if used as a back-up for existing IDSs. These were the main underlying objectives of this research work.

11. Future work

The following should be considered for further investigation: to re-determine the upper and lower limits of the probability of receiving an abnormal packet given that a normal packet was transmitted, $P(A_R/N_S)$ for matrix M; and to consider a model with multiple entry points. Implementation of this IDS technique (prototype) should be done in order to further justify the contributions made so far. The performance of the IDS techniques should be determined based on the following metrics:

- False positive rate (FPR);
- False negative rate (FNR); and
- Crossover error rate (CER).

The possibility of extending this developed technique to secure wireless networks should be considered after the performance study.

12. References

Akujuobi, C. M. & Ampah, N. K. (2007). Enterprise network intrusion detection and prevention system. *Society of Photographic Instrumentation Engineers Defense and Security Symposium*: Vol. 6538, pp. 1-12

Akujuobi, C. M. & Ampah, N. K. (2009). Modeling Intrusion Detection with Self Similar Traffic in Enterprise Networks. *Handbook of Research on Telecommunications Planning and Management, Information Science Reference,* (pp.)

Akujuobi, C. M.; Ampah, N. K. & Sadiku, M. N. O. (2007a). An Intrusion Detection Technique Based on Change in Hurst Parameter with Application to Network Security. *International Journal of Computer Science and Network Security,* 5(7), 55–64

Akujuobi, C. M.; Ampah, N. K. & Sadiku, M. N. O. (2007b). Application of Signal Detection and Estimation Theory to Network Security. *International Symposium on Consumer Electronics,* pp. 1-6

Akujuobi, C. M.; Ampah, N. K. & Sadiku, M. N. O. (2007c). Application of Wavelets and Self-similarity to Enterprise Network Intrusion Detection and Prevention Systems. *International Symposium on Consumer Electronics,* pp. 1-6

Anwar, M. M.; Zafar, M. F. & Ahmed, Z. (2007). A proposed preventive information security system. *International Conference on Electrical Engineering,* pp. 1-6

Beheshti, M. & Wasniowski, R. A. (2007). Data fusion support for Intrusion Detection and Prevention. *International Conference on Information Technology,* pp. 966-966

Biermann, E.; Cloete, E. & Venter, L. M. (2001). A comparison of intrusion detection systems. *Computers and Security* 8(20), (676–683)

Bignell, K. B. (2006). Authentication in the Internet Banking Environment; Towards developing a strategy for fraud detection. *International Conference on Internet Surveillance and Protection,* pp. 23-23

Bringas, P. G. (2007). Intensive use of Bayesian Belief Network for the unified, flexible and adaptable analysis of misuses and anomalies in network intrusion detection and prevention systems. *International Conference on Database and Expert Systems Applications,* pp. 365-371

Bruschi, D.; Cavallaro, L. & Lanzi, A. (2007). An effective technique for preventing Mimicry and Impossible Paths Execution Attacks. *International Conference on Performance, Computing, and Communications,* pp. 418-425

Cannady, J. (2009). Distributed Detection of Attacks in Mobile Ad Hoc Networks Using Learning Vector Quantization. *Third International Conference on Network and System Security,* pp. 571–574

Capuzzi, G.; Spalazzi, L. & Pagliarecci, F. (2006). IRSS: Incident Response Support System. *International Symposium on Collaborative Technologies and Systems,* pp. 81-88

Chaboya, D. J.; Raines, R. A.; Baldwin, R. O. & Mullins, B. E. (2006). Network Intrusion Detection: Automated and manual methods prone to attacks and evasion. *Security and Privacy Magazine,* 6(4) (36-43)

Changxin, S. & Ke, M. (2009). Design of Intrusion Detection System Based on Data Mining Algorithm. *International Conference on Signal Processing Systems,* pp. 370–373

Chunmei, Y.; Mingchu, L.; Jianbo, M. & Jizhou, S. (2004). Honeypot and scan detection in intrusion detection system. *Proceedings of Electrical and Computer Engineering,* pp. 1107–1110

Colon Osorio, F. C. (2007). Using Byzantine Agreement in the design of IPS Systems. *International Conference on Performance, Computing, and Communications,* pp. 528-537

Fadia, A. (2006). *Network Security: A Hacker's Perspective.* Boston, Massachusetts: Thomson Course Technology.

Ihn-Han, B. & Olariu, S. (2009). A Weighted-Dissimilarity-Based Anomaly Detection Method for Mobile Wireless Networks. *International Conference on Computational Science and Engineering*, pp. 29–34

Janakiraman, R.; Waldvogel, M. & Qi Zhang (2003). Indra:a peer-to-peer approach to network intrusion detection and prevention. *International Workshops on Enabling Technologies: Infrastructures for Collaborative Enterprises*, pp. 226-231

Jing, Z.; HouKuan, H.; ShengFeng, T. & Xiang, Z. (2009). Applications of HMM in Protocol Anomaly Detection. *International Joint Conference on Computational Sciences and Optimization*, pp. 347–349

Jing-Wen, T.; Mei-Juan, G.; Ling-Fang, H. & Shi-Ru, Z. (2009). Community intrusion detection system based on wavelet neural network. *International Conference on Machine Learning and Cybernetics*: Vol. 2, pp. 1026 - 1030

Jou, Y. F.; Gong, F.; Sargor, C.; Wu, S.; Wu, S. F.; Chang, H. C. & Wang, F. (2000). Design and implementation of a scalable intrusion detection system for the protection of network infrastructure. *Defense Advanced Research Projects Agency Information Survivability Conference and Exposition*: Vol. 2, pp. 69–83

Kayacik, H. G.; Zincir-Heywood, A. N. & Heywood, M. I. (2004). On dataset biases in a learning system with minimum a priori information for intrusion detection. *Communication Networks and Services Research Conference*, pp. 181–189

Khoshgoftaar, T. M. & Abushadi, M. E. (2004). Resource-sensitive intrusion detection models for network traffic. *High Assurance Systems Engineering Symposium*, pp. 249–258

Ko, C. (2003). System health and intrusion monitoring (SHIM): project summary. *Defense Advanced Research Projects Agency Information Survivability Conference and Exposition*: Vol. 2, pp. 202–207

Krizhanovsky, A., & Marasanov, A. (2007). An approach for adaptive Intrusion Prevention based on The Danger. *2nd. International Conference on Availability, Reliability and Security*, pp. 1135-1142

Kui, Z. (2009). A Danger Model Based Anomaly Detection Method for Wireless Sensor Networks. *Second International Symposium on Knowledge Acquisition and Modeling*, pp. 11–14

Labbe, K. G.; Rowe, N. G. & Fulp, J. D. (2006). A methodology for evaluation of Host-Based intrusion prevention systems and its application. *Information Assurance Workshop*, pp. 378-379

Leinwand, A. & Conroy K. F. (1996). *Network Management: A Practical Perspective.* New York, NY: Addison-Wesley

Lixia, X.; Dan, Z. & Hongyu, Y. (2009). Research on SVM Based Network Intrusion Detection Classification. *Sixth International Conference on Fuzzy Systems and Knowledge Discovery*, pp. 362–366

Mitrokotsa, A.; Komninos, N. & Douligeris, C. (2007). Intrusion Detection with Neural Networks and Watermarking Techniques for MANET. *International Conference on Pervasive Services*, pp. 966-966

Momenzadeh, A.; Javadi, H.H.S. & Dezfouli, M.A. (2009). Design an Efficient System for Intrusion Detection via Evolutionary Fuzzy System. *11th International Conference on Computer Modeling and Simulation*, pp. 89–94

Muthuprasanna, M.; Ke, W. & Kothari, S. (2006). Eliminating SQL Injection Attacks - A Transport Defense Mechanism. *3rd International Symposium on Web Site Evolution*, pp. 22-23

Nassar, M.; State, R. & Festor, O. (2007). VoIP honeypot architecture. *International Symposium on Integrated Network Management*, pp. 109-118

Niccolini, S.; Garroppo, R. G.; Giordano, S.; Risi, G. & Ventura, S. (2006). SIP intrusion detection and prevention: recommendation and prototype recommendation. *1st. Workshop on VoIP Management and Security*, pp. 47-52

Onut, I. V. & Ghorbani, A. A. (2006). Toward a feature classification scheme for network intrusion detection. *4th Annual Communication and Networks and Service Research Conference*, pp. 8

Otrok, H.; Debbabi, M.; Assi, C. & Bhattacharya, P. (2007). A cooperative approach for analyzing Intrusion in Mobile Ad hoc Networks. *27th. International Conference on Distributing Computing Systems Workshops*, pp. 86-86

Paez, R. & Torres, M. (2009). Laocoonte: An agent based Intrusion Detection System. *International Symposium on Collaborative Technologies and System*, pp. 217–224

Paulson, L. D. (2002). Stopping intruders outside the gates. *Computer*, 11(35), pp. (20–22)

Piromsopa, K. & Enbody, R. J. (2006a). Buffer-Overflow Protection: The theory. *International Conference on Electro/information Technology*, pp. 454-458

Piromsopa, K. & Enbody, R. J.(2006b). Arbitrary copy: Buffer-Overflow Protections. *International Conference on Electro/information Technology*, pp. 580-584

Piscaglia, P. & Maccq, B. (1996). Multiresolution lossless compression scheme. *International Conference on Image Processing*: Vol. 1, pp. 69-72

Ramana, R. K.; Singh, S. & Varghese, G. (2007). On scalable attack detection in the network. *Association for Computing Machinery Transactions on Networking*, 1(15), pp. (31-44)

Ransbottom, J. S. & Jacoby, G. A. (2006). Monitoring mobile device vitals for Effective Reporting. *Military Communication Conference*, pp. 1-7

Sampathkumar, V.; Bose, S.; Anand, K. & Kannan, A. (2007). An intelligent agent based approach for intrusion detection and prevention in ad hoc networks. *International Conference on Signal Processing Communications and Networking*, pp. 534-536

Satti, M. M., & Garner, B. J. (2001). Information security on internet enterprise managed intrusion detection system (EMIDS). *International Multitopic Conference*, pp. 234-238

Sher, M., & Magedanz, T. (2007). Protecting IP Multimedia Subsystem (IMS) server delivery platform from Time Independent Attacks. *3rd International Symposium on Information Assurance and Security*, pp. 171-176

Stallings W. (2003). *Cryptography and Network Security: Principles and Practices*. India: Pearson Education, Inc.

Sun, B.; Xiao, Y. & Wang, R. (2007). Detection of fraudulent usage in wireless networks. *Transactions on Vehicular Technology*, 6(56), pp. (3912-3923)

Tront, J.G. & Marchany, R.C. (2004). Internet Security: Intrusion Detection and Prevention. *37th Annual Hawaii International Conference on System Sciences*, pp. 188-188

Vokorokos, L.; Kleinova, A. & Latka, O. (2006). Network security on the intrusion detection system level. *International Conference on Intelligent Engineering Systems*, pp. 534-536

Weaver, N.; Paxson, V. & Sommer, R. (2007). Work in progress: Bro-LAN Pervasive network inspection and control for LAN traffic. *Securecomm and Workshops*, pp. 1-2

Weber, W. (1999). Firewall Basics. *4th. International Conference on Telecommunications in Modern Satellite, Cable and Broadcasting Services*: Vol. 1, pp. 300-305

Wei, W.; Xiangliang, Z.; Gombault, S. & Knapskog, S.J. (2009). Attribute Normalization in Network Intrusion Detection. *10th International Symposium on Pervasive Systems, Algorithms, and Networks*, pp. 448–453

Weinberg, Y.; Tzur-David, S.; Dolev, D. & Anker, T. (2006). High performance string matching algorithm for a network intrusion prevention system. *Workshop on High Performance Switching and Routing*, pp. 7

Xinidis, K.; Charitakis, I.; Antonatos, S.; Anagnostakis, K. G. & Markatos, E. P. (2006). An active splitter architecture for intrusion detection and prevention. *Transactions on Dependable and Secure Computing*, 1(3), pp. (31- 44)

Yau, S. S. & Xinyu Zhang (1999). Computer networks intrusion detection, assessment and prevention based on security dependency relation. *Computer Software and Applications Conference*, pp. 86–91

Yee, C. G.; Rao, G. V. S. & Radha, K. (2006). A hybrid approach to intrusion detection and prevention business intelligent applications. *International Symposium on Communications and Information Technologies*, pp. 847-850

Yung-Da, W. & Paulik, M. J. (1996). A discrete wavelet model for target recognision. *39th Midwest Symposium on Circuit and Systems*: Vol. 2, pp. 835-838

Zhaoyu, L. & Uppala, R. (2006). A dynamic countermeasure method for large-scale network attacks. *International Symposium on Dependable, Autonomic and Secure Computing*, pp. 163-170

Zheng-De, Z.; Zhi-Guo, L.; Dong, Z. & Fei-Teng, J. (2006). Study on joint prevention technique of information security in SUN. *International Conference on Machine Learning and Cybernetics*, pp. 2823-2827

Zhou, C.; Liu, Y. & Zhang, H. (2006). A pattern matching based Network Intrusion Detection System. *9th. International Conference on Control, Automation, Robotics and Vision*, pp. 1-4

Ziemer, R. E., & Tranter, W. H. (5). (2002). *Principles of Communications: Systems, Modulation and Noise.* Wiley

15

Signal Processing Methodology for Network Anomaly Detection

Rafał Renk[2,3] , Michał Choraś[1,3],
Łukasz Saganowski[1,3], Witold Hołubowicz[2,3]
[1]*University of Technology and Life Sciences, Bydgoszcz*
[2]*Adam Mickiewicz University, Poznań*
[3]*ITTI Ltd. Poznań*
Poland

1. Introduction

Intrusion Detection Systems (IDS) can be classified as belonging to two main groups depending on the detection technique employed:

- signature-based detection,
- anomaly detection.

Currently, most IDS systems have problems in recognizing new attacks (0-day exploits) since they are based on the signature-based approach. In such mode, when system does not have an attack signature in database, such attack is not detected. Another drawback of current IDS systems is that the used parameters and features do not contain all the necessary information about traffic and events in the network (Coppolino at al., 2009).

On the other hand, anomaly detection techniques rely on the existence of a reliable characterization of what is normal and what is not, in a particular networking scenario. More precisely, anomaly detection techniques base their evaluations on a model of what is normal, and classify as anomalous all the events that fall outside such a model.

In this paper, a new solution for Anomaly Detection System (ADS) system based on signal processing algorithm is presented. ADS analyzes traffic from internet connection in certain point of a computer network. The proposed ADS system uses redundant signal decomposition method based on Matching Pursuit algorithm.

Our original methodology for network security anomaly detection based on Matching Pursuit is presented and evaluated using network data traces. We also compared Matching Pursuit approach to Discrete Wavelet Transform used by other researchers.

The paper is structures as follows: firstly, in Section 2 the motivation to use signal processing techniques in intrusion and anomaly detection systems is provided. In Section 3 the anomaly detection system based on the Matching Pursuit is presented in detail. The effectiveness of the proposed system is evaluated in Sections 4 and 5 where the comparison to the state-of-the-art method based on Discrete Wavelet Transform is shown.

Feature ID	Feature Description
1	ICMP flows/time period
2	ICMP in bytes/time period
3	ICMP out bytes/time period
4	ICMP in frames/time period
5	ICMP out frames/time period
6	TCP flows/time period
7	TCP input bytes/time period
8	TCP out bytes/time period
9	TCP in frames/time period
10	TCP out frames/time period
11	UDP flows/time period
12	UDP in bytes/time period
13	UDP out bytes/time period
14	UDP in frames/time period
15	UDP out frames/time period

Table 1. Network traffic parameters

2. Signal processing techniques applied to anomaly detection

Signal processing techniques have found application in Network Intrusion Detection Systems because of their ability to detect novel intrusions and attacks, which cannot be achieved by signature-based approaches (Esposito et al., 2005). It has been shown that network traffic presents several relevant statistical properties when analyzed at different levels (e.g. self-similarity, long range dependence, entropy variations, etc.) (Esposito et al., 2005)(Cheng et al., 2002).
Approaches based on signal processing and on statistical analysis can be powerful in decomposing the signals related to network traffic, giving the ability to distinguish between trends, noise, and actual anomalous events. Wavelet-based approaches, maximum entropy estimation, principal component analysis techniques, and spectral analysis, are examples in this regard which have been investigated in the recent years by the research community (Cheng et al., 2002)(Barford et al., 2002)(Huang et al., 2001)(Li & Lee, 2003)(Dainotti et al., 2006). However, Discrete Wavelet Transform provides a large amount of coefficients which not necessarily reflect required features of the network signals.
Therefore, in this paper we propose another signal processing and decomposition method for anomaly/intrusion detection in networked systems. We developed original Anomaly Detection Type *IDS* algorithm based on Matching Pursuit. As to our best knowledge, we have not met any other IDS system based on matching pursuit.
ADS based on Matching Pursuit uses Dictionary of Base Functions - *BFD* to decompose input 1D traffic signal (1D signal may represent for example packets per second) into set of based functions called also atoms. The proposed *BFD* has ability to approximate traffic signal.
In the proposed system we use 15 network traffic parameters shown in Table 1.

3. Anomaly detection system based on matching pursuit

Matching Pursuit is a known signal processing technique used for instance in audio compression, image and video compression (Mallat et al., 1993)(Neff et al., 2002)(Figureas

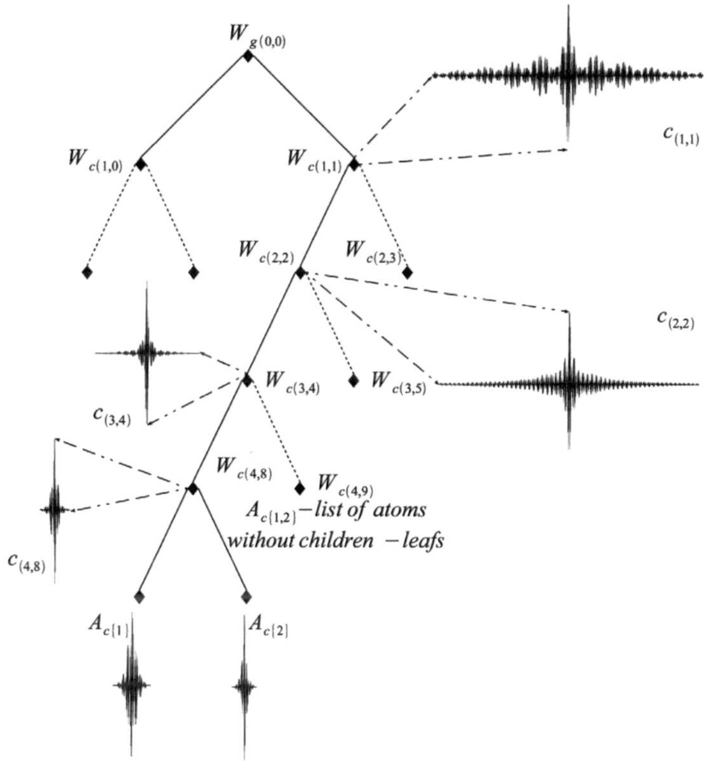

Fig. 1. Example dictionary structure

et al., 2006)(Shaopeng et al., 2002)(Daudet, 2010). However, as to our best knowledge, we are the first to use Matching Pursuit for intrusion and anomaly detection in computer networks. Matching Pursuit signal decomposition was proposed by Mallat and Zhang (Mallat et al., 1993). Matching Pursuit is a greedy algorithm that decomposes any signal into a linear expansion of waveforms which are taken from an overcomplete dictionary D. The dictionary D is an overcomplete set of base functions called also atoms.

$$D = \{\alpha_\gamma : \gamma \in \Gamma\} \tag{1}$$

where every atom α_γ from dictionary has norm equal to 1:

$$\|\alpha_\gamma\| = 1 \tag{2}$$

Γ represents set of indexes for atom transformation parameters such as translation and scaling. Signal s has various representations for dictionary D. Signal can be approximated by set of atoms α_k from dictionary and projection coefficients c_k:

$$s = \sum_{n=0}^{|D|-1} c_k \alpha_k \tag{3}$$

In the basic Matching Pursuit algorithm atoms are selected in every step from entire dictionary which has flat structure. In this case algorithm causes significant processor burden. Therefore, a dictionary with internal structure was used in our coder. Such dictionary is built from: atoms and centered atoms. Centered atoms group such atoms from D that are as correlated (to each other) as possible.
To calculate the measure of correlation between atoms, the function $o(a,b)$ can be used (Jost et al., 2005):

$$o(a,b) = \sqrt{1 - \left(\frac{|\langle a,b \rangle|}{\|a\|_2 \|b\|_2}\right)^2} \tag{4}$$

The quality of centered atom can be estimated according to (5):

$$O_{k,l} = \frac{1}{|LP_{k,l}|} \sum_{i \in LP_{k,l}} o\left(A_{c(i)}, W_{c(k,l)}\right) \tag{5}$$

$LP_{k,l}$ is a set of atoms grouped by centered atom. $O_{k,l}$ is mean of local distances from centered atom $W_{c(k,l)}$ to the atoms $A_{c(i)}$ which are strongly correlated with $A_{c(i)}$.
Example dictionary structure was presented in Figure 1. Atom tree consist of root node W_g and every centroid consist of two children. Parameter A_c represents leaf nodes (without children).
Centroid $W_{c(k,l)}$ represents atoms $A_{c(i)}$ which belong to the set $i \in LP_{k,l}$. List of atoms $LP_{k,l}$ should be selected according to the Equation 6:

$$\max_{i \in LP_{k,l}} o\left(A_{c(i)}, W_{c(k,l)}\right) \leq \min_{t \in D \setminus LP_{k,l}} o\left(A_{c(t)}, W_{c(k,l)}\right) \tag{6}$$

In the proposed ADS solution $1D$ real Gabor base function (Equation 7) was used to build dictionary (Troop, 2004)(Gribonval, 2001).

$$\alpha_{u,s,\xi,\phi}(t) = c_{u,s,\xi,\phi}\alpha\left(\frac{t-u}{s}\right)\cos(2\pi\xi(t-u)+\phi) \tag{7}$$

where:

$$\alpha(t) = \frac{1}{\sqrt{s}} e^{-\pi t^2} \tag{8}$$

$c_{u,s,\xi,\phi}$ - is a normalizing constant used to achieve atom unit energy.
In order to create overcomplete set of $1D$ base functions dictionary D was built by varying subsequent atom parameters: Frequency ξ and Phase ϕ, Position u, Scale s. Base functions dictionary D was created with using 10 different scales (dyadic scales) and 50 different frequencies.
Traffic Parameters are used to create one dimensional signal. This signal is decomposed with the use of Matching Pursuit transformation. After MP decomposition we achieved projection coefficients c_k which are used for creating normal traffic profiles.

Network Traffic Feature	Total number of of attack	Detected number of attack	Detection Rate [%]
ICMP flows/minute	73	61	84.93
ICMP in bytes/minute	73	31	43.83
ICMP out bytes/minute	73	39	54.79
ICMP in frames/minute	73	59	82.19
ICMP out frames/minute	73	65	90.41
TCP flows/minute	73	68	94.52
TCP in bytes/minute	73	32	46.57
TCP out bytes/minute	73	31	45.20
TCP in frames/minute	73	57	79.45
TCP out frames/minute	73	54	76.71
UDP flows/minute	73	41	58.90
UDP in bytes/minute	73	52	73.97
UDP out bytes/minute	73	73	100.00
UDP in frames/minute	73	52	73.97
UDP out frames/minute	73	70	98.63

Table 2. Detection Rate for W5D1 (Fifth Week, Day 1) (DARPA, 2000) trace

Matching Pursuit (Mallat et al., 1993),(Jost et al., 2005) algorithm (stop condition of the MP algorithm) was modified in order to encode only sufficient number of atoms. This number of atoms may be different for a given traffic (signal) analysis window (for e.g. for $10min.$ analysis window number of encoded atoms may be between 3 and max 10). This operation causes a significant reduction of the algorithm execution time.
Normal traffic profiles are calculated using input traffic without attack and anomalies. Normal profiles are calculated separately for every traffic feature. Our ADS system compares current traffic traces (to be analyzed) with the reference profiles calculated during normal work

Network Traffic Feature	Total number of of attack	Detected number of attack	Detection Rate [%]
ICMP flows/minute	68	49	72.06
ICMP in bytes/minute	68	56	82.35
ICMP out bytes/minute	68	54	79.41
ICMP in frames/minute	68	59	86.76
ICMP out frames/minute	68	56	82.35
TCP flows/minute	68	37	54.41
TCP in bytes/minute	68	41	60.29
TCP out bytes/minute	68	23	33.82
TCP in frames/minute	68	31	45.58
TCP out frames/minute	68	32	47.05
UDP flows/minute	68	66	97.05
UDP in bytes/minute	68	62	91.17
UDP out bytes/minute	68	60	88.23
UDP in frames/minute	68	62	91.18
UDP out frames/minute	68	60	88.24

Table 3. Detection Rate for W5D5 (Fifth Week, Day 5) (DARPA, 2000) trace

TCP trace (packet/second) (MAWI, 2005)	Window1 MPMP	Window2 MPMP	Window3 MPMP	MPMP for trace	MPMP for normal trace
Mawi 2004.03.06 tcp	210.34	172.58	239.41	245.01	240.00
Mawi 2004.03.13 tcp	280.01	214.01	215.46	236.33	240.00
Mawi 20.03.2004 tcp (attacked: Witty)	**322.56**	**365.24**	**351.66**	346.48	240.00
Mawi 25.03.2004 tcp (attacked: Slammer)	**329.17**	**485.34**	**385.50**	400.00	240.00

Table 4. Matching Pursuit Mean Projection - MP-MP for TCP trace (20 min. analysis window)

(stored in a database). ADS system makes an alarm when difference between profiles exceed certain threshold (we usually use the threshold value equal to 30%).

4. Evaluation of the proposed anomaly detection system based on matching pursuit

In our previous work we showed the first results of the Matching Pursuit methodology for anomaly detection using only one network traffic metric (feature), namely packets per second (Saganowski et al. , 2009). Hereby, we in our anomaly detection system, we correlate much more network traffic features (Table 1).
Performance of our approach was evaluated with the use of the following trace bases:

- (DARPA, 2000),
- (MAWI, 2005),
- (CAIDA, 2004),
- (UNINA, 2009) (University of Napoli network traces).

The test data contains attacks that fall into four main categories (Wei et al., 2009) such as:

1. DOS/DDOS: denial-of-service, e.g. syn flood,
2. R2L: unauthorized access from a remote machine, e.g. guessing password,
3. U2R: unauthorized access to local superuser (root) privileges, e.g., various "buffer overflow" attacks,
4. PROBING: surveillance and other probing, e.g., port scanning.

UDP trace (packet/second) (MAWI, 2005)	Window1 MPMP	Window2 MPMP	Window3 MPMP	MPMP for trace	MPMP for normal trace
Mawi 2004.03.06 tcp	16.06	13.80	17.11	15.65	16.94
Mawi 2004.03.13 tcp	20.28	17.04	17.40	18.24	16.94
Mawi 20.03.2004 tcp (attacked: Witty)	**38.12**	**75.43**	**61.78**	58.44	16.94
Mawi 25.03.2004 tcp (attacked: Slammer)	**56.13**	**51.75**	**38.93**	48.93	16.94

Table 5. Matching Pursuit Mean Projection - MP-MP for UDP trace (20 min. analysis window)

TCP trace (packet/second) (CAIDA, 2004)	Window1 MPMP	Window2 MPMP	Window3 MPMP	MPMP for trace	MPMP for normal trace
Backscatter 2008.11.15	147.64	**411.78**	**356.65**	305.35	153.66
Backscatter 2008.08.20	**208.40**	161.28	153.47	147.38	153.66

Table 6. Matching Pursuit Mean Projection - MP-MP for TCP trace with DDoS attacks (20 min. analysis window)

For experiments we chose 20 minutes analysis window because most of attacks (about 85%) ends within this time period. We extracted 16 traffic features in order to create 1D signals for Matching Pursuit - Mean Projection analysis. Traffic features were calculated with the use of 1 minute time period.
In Table 2 and Table 3 detection rates achieved for DARPA benchmark trace base are presented. These are results achieved for two test days. Detection results were compared to the list of attacks which should exist in this two testing days.
In Table 4 and Table 5 there are results for MAWI test base. Bold numbers in tables point to existence of anomalies/attacks in certain window.
In Table 6 there are results achieved for CAIDA test base. Traces consist of DDoS attacks and every trace represents 1 hour of the network traffic.

5. Comparison of the matching pursuit with standard DWT using 15 traffic parameters

The basic idea of wavelet transform is to decompose the input signal into family of some specific functions that are called wavelets. Wavelets are functions that are generated through a process of dilations and translations of one single function, which is usually called "mother wavelet". The concept of wavelet transform was defined in (Grossman & Morlet , 1985). In case of IDS system signal represents parameters of network traffic (such as number of packets per second). Anomaly Detection System based on DWT and using 15 network features was presented in (Wei et al., 2009).
In Table 7 comparison of our anomaly detection methodology to state-of-the-art DWT based (Wei et al., 2009) signal processing ADS was presented. Both solutions were tested with the use of the same DARPA (DARPA, 2000) test traces. DARPA benchmark traces consist of attacks which belong to every layer of TCP/IP protocols stack.
In Table 7 the results for W5D1 (Week 5 Day 1) testday are reported. We used all 15 traffic parameters presented in Table 1 during systems testing.
Detection rate and false positive rate achieved by our methodology based on Matching Pursuit is better than in DWT based system presented in (Wei et al., 2009).
Detection rate is changing depending on the particular traffic feature. To recognize 100% of anomalies for DARPA testbed we have to use 1 to max 4 traffic features.
We also significantly reduced false positive parameter in comparison to DWT-based ADS (Wei et al., 2009). It is very important parameter in ADS systems, since the number of false positives can not be overwhelming.

6. Conclusions

In the article our developments in feature extraction for Anomaly Detection Systems are presented. The major contributions of our work is a novel algorithm for detecting anomalies

Traffic Feature	MP-MP DR[%]	MP-MP FP[%]	DWT DR[%]	DWT FP[%]
ICMP flows/minute	68.49	20.54	14.00	79.33
ICMP in bytes/minute	79.45	27.39	83.33	416.00
ICMP out bytes/minute	73.97	32.87	83.33	416.00
ICMP in frames/minute	78.08	27.39	32.00	112.00
ICMP out frames/minute	72.60	30.13	32.00	112.00
TCP flows/minute	89.04	34.24	26.67	74.67
TCP in bytes/minute	47.94	32.87	8.67	23.33
TCP out bytes/minute	80.82	27.39	8.67	23.33
TCP in frames/minute	36.98	26.02	2.00	36.00
TCP out frames/minute	38.35	27.39	2.00	36.00
UDP flows/minute	89.04	41.09	10.00	74.67
UDP in bytes/minute	98.63	41.09	11.33	66.67
UDP out bytes/minute	100.00	46.57	11.33	66.67
UDP in frames/minute	98.63	39.72	12.67	66.67
UDP out frames/minute	100.00	46.57	12.67	66.67

Table 7. Proposed MP-MP ADS in comparision to DWT based ADS (Wei et al., 2009). Both solutions were tested with the use of DARPA (DARPA, 2000) testbed (results in table are for Week5 Day1 testday; DR-Detection Rate [%], FP-False Positive [%])

based on signal decomposition. In the classification/decision module we proposed to use original matching pursuit features such as mean projection. As to our best knowledge, we are the first to propose anomaly detection system based on Matching Pursuit.
We tested and evaluated the proposed approach and showed that experimental results proved the effectiveness of the proposed method. We also provided the comparison of the Matching Pursuit methods to DWT-based anomaly detection and reported better results in terms of detection rate and false positives.
Our developments can be used in many deployments and applications, for instance for military network security enhancement or critical infrastructures information systems security.

Test Days	W5D1	W5D2	W5D3	W5D4	W5D5
DR [%] for all attack instances - DWT ((Wei et al., 2009))	94.67	66.1	49.52	74.33	26.7
DR [%] for all attack instances - MPMP (Matching Pursuit Mean Projection)	100	100	100	100	100
DR [%] attack types (DoS, U2R,R2L,PROBE) - DWT ((Wei et al., 2009))	100	75	71.43	88.89	74.1
DR [%] attack types (DoS, U2R,R2L,PROBE) - MPMP (Matching Pursuit Mean Projection)	100	100	100	100	100

Table 8. Cumulative DR - detection rate takes into consideration attacks recognized by all traffic features presented in Table 1. Results were compared to results achieved for fifth test week (Week5 Day1-5) of (DARPA, 2000) traces.

7. Acknowledgment

This work partially supported by Polish Ministry of Science and Higher Education funds allocated for the years 2010-2012 (Research Project number OR00012511).

8. References

Coppolino, L.; D'Antonio, L.; Esposito, M.; Romano L. (2009). Exploiting diversity and correlation to improve the performance of intrusion detection systems, *Proc. of IFIP/IEEE International Conference on Network and Service*, 2009.

Esposito, M.; Mazzariello, C.; Oliviero, F.; Romano, S.P.; Sansone, C. (2005). Evaluating Pattern Recognition Techniques in Intrusion Detection Systems, *PRIS*, pp. 144-153, 2005.

Esposito, M.; Mazzariello, C.; Oliviero, F.; Romano, S.P.; Sansone, C. (2005). Real Time Detection of Novel Attacks by Means of Data Mining Techniques, *ICEIS*, pp. 120-127, 2005.

Barford, P.; Kline, J.; Plonka, D.; Ron, A. (2002). A signal analysis of network traffic anomalies, *ACM SIGCOMM Internet Measurement Workshop*,2002.

Huang, P.; Feldmann, A.; Willinger, W. (2001). A non-intrusive, wavelet-based approach to detecting network performance problems, *ACM SIGCOMM Internet Measurement Workshop*, Nov. 2001.

Li, L. & Lee, G. (2003). DDos attack detection and wavelets, *IEEE ICCCN03*, pp. 421-427, Oct. 2003.

Dainotti, A.; Pescape, A.; Ventre, G. (2006). Wavelet-based Detection of DoS Attacks. *IEEE GLOBECOM*, San Francisco USA, Nov 2006.

Neff, R.; Zakhor, A.; (2002). Matching Pursuit Video Coding - Part I: Dictionary Approximation. *IEEE Transactions on Circuits and Systems for Video Technology*, vol.12, no. 1, pp. 13-26, 2002r.

Figueras, R.M.; Vandergheynst, P.; Frossard, P. (2006). Low-Rate and Flexible Image Coding With Redundant Representations. *IEEE Transactions on Image Processing*, vol. 15, no. 3, pp. 726-739, march 2006r.

Shaopeng, S.; Junxun, Y.; Yongcong, Y.; Raed, A.M. (2002). A low bit-rate audio coder based on modified sinusoidal model. *IEEE 2002 International Conference on Communications, Circuits and Systems and West Sino Expositions Proceedings* , vol.1, pp. 648- 652, July 2002.

Daudet, L. (2010). Audio Sparse Decompositions in Parallel. *IEEE Signal Processing Magazine*, vol.27, no.2, pp.90-96, March 2010.

Troop J.A. (2004). Greed is Good: Algorithmic Results for Sparse Approximation. *IEEE Transactions on Information Theory*, vol. 50, no. 10, October 2004.

Gribonval R. (2001). Fast Matching Pursuit with a Multiscale Dictionary of Gaussian Chirps. *IEEE Transactions on Signal Processing*, vol. 49, no. 5, May 2001.

Cheng, C.M.; Kung, H.T.; Tan, K.S. (2002). Use of spectral analysis in defense against DoS attacks, *IEEE GLOBECOM 2002*, pp. 2143-2148.

DAPRA, (2000). DARPA traces, *http://www.ll.mit.edu/mission/communications/ist/corpora/* .

MAWI, (2005). MAWI traces, *WIDE Project: MAWI Working Group Traffic Archive at tracer.csl.sony.co.jp/mawi/* .

CAIDA, (2004). CAIDA traces, *The CAIDA Dataset on the Witty Worm - March 19-24, Colleen Shanon and David Moore, www.caida.org/passive/witty.*

UNINA, (2009). UNINA traces, *http://www.grid.unina.it/Traffic/Traces/ttraces.php.*

Wei, L.; Ghorbani A. (2009). Network Anomaly Detection Based on Wavelet Analysis, *EURASIP Journal on Advances in Signal Processing*, Volume 2009, Article ID 837601, 16 pages.

Mallat, S.; Zhang, (1993).Matching Pursuit with time-frequency dictionaries., *IEEE Transactions on Signal Processing*, vol. 41, no 12, pp. 3397-3415, Dec 1993.

Jost, P.; Vandergheynst P.; Frossard, P. (2005). Tree-Based Pursuit: Algorithm and Properties., *Swiss Federal Institute of Technology Lausanne (EPFL), Signal Processing Institute Technical Report*, ,TR-ITS-2005.013, May 17th, 2005.

Grossman, A.; Morlet, J. (1985). Decompositions of Functions into Wavelets of Constant Shape, and Related Transforms. *Mathematics and Physics: Lectures an Recent Results*, L. Streit, 1985.

Saganowski, Ł.; Choraś, M.; Renk, R.; Hołubowicz, W. (2009). A Novel Signal-Based Approach to Anomaly Detection in IDS Systems, and Related Transforms. *M. Kolehmainen et al. (Eds.): ICANNGA 2009* ,LNCS 5495, pp. 527–536, Springer 2009.

16

Graphics Processor-based High Performance Pattern Matching Mechanism for Network Intrusion Detection

Nen-Fu Huang, Yen-Ming Chu and Hsien-Wen Hsu
National Tsing Hua University
Taiwan

1. Introduction

As high-speed networking technology has progressed, the current network environment comprises many applications. However, many users still feel uncertain about these network applications due to security issues. Intrusion detection and prevention systems (IDS/IPS) are designed to detect and identify diverse threats over the network, such as worms, virus, spyware, and malicious codes, by performing deep packet inspection on packet payloads. Deep packet inspection is used to perform various processing operations in the entire packet, including the header and payload. Therefore, searching keywords in each traffic stream forms a bottleneck. That is, string matching is always an important issue as well as significant challenge in high speed network processing. For instance, Snort (Roesch, 1999), the most famous and popular open source IDS, takes over 2,500 patterns as signatures and takes more than 80% of CPU time for pattern matching. Thus, IDS need an efficient pattern matching algorithm or other mechanisms to speed up this key operation. Otherwise, an under-performing system not only becomes the network bottleneck but also misses some critical attacks.

Pattern matching algorithms have been studied for a long time, such algorithms include the Boyer Moore algorithm which solves single-pattern matching problem (Boyer & Moore, 1977) and the Aho-Corasick (AC) (Aho & Corasick, 1975) and Wu-Manber (Wu & Manber, 1994) algorithms, which solve multi-pattern string-matching problems. Research in this field has recently become popular again owing to the requirements for processing packets, especially for deep packet inspection applications. Various new concepts and algorithms have been proposed and implemented, such as Bitmap AC (Tuck et al., 2004), parallel bloom-filter (Dharmapurikar et al., 2004), reconfigure silicon hardware (Moscola et al., 2003) and TCAM-based mechanism (Yu et al., 2004).

Implementations of IDS can be categorized into hardware-based approaches and software-based approaches. The design concept for data structures and algorithms are usually different for these two implementations. The hardware approach is often used for network-based IDS, which is usually placed in the entrance of a local area network (LAN) and is responsible for scanning suspicious packets through it. Most of them store the famous Snort signatures, which are the collection of the characteristic of many network attacks, in the database to perform pattern matching. In order to process packets quickly and flexibly, parallel processing is the main architecture employed for network processing. The network processor (NP) is the most representative of these implementations. However, traditional network processors still suffer from poor performance and high cost when perform deep packet inspection, even though applying network processors for pattern matching has been proposed (Liu et al., 2004). Hence, many network security chip vendors have released special-purpose silicon products for accelerating the work of pattern matching. Nevertheless, such solutions are always expensive because of insufficient sales volume in the market.

On the other hand, software-based solutions, such as anti-virus software, personal firewalls, are very popular, especially in personal computers and servers. According to the reports, the security software market in Asia/Pacific (excluding Japan) is expect to grow up to over $US1100 millions in 2007 (IDC, 2006, Asia) and the market in Japan will also reach $US1927 million in 2010 (IDC, 2006, Japan), respectively. In terms of software, pattern matching is still necessary to detect network intrusion or to scan suspicious files. Form example, some famous network security software, such as Norton anti-virus, Trend-Micro pc-cillin, and Kaspersky anti-virus, have implemented the intrusion detection component in it. That is, host-based IDS becomes more and more common nowadays. However, the task of pattern matching slows down the system performance significantly because there is no additional hardware for accelerating. The problem is more crucial for servers, which often have to handle hundreds to thousands of connections simultaneously.

This study has found that graphics processors could constitute a solution for end hosts to perform pattern matching efficiently. With the parallel nature of graphics processors, the performance of pattern matching is greatly improved, even outperforms some previous hardware solutions. The personal computer has now become a standard consumer electronic device, particularly because of its ability to play PC/TV games, which increasingly require 3D processing. Players now demand for real-time, smooth and vivid frame transition, leading to the rapid development of graphics related technologies. Graphics processors are capable of increasingly powerful computation, even surpassing that of general processors in floating point computation. Developers of games or multimedia can design their own features by programming the graphics processor. This feature also catches the eye of developers of software other than games or graphics. Non-graphics applications using the programming power of graphics processors are called *General-Purpose Computations on Graphics Processor Units* (GPGPU).

This study proposes a novel approach and architecture to speed up pattern matching by using the GPUs. GPU is also capable of processing network traffic of multiple sessions in parallel. The contributions of this study can be summarized as follows:

- **Generic:** The proposed architecture is generic, and can be integrated with other systems accelerating pattern matching, such as network security system or content-intuitive systems.
- **Economics**: The GPUs are commodity and cost-effective. For example, the solution using NVIDIA GeForce 6800GT (NVIDIA GeForce 6800, 2005) costs 1/10 of other silicon solutions with the same performance.
- **Effective Utilization**: In general, the graphics processing sub-system is often idle in a PC. The computation power of GPU is not always fully utilized even when running games and other GPU-consuming applications. Hence, using a GPU to reduce the system load when performing pattern matching computations, such as virus scans or intrusion prevention, or using a GPU as a co-processor, could improve the performance of systems or applications.

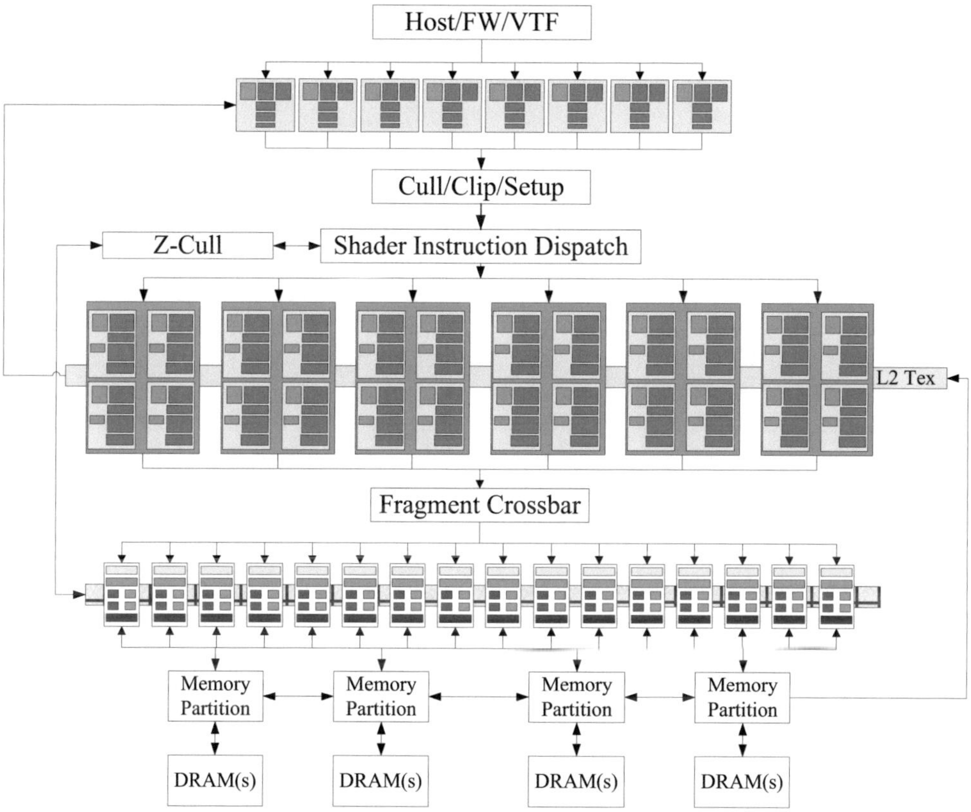

Fig. 1. NVIDIA GeForce 7900 GTX architecture

- **High Performance**: This study demonstrates that the proposed concept and mechanism work well. Experimental results indicate that the performance of the proposed mechanism (programming the GPUs by OpenGL Application Program Interface (Wright & Sweet, 2000)) is almost thrice that of a system using only a general processor (CPU). Moreover, considering a system environment designed for GPUs, the proposed system could reach 6.4Gbps throughput, and costs under $400 overall.

The rest of this chapter is organized as follows. Section 2 provides related research concerning pattern matching and GPU architecture. The architecture and operation of the proposed GPU-based pattern matching mechanism are presented in Section 3. Section 4 focuses on the performance evaluation, and provides a complete performance analysis of the proposed system. Finally, conclusions and future work are given in Section 5.

2. Related works

The proposed scheme integrates the pattern matching algorithms and the computing power of commodity GPUs. The AC algorithm is a simple, but efficient string matching algorithm to locate all occurrences of a finite set of keywords in a text string. It constructs a finite state automaton first by preprocessing a set of keywords and then applies that automaton to the input string. AC algorithm has best performance in worst case. In the following section, the GPU hardware architecture is described in detail since the rendering pipeline in GPUs is the key function in the proposed scheme. Works using GPUs for non-graphics applications are introduced in the end of this section.

2.1 GPU architecture

This section introduces the architecture and features of current GPUs. Due to market demand and the growth in semiconductor technology, the two major GPU suppliers, namely ATI (ATI Tech.) and NVIDIA (NVIDIA Corp.), are continuously improving the computing power of GPUs. The two currently most powerful GPUs, ATI X1900 and NVIDIA GeForce 7900 GTX, have hardware optimized for floating-point arithmetic. GPUs perform better than CPUs in many data parallel computations because of the strongly parallel nature of GPUs.

Fig. 1 depicts the architecture of NVIDIA's last flagship GPU, the GeForce7900 GTX, which has eight vertex shaders, 24 fragment shaders, and a core clock of 650 MHz. It uses GDDR3 memory with a bandwidth of 51.2 Gigabytes per second and a work clock of 800 MHz. Unlike CPUs, today's GPUs have higher off-chip memory clock rates than core clock rates. This feature can prevent the memory stall caused by heavy demand for memory access in shaders. For this study, the most important components in GPUs are the programmable vertex shaders and fragment shaders. A GPU program usually performs better with more vertex and fragment shaders.

In computer graphics, the procedure that transforms the vertices, colors, and coordinates information into the 2D or 3D images on the screen is called rendering pipeline (Fig. 2). The pipeline has three major portions. The vertex shaders are at the front, followed by the rasterizer, with the fragment shaders at the back of the pipeline. The input of vertex shaders comprises geometric information, including vertices and colors. The coordinates of vertices are transformed to the positions rendered on screen according to the default or user-defined coordinate matrix. The vertex shaders then perform the lighting computation for each vertex, and determine their colors. The rasterizer, which is a non-programmable fixed function in GPUs, produces every triangle of a polygon based on the processed vertices and the connectivity between them (Triangle Setup), and colors every triangle linearly (Digital Differential Analyzer). The fragment shaders process every pixel outputted by the rasterizer, and generate real pixels on the screen. Those pixels that have not been processed by fragment shaders are also called potential pixels. The first and most important job of the fragment shaders is texture mapping, which map textures polygon faces. The fragment shaders then perform alpha, stencil, and depth test to determine whether to render or discard pixels. Finally, the GPU blends test results with the pixels that have been rendered to target. The GPU writes results to the rendering target and draw them on screen at the end of the rendering pipeline. The rendering target is generally a frame buffer or texture memory. A rendering pass is the procedure in which a collection of data passes through the rendering pipeline and outputs to the rendering target.

Since the float-point computing power of GPUs grows much faster than the off-chip memory bandwidth (Pharr & Fernando, 2005) and the on-chip cache is small, accessing data from off-chip memory is rather expensive. Hence, GPUs require high arithmetic intensity.

The number of logic operations must be maximized, whereas the amount of communications between GPUs and memory need to be minimized.

To build high performance GPU program, besides avoiding heavily access to off-chip memory, the data structure needs to be designed carefully to exploit the cache. The CPU was originally designed for general-purpose applications, and must function in different conditions, so has a higher control capacity than data-path capacity, making the CPU appropriate for sequential tasks. Conversely, a GPU is special-purpose hardware designed for computer graphics and has less control logic hardware than a CPU. However, GPUs are optimized for parallel computing. Algorithms should be designed to consider the parallel nature of a modern GPU to optimize a program's performance.

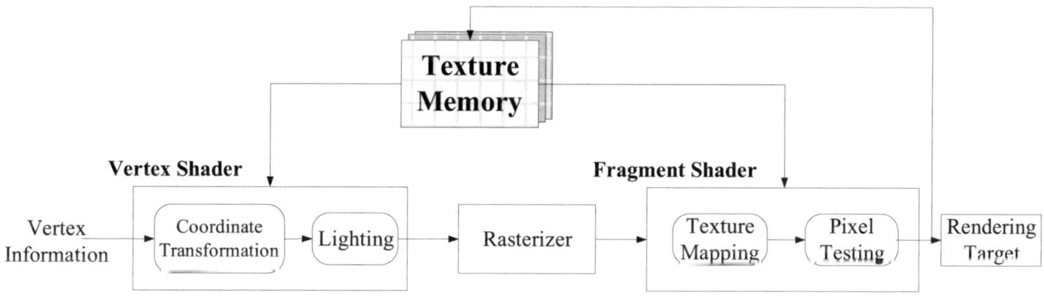

Fig. 2. Typical 3D pipeline

2.2 GPGPU

GPGPU signifies General-Purpose computation on GPUs (GPGPU, Online). As discussed in the previous section, commodity graphics processing units are becoming increasingly powerful. Researchers have developed various algorithms and systems based on GPUs to improve the performance of CPU-oriented programs (Trancoso & Charalambous, 2005). Cook (Cook et al., 2005) is the first to apply GPU to cryptography. They demonstrated the feasibility of utilizing GPUs for cryptographic processing to offload symmetric key encryption from CPU, and proved that block cipher algorithms are unsuitable for application with GPUs. Moreover, various GPU-based pattern-matching applications are popular (Vasiliadis et al., 2008) (Smith, 2009) (Goyal, 2008).

A number of works have been studied to process the stream data in a SIMD fashion. For instance, Lai applied Imagine Processor to Bloom Filter (Kapasi et al., 2002). However, these are neither implemented on a commodity GPU, nor analyzed from the viewpoint of computer graphics.

Recently, Advanced Micro Devices (AMD) and ATI Technologies, which jointed together on October 25, 2006, has released the first GPGPU product named AMD stream processor (AMD Stream Processor, Online) and announced at the Supercomputing 2006 (Supercomputing06, 2006) trade show. The AMD stream processor makes use of AMD's new technology called *CLOSE TO METAL* (CTM) to provide users a more powerful interface to develop applications based on GPUs. The parallel processing power of it is used for a wide range of applications, such as financial analysis, seismic migration analysis, and life sciences research, providing organizations and researchers now have the ability to process incredible amounts of information in significantly less time.

3. Packet inspection scheme using GPUs

The proposed procedure is a parallel byte streams pattern matching scheme which is suitable for any automaton-based string matching algorithm. AC is a well known representative of automaton-based algorithm. The AC algorithm is a sequential task model, in which one task can process only one byte stream. This study combines several sequential AC tasks to form one complex task that can process multiple byte streams, each is independent of the others. With the task parallelism of GPU, the fragment shaders can match multiple byte streams with patterns simultaneously, enabling independent pattern matching tasks to be executed at the same time. When several fragment shaders want to access data in the GPU memory, GPU can provide simultaneous memory access for decreasing the latency of data access and achieve data parallelism because of its multiple memory controllers. In theory, increasing the number of fragment shaders running in GPU raises the number of byte streams that are processed in parallel, thus improving performance. Therefore, the GPU must be provided as many byte streams as possible in order to prevent any fragment shader in the GPU from being idle.

The proposed approach can be applied in host-based IDS since GPU is almost available in every PC nowadays. It's particularly suitable for servers, which are very common to serve many connections simultaneously. The proposed scheme is expected to perform better in the network environment if the number of concurrent sessions exceeds some threshold. The later performance analysis uses the Defcon9 (Defcon 9, 2001) as network packet for input byte streams, and uses Snort's patterns as our patterns (Roesch, 1999). With the combination of the CPU and the GPU (GPU is the CPU's co-processor), the feasibility of the proposed approach is analyzed. Using real network traffic and real IDS patterns in our experiment also demonstrates that the proposed approach is very suitable for working in a high-speed network environment with multiple connection sessions.

The proposed approach is divided into three parts, namely *Data Flow*, *Data Structure*, and *Control Flow*. *Data Flow* transforms the original finite state automaton constructed with predefined patterns into another form that can be run in the GPU. That is, *Data Flow* must modify the layout of data in the CPU to fit that in the GPU. The major task of *Data Flow* is to execute the state transitions of multiple byte streams in GPUs. *Data Structure* is responsible for changing the data format between the CPU and GPU. Notably, casting operations may be necessary during processing due to the different data formats in GPU. Since casting operations decrease the throughput, an appropriate data structure must be chosen. *Control Flow* is responsible for the communication setup between the CPU and GPU. Additionally, *Control Flow* administers the overall operations of the proposed approach, and performs the program flow. The *Control Flow* constitutes the framework bottleneck, which is discussed later.

3.1 Model framework

Three data structures have to be maintained in the GPU texture memory. *Automata texture* is used to store the finite state automaton; *Text texture* is used to store multiple input streams, and *State texture* is employed to store the current states of input streams in the finite state automaton (Fig. 3). The dimensions of the *Text texture* and *State texture* are determined from the number of input streams in the system. For instance, if the number of input streams is 256, then the dimensions of *Text texture* and *State texture* can be configured as 16×16. The dimensions of rendering targets are set to 16×16, and the rasterizer in the GPU maps one pixel in the textures to one fragment. Therefore, the fragment shaders can process one single pixel in the textures (called a *texel*) at once. If one GPU has 16 fragment shaders, and 256 pixels need to be processed, then each fragment shader should handle 16 pixels within one rendering pass.

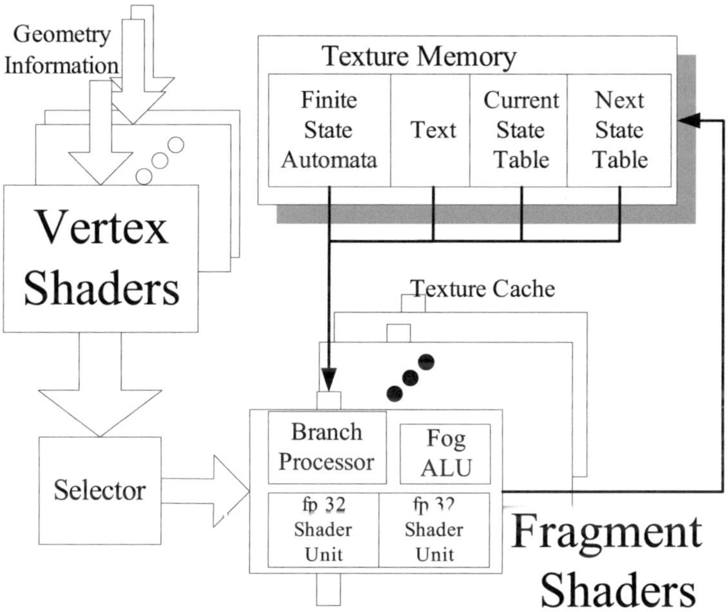

Fig. 3. The block diagram of pattern matching engine

Fig. 3 shows the flowchart of the proposed approach, which is described as follows:

Step 1. Construct the pre-defined patterns into finite state automata. Through some preprocessing like basic data format and address translation, the finite state automata are transformed into *Automata texture*, which are then downloaded from system memory to GPU texture memory via a high speed memory bus. The *Automata texture* cannot be modified once the operation is finished. If new patterns are to be added into the finite state automaton, then one new finite state automaton must be re-constructed.

Step 2. Define and allocate *State texture* and *Text texture*. The texture memory cannot be read and written in the meanwhile. Therefore, two state textures, *Current State texture* and *Next State texture*, are defined to read the current state and write the next state.

Step 3. Program the fragment shaders in the GPU by shading language (Rost, 2009). All required data are stored in the texture memory. The geometry information in Fig. 3 is utilized only to map *Text* and *Current State textures* to the rendering target. All fragment shaders execute the following instructions:

1. Obtain an input symbol from *Text texture*,
2. Obtain the current state from *Current State texture*, and
3. Apply the input symbol and current state as one index to obtain the next state from *Automata texture*.
4. Write the next state into *Next State texture* for use in the next rendering pass.

Step 4. Read in and transform the streams into *Text texture*, then download *Text texture* from system memory to texture memory in the GPU. The fragment shaders process every texel in the *Text texture* based on the pre-defined shader instructions in Step 3. Modern commodity GPUs always have multiple fragments shaders. This study assumes that the performance of the proposed approach improves with increasing number of fragment shaders. The number of concurrent input streams (denoted as S) does not have to be the same as the number of fragment shaders (denoted as FS). However, if $S < FS$, then some fragment shaders remain idle. If $S >= FS$, then the hardware driver automatically dispatches input streams to the idle fragment shaders. The fragment shaders return the matching results to the system memory from the texture memory after each rendering pass.

3.2 Data flow

Programming on a GPU is very different from programming on a CPU. It is not trivial to write a general-purpose application on GPUs due to few supported libraries and limited usage of branch/logic operations. Additionally, it is not convenient to access memory like programming in C language. Besides temporary variables, the memory allowed to read and write is texture memory. However, texture memory cannot be read and written arbitrarily. Vertex shaders and fragment shaders can read from texture memory, but cannot write to it directly. The results must be written into texture memory at the end of the rendering pipeline.
The pre-constructed finite state automaton is converted into the format suitable for GPU memory, through which fragment shaders can access data. The proposed approach utilizes pixels in *Automata texture* to represent each state in the finite state automaton (one pixel can carry 1~4 states, as discussed in the next section). GPUs operate according to the stream-kernel principle, in which a stream is a data collection of the same data type and needing similar operations, and a kernel comprises functions that operate on every element in the stream. Streams can provide the GPU parallel data, and each element in different streams is independent of the kernel. In *Data Flow*, taking the input symbols that the CPU transfers to the GPU steadily as streams and the multiple fragment shaders in the GPU as the computation kernel. Each input symbol processed by different fragment shaders is independent. *Data Flow* is described as follows.

Construction Phase

In the *Construction Phase*, the pre-constructed finite state automaton is represented by a deterministic finite automaton (DFA) table. Assuming that the size of symbol space is n, each state in the finite state automaton will be expanded to n next states. For example, for the ASCII-based 8-bit codes, the symbol space $n = 256$ (0x00-0xff). If the finite state automaton contains k states, then one DFA table with dimensions $n \times k$ must be maintained in memory. Considering the patterns in the Snort project as example, the compiled finite state automaton contains about 22000 states. Hence, one *Automata texture* with $n \times 22000$ pixels should be maintained. Since the dimension of a texture is limited to 4096×4096, the finite state automaton may need to be transformed, in case its dimensions exceed the limit of the fitting layout (the actual layout in GPU memory is shown later). Of course, there is no need to maintain one big 4096×4096 texture for every finite state automaton. The dimension can be adjusted according to the size of the finite state automaton. For example, one finite state automaton contains 1024 states, then its DFA needs to be mapped to one texture with

$1024 \times n$ pixels, so one texture (square) with dimensions $(1024 \times n)^{1/2} \times (1024 \times n)^{1/2}$ is adequate. The memory structure in the GPU memory is two-dimensional, but that in the CPU is one-dimensional. The following procedure is used for translation between the two different dimensions.

Procedure DataAddressing (*T, H, W, A, K, S*)
Input: Deterministic Finite Automaton table: *T*, the height of DFA table: *H*, the width of DFA table: *W*, the dimension of element space: *A*, the amount of states: *K*, and the set of states: *S*
Output: One two-dimensional texture in GPU memory: *GT*, transformed from the one-dimensional DFA table.
Load DFA table *T*;
Initialize: $t \leftarrow \emptyset$, $z \leftarrow \emptyset$, $offset \leftarrow \emptyset$;
For each $S[t]$ **do**
    $r \leftarrow$ the remainder of t dividing by H;
    $p \leftarrow$ the quotient of W dividing by A;
    $q \leftarrow$ the quotient of t dividing by W;
    offset $\leftarrow$ multiply(A, sum(multiply(r, p), q));
    While $z < A$ **do**
        If $T[t, z] \neq$ NULL **then**
            Load data from T at index (t, z) to GT at index (sum(*offset*, z), z);
        Else
            Continue;
        Increase z by 1;
    End
End
Return;

Search Phase

The *Search Phase* utilizes the programmable fragment shaders in GPUs. Numerous shading languages like GLSL, HLSL, Cg, Brook (Buck et al., 2004), and assembly language can be used to accomplish such purpose. This study applies GLSL and OpenGL (Wright & Sweet, 2000) to program fragment shaders. Fragment shaders follow the SIMD programming model, which implies the same instructions are executed simultaneously on different data. The following search procedure is invoked by fragment shaders to perform state transitions. The input symbol is first obtained from the *Text texture* in GPU memory. The current state information is then obtained from *Current State texture* in the same way. The next state can be fetched by taking the input symbol and current state as an index of the *Automata texture*. *Render-to-texture*, which rendered computation results to texture rather than frame buffer, is then adopted to write the next states into the *Next State texture* for the next rendering pass. Additionally, the next states are transferred to the system memory for post-processing of pattern matching by CPUs. Although three memory lookup operations are executed in the above procedure, the speed of off-chip memory access inside GPUs is very fast, even up to 51 GB/s. The latency of these three memory lookups is assumed to be low.

Procedure Search (*AT, IT, CT, H, W, A, P*);
Input: The DFA texture: *AT*, the input symbol texture: *IT*, the current state texture: *CT*, the height of the rendering target: *H*, the width of the rendering: *W*, and the dimension of element space: *A*, the corresponding position in rendering target: *P*
Output: The next state information in DFA: *NS*;
Initialize: s $\leftarrow \emptyset$, c $\leftarrow \emptyset$, x $\leftarrow \emptyset$, y $\leftarrow \emptyset$;
Fetch an input symbol from *IT* at *P*, and store in *s*;
Fetch current state from *CT* at *P*, and store in *c*;
Round up and down *s* for accuracy;
If (*s* = NULL) **then**
    Return;
Else
    $r \leftarrow$ the remainder of *c* dividing by *H*;
    $r' \leftarrow$ the quotient of *c* dividing by *H*;
    $x \leftarrow$ sum(multiply(*r*, *A*), *s*);
    $y \leftarrow r'$;
    $NS \leftarrow$ Lookup(*AT*, *x*, *y*); /* Lookup next state from *AT* */
    If (*NS* is an accepted state) **then**
        Set accepted flag;
        Return True;
    Else
        Return True;
Return False;

3.3 Data structure

This section introduces how to represent the DFA table in GPU, and discusses memory optimization issues. The DFA table and other data needed are stored in the GPU texture memory. Accordingly, all data in system memory must be transformed into the texture data format, namely pixels. Since data are stored in pixels, the chosen pixel format significantly affects the size of GPU memory required. Additionally, the processing time of the *Search Phase* varies according to the pixel format. Common OpenGL pixel formats include color index, grayscale, RGB, and RGBA. RGBA and grayscale pixel format are considered here as examples.

RGBA Pixel Format

Assuming that each pixel contains four 32-bit components: Red(*R*), Green(*G*), Blue(*B*), and Alpha(*A*). The state information of a finite state automaton is stored as *R* values in pixels (Fig. 4), so that one state is represented as one pixel. Although modern GPUs support 16-bit floating-point format, its precision is far lower than that of 32-bit floating-point format. For instance, if the NVIDIA fp16 float is used, the element 3079 cannot be addressed, since the closest representable numbers of fp16 float are 3078 and 3080. This inaccuracy seriously affects computations. The fp16 float is not used in this study. Supposing that the space of input symbols ranges between 0x00 and 0xff, the Snort patterns have over than 22,000 states, each then can be expanded to 256 next states. Therefore, about 5 millions pixels are needed to store the entire DFA table. The limit of the texture dimension in GPUs is 4096×4096, meaning that one single texture contains at most 2^{24} pixels (16 millions). Therefore, storing entire DFA table of the Snort rules into one big texture has no problem. Additionally, modern GPU technology performs all computations with floating-point arithmetic. Floating-point related operations in modern GPU hardware are improving. Therefore, floating-point arithmetic gives the best performance for finite state automaton data format and related computations.

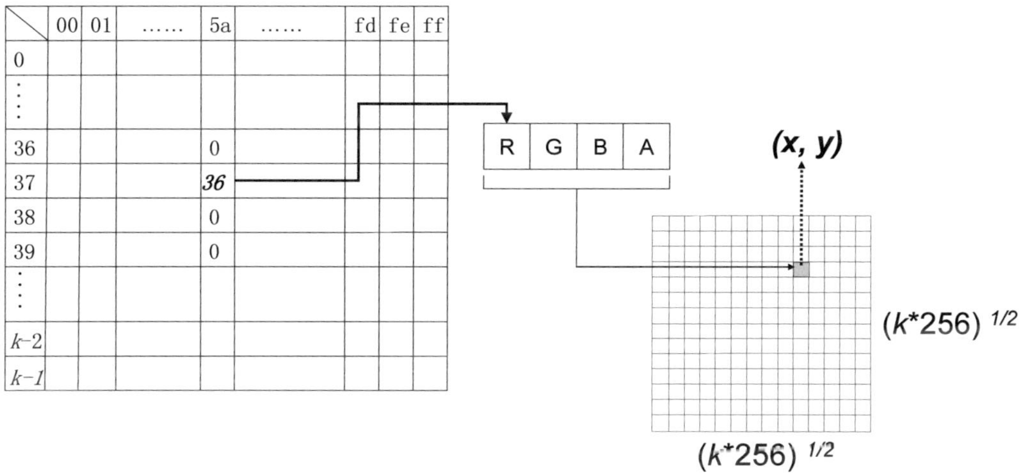

Fig. 4. Illustration of data packing

In Fig.4, the left side is a DFA table and the right side is a texture (square) with dimensions $(k \times 256)^{1/2} \times (k \times 256)^{1/2}$. The space of input symbols ranges between 0x00 and 0xff. The number of states is given as k. The dotted line indicates the mapping from state 37 to the R component of a pixel while reading in input symbol "5a". The coordinate (x, y) is derived from the mentioned Search Procedure.

In the above example, the state information of DFA table is stored in the R component of pixels, while the other three components, G, B, and A, are wasted. To fully utilize the components of pixels, the original patterns can be split into four groups, such that the number of states in each group are almost equal. The same component in different pixels comprises one finite state automaton. That is, the four finite state automata are traversed by fragment shaders concurrently. In this way, the four finite state automata, each with at most 65536 states, can theoretically be packed into one single big texture. Naturally, fragment shaders must execute extra instructions to perform all pattern matching operations. The processing time would be slower than in the case that only R component is used.

Grayscale Pixel Format

The grayscale texture can be adopted to represent one DFA table rather than applying all components, namely R, G, B, and A. Pixels in a grayscale texture have only a grayscale component. By assigning each grayscale component one 16-bit unsigned integer, 2^{16} states can be expressed at most. However, the grayscale value is clamped as a float-point number between 0.0 and 1.0 in OpenGL. Hence, extra computations are required to restore the state information to the original integer representation.

3.4 Control flow

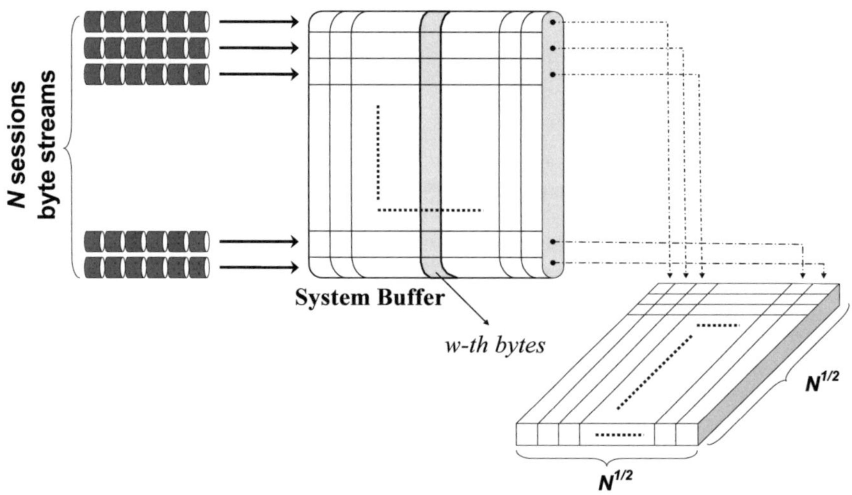

Fig. 5. Illustration for packing *N* byte-streams into the Text texture ($N^{1/2} \times N^{1/2}$)

In *Control Flow*, OpenGL is used to control the flow of the proposed approach. The implementation follows the general computer graphics programming model, except that the data are not intended to be displayed on the screen. The focus is the communications between the CPU and GPU. Beyond that, the *Control Flow* is also responsible for pre-processing of byte streams in CPU and post-processing of pattern matching. For illustration, considering the input phase, as shown in Fig. 5, *N* input byte streams need to be processed. First, all input streams are read into a buffer, and the *w*-th byte of each input stream is copied and placed into the *Text texture* in row-major order before starting the *w*-th rendering pass. This texture is then transferred to the GPU memory. The rendering pipeline can then be initialized and started. CPU has to trigger these operations every time before starting the rendering pipeline. As for the output phase, the results, which are rendered at the end of the rendering pipeline, are then transferred from GPU memory to system memory. The results are the accepted states in finite state automata. CPUs need to do computations with the accepted states for getting the corresponding matched patterns. We can use matched patterns or other related information as the matching results, and *Automata texture* is the only structure we have to modify.

4. Evaluation and analysis

The previous section demonstrated how finite state automata on GPUs function. The fingerprint of finite state automata is shown in the following section. Next, an attempt is made to demonstrate the performance of the proposed data flow with commodity GPUs by using the performance profiling tool released by NVIDIA for measuring unbiased throughput. Various pixel formats are also analyzed and compared with respect to the performance of the fragment shaders. *Data Flow* is then integrated with *Control Flow* to compare performance of the proposed approach with that of other AC algorithm-based implementations.

4.1 Memory fingerprint

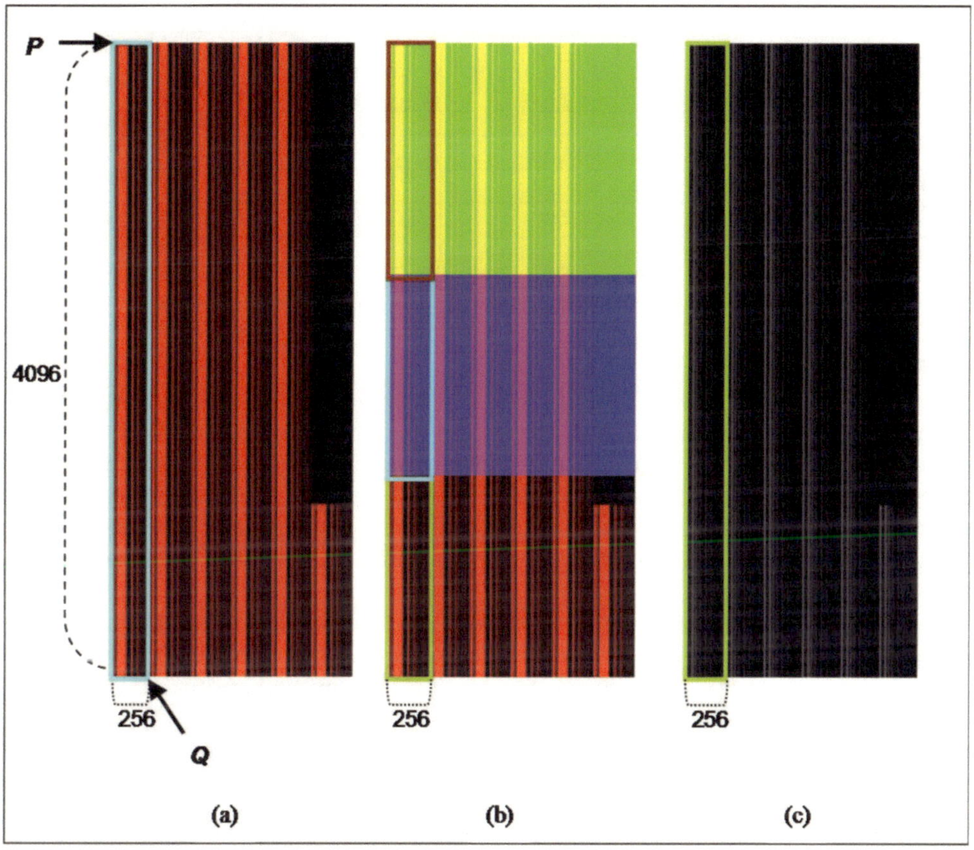

Fig. 6. The fingerprint of finite state automata

The images in Fig. 6 show the layouts of finite state automata (for Snort patterns), which are located in GPU memory. The lower left corner of these images is the origin pixel, and it represents the next state which current state is 0 and input symbol is 0. From the origin to the point *P* are the pixels with current states ranged from 0 to 4095 in order and input symbol 0. Similarly, from the origin to the point *Q* are the pixels with input symbols from 0 to 255 and current state 0.This rectangle with a width of 256 pixels and a height of 4096 pixels could contain all next states with current state from 0 to 4095 (Fig. 6(a)). In the same way, we could divide Fig. 6(a) into six rectangles, and it can carry $4096 \times 6 \times 256$ next states. Fig. 6(a) means the layout of finite state automaton located GPU memory which only utilizes *R* value of one pixel. Pixels with non-zero next state are red while pixels with zero next state are black.

As for the case that all *R*, *G*, *B*, and *A* components are used, pixels are black if four next states are all zero (Fig. 6(b)). When only the *R* component is utilized, the pixels are red. Moreover, when only the *G* component is utilized, the pixels are green. Similarly, the pixels are blue only if *B* component is utilized. Furthermore, the pixels are yellow if both *R* and *G* components are employed. Fig. 6(c) represents the layout in which grayscale pixel format is applied.

GPU / Pixel Format		Memory Size (Mbytes)		GeForce 6200 (NV44)	GeForce 6600 GT (NV43-GT)	GeForce 6800 Ultra (NV40)	GeForce 7800 GT (G70)
		64K states	Snort 2.4 (Apr.06)	4 fragment shaders	8 fragment shaders	16 fragment shaders	24 fragment shaders
Strategy	1	256	84.36	933.36	2666.64	4266.64	6400.00
	2	64	21.09	622.24	1777.76	2844.48	4266.64
	3	32	10.54	700.00	2000.00	3200.00	5485.68

Unit: Mbps

Table 1. Memory required and the throughput with different GPUs

4.2 Performance analysis

NVShaderPerf (NVIDIA ShaderPerf 2, 2008) is a command line utility to report shader performance metrics. It can produce the scheduling information based on instructions executed in shaders. In order to evaluate the proposed data flow, the pixel processing throughput is treated as the performance metric. In this section, the instructions executed in pixel shaders are different according to the pixel formats adopted in the three strategies. Although the purposes of these strategies are the same, the test result of these strategies varies.

To compare with other related works impartially, the *Control Flow* was separated from this experiment. This is because *Control Flow* involves interaction between the operating system platform and device driver, which is not the focus of the proposed approach. The details are provided in the next section.

Strategy 1 in TABLE 1 applies only the *R* component of pixels to represent the state information. Although the other three components, *G*, *B*, and *A*, are not used in Strategy 1, the operation is succinct. Strategy 1 obtains the optimum throughput among all. Assuming the space of input symbols ranges between 0x00 and 0xff, Strategy 1's deterministic finite state automaton has a maximum of 2^{24} next states since the texture dimension is limited to 4096 ×4096. Each component of *RGBA* is 32-bit, such that Strategy 1 would consume 256MB GPU memory (4Bytes × 4 × 4096 × 4096) if the texture dimension is set to 4096 × 4096. On the contrary, Strategy 2 applies all components to represent states of four finite state automata. The GPU pixel utilization of Strategy 2 is 4 times efficient of Strategy 1; i.e., Strategy 2 requires only 1/4 of the memory of Strategy 1. However, the amount of memory access in Strategy 2 is also 4 times Strategy 1. Strategy 3 adopts the grayscale component of pixels, and every component is 16-bit. The DFA with 2^{16} states requires 32MB of GPU memory in Strategy 3. All computations inside the GPU are based on 32-bit floating-point numbers. If 16-bit grayscale components are utilized for finite state automata, then shaders must perform extra computations for accuracy. These computations have significant overheads. Hence, Strategy 1 had the best throughput, and Strategy 3 was slightly worse than Strategy 1. The proposed approach is flexible, since it seeks a tradeoff between the number of patterns and throughput. Similar approaches are common in commercial Graphics Processor products.

Fig. 7 shows the performance comparison between the proposed approach and other famous related proposals. The algorithm proposed by Tuck (Tuck et al., 2004) applies an accessible embedded memory of 1024 bits, which is implemented in on-chip. The design cost can be assumed far more than the proposed approach using GPUs located in PCs originally. Even though Tuck's ASIC design performs better than the proposed system, the superiority of GPUs can be discovered. TABLE I also shows that the number of fragment shaders raises with each new generation of GPUs. Therefore, the proposed approach with the new GPU architecture performs better than that with older GPU architecture. The GF7800-1 approach in Fig. 7 even outperforms other implementations which used specific hardware (Cho et al., 2002), (Tuck et al., 2004), (Bos & Huang, 2005), (Song et al., 2005).

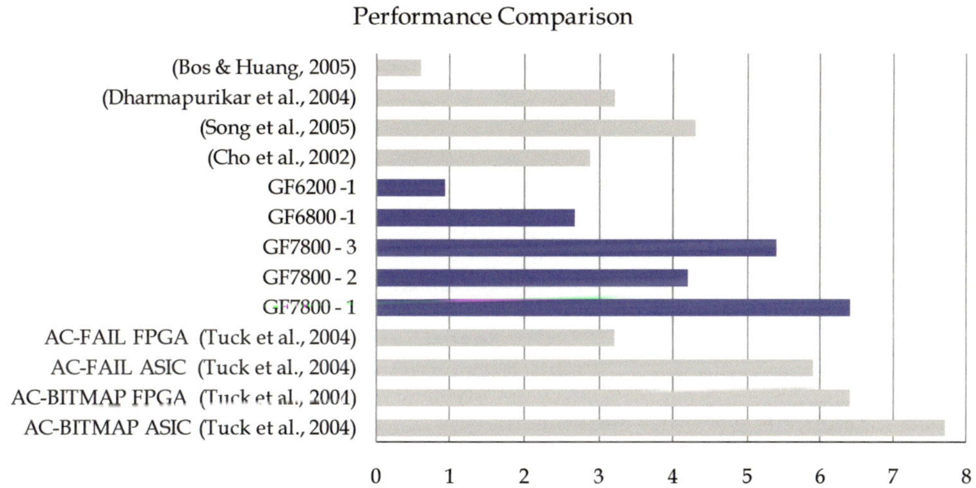

Fig. 7. The performance comparison between the proposed approach and other famous related proposal

4.3 System overhead

Fig. 7 indicates that the proposed solution is potentially as good as other FPGA or ASIC solutions. However, our proposed method is software-based since the GPU can be programmed through shader languages and almost every PC has GPU installed in it. It is considerable that the performance of a software-based solution is almost as good as that of hardware-based solutions. In this section, the proposed approach is integrated with commodity graphics cards in home PCs and designed to cooperate with other software in the operating system. The experimental environment was configured as follows:

Processor: AMD Sempron 2500+
Operating system: Windows XP Service Pack 2
System main memory: 512 DDR memory
Graphics card: NVIDIA GeForce 7600 GT with 12 fragment shaders
Graphics API: OpenGL

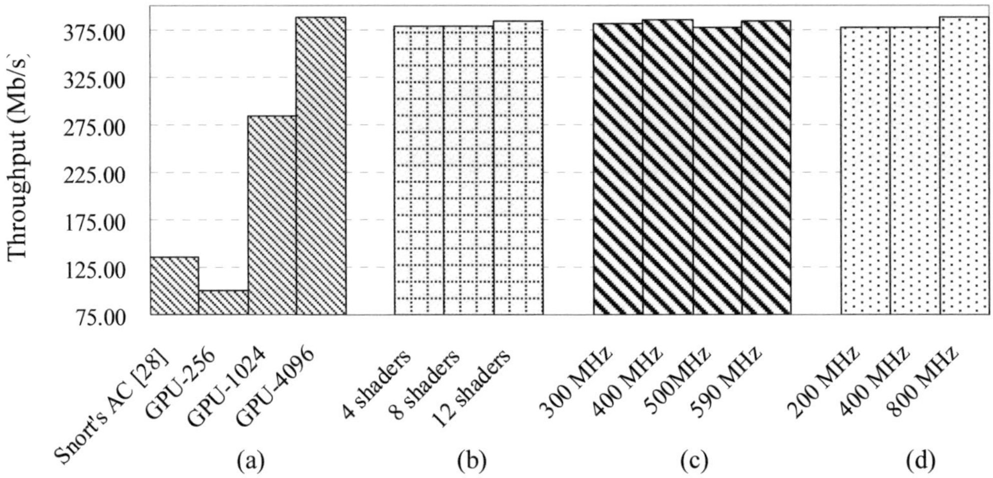

Fig. 8. (a) Performance of AC algorithm and the proposed approach. This experiment compared the performance of AC algorithm and the proposed approach with different number of sessions. (Number of sessions: GPU-256: 256, GPU-1024: 1024, GPU-4096: 4096); (b) Performance of the proposed approach with different number of fragment shaders; (c) Performance of the proposed approach at different GPU core clock rates; (d) Performance of the proposed approach at different GPU memory clock rates

The Snort 2.4 patterns were also taken as the keyword patterns, as in other related work. The Defcon9 trace is taken as the testing data for pattern matching. As shown in Fig. 8(a), the software performance between the proposed approach with various amount of sessions and the Snort's AC implementation (Norton, 2004) is compared. Multiple-session and single-session solutions were compared since traffic from a large network is an aggregation of many sessions. It shows that the proposed approach performs better than AC algorithm when processing 1024 or 4096 sessions, as well as the number of sessions raises. The AC algorithm is a sequential task model which naturally performs worse than a parallel task model. Thus it is always slower than the proposed approach once the benefit of parallel processing is greater than the overhead of using OpenGL API. From another perspective, this feature is advantageous for pattern-matching intuitive software, such as anti-virus software or intrusion detection systems on PCs. For instance, anti-virus software can scan multiple files simultaneously. Therefore, The GPU resources of PCs can be fully exploited.

Fig. 8(b) shows the performance of the proposed approach with various numbers of fragment shaders. The throughput rises with increasing numbers of fragment shaders. However, using 12 fragment shaders did not produce a significant performance improvement, which is not consistent with previous assumptions. The gDEBugger (Graphic Remedy gDEBugger, 2005) profile indicates that the proposed approach is CPU-bound. The number of fragment shaders has minor effect on the entire architecture, since a GPU can finish its job and return results to CPU within 20 microseconds with either 4 or 12 fragment shaders. The experimental results also imply that the proposed approach can reach the peak performance when using a GPU-based system.

Fig. 8(c) demonstrates that the core clock rate has a slight impact on performance. The difference between the maximum and minimum throughput was less than 10 Mbps. The performance was assumed to be better at a higher clock rate, but Fig. 8(c) shows the opposite results. The performance dropped at high clock rates because our implementation determined the throughput using traffic divided by processing time. The difference in processing time with various clock rates was less than 0.5 seconds. The proposed implementation was possibly interrupted or preempted by other operating system (Microsoft Windows) application threads, influencing our testing processing time and producing a non-reasonable result. Fig. 8(d) shows the testing result after adjusting the clock rate of the GPU memory, demonstrating that the performance of the proposed approach is directly proportional to the clock rate of GPU memory.

Fig. 8(b)-(d) show that the proposed approach performs well while the degree of parallelism is above a threshold, and the processing power of GPUs is never the bottleneck of the overall system. The GPU remains idle at most processing time period. The interaction between applications, OpenGL, OS, and device driver slows down the proposed system. Moreover, the data from CPU to GPU in every rendering pass is below 10KB. The proposed approach does not benefit from the high-speed PCI-E bus. Even though the proposed approach can perform better than other implementations in software, it has particularly strong potential when GPU and high-bandwidth bus are fully exploited.

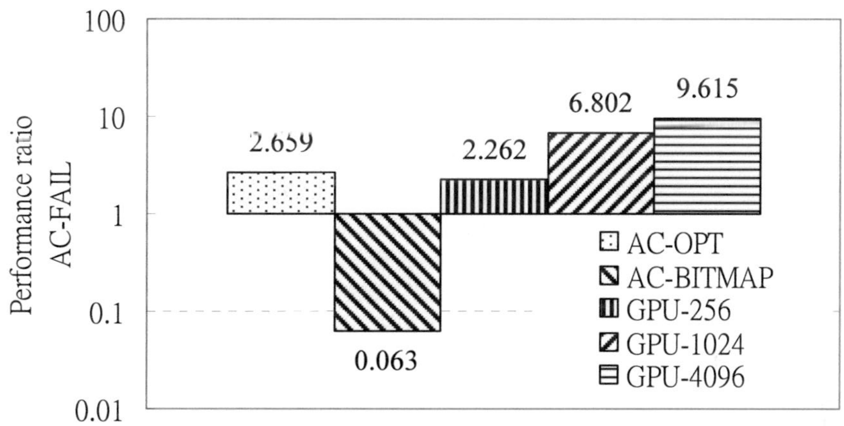

Fig. 9. Performance ratio of various AC implementations to AC-FAIL

Fig. 9 compares the software performance of the proposed approach and Tuck's algorithm (Tuck et al., 2004) with the performance of Tuck's AC-FAIL approach as the baseline. The proposed approach had a performance which is 9.615 times that of AC-FAIL when 4096 sessions were processed simultaneously, and even outperformed the optimized software approach in Tuck's algorithm. Although the GPU was used as the pattern matching accelerator, the proposed approach is still classified as a pure software application, since it utilizes no specific hardware. A graphics card is included in every modern personal computer, and therefore includes no extra cost. The proposed approach utilizes existing system resources.

5. Conclusion

This chapter discusses pattern matching algorithm and research about GPU, and presents a novel scheme that employs the GPU as an accelerator for multi-session deep packet inspection. This study is the first to consider the application of a GPU for this purpose. Several parameters are analyzed, such as the pixel formats employed by finite state automata and the number of shaders. The measurement and analysis show that the proposed scheme is better than other explored approaches, and the idea of pattern matching on the GPU is feasible. High-performing IDS within a host is possible to be made by applying this new concept for network processing, especially useful for servers to provide reliable services for multiple connections concurrently.

There are still many details that could be further improved in the future. First, GPUs are originally designed for graphics processing, so they have very good performance in matrix operations and have great power of floating point computation. For example, it can do multiply-add operations within one instruction. Problems such as how to store data in floating point format compactly or how to take the advantages of some special instructions designed for GPUs, need to be investigated deeply. As mentioned above, the proposed approach is appropriate for most automaton-based works, and the parallel nature of GPUs is particularly fitting for implementing various FSM-based algorithms for speedup (Tan et al., 2006). A suitable pattern matching algorithm may be found by further utilizing these virtues to exploit the power of GPUs. Additionally, GPU applications need high arithmetic intensity for peak performance. Therefore, rather than automaton-based pattern matching algorithms, hash-based algorithms, such as Wu-Manber or Bloom Filter, could also be utilized in GPUs. Second, GPGPU research usually focus on how to program fragment shaders regardless of programming vertex shader since it has limited operations on texture memory before, but the trend seems to change recently. Because some vertex shaders in GPUs can store data into the texture memory now, people try to use vertex shader to increase performance. All GPU-based algorithms might be improved by combining these two powerful processors, for instance, preprocessing in vertex shaders and taking other operations in fragment shaders. Third, as we mentioned in section II, AMD has released a stream processor, which is aimed at the GPGPU applications. With the new thin hardware interface called *CLOSE TO METAL* (CTM) proposed by AMD, programmers now could directly control the graphics kernel instead of using 3D application programming interfaces (APIs) which are originally designed for 3D rendering, such as OpenGL, DirectX, or with the compilation of GLSL, Cg and other shading languages. Therefore, the CTM can improve at least 8x throughput compare to 3D APIs. Thus, the system overhead generated by OpenGL APIs in our proposed method, has great chance to be solved in the near future. Finally, the main focus of future research will be NPGPU, a high-speed network packet processing application based on GPUs, like longest prefix matching, packet classification and network intrusion detection. With the rapid development of GPUs recently, as its programmability and flexibility increased, more friendly GPGPU development platform released, and the parallel nature of GPUs is consistent with the characteristic of simultaneous network connections, we ambitiously expect the diverse network applications based on GPUs will explode.

6. References

Aho, A. & Corasick, M. J. (1975). Efficient string matching: An aid to bibliographic search. *Communications of the ACM*, Vol. 18, No 6, (Jun. 1975), pp. 333–340, ISSN-0001-0782.

AMD Stream Processor™. [Online]. Available: *http://ati.amd.com/products/streamprocessor/index.html*

ATI Technologies Inc. , [Online]. Available: *http://www.ati.com/*

Bos, H. & Huang, K. (2005). Towards software-based signature detection for intrusion prevention on the network card, *Proceedings of Eighth International Symposium on Recent Advances in Intrusion Detection (RAID2005)*, pp. 102-123, Seattle, Washington, Sep. 2005.

Boyer, R. S. & Moore, J. S. (1977). A fast string searching algorithm, *Communications of the ACM,* Vol. 20, No. 10, (Oct. 1977), pp. 761–772, ISSN-0001-0782.

Buck, I.; Foley, T.; Horn, D.; Sugerman, J.; Fatahalian, K.; Houston, M. & Hanrahan, P. (2004). Brook for GPUs: Stream computing on graphics hardware, *ACM Transactions on Graphics (SIGGRAPH)*, Vol. 23, No. 3, (Aug. 2004), pp. 777–786, ISSN- 0730-0301.

Cho, Y. H.; Navab, S. & Mangione-Smith, W. (2002). Specialized hardware for deep network packet filtering, *Lecture Notes In Computer Science*, Vol. 2438, (Sep. 2002), pp. 452-461, ISBN-3-540-44108-5.

Cook, D. L.; Ioannidis, J.; Keromytis, A. D. & Luck, J. (2005). CryptoGraphics: Secret key cryptography using graphics cards, *Proceedings of the RSA Conference, Cryptographer's Track (CT-RSA 2005)*, pp. 334–350, San Francisco, Feb. 2005.

Defcon 9 (2001). [Online]. Available: *http://www.defcon.org*

Dharmapurikar, S.; Krishnamurthy, P.; Sproull, T. & Lockwood, J. (2004). Deep packet inspection using parallel Bloom filters, *IEEE Micro*, Vol. 24, No. 1, (Aug. 2004), pp. 52–61. ISBN- 0-7695-2012-x.

Goyal, N.; Ormont, J.; Smith, R.; Sankaralingam, K. & Estan, C. (2008). Signature matching in network processing using SIMD/GPU architectures. Technical Report TR1628, University of Wisconsin at Madison, 2008.

GPGPU: General-Purpose Computation on GPUs. [Online]. Available: *http://www.gpgpu.org*

Graphic Remedy gDEBugger (2005). [Online]. Available: *http://www.gremedy.com*

IDC 2006 research report. (2006). Asia/Pacific Semiannual Security Software Tracker. [Online]. Available: *http://www.idc.com/getdoc.jsp?containerId=IDC_P5559*

IDC 2006 research report. (2006). Japan Security Software 2006-2010 Forecast and 2005 Vendor Shares. [Online]. Available: *http://www.gii.co.jp/english/id44743-vend-share.html*

Liu, R.T.; Huang, N.F.; Chen, C.H. & Kao, C.N. (2004). A Fast String Matching Algorithm for Network Processor-based Intrusion Detection Systems, *ACM Transactions on Embedded Computer Systems*, Vol. 3, No. 3, (Aug. 2004), pp. 614 - 633, ISSN-1539-9087.

Kapasi, U. & Dally, W. J. et al. (2002) The Imagine stream processor, *Proceedings of* the *IEEE International Conference on Computer Design*, pp. 282–288, ISBN- 0-7695-1700-5, Freiburg, Germany, Sep. 2002, IEEE.

Moscola, J.; Lockwood, J.; Loui, R. P. & Pachos, M. (2003). Implementation of a content-scanning module for an internet firewall, *Proceedings of the IEEE Symposium on Field-Programmable Custom Computing Machines (FCCM)*, pp. 31–38, ISBN-0-7695-1979-2, Napa, CA, April 2003, IEEE.

Norton, M. (2004). Optimizing Pattern Matching for Intrusion Detection, Jul. 2004. [Online]. Available: *http://docs.idsresearch.org/OptimizingPatternMatchingForIDS.pdf*

NVIDIA Corporation Inc. , [Online]. Available: *http://www.nvidia.com/*

NVIDIA GeForce 6800, (2005). [Online]. Available: *http://www.nvidia.com/page/geforce_6800.html*

NVIDIA ShaderPerf 2 (2008). NVIDIA developer tools: NVShaderPerf, [Online]. Available: *http://developer.NVIDIA.com/object/nvshaderperf_home.html*

Pharr, M. & Fernando, R. (2005). *GPU Gems 2*, Addison Wesley Publishing Company, ISBN-978-0321335593, New York.

Roesch, M. (1999). Snort: Lightweight intrusion detection for networks, *Proceedings of the 1999 USENIX LISA Systems Administration Conference*, November 1999. [Online]. Available: *http://www.snort.org/*

Rost, R. J. et al. (2009) *OpenGL(R) shading language*, 3rd edition, Addison Wesley Professional, ISBN-978-0321637635.

Smith, R.; Goyal, N.; Ormont, J.; Sankaralingam, K. & Estan, C. (2009). Evaluating GPUs for network packet signature matching. *Proceedings of the IEEE International Symposium on Performance Analysis of Systems and Software (ISPASS 2009)*, pp. 175–184, ISBN-978-1-4244-4184-6, Boston, MA, April 2009, IEEE.

Song, T.; Zhang, W.; Tang, Z. & Wang, D. (2005). Alphabet based selected character decoding for area efficient pattern matching architecture on FPGAs, *Proceedings of the Second International Conference on Embedded Software and Systems (ICESS'05)*, pp. 276–283, ISBN-0-7695-2512-1, Xian, China, Dec. 2005, IEEE.

Supercomputing06. (2006). The international Conference for High Performance Computing, Networking, Storage and Analysis. [Online] Available: *http://sc06.supercomputing.org/*

Tan,L.; Brotherton, B. & Sherwood, T. (2006). Bit-split string-matching engines for intrusion detection and prevention, *ACM Transactions on Architecture and Code Optimization (TACO)*, Vol. 3 No. 1, pp. 3-34, ISSN-1544-3566.

Trancoso, P. & Charalambous, M. (2005). Exploring graphics processor performance for general purpose applications, *Proceedings of the 8th Euromicro Conference on Digital System Design (DSD'05)*, pp. 306–313, ISBN-0-7695-2433-8, Porto, Portugal, August 2005, IEEE.

Tuck, N.; Sherwood, T.; Calder, B. & Varghese, G. (2004). Deterministic memory-efficient string matching algorithms for intrusion detection, In *Proceedings of the IEEE Infocom Conference*, pp. 333–340, ISBN-0-7803-8355-9, Hong Kong, March 2004, IEEE.

Vasiliadis, G.; Antonatos, S.; Polychronakis, M.; Markatos, E. P. & Ioannidis, S. (2008). Gnort: High performance network intrusion detection using graphics processors, *Lecture Notes In Computer Science*, Vol. 5230, (Sep. 2008), pp. 116-134, ISBN-978-3-540-87402-7.

Wright, R. S. & Sweet, M. (2007). *OpenGL SuperBible, 4th edition,* Addison Wesley, ISBN-978-0321498823, New York.

Wu, S. & Manber, U. (1994). A fast algorithm for multi-pattern searching, Technical Report TR-94-17, Department of Computer Science, University of Arizona, 1994.

Yu, F.; Katz, R. H. & Lakshman, T. V. (2004). Gigabit rate packet pattern-matching using TCAM, *Proceedings of the 12th IEEE International Conference on Network Protocols (ICNP 2004)*, pp.174–183, ISBN 0-7695-2161-4, Berlin, Germany, Oct. 2004, IEEE.

17

Analysis of Timing Requirements for Intrusion Detection and Prevention using Fault Tree with Time Dependencies

Pawel Skrobanek and Marek Woda
Institute of Computer Science, Automatic Control, and Robotics
Wroclaw University of Technology, Wroclaw,
Poland

1. Introduction

In-depth analysis of an attack strategy enables possibility to prevent it or when it is inevitable to minimize its adverse effects. Intrusion detection systems (IDS) base their operation on the built-in patterns of various attack strategies. Aforementioned strategies can be represented by different means like: augmented goal-tree [6], attack trees [17] (originated from on fault trees), attack graphs [14], or augmented software fault trees [4].

In augmented goal tree representation [6], the attack is expressed by sequences of logically related steps. The root of this tree is the goal of the attack, e.g., "Modification of a file". The sub-goals are associated with the roots of the sub-trees. The basic constructs are the OR, AND, Ordered-AND constructs. For example, in order to achieve the sub-goal represented as the root of the Ordered-AND construct, all sub-sub-goals have to be reached in required order.

Fault tree analysis (FTA) [3], which is a base of the attack tree [17] analysis, is a deductive probabilistic assessment technique. The FTA is the backward approach. In the fault tree, the root is associated with the top event being the hazard, e.g. "The Intrusion takes control over the Victim". Then direct causes of the hazard are considered. Next, the causes of the above causes are analyzed. Hence, different ways in which the hazard can occur are investigated. The FTA can be used to determine the following: minimal cut sets of faults that cause a hazard, probabilities of the hazard and faults. Therefore, the FTA can be used in identification which events are critical and should therefore be subjected to monitoring.

Traditional Fault Trees (FT) are widely criticized [14] due to many, widely known drawbacks, like inability to model multiple attack attempts, time dependencies, or access controls as well as for luck of modeling cycles.

In the attacks graphs [14], nodes symbolize the class of machines the attacker accessed and as well user level of privileges. The arcs are labeled by attackers' activities. By assigning probabilities of success on the arcs, one can identify the attack paths with the highest probability of success.

Augmented software fault trees [4] were defined in order to overcome disadvantages of the classical fault trees. In this approach, a trust, a context, and temporal orderings can be defined. The trust relationship expresses that some members of a distributed system trust other members of the system. Context describes which subsets of intrusive events occur in some context. The activities of attackers and network are time dependent. Event and conditions involved in an intrusion often must occur in a particular order. In order to express the temporal orderings, the interval temporal logic [1] is applied. In this logic, the structure of time is a simple linear model of time, i.e., there is one past and one future only. Therefore, the attack scenario is a deterministic one.

The fault tree with time dependencies (FTTD) [9], [10] can express non-deterministic attacks too. In the chapter, FTTD are used to describe attacks with emphasis put on timing properties. In the FTTD, event duration times, delay times between the cause events and the result event can be described by the time intervals given by its minimal and the maximal lengths. FTTD are used in verification whether the IDS reacts sufficiently quick on the attack in order to avoid the results of the attack.

The fault trees could constitute a basis for increased security awareness in any organization by supporting IT infrastructure audit preparation by drawing conclusion out of FT analysis and based on that security survey creation [20].

The structure of the chapter is the following. In, Section 2, models of two attacks (SYN-Flood called "The Victim trusts the Intruder" and generic "The Intruder has access to data in server") are described. In Section 3, FTTD in general, and FTTD for this attack are presented. Then the analysis of timing properties of this attack using the FTTD is given. In Section 4, authors exemplify protections against the attacks and present methods that increase security awareness and facilitate enforcing the desired security level. In the last section, conclusions are being stated.

The details of the TCP/IP protocol are given in [7], [8], [12], [15] and [16].

2. System description

We base our analysis on two cases, exemplified by following attack examples:

1. "The Intruder has access to data in server",
2. "The Victim trusts the Intruder".

2.1 Example #1: "The Intruder has access to the data stored on server"

Analyzed system is illustrated by Figure 1. There are two possible situations shown:

a. The intruder have access to the terminal T, onsite (within company's network) or uses trusted VPN connection (accessing INTRANET from outside) impersonated as a trusted employee with appropriate credentials (that were stolen or extracted during snooping or eavesdropping).
b. Once data on a server is not properly secured, or data access is not authenticated from within INTRANET, an Intruder can easily breach security or bypass access rights (e.g. weak, well known or no password) or access data directly when hooked up to intranet with his own machine.

Following assumptions (for example #1) were taken:

- there might be basic (based on password type "something I know") or advanced authentication smart card / token
- TCP/IP system access with MAC address verification
- vital company data is stored on server
- credentials can be stolen or snooped
- MAC address can be altered

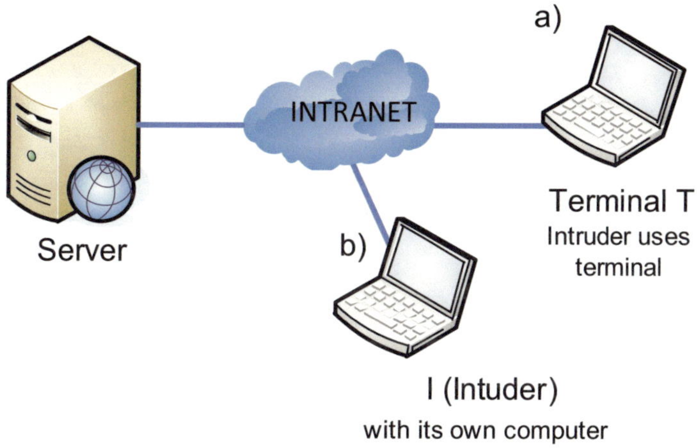

Fig. 1. (Example #1) Scenario - "The Intruder has access to the data stored on server"

2.2 Example #2: "The Victim trusts the Intruder"

This attack was already quite thoroughly described in [21]. Analyzed system is illustrated by Figure 2.
The "The Victim trusts the Intruder" attack is based on a SYN-Flood attack and goes as follows:

Fig. 2. (Example #2) Scenario - "Intruder-Victim-Host A"

I (Intruder) wants to pretend itself as A when talking to V. In response to the SYN packet that presumably came from A (in fact it came from I), V will reply with the ACK packet to start up a connection with A. When A sees the ACK to a request not generated by itself, it will send the RESET packet, and V drops the connection with I. In this case, the attack would fail. This situation is depicted in Figure 3.
Steps of scenarios (depicted in Figure 3) go as follows:

- Intruder sends SYN packet to V signed as Host A (a,b),
- V sends ACK packet to Host A (c),
- Host A receives ACK packet (although it has not yet sent SYN package) (d),
- Host sends RESET packet and finally connection is not being established (e, f, g).

However, let us suppose that the attacker I uses SYN-Flood. In this case, I and its co-operators send large number of SYN packets to A. This will keep A so busy, that the ACK packet sent from V is dropped and will go unnoticed by A. As a result, A will not send the RESET packet, and I can spoof A (see Fig. 4.).

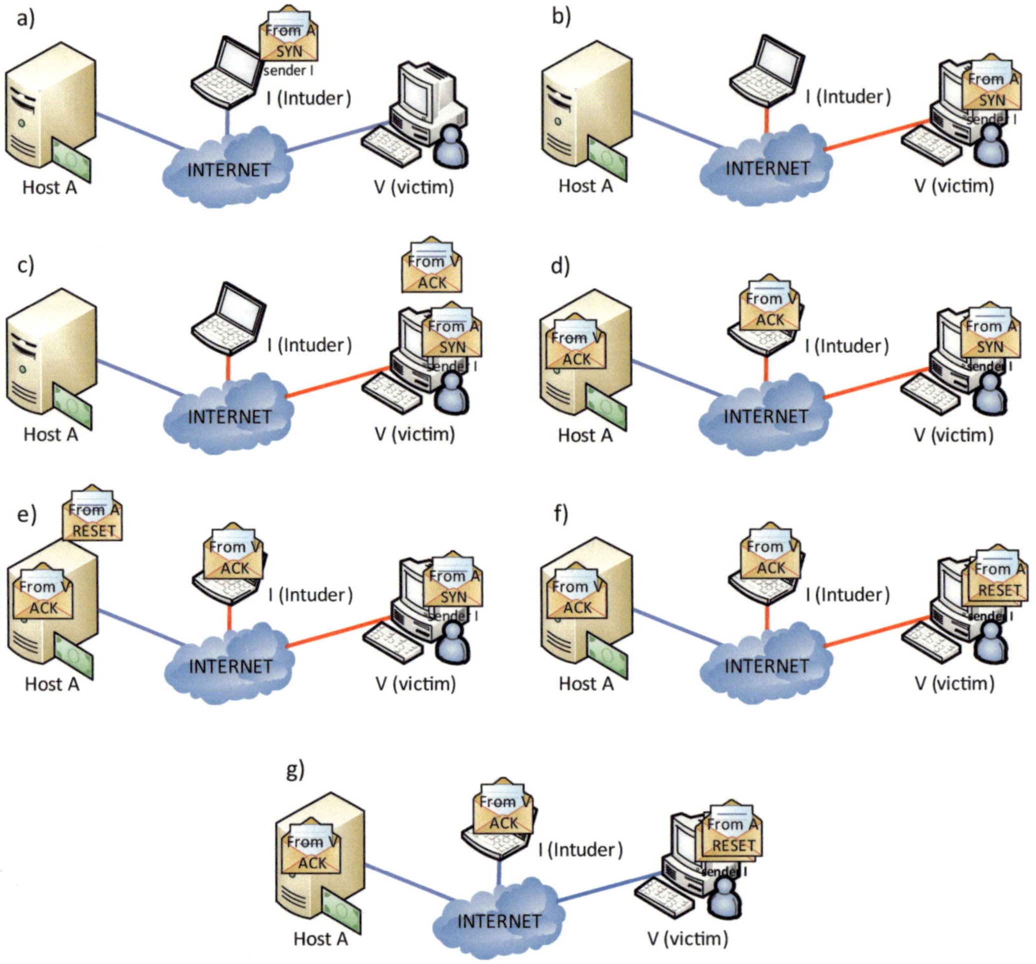

Fig. 3. "The Victim trusts the Intruder" scenario - unsuccessful attack

Steps of scenarios (depicted in Figure 4) go as follows:

- Intruder starts flooding with message Host A - DoS attack attempt
- Denial of Service attack is successful (a),
- V sends ACK packet to Host A (b),
- ACK packet is being lost (or delivery and then answer to this packet is greatly delayed)
- Connection with Intruder is established (c).

The assumptions, more detailed system description and analysis is given in [21].

3. Fault trees with time dependencies

Fault tree with time dependencies (FTTD) technique is a top-down approach. It starts from identifying all hazards (dangerous situations) in a system and their duration time.
Subsequently, for each hazard, a set of such events with time parameters that can cause the hazard is generated. The steps of the construction of the FTTD and its analysis are given in Fig.5.

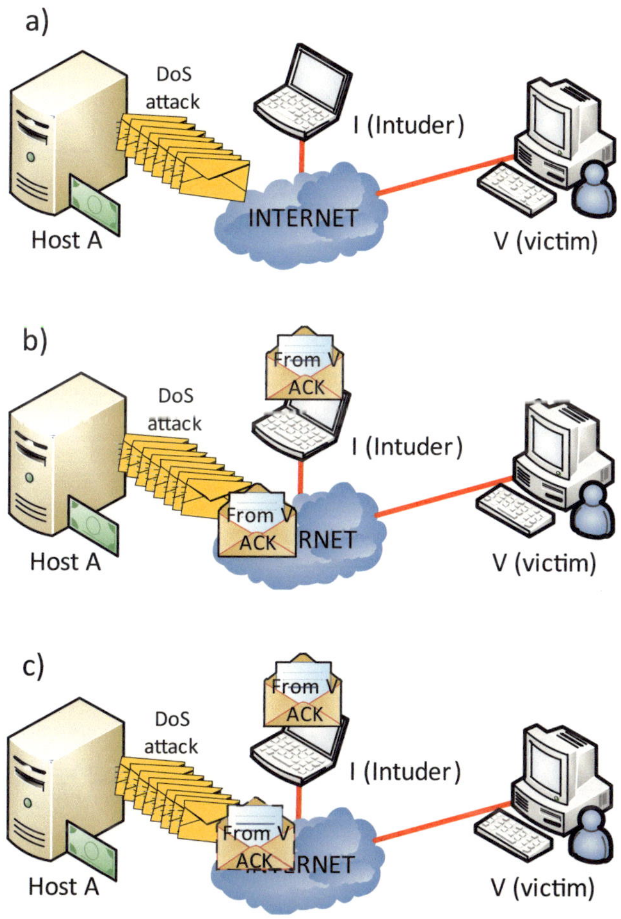

Fig. 4. "The Victim trusts the Intruder" attack based on Syn-Flood

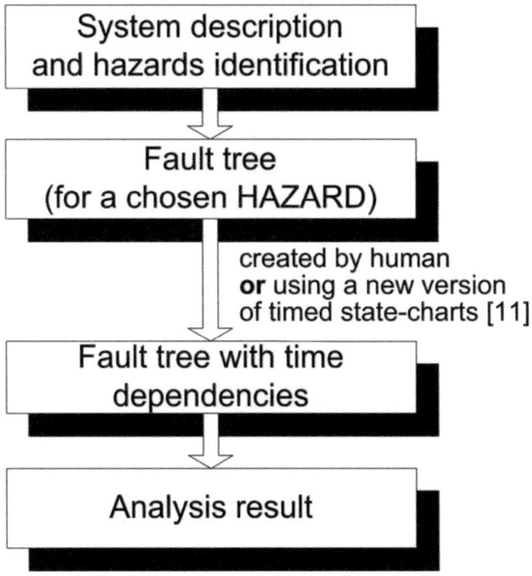

Fig. 5. The steps of the FTTD analysis

If the hazard cannot occur, or the hazard occurrence probability is on an accepted level, or the product of the hazard occurrence probability by the hazard cost is on accepted level, then we finish the analysis. Otherwise, additional security support, e.g., monitoring and security system is indispensable, as it will be shown.

3.1 The notation of the FTTD

The notations of basic gates and events are presented in Fig.6. The tool for FTTD with basic gates analysis has been presented in paper [19]. The library, as a pattern for Visio application, that allows us to draw the FTTD and to save it in file that can be analysis with tool [18]. Time dependencies can be given numerically or parametrically.

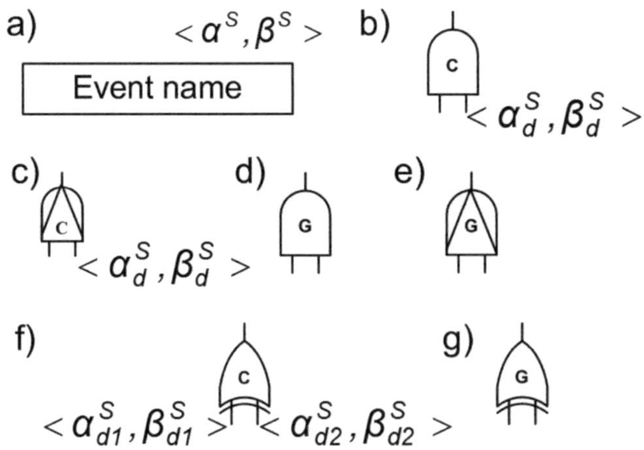

Fig. 6. The notations for a) events, c) causal AND gates, d) causal priority AND gates, d) generalization AND gates, e) generalization priority AND gates, f) causal XOR gates, g) generalization XOR gates

In the generalization gates output event is the same as one of the input events (for XOR gate) or occur when the input events coexist (for AND gate) – start corresponds to the start of event which has occurred later, and the end corresponds to end of the event which has ended earlier.

In causal gates the output event is the result of event (XOR gate) or coexistent events (AND gate) and can occur with delay to start of the cause (XOR gate) or the causes (AND gate). Duration time of the event does not depend on the cause.

An event can be an input of the gate (cause) or be an output of the gate (effect).

The meaning of symbols is as follows:

- α^S, β^S – such static parameters for the events that express the minimal and maximal duration time of the event,
- static parameters α^S, β^S for the causal AND gate are the minimal and maximal delays between the causes and the effect,
- static parameters $<\alpha^S_{d1},\beta^S_{d1}>$, $<\alpha^S_{d2},\beta^S_{d2}>$ for the causal XOR gate are the minimal and maximal delays between the two causes (1,2) and the effect; if one input is used then the parameters for second input are omitted.

The static parameters are the results of system architecture, parameters of the system components, algorithms, code execution time, and physics laws. Examples of the parameters could be the minimal and maximal times of: a transmission of a signal in the air, chemical reaction in chemical process industry, code execution, establishing the network connection, discovering the SYN-flood activity. If a duration time of an event is not known then it can be assumed that the minimal duration time is equal to 0, while the maximal one is infinity. In this case we will use the notation $<0, \infty>$. For the immediate events will use the symbol $<0,0>$.

In order to analyze the FTTD, dynamic time parameters of their events and gates have to be known. These parameters concern: the duration times of the event occurrences, delay times of the gates, and the relations among the start and end time instants of the event occurrences associated with the gates. Instead of the event occurrence, we will shortly write: event. Definitions of the FTTD gates that have been described above, will be stated below, more detailed information can be found [5], [9], [10], [13].

We will use the following notation:

- xs, xe , respectively, represents: the start, the end, respectively, of the event x,
- $\tau(xs)$ - are the time instances when the event x started,
- $\tau(xe)$ - are the time instances when the event x ended.

3.2 The causal XOR gate

Definition 1. Causal XOR gate:

$$occur(z) \Rightarrow (occur\ (x)\ and\ (\ duration(x) \geq \alpha^S_{d1} \wedge \tau(xs) + \alpha^S_{d1} \leq \tau(zs) \leq \tau(xs) + \beta^S_{d1}))$$

$$\oplus\ (occur\ (y)\ and\ (duration(y) \geq \alpha^S_{d2} \wedge \tau(ys) + \alpha^S_{d2} \leq \tau(zs) \leq \tau(ys) + \beta^S_{d2}))$$

where:

- α^S_{d1}, β^S_{d1} - respectively, the minimal and the maximal delays times between the occurrence of the cause x and the effect z
- α^S_{d2}, β^S_{d2} – respectively, the minimal and the maximal delays time between the occurrence of the cause y and the effect z,
- occur(z) – the predicate, the event z come into being in time, analogically: occur(x), occur(y),

- duration(x) - the predicate, event *x* duration in time, analogically: duration(y),
- ⊕, ∧ – the logical symbol denotes respectively, "exclusive disjunction", "logical conjunction".

The models of the causal XOR gates can be generalized by the causal XOR gates with: more than two input events and for one input only.
The Causal XOR gate with output event z and two inputs events x, y is given in Fig.7.

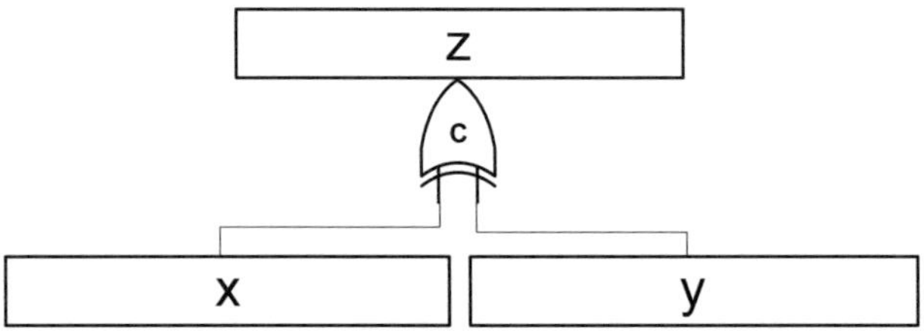

Fig. 7. The Causal XOR gate

The time relations between event *x* (cause) end event *z* (effect) are given in Fig. 8.

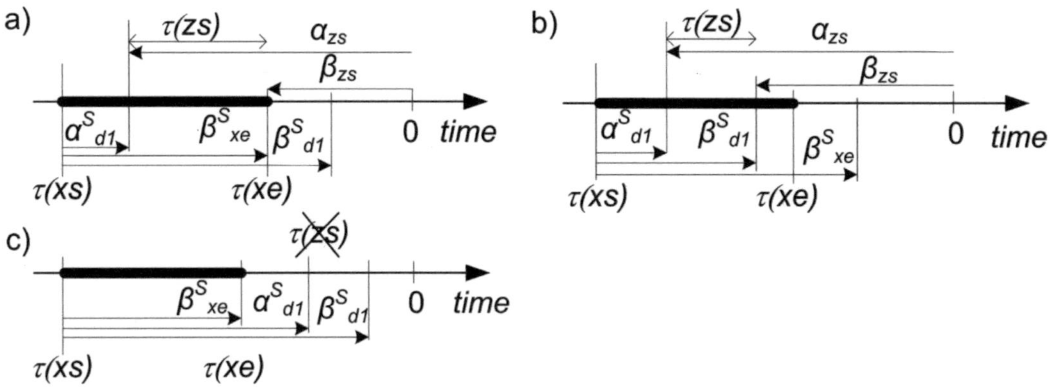

Fig. 8. The time relations between event *x* (cause) and event *z* (effect) for causal XOR gate

In causal XOR Gate the effect (event *z*) must occur not earlier that $\alpha^S{}_{d1}$ and not later that $\beta^S{}_{d2}$ counting from the start of causes (event *x*). Additionally, the effect can occur only before the end of cause (before τ(xe)). There are some examples (presented in Fig. 5) of time intervals in which event *z* can occur:

- start of the event *z* must occur between: $\tau(xs)+ \alpha^S{}_{d1}$ and $\tau(xs)+ \beta^S{}_{xe}$ (see Fig. 5a), because maximal duration of the event *x* is smaller than maximal delay time between causes and effect ($\beta^S{}_{xe}\leq \beta^S{}_{d1}$),
- start of the event *z* must occur between: $\tau(xs)+ \alpha^S{}_{d1}$ and $\tau(xs)+ \beta^S{}_{d1}$ (see Fig. 5b), because maximal delay time between causes and effect is smaller than maximal duration of the event *x* ($\beta^S{}_{xe}\leq \beta^S{}_{d1}$),
- event *z* cannot occur, because duration of the event *x* is too small (see Fig. 5c).

Let us assume minimal and maximal time for start and end of the event *z* are respectively α_{zs}, β_{zs}, therefore $\alpha_{zs}\leq\tau(xs)\leq\beta_{zs}$. Knowing that $\tau(xs)+ \alpha^S{}_{d1}\leq \tau(zs)$ and $\tau(zs)\leq \tau(xs)+ \min\{ \beta^S{}_{d1}, \beta^S{}_{xe}\}$ hence $\alpha_{zs}= \tau(xs)+ \alpha^S{}_{d1}$ and $\beta_{zs}= \tau(xs)+ \min\{ \beta^S{}_{d1}, \beta^S{}_{xe}\}$ – we have knowledge about time relation between causes and effect.

On the other hand, if α_{zs}, β_{zs} are known then we can calculate minimal and maximal time in which event x can occur - what it can cause effect z (we can calculate α_{xs}, β_{xs}). This knowledge allows us for elaboration of the inequalities - equalities system for each gate. Derivations of those formulas are of no requirement for our discussion (more information are given in [10], [13]), only the basic knowledge of the gate model and final form of its inequalities-equalities system is required. For causal XOR gate the inequalities-equalities system is given by formula (1).
It is possible to use fault tree with time dependencies tools [18] as well. Using such tools it is essential for the construction the fault tree to use the toolbox in MS Visio or to prepare a file as it was shown in [19].

$$\begin{cases} \alpha_{d1}^{S} \le \beta_{xe}^{S} \\ \alpha_{xs} = \alpha_{zs} - min\{\beta_{d1}^{S}, \beta_{xe}^{S}\}, \quad \beta_{xs} = \beta_{zs} - \alpha_{d1}^{S} \\ \alpha_{xe} = \alpha_{zs}, \beta_{xe} = \beta_{xs} + \beta_{xe}^{S} \end{cases} \qquad (1a)$$

$$\oplus \begin{cases} \alpha_{d2}^{S} \le \beta_{ye}^{S} \\ \alpha_{ys} = \alpha_{zs} - min\{\beta_{d2}^{S}, \beta_{ye}^{S}\}, \ \beta_{ys} = \beta_{zs} - \alpha_{d2}^{s} \\ \alpha_{ye} = \alpha_{zs}, \ \beta_{ye} = \beta_{ys} + \beta_{ye}^{S} \end{cases} \qquad (1b)$$

(1)

3.3 The generalization AND gate

Definition 2. Generalization AND gate:

occur(z) $\Rightarrow$ occur(x) $\wedge$ occur(y) $\wedge$ overlap(x, y) $\wedge$
max(τ (xs), τ (ys)) = τ (zs) $\wedge$ min(τ (xe), τ (ye)) = τ (ze)

where:

- overlap(x,y) - the predicate, the events x and y overlap in time.

The examples of time relations between events x and y (causes) end event z (effect) are given in Fig. 9.

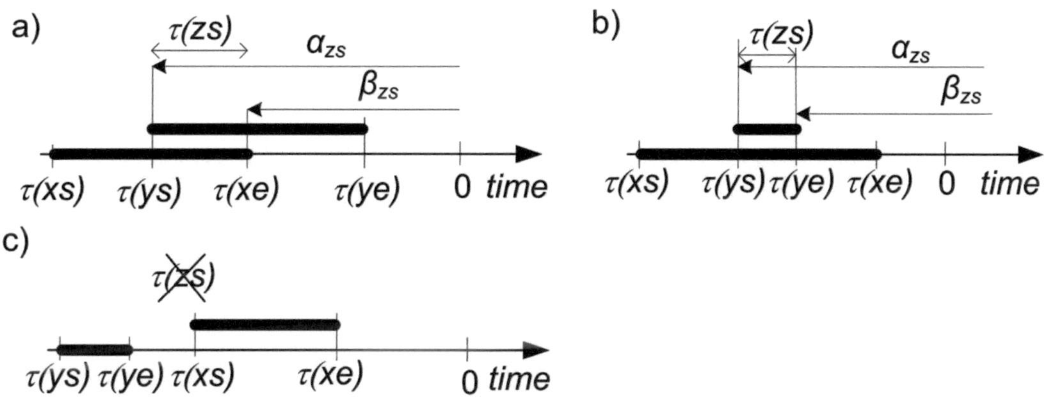

Fig. 9. The time relations between event x (cause) and event z (effect) for generalization AND gate

The inequalities-equalities system is given by formula (2).

$$
\begin{aligned}
&\begin{cases} \alpha_{xs} = \alpha_{zs}, \beta_{xs} = \beta_{zs}, \alpha_{xe} = \alpha_{ye}, \beta_{xe} = \beta_{xs} + \beta_{xe}^{S} \\ \alpha_{ys} = \alpha_{xs} - \beta_{ye}^{S}, \beta_{ys} = \beta_{xs}, \alpha_{ye} = \alpha_{ze}, \beta_{ye} = \beta_{ze} \end{cases} && \text{(2a)} \\
\oplus &\begin{cases} \alpha_{ye}^{S} \le \beta_{xe}^{S} \\ \alpha_{ys} = \alpha_{zs}, \beta_{ys} = \beta_{zs}, \alpha_{ye} = \alpha_{ze}, \beta_{ye} = \beta_{ze} \\ \alpha_{xs} = \alpha_{ye} - \beta_{xe}^{S}, \beta_{xs} = \beta_{ys}, \alpha_{xe} = \alpha_{ye}, \beta_{xe} = \beta_{xs} + \beta_{xe}^{S} \end{cases} && \text{(2b)} \\
\oplus &\begin{cases} \alpha_{ys} = \alpha_{zs}, \beta_{ys} = \beta_{zs}, \alpha_{ye} = \alpha_{xe}, \beta_{ye} = \beta_{ys} + \beta_{ye}^{S} \\ \alpha_{xs} = \alpha_{ys} - \beta_{xe}^{S}, \beta_{xs} = \beta_{ys}, \alpha_{xe} = \alpha_{ze}, \beta_{xe} = \beta_{ze} \end{cases} && \text{(2c)} \\
\oplus &\begin{cases} \alpha_{xe}^{S} \le \beta_{ye}^{S} \\ \alpha_{xs} = \alpha_{zs}, \beta_{xs} = \beta_{zs}, \alpha_{xe} = \alpha_{ze}, \beta_{xe} = \beta_{ze} \\ \alpha_{ys} = \alpha_{xe} - \beta_{ye}^{S}, \beta_{ys} = \beta_{xs}, \alpha_{ye} = \alpha_{xe}, \beta_{ye} = \beta_{ys} + \beta_{ye}^{S} \end{cases} && \text{(2d)}
\end{aligned}
\qquad (2)
$$

3.4 The generalization XOR gate

Definition 3. Generalization XOR gate:

$occur(z) \Rightarrow (occur(x) \wedge x = z) \oplus (occur(y) \wedge y = z)$

The example of time relations between events x (cause) and event z (effect) are given in Fig. 10.

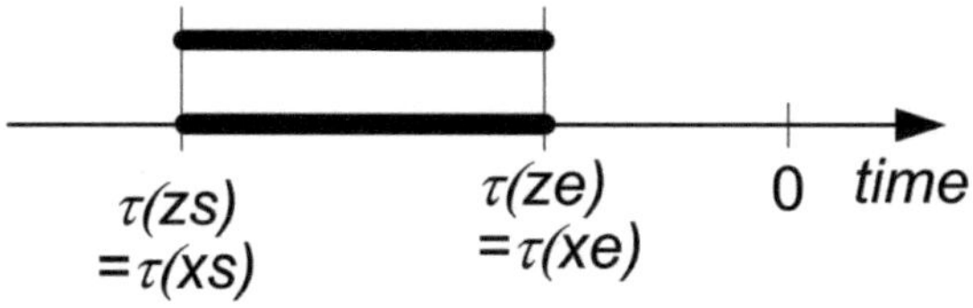

Fig. 10. The time relations between event x (cause) and event z (effect) for generalization XOR gate

The inequalities-equalities system is given by formula (3).

$$
\begin{aligned}
&\begin{cases} \alpha_{xs} = \alpha_{zs}, \beta_{xs} = \beta_{zs} \\ \alpha_{xe} = \alpha_{ze}, \beta_{xe} = \beta_{ze} \end{cases} && \text{(3a)} \\
\oplus &\begin{cases} \alpha_{ys} = \alpha_{zs}, \beta_{ys} = \beta_{zs} \\ \alpha_{ye} = \alpha_{ze}, \beta_{ye} = \beta_{ze} \end{cases} && \text{(3b)}
\end{aligned}
\qquad (3)
$$

The other gates are not presented here as they do not occur in the FTTDs for given examples.

The inequalities – equalities systems for other gates can be found in papers [9], [10], [13]. These systems are used in backward analysis from the hazard event to primary events.

4. FTTD analysis

In order to simplify the interpretation of the result analysis, the conventional moment of time „0" has to be established as start of the hazard, therefore:

$$\alpha_{hs} = 0 \text{ and } \beta_{hs} = 0 \tag{4}$$

We start the FTTD analysis by identifying the time interval, when the hazard can occur using formula (4). More information about it is given in [10].

$$\alpha_{he} = \alpha^{S}_{he} \text{ and } \beta_{he} = \alpha^{S}_{he} \tag{5}$$

Then, we consider the causes that can directly lead to the hazard and time relations between these causes and the hazard occurrences using formulas for adequate gates (for each hazard is the output event). Then we consider causes for the above causes, etc.
As a result of this analysis, the following pairs for the events are obtained:
$<\alpha_{zs}, \beta_{zs}>$, $<\alpha_{ze}, \beta_{ze}>$ where:

- α_{zs}, β_{zs}, respectively, are be the earliest, the latest time instant of the start of the event z,
- α_{ze}, β_{ze}, respectively, be the earliest, the latest time instant of the end of the event z.

These are time constraints imposed on events occurrence time in order to cause the hazard.

4.1 FTTD analysis - example #1

The fault tree for the system (called example #1 - depicted on Fig. 1.) can be found at Fig. 11. The left sub-tree (composed of events: 2, 4, 5, 6, 7) corresponds to the scenario (a) represented by Fig. 1 - the intruder uses the terminal T impersonated as the worker to get

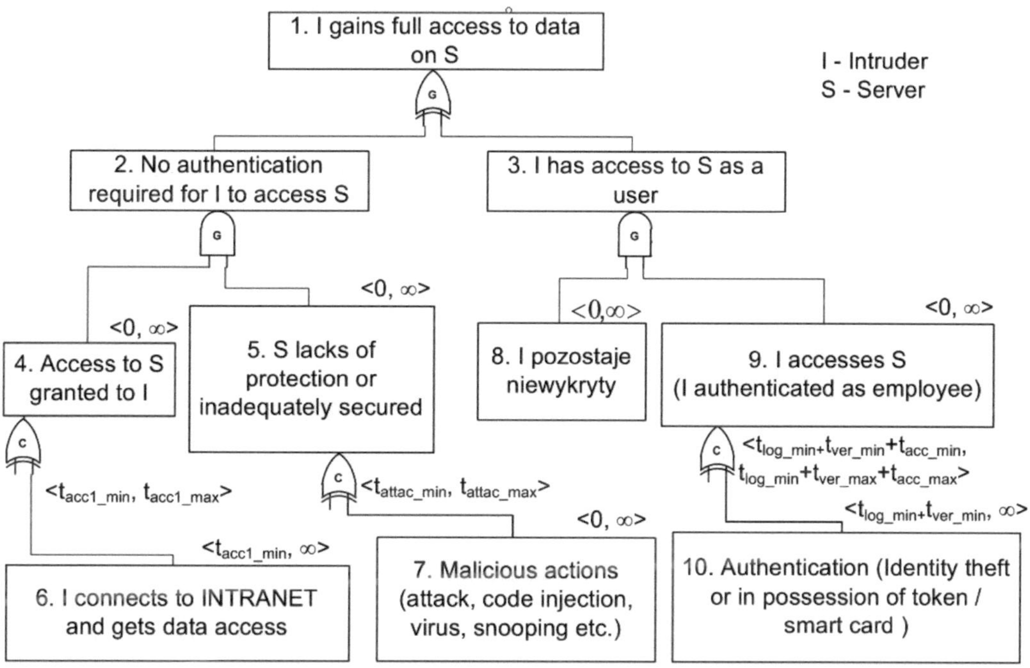

Fig. 11. The FTTD for Example #1

access to data. The right sub-tree (composed events 3, 8, 9, 10) corresponds to the scenario (b) in which Intruder uses his own laptop to get direct access to compromised (unsecured) server.

Following steps should be undertaken in order to get meaningful result after the FTTD analysis.

STEP 1: The calculations of the time parameters for HAZARD (event 1) using formulas (4) and (5) are being done. As hazard is the output event in a generalization gate, the static parameters for hazard must be obtained from the input event. If they are equal, then we have one case (as in our case), if they are not - we must consider more cases as it was shown in [13].

Hence: **1 <0,0> <0, ∞>**, where: 1 – number of top event, $<\alpha_{1s}=0, \beta_{1s}=0> < \alpha_{1e}=0, \beta_{1e}=\infty>$. The event 1 starts in time instant "0" ($\alpha_{1s} \le \tau(1s) \le \beta_{1s}$, then $0 \le \tau(1s) \le 0$ and $\tau(1s)=0$), the event 1 end instant satisfies the inequalities $0 \le \tau(xe) \le \infty$.

STEP 2: The calculations for the events 2 and 3.

We make the calculation from formulas (3) for the generalization XOR gate.

We have: 2 <0,0> <0, ∞>

xor 3 <0,0> <0, ∞>

STEP 3: The calculations for the events 4 and 5.

We make the calculation from formulas (2) for the generalization of AND gate and for time parameters for the event 2: $<\alpha_{2s}=0, \beta_{2s}=0> < \alpha_{2e}=0, \beta_{2e}=\infty>$.

We have: (4 <0,0> <0, ∞> and 5 <-∞,0> <0, ∞>)

xor (4 <-∞,0> <0, ∞>) and 5<0,0> <0, ∞>)

We have two cases (the following two are the equal):

- the event 5 occurs before the event 4 (then event 5 start must satisfy the inequalities: $-\infty \le \tau(5s) \le 0$) and the event 5 must end not earlier than event 4 starts (the event 5 end instant must satisfy the inequalities: $0 \le \tau(5e) \le \infty$); the event 4 start is in time instant "0", the event 4 end satisfies the inequalities $0 \le \tau(4e) \le \infty$,
- the event 4 occurs before the event 5 and the event 4 must end not earlier than the event 5 starts: ($-\infty \le \tau(2s) \le 0$, $0 \le \tau(2e) \le \infty$, $0 \le \tau(3s) \le 0$, $0 \le \tau(3e) \le \infty$).

STEP 4: The calculation for the event 8 and 9 – are analogous as for 4 and 5 using formulas(2).

NEXT STEPS: We analyze remaining events using formula (1b). The result of the analysis is depicted on Fig. 12.

Each rectangle at Fig. 12 has the Minimal Cut Set (MCS). According to the paper [3] (excluding inscription: *or in a proper time*): Minimal cut set (MCS) - is such minimal set of events that if they all occur simultaneously (or in a proper sequence *or in a proper time*) then the top event occurs. If one event from MCS does not occur, then it causes that top event will also not occur.

Words in bracket:

- „in a proper sequence" - extends standard definition of MCS of FTA to events occurring sequence dependencies,
- „*in a proper time*" - extends standard definition of MCS of FTA to time dependencies, what is required for the FTTD.

MCS for FTTD includes events with time conditions. For the event i we have:

$$i <\alpha_{is}, \beta_{is}> < \alpha_{ie}, \beta_{ie}>$$

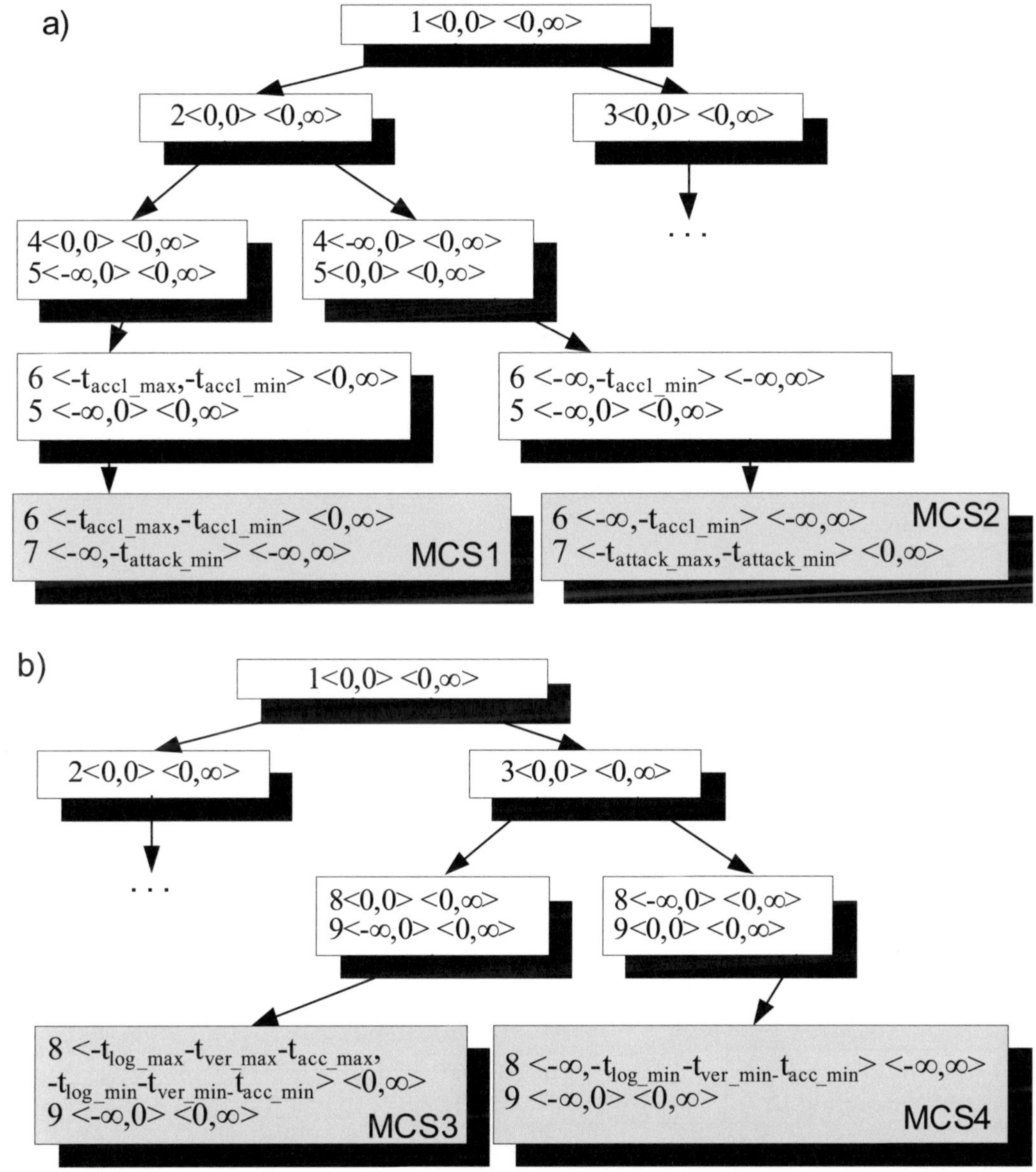

Fig. 12. FT analysis for Example #1 a) left sub-tree, b) right sub-tree

The time conditions denotes, respectively: the earliest (α_{is}) and the latest (β_{is}) time instants of the event i start, and the earliest (α_{ie}) and the latest (β_{ie}) time instants of the event i end. In order to cause the hazard (top event), the event i start instant ($\tau(is)$) and the event i end instant ($\tau(ie)$) must satisfy the inequalities: $\alpha_{is} \leq \tau(is) \leq \beta_{is}$, $\alpha_{ie} \leq \tau(ie) \leq \beta_{ie}$.

The α_{is}, β_{is}, α_{ie}, β_{ie} can be counted with respect to reference time instant 0 (e.g. we assume $\beta_{1s}=0$, see [10]).

If one event from MCS will not occur in the proper time (e.g. as result of introduced insurance, catalysts, equipment with proper parameters), it causes that the top event will also not occur.

Finally, the sets marked with gray color have been obtained. The final MCS have only events which are leaves of the FTTD.

Interpretation for the MCS1 and MCS2:

- Events 6 and 7 must occur together to cause the effect, we known that the duration time before effect must be minimally equal to t_{acc1_min} (from MCS1), t_{attack_min} (from MCS2), therefore

$$\min\{t_{acc1\_min}, t_{attack\_min}\}$$

Interpretation for the MCS2 and MCS3:

- analogically as it was for the events 6 and 7, it has minimal hazard time equal to

$$t_{log\_min}+t_{ver\_min}+t_{acc\_min}.$$

The use of FTTD is this case is not required; however taking advantage of formal methods is beneficial; it prevents creation an unequivocal description, we are able to make the precise specification and allow avoiding omission not so obvious aspects.

4.2 FTTD analysis - example #2

The fault tree for the system (example #2 - depicted on Fig. 2.) can be found at Fig. 13 (for more detailed information please refer to [21]).

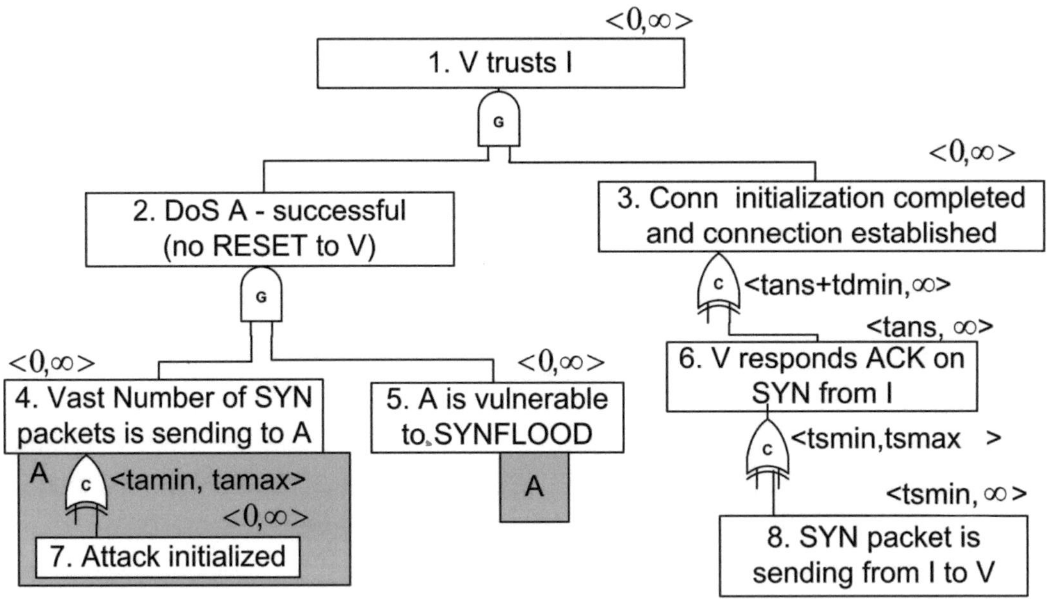

Fig. 13. The FTTD for "V trusts I" attack

As it was presented in [21], the time parameters for the XOR causal gates of the right part of the FTTD are as follows:

- tsmin, tsmax - the minimal and maximal time of sending the SYN packet from the I to V,
- tans – time of preparing the acknowledgement ACK on the SYN packet, it is the activity of V,

- tdmin - minimal time of establishing the connection between I and V after time instant when V have sent the ACK.

Event "Attack initialised" means the sending of the first SYN packet from V to A, i.e., SYN-Flood has been started.

The time parameters for the XOR causal gate of the left part of the FTTD are as follows:

- tamin, tamax - minimal and maximal lengths of time interval which is sufficient to send such a number of SYN packets from I to A that A cannot generate the RESET packet.

The event "A is vulnerable to SYN-Flood" means that there are no such facilities at A that A can avoid the SYN-Flood.

If the events 4. and 5. are overlapped in time then the Denial of Service occurs and A cannot send the RESET packet to V ("DoS A - successful (no RESET to V)").

Let the events 2. and 3. are overlapped in time. Hence, the connection between I and V has been established, and A is not able to send the RESET packet to V. Therefore, "V trusts I".

The more detailed analysis was shown in [21]. Result of the analysis is depicted on Fig. 8.

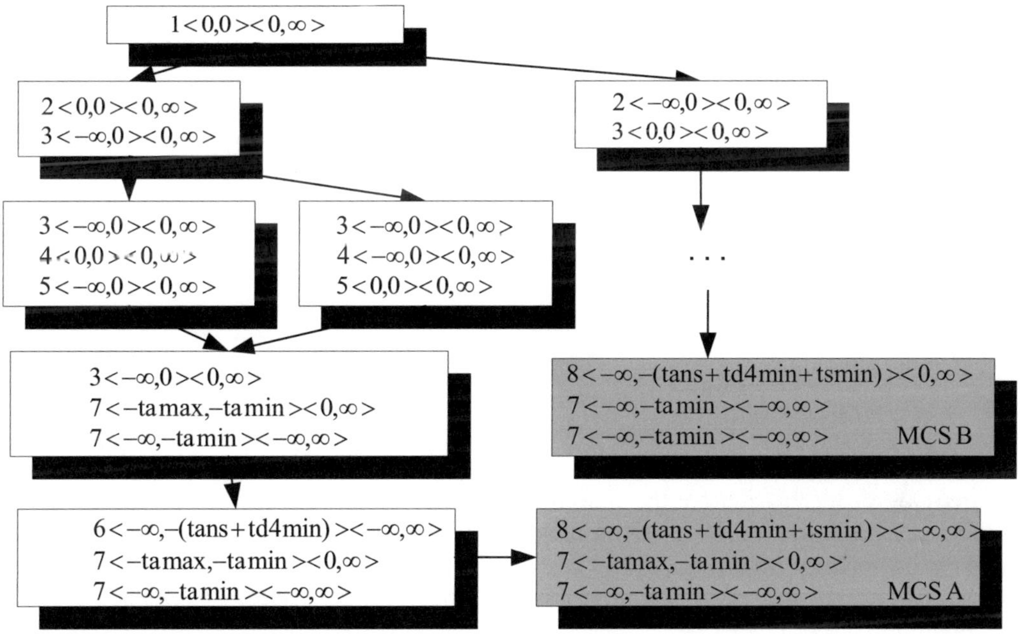

Fig. 14. The analysis result

Interpretation for the MCS A (please refer to [21]):

1. time intervals connected with the event 7 are different; so after calculating the common part, we have: 7 <-tamax,-tamin> <0,∞> and 8 <-∞, -(tans+tdmin+tsmin)> <-∞,∞>,
2. counting from sending the SYN package (the event 8), the hazard "V trusts I" will occur minimally after tans+tdmin+tsmin time units, but the attack needs to last until the event "V trusts I".

Interpretation for the MCS B:

The hazard can occur, when the event "Attack initialized" starts not later than tamin before the hazard. Analogically the event 8 starts not later than tans+tdmin+tsmin and ends - not earlier than in 0 time instant.

5. Application of result received in analysis

5.1 System with protection

The abovementioned timing properties can be used in designing protections and services. Now three proposals will be presented.

1. If the time connected with service activity of one SYN packet is t_{SYN}, then the amount of packets that can be serviced by server in time before "V truts I" is about (tans+tdmin+tsmin)/t_{SYN}. Hence, these packet numbers can be used for construction of the firewall rules or for specification of the requirements of attack detection,
2. if in order to avoid the vulnerability to SYN-Flood attack, a protection, e.g. SYN Cookies, should be introduced or reintroduced in time no longer than t_{amin}; but if the computer Intruder sends the packet (SYN to the V) simultaneously with the attack initialization, then the protection has to complete its procedure in time not longer than max {tamin, tans+tdmin+tsmin},
3. if the security is more important than functionality, then knowing the time parameters connected with the attack is essential, we can, e.g. monitor the load of the server (the testing of the SYN packets). If the server cannot respond before the time $t_{ans}+t_{dmin}+t_{smin}$, then the RESET packets can reset all connections,
4. Vulnerability of the server during the attack cannot be greater than min{t_{acc1_min}, t_{attack_min}}, hence we are able to periodically verify server protection,
5. Intruder must be detected in $t_{log\_min}+t_{ver\_min}+t_{acc\_min}$ time units; therefore e.g. "visual" verification of employees by a guard or cameras with face recognition system should be introduced.

5.2 Safety audit procedure

The efficient and safe IT assets management requires detailed knowledge of the infrastructure and underlying inventory items. All information that one may need for that purpose can be acquired during a security audit.

The security audit is a process in which collection and evaluation of "evidence and premises" is taking place in order to determine whether the computer system and related resources are properly secured; to retain data integrity and desired level of security, and to provide relevant and reliable information that allow quickly and effectively achieve organization security objectives. Audit results can influence on resources utilization (to be used sparingly), enforce internal control mechanisms to provide reasonable means to assure that operational objectives be achieved and help control IT environment by enabling protection against adverse events or ultimately help in detection on time to minimize the effects that might have been already caused.

The fault trees can be used to support construction of security audit procedure. The common knowledge is that any system as a whole is as weak as its weakest component, so each protection is equally important. Having this in mind, along with fault tree constructed and then analyzed one can be tempted to create a security survey that will constitute a basis for fully-fledged security audit. Conclusions drawn after the analysis can be formulated as questions for administrators toward the systems that are about to be secured.

Let us focus on two examples based on aforementioned assumptions:

1. Having considered Fault Trees without time dependencies, one knows that events 4, 5 and 8 are only prerequisites for hazard to occur. Based on that following questions may be added to a security survey:

- Is system still synflood attack prone?
- Has synflood susceptibility been eliminated or considerably restricted?
- Had SYN packets number being received from one source been limited?
- If in a corporate environment, has any additional authentication (client's terminal and server) mechanism been introduced?

2. Having analyzed FT and a monitoring tool in place, one may want to create a metric that will be delivering information about a number of incoming packets in a defined timeframe.

These are just simple examples that could be extended in a wide variety of cases to enforce security awareness and apply security rules. What's more based on the response from the security survey generic firewall rules may be created and instantly adapted e.g.

If system Y attack X prone then block INCOMING communication using protocol XYZ on port xxx.

Having in mind example #1, one may be tempted to draw some conclusions out of its analysis.

1. Any person that is logged in should be double checked if he/she is the really the one that has been logged as. So following security rule can be established

If a user is successfully logged, an additional identity check should be performed not later than … since the time when authentication was successful.

2. Automated security check ups should be employed as a part of periodical audit routines (penetration tests, scripting based logging procedures etc.)

6. Conclusions

In the chapter, the FTTD analysis has been applied in pursue for such minimal sets of causes with time relations that can lead to the hazard. The hazard is the event when the security requirements are violated. It has been shown that the time relations between the events and the hazard could be applied in: construction of protections against the hazard occurrence or such a choice of network parameters that the hazard can be avoided. Additionally, the fault tree can be used for identification of security threats; and its analysis may help in introduction of attacks remedial measures, like discussed example of safety audit procedure. The FTTD analysis can be used not only for analysis of faults consequences, but it can be applied for checking whether a design of a network satisfies some safety requirements, too. What is more, there are such tools that can automate and help with the analysis of FTTD with four types of gates: generalization AND, XOR, priority AND and causal AND, XOR, priority AND.

7. References

[1] J. F. Allen, G. Ferguson, "Actions and events in interval temporal logic", Journal of Logic and Computation, Vol. 4, 1994, No. 5, pp. 531-579.

[2] D. J. Bernstein's, SYN Cookies explanation, http://cr.yp.to/syncookies.html

[3] "Fault Tree Analysis (FTA)", International Technical Commission, IEC Standard, Publication 1025, 1990.

[4] G. Helmer, J. Wong, M. Slagell, V. Honavar, L. Miller, Y. Wang, "Software Fault Tree and Colored Petri Net Based Specification, Design and Implementation of Agent-Based Intrusion Detection System", 2002.

[5] J. Górski, J. Magott, A. Wardziński, "Modelling Fault Trees Using Petri Nets", in: Proc. SAFECOMP'95, Belgirate, Italy, LNCS, Springer-Verlag, 1995.
[6] M. Y. Huang, T. M. Wicks, "A Large-scale Distributed Intrusion Detection Framework Based on Attack Strategy Analysis", Computer Networks, Vol. 31, 1999, No. 23-24, pp. 2465-2475.
[7] Introduction to TCP/IP (http://www.yale.edu/pclt/COMM/TCPIP.HTM)
[8] John Kristoff - Overview of TCP (Fundamental concepts behind TCP and how it is used to transport data between two endpoints) (http://condor.depaul.edu/~jkristof/technotes/tcp.html)
[9] J. Magott, P. Skrobanek, "A method of analysis of fault trees with time dependencies", in: Proc. SAFECOMP'2000, Rotterdam, The Netherlands, LNCS, Vol. 1943, Springer-Verlag, 2000, 176-186.
[10] J. Magott, P. Skrobanek, "Method of Time Petri Net Analysis for Analysis of Fault Trees with Time Dependencies", IEE Proceedings - Computers and Digital Techniques, 2002, Vol. 149, No. 6, pp. 257-271.
[11] J. Magott, P. Skrobanek, "Partially automatic generation of fault-trees with time dependencies", in: Proc. Dependability of Computer Systems", DepCoS '06, Szklarska Poręba, Poland, IEEE Computer Society Press, 2006, 43-50.
[12] W. Richard Stevens, Detailed tutorial on TCP/IP, (http://www.goldfish.org/books/TCPIP%20Illustrated%20Vol%201/)
[13] P.Skrobanek, "A method of analysis of fault tree with time dependencies for safety-related systems" (in Polish), Ph. D. Thesis, Technical University of Wrocław, Poland, report: PRE. 24/2005 (http://www.dbc.wroc.pl/dlibra/doccontent2?id=1142&from=&from=metadatasearch&dirids=1)
[14] L. P. Swiler, C. Phillips, "A Graph-Based System for Network-Vulnerability Analysis", in: New Security Paradigms Workshop, Charlottesville, VA, USA, 1998, pp. 71-79.
[15] The basics of Transmission Control Protocol (http://tcp.mywebcities.com/)
[16] TCP, Transmission Control Protocol (http://www.networksorcery.com/enp/protocol/tcp.htm)
[17] G. D. Wyss, B. Schneier, T. R. Gaylor, "Probabilistic Logic Modeling of Hybrid Network Architectures", in: Proc. 21st IEEE Conference on Local Computer Networks.
[18] https://snow.iiar.pwr.wroc.pl:36914/FaultTreeWeb/
[19] M. Jureczko, P.Skrobanek, "Tool for analysis of the fault tree with time dependencies", Electrotechnical Review, 2010, R. 86, nr 9 s. 179-183
[20] Bierć P., „The safety analysis of PostgreSQL Server with PHP access using fault tree analysis", M. A. Thesis, (in Polish), Wroclaw University of Technology, Wroclaw, Poland, 2007
[21] J. Magott, P. Skrobanek, M. Woda, Analysis of timing requirements for intrusion detection systems, in: Proc. Dependability of Computer Systems, DepCoS-RELCOMEX '07, Szklarska Poręba, Poland, IEEE Computer Society Press, 2007, 278-285.